LOUIS THE BELOVED
The Life of Louis XV

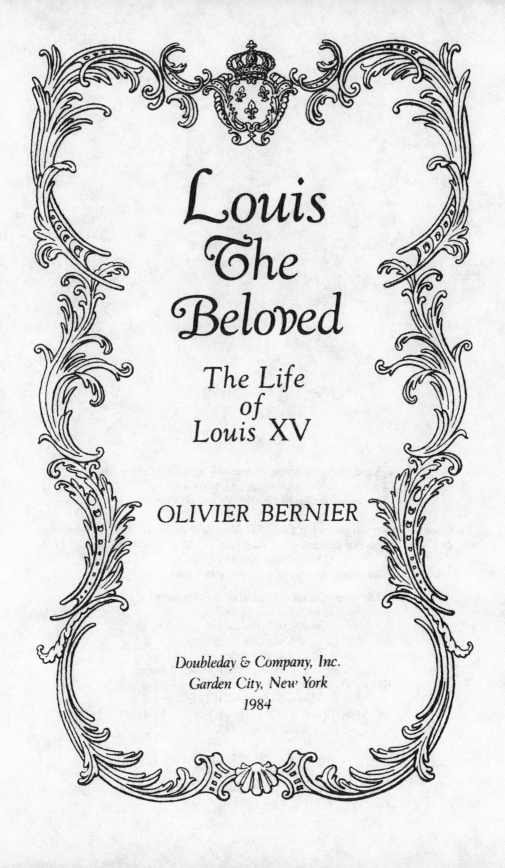

Louis The Beloved

The Life of Louis XV

OLIVIER BERNIER

Doubleday & Company, Inc.
Garden City, New York
1984

Title page and chapter opening decorations by Antony Groves-Raines
Genealogical chart by David Gatti
Book design by Beverley Vawter Gallegos

Engravings of equestrian portrait of Louis XV, Mme de Pompadour, château of Bellevue,
duc de Choiseul, theatrical costumes, and King Frederick II of Prussia are courtesy of the
Metropolitan Museum of Art.
All others courtesy of the New York Public Library.

Library of Congress Cataloging in Publication Data
Bernier, Olivier.
Louis the Beloved. The Life of Louis XV.
Bibliography: p. 258
Includes index.
1. Louis XV, King of France, 1710–1774.   2. France—
History—Louis XV, 1715–1774.   3. France—Kings and
rulers—Biography.   I. Title.
DC134.B47   1984   944′.034′0924 [B]   82–46027
ISBN 0-385-18402-6

Contents

List of
Eighteenth-Century
Engravings

Preface

WHEN he was a frail five-year-old child, the peace of Europe depended on his survival; when he was in his early thirties, he led his army into battle and won a great victory; when he reached sixty, appalled by the ineffectiveness of his own government, he carried through far-reaching and effective reforms: the century of Louis XV, Voltaire called it, and at the time few doubted that his fifty-nine-year reign was one of the most important in French history.

Indeed, Louis XV seemed to have every quality needed to join Louis XIV, his great-grandfather, on that short list of monarchs who have deserved well of France. He was hard-working, conscientious, tolerant and kind. He cared about the welfare of the state but also about the comfort of the people, so that his was an era of unprecedented prosperity. Almost uniquely, he preserved France from invasion. He understood and patronized the arts, and commissioned buildings—the Petit Trianon, for instance—which remind us that perfection is within reach. He married early, fathered nine children and then, true to the spirit of the time, went on to love a succession of beautiful women. Then, at the last, he broke the power of a selfish, reactionary elite so that the burden of taxation no longer rested exclusively on the shoulders of the poor. Why, then, is there not a long shelf of books about this wise and attractive monarch?

One reason, which will probably surprise no modern statesman, was that he cared nothing about publicity: let people attack him as they might, he paid no attention and never condescended to answer. As a result, by the seventeen sixties disappointed factions at court were financing a flood of scurrilous pamphlets in which the King was pictured as a worn-out debauchee ruled by the whims of his mistress—an attitude summed up in the wholly apocryphal "after me the deluge." Then, because during the Revolution many people still remembered just how pleasant life had been under Louis XV, it became obvious that toppling his grandson, Louis XVI, wasn't enough. It was the monarchy itself that must become an object of scorn and hatred, so a whole new wave of pamphlets was written to attack the memory of Louis XV, and these often took the form of fake memoirs in which the public was offered the picture of a selfish, lazy rake.

Then, too, attacks came from a completely different side: in 1756, Louis XV broke with France's traditional hostility to the Habsburgs because he realized that Prussia, not Austria, had become the danger to peace. Just how right he was the nineteenth century proved all too abundantly, but in his own lifetime he was attacked by all those—and they were a majority—who followed blindly after Prussia, so that it soon became an accepted notion that the reversal of alliances had been a disaster. Soon, the new policy was portrayed as Madame de Pompadour's work: she had supposedly sold France for a few polite letters from the Empress Maria Theresa. Curiously, the fact that these letters never existed did nothing to stop the many attacks on King and favorite.

Actually, it is no wonder: in Louis XV's lifetime, these attacks at least served to express the rage of an impotent faction; during the Revolution, they were eagerly seized on as propaganda fodder; and when, in the eighteen sixties, histories of the eighteenth century finally began to appear, their authors, who cared more for drama and "revelations" than truth, simply copied all the tired old lies. A feckless monarch obviously made for better copy than a wise and conscientious one. One example of this attitude will suffice. There exist two detailed accounts of the death of Louis XV, one by the duc de Croy, who was an eyewitness, a man of enormous conscience and exacting veracity; and the other by an anonymous author who published his description in 1791. That alone should be enough to discredit him, as should the clearly revolutionary vocabulary he uses; but his story is far more entertaining than Croy's. Why settle for a brave and Christian death when you can have a burlesque parodied from the comedies of Molière? Of course, the burlesque prevailed.

Since then, there have been studies of different aspects of the reign of Louis XV—books like Jean Egret's *Louis XV et l'opposition parlementaire,* which focuses on the Parlement's tenacious opposition to King and reform; monographs on various economic aspects of the century; and one serious attempt at putting Louis XV and his era back into perspective, Pierre Gaxotte's *Le Siècle de Louis XV.* None of these books, however, focuses on the personality and achievements of the King himself; and Jacques Levron's affectionate biography, while excellent in its images of life at Versailles, leaves out most of Louis XV's political life. Clearly, it is time to take a fresh look at the life and reign of this long-maligned King.

Nor is this an impossible enterprise. It is not so very difficult to separate the fake letters from the real, the phony memoirs from the authentic. Then, too, there is an abundance of material on which the cautious author can lean: Louis XV was a great letter writer, several of his courtiers and ministers recorded everything they saw, and, of course, all his state papers are intact. Thus, the very bulk of his correspondence, the care with which he annotated the registers of court and government expenditure are enough to dispel, once and for all, the myth of the King's laziness. We know, too, just how well the economy did during his reign, how stable the currency remained. Finally, museums all over the world proudly exhibit the glorious objects made for Louis XV, while his rooms at Versailles remain today almost exactly as he saw them himself. The concerned observer can, therefore, find out just what happened from 1715 to 1774 and even, to a considerable extent, just how the King himself felt about the persons and events of his reign.

A good biographer must, of course, remain unbiased, but it is possible to be fair and yet react to the personality which emerges from the words of contemporary witnesses and documents. When we discover a gifted, honorable and compassionate man who, after a long struggle with his feelings of inferiority, became one of the greatest statesmen of the ancien régime, then it is only natural to feel affection and respect. Historical truth must be unearthed if we want to understand our own day; to see a good man maligned calls for redress. It is the purpose of *Louis the Beloved* to show that monarch, at last, for the man he really was.

THE FRENCH BOURBONS TO 1793

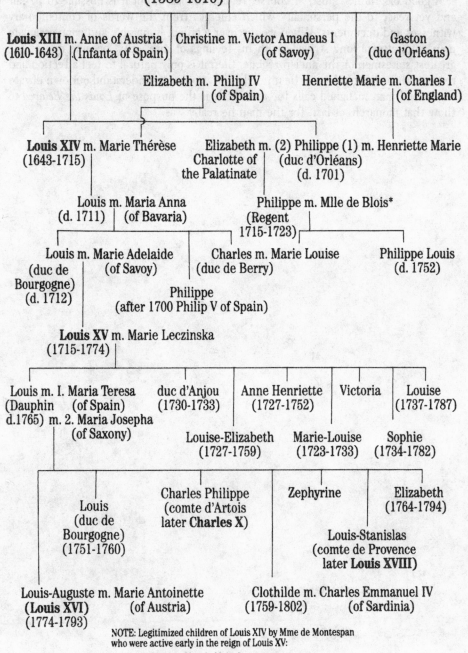

Henri IV m. Marie de' Medici
(1589-1610)

Louis XIII m. Anne of Austria   Christine m. Victor Amadeus I   Gaston
(1610-1643) (Infanta of Spain)   (of Savoy)   (duc d'Orléans)

Elizabeth m. Philip IV   Henriette Marie m. Charles I
(of Spain)   (of England)

Louis XIV m. Marie Thérèse   Elizabeth m. (2) Philippe (1) m. Henriette Marie
(1643-1715)   Charlotte of   (duc d'Orléans)
         the Palatinate   (d. 1701)

Louis m. Maria Anna   Philippe m. Mlle de Blois*
(d. 1711) (of Bavaria)   (Regent
          1715-1723)

Louis m. Marie Adelaide   Charles m. Marie Louise   Philippe Louis
(duc de (of Savoy)   (duc de Berry)   (d. 1752)
Bourgogne)
(d. 1712)   Philippe
      (after 1700 Philip V of Spain)

Louis XV m. Marie Leczinska
(1715-1774)

Louis m. I. Maria Teresa   duc d'Anjou   Anne Henriette   Victoria   Louise
(Dauphin (of Spain)   (1730-1733)   (1727-1752)   (1737-1787)
d.1765) m. 2. Maria Josepha
      (of Saxony)   Louise-Elizabeth   Marie-Louise   Sophie
                  (1727-1759)   (1723-1733)   (1734-1782)

             Charles Philippe   Zephyrine   Elizabeth
             (comte d'Artois   (1764-1794)
     Louis   later **Charles X**)
    (duc de   Louis-Stanislas
   Bourgogne)   (comte de Provence
   (1751-1760)   later **Louis XVIII**)

Louis-Auguste m. Marie Antoinette   Clothilde m. Charles Emmanuel IV
(Louis XVI) (of Austria)   (1759-1802) (of Sardinia)
(1774-1793)

NOTE: Legitimized children of Louis XIV by Mme de Montespan
who were active early in the reign of Louis XV:

Louis-Auguste (duc de Maine)
Louise-Françoise (Mlle de Nantes) m. Louis, duc de Bourbon
Françoise-Marie (*Mlle de Blois) m. Philippe, duc d'Orléans
Louis-Alexandre (comte de Toulouse)

LOUIS THE BELOVED
The Life of Louis XV

Chapter One

A Very Young King

AT eight-twenty, on the morning of September 1, 1715, a very old King lay dying in his red and gold bedroom at the heart of the great Palace of Versailles. Not far away, in one of the wings, a five-year-old orphan, richly dressed in black velvet, stood alone, his governess far behind him. Within minutes, he heard a great noise coming closer. The doors burst open; before him, bowing deeply, stood his great-uncle, the duc d'Orléans, followed by the Princes of the Blood Royal and the rest of the court. "As soon as the child heard himself called 'Sire' and 'Your Majesty,' he burst into tears and sobs even though no one had told him that [Louis XIV] was dead."[1] The reign of Louis XV had begun.

It is no great wonder that the child reacted so quickly and strongly to the death of his infinitely remote great-grandfather. Death was already horribly familiar: only three years earlier he had lost his father, his mother and brother. Now he was alone. He scarcely knew the great-uncle who led the little troupe of princes; only his governess, the duchesse de Ventadour, was close to him: she was the only familiar figure. In that huge palace, before that enormous crowd of courtiers who surged behind the princes and tried to catch the new King's attention, the weight of the world had passed onto that sobbing boy; and young though he was, he knew it full well.

That dreadful shock was no surprise. For a month already, Louis XIV had been declining visibly. In London, they were placing bets on the exact date of his death. All through Europe the statesmen were feeling a mixture of relief and anxiety: relief because they would soon be rid of the man who had determined the course of Continental politics for so long, anxiety because he left a sickly five-year-old as his successor. If the little boy died, the complex settlement reached at Utrecht only two years before might well become obsolete, and no one wanted the European war to start all over again.

It all depended now on the life of that child, the sole survivor of a once numerous family. In a mere three years, Louis XIV had lost his only son; his eldest grandson, the duc de Bourgogne; his youngest grandson, the duc de Berry; as well as his eldest great-grandson and the granddaughter by marriage, the duchesse de Bourgogne, who had brightened his old age. The succession which, in 1712, had seemed utterly secure now, in late August 1715, had become a terrifying riddle. That the old King would soon be dead everyone, including himself, could see. That the little boy would live long enough to succeed seemed extremely probable, but, then, child mortality was appallingly high, the Dauphin himself terribly fragile. When he followed his great-grandfather to the tomb, as everyone assumed he must, two men would have conflicting claims to the throne. One was Philip V, King of Spain and the Indies, the second of Louis XIV's grandsons. Upon leaving France he had formally renounced all claims to the succession, but it was known that he repented having done so. The other claimant was the duc d'Orléans, Louis XIV's nephew, the son of his brother and the grandson of Louis XIII. If the eldest branch of the Bourbon family, as represented by Louis XIV's descendants, failed, then the younger branch, issued from Louis XIV's younger brother, was next in line. One thing was, at any rate, certain: for the moment, by right of birth the duc d'Orléans must soon be Regent of France. It was an easy and widely shared assumption that he would clear his way to the throne by arranging the little boy's demise.

Still, nothing was changed at Versailles. The monarch who took pride in the fact that anyone, anywhere in Europe, could look at his clock and know just what the King of France was doing kept all the rigors of the etiquette in force. For the last week of his life he no longer left his bedroom, but the successive waves of courtiers came in according to the same rules as ever; the King's Music still played during his meals (except for the last three days, when he could bear it no longer); and the splendid autocrat went about taking leave of his court in the same masterful yet enormously polite manner he had perfected during his seventy-two-year reign. No one, except his helpless doctors, realized that he was in constant agonizing pain as gangrene, inch by inch, crept up his leg.

Some of the adieus were said not in private—the whole court was watching—but, at any rate, inaudibly to anyone except the person so favored. One after the other, the King spoke to his bastard, but now legitimized, children, to the Princes of the Blood Royal, to the duc d'Orléans; and then he called for the Dauphin.

"At noon [on August 26]," wrote that most devoted of courtiers, the marquis de Dangeau, "His Majesty had the little Dauphin brought in to his room and, after having kissed him, he said: 'Sweet child, you are about to be a great king, but your whole happiness will depend on your submitting to God, and on the care you have to relieve your people of their burden. In order to do this you must, whenever you can, avoid making war: it is the ruin of the people. Do not follow the bad example I have given you on this point. Often, I have started wars without sufficient cause and continued them to satisfy my pride. Do not imitate me, be a peaceful ruler, and let your main object be to look after your subjects. Take advantage of the education Madame la duchesse de Ventadour [the Dauphin's governess] is giving you, obey her and follow the advice of Father Le Tellier when it comes to serving God: I give him to you as your confessor.

"'As for you, Madame [he said to Madame de Ventadour], I owe you much gratitude for the care with which you are bringing up this child and for the tenderness you show him. I ask that you continue in the same fashion, and I urge him to give you every proof possible of his gratitude.' After this, he still kissed the Dauphin twice and gave him his blessing."[2] It was a moving scene and made a lasting impression on the child, but even then there was another farewell to be said. The King called his courtiers to him after the Dauphin had been taken from the room. Crowding around the bed, they listened in complete silence to the King who had ruled them so firmly and so long. "Messieurs," he said, "I am pleased with your services; you have served me faithfully and with the desire to please. I am sorry I could not reward you better; these last years have not allowed me to do so. Serve the Dauphin with the same affection you have shown me; he is only a five-year-old child who may have many setbacks, for I remember having had many myself when I was young.* I am going, but the State will remain. Be faithful to it and let your example inspire all my other subjects. Always remain united and in accord—that is the strength of a state—and always obey the orders my nephew [the duc d'Orléans] will give you: he will govern the kingdom. I hope that you will do your duty and also that you will remember me sometimes." At that, according to Dangeau, "we all burst into tears and nothing could begin to describe the sobs, sorrow and despair of all those present."[3]

After that, Louis XIV confessed and received the last rites, but he was too strong to die. For five more days the gangrene crept up slowly and the King suffered patiently, finally slipping into a coma; then, on September 1, at eight twenty-two in the morning, the Sun King died "without any effort, just like a candle flickering out."[4]

Just as, in France, the enormously complex etiquette carefully defined levels of distinction and precedence, so the King enjoyed a status different from that of ordinary men, be they ever so noble. He was halfway between man and God, whose anointed and spokesman he knew himself to be and to whom alone he was responsible. More than just a monarch, he had become a demigod. He was an absolute ruler whose orders no one could gainsay. All the good things of life—places, promotions, pensions, titles—were in his gift alone. More, it had been one of Louis XIV's greatest achievements to tame the once rebellious nobility so that attendance on the King's person became the most desirable of privileges. Handing the monarch his nightshirt, holding his candle, serving his meals on bended knee—all those tasks once reserved to menials were eagerly sought by the proudest noblemen in the realm. Only those men—and women—who were always present before His Majesty could hope for preferment: if ever, upon being asked for a favor, the King said of the solicitor, "I don't know him," the wretch knew he had no more hope.

Louis XIV had brought about this enslavement of the nobility partly through a carefully calculated system of rewards, partly by refusing his father's example in allowing a prime minister to run the government. All through Versailles we can still see paintings and tapestries entitled "The King rules by himself." That meant not only that it was the King in person who determined policy but also that it was he alone who gave out the rewards. Then, too, the Sun King had understood the power of fashion and made his court the most splendid, most desirable place in France. He built his great palace, soon to be imitated all over Europe, and made sure that life there became a series of dazzling entertainments. Further, because he urged his

---

* An allusion to the troubled period of the Fronde, which was marked by revolts against the Queen Regent and the King's authority.

courtiers to live and dress as luxuriously as possible, thus spending far more than their incomes, he made sure that they would come begging for places and pensions. Soon, exile to one's own country castle became a fate worse than death.

Of course, this kind of concentration on the monarch's person meant that he must meet the almost impossible standards Louis XIV set for himself. Henceforth, a king of France must be perfectly content to spend his every waking moment on display, renouncing privacy even in the most private occupations. More unlikely still he must find the actual process of government enjoyable so that hard work, far from being a chore, would become almost an amusement: without that sort of single-minded concentration on the King's part, the system simply wouldn't work. All depended on his being a blend of savvy prime minister and constantly paraded mass idol. Now, on September 1, 1715, only one thing was obvious: for a few years at least, the system must change. A five-year-old child, semidivine though he might be, could not be the sort of monarch Louis XIV had been. The government, therefore, along with the almost endless stream of favors at the King's disposal, must be controlled by someone else. What everyone in Paris and Versailles wondered about that day was who that person would turn out to be.

In theory and according to custom, the Regent of France must be the member of the Royal Family closest to the King by blood: his mother, as had been the case for Louis XIV, or an uncle. Since Louis XV's only surviving uncle was now King of Spain, that left only Philippe, duc d'Orléans. The duc was Louis XIII's grandson, and thus Louis XIV's nephew, and Louis XV's first cousin twice removed. He was also the new King's great-uncle because his half-sister had married the Duke of Savoy, whose daughter was the boy's mother. That the duc d'Orléans must now become Regent no one disputed, but Louis XIV had left a will. There was no telling, therefore, how severely he might have restricted his nephew's powers. If he had curbed them radically enough, then the duc du Maine was the coming man.

Bastards, whether officially recognized or not, were hardly a novelty. In 1715, several of the important people at Court were descended from the illegitimate children of earlier kings, but now there was a difference. Louis XIV had had an unusually large brood of bastards and recognized them all: that was perfectly normal and according to precedent. But then he had gone a very large step further: first, he married them to members of the legitimate Royal Family: the duchesse d'Orléans, for instance, the wife of the putative Regent, was one of the *légitimés,* as they were called; and, as the King's own daughter, she made it very plain that she thought herself more important than her husband, who, legitimate though he might be, was only the grandson of a king.

This, the traditionalists felt, was already pretty shocking. Worse soon followed. First, the légitimés were raised to a status halfway between the dukes and the Princes of the Blood Royal: until then, they had taken precedence according to the date of their peerage (which meant behind a lot of dukes) and had been granted the same privileges as those accorded the other peers.* Then, in the most drastic change of all, Louis XIV declared them able to succeed to the throne if the legitimate Royal Family (i.e., the descendants of Louis XIII) became extinct. While, in 1715, two of the

---

* With exceedingly rare exceptions, only dukes were also peers.

King's bastard sons lived, only one, the duc du Maine, was a serious contender for power.

All through the previous decade, Louis XIV had made his fondness for the duc du Maine perfectly obvious. He had given him great military commands, most recently that of the Household troops, vast sums of money, special *entrées,** and had married him to Bénédicte de Bourbon, the daughter of the First Prince of the Blood. The reason for all this preferment, aside from du Maine's carefully cultivated but undoubted charm, was simple and well known: the King's secret wife, Mme de Maintenon, had once been the Governess of the légitimés (that, in fact, was how she had met the monarch). As such, she had grown inordinately fond of the duc du Maine because, when he was a sickly, fragile child, she had saved his life again and again. Even as an adult, Maine remained thin and spindly; he limped, and his sharp-featured face was anything but attractive. He was as unappetizing morally as he was unappealing physically. A liar, a cheat and a coward, he was given to slandering his betters, carefully buttering up anyone who might be of help to him while abasing himself before those whose power he feared: he advanced himself in the King's favor by dint of assiduous flattery. As for his wife, a brilliantly intelligent woman with a lively appreciation of the arts, she was determined to make up for being a bastard's wife by pushing her husband to power and, who knew, perhaps even one day the throne. So she, too, schemed and toadied. If, as seemed probable, the du Maines had convinced Louis XIV that they were more deserving than the duc d'Orléans, then they, and they alone, would now rule France.

Still, they had several obstacles to overcome: the traditional feeling against illegitimate children who presumed; the duc d'Orléans's obvious right to the Regency; and their own unpopularity in many quarters. That, they thought, might be balanced by Orléans's own ill repute. When death had followed death in the Royal Family, and brought Orléans closer and closer to the throne, whispers (probably started by the duchesse du Maine) had been heard to suggest that the dear departed had probably been poisoned by the duc d'Orléans: everyone knew that the duc was fond of chemistry and even kept a laboratory fully stocked in his Paris palace. Now Louis XV would be the next victim, they hinted. If the new King were to be protected, therefore, Orléans must be powerless.

The first step in that direction had already been taken a little earlier by the old King when he had given the duc du Maine command of the Household troops and left a clause of his will appointing him Superintendent of the future king's education. By controlling both the armed forces guarding the palace and the personnel around the child, the duc du Maine would obviously be able to protect Louis XV from any dastardly attempt; he would also, of course, control the source of power. These twin appointments went even further than it first seemed: the duc du Maine could have the Regent arrested at any time since he alone controlled the troops and would, at the same time, be able to claim he was merely conveying the King's orders. Whatever appearance of power the duc d'Orléans might retain, it would be meaningless since, in case of conflict, he would never be able to enforce his orders. In any case, the duc du Maine would obviously represent the rising sun. The Regency, after all, would

* Entrées were the right of entering the King's bedroom before the rest of the Court.

end the day Louis XV became thirteen, in a mere eight years. That day the King
could, if he chose, appoint an all-powerful prime minister. Obviously, the person
closest to him would be in the best position to bag the prize.

All that was bad enough, but, as the duc d'Orléans found out on September 1,
there was worse to come. In his will, Louis XIV had indeed specified that the duc
d'Orléans was to be Regent, but he then added that all decisions and all appointments were to be the responsibility of a Council of Regency so composed that the
Regent would be in the minority and the duc du Maine in the majority, with the
obvious consequence that the Regent would be a mere figurehead while the duc du
Maine was the actual ruler. Coming from a monarch who, on his deathbed, had
urged his courtiers to remain united, these arrangements were nothing short of
stupefying, since their first, most immediate, consequence would be an attempt by
the duc d'Orléans to regain the plenitude of power normally granted the Regent,
while the duc du Maine would struggle equally hard to retain the advantage. The
Court would be split between the two, with obvious results: a repetition of the
Fronde, the civil war which had torn France in two during Louis XIV's own minority.

That the old King had been fond of his bastard son is certain; so, at Mme de
Maintenon's urging, he did his best, but without really believing that his will would
ever take effect. He very nearly said as much to the Premier Président of the Parlement de Paris when he handed him the sealed envelope, and with good reason. Both
his grandfather, Henri IV, and his father, Louis XIII, had died leaving a child to
succeed the throne; both had attempted, in their wills, to restrict the powers of the
Regent; and in both cases the wills were, within twenty-four hours of the King's
death, declared invalid by the Parlement. The only question, therefore, on that busy
morning was whether the duc d'Orléans could strike a deal with that peculiar institution.

The Parlement de Paris, its name notwithstanding, was not a real parliament at all:
it was merely one of twelve geographically defined courts of justice scattered
throughout the realm. Its members bought or inherited their offices, so that wealth,
not election or even competence, decided on whether a man could join the Parlement. Only the Premier Président, the chief magistrate, and the Attorney General
were appointed by the King and, therefore, did not own their seats. As a result, they,
and they alone, could be dismissed. Altogether, the Parlement de Paris numbered
some two hundred and thirty judges *(conseillers)* and ten superior magistrates *(présidents)*. It differed from the provincial parlements in four ways: it had more members;
its jurisdiction, which spread over one third of the kingdom, was exceptionally large;
it was the only court in which a Peer could be tried, the only one in which every
Peer, as he came of age or succeeded to his title, must officially be declared in
possession, and in which he could, thereafter, sit as a judge if he so chose; finally,
because of its geographical proximity to the King, it was the first to register his edicts.

At first, in the fourteenth century, the registration of the edicts had been purely a
matter of record. The new laws were entered into a register so that one authorized
text could always be cited; but, little by little, the Parlement took a new function onto
itself: when it felt that the new edict was faulty—because it was poorly drafted,
perhaps, or because it contradicted some earlier law—the court presented "remon-

strances" to the King. In the beginning, these were purely technical. By the fifteenth century, they had begun to take on political overtones: the Parlement, in effect, would ask the King to reconsider what it felt to be a wrong decision or, most often, an overly heavy tax. The King, however, was always free to reject a remonstrance, and, if he did, the Parlement must register the new edict, no matter how much it was opposed to it. Soon, it went a step further and began remonstrating not only to the edict itself but to the letters of command *(lettres de jussion)*, ordering it to register the edict despite its remonstrances; so a new procedure developed, the "bed of justice" *(lit de justice)*.* When a complete deadlock was reached, the King came in full state to the Parlement and ordered, in person, the registration of the edict. Since France had always been, in theory at least, an absolute monarchy, there was no disobeying the King, and the edict was well and truly registered.

In reality, however, matters had not proceeded so smoothly. Whenever, for any reason, the government's power declined—after a disastrous military defeat, for instance, or when the King was a minor—the Parlement tried to grab as much power as it could. Its most recent attempt, during the minority of Louis XIV, had come close to installing an oligarchy in which a few rich men sitting in the Parlement would rule France instead of the King. In the event, the Fronde failed and, a few years later, Louis XIV, who took a very bleak view of rebellious institutions, had held a lit de justice in which the Parlement lost the right to delay the registration of the King's edicts and was in effect silenced. For the rest of the reign, therefore, it had become once again a purely judicial body which, almost incidentally, kept the register of the laws.

Now Louis XIV was dead, and everyone remembered that it had been the Parlement that had annulled the wills of both Henri IV and Louis XIII. Obviously, the question was: would it do so again to this latest of royal wills? Since in the ancien régime tradition carried enormous weight, it was assumed by everyone that what the earlier parlements had done could be done again in 1715. Besides, it was accepted doctrine that in France the King's will was supreme but limited to his own lifetime. It followed that any will disposing of the government after the King's death was, on the face of it, invalid.

Clearly, it was all a question of reciprocity. The duc d'Orléans naturally wanted a solemn affirmation of his untrammeled power as Regent. The Parlement, on the other hand, wanted to recover its right to remonstrate and delay registration: the makings of a deal were obvious. It surprised no one, therefore, when the duc d'Orléans was seen conferring with the Premier Président. Even when that magistrate announced a solemn session of the Parlement and Peers for the next day so as to read the King's will, however, the duc du Maine didn't worry. The Premier Président owed his place to the duc and was well known to be among his followers. What the du Maines forgot was that the cowardly often abandon their old friends when they see power elsewhere.

It is only fair to say, in defense of the duc du Maine's blindness, that everyone had obeyed the late King so promptly and for so many years that the very notion of flouting his will seemed almost incomprehensible. Then, too, the du Maines had

* So called because the King sat on a bedlike mound of cushions.

recently backed the Parlement in its dispute with the Peers over one of those minor points of etiquette* which loomed so large in the life of the ancien régime. Further, the duc d'Orléans's reputation was such that, surely, no one would work for him: until that day, his isolation at Court had been complete. Finally, the only Prince of the Blood then of age to make his reputation felt, the duc de Bourbon, was the duchesse du Maine's own nephew. Now, the duc du Maine took over the King's care, as was his right and, after consulting his brother, the comte de Toulouse, he waited for the morrow without apprehension; but all through the huge palace the courtiers gathered and tried anxiously to predict the future. It soon became obvious that they had made their decision: while the duc du Maine was left alone with a few close followers, it was the duc d'Orléans who was suddenly surrounded by a fawning court.

By seven o'clock the next morning, the great hall of the Parlement was already full; soon the légitimés came in, followed by the duc de Bourbon and the Regent. The Peers sat on their high benches, the conseillers and présidents, in their scarlet robes, sat below. With the proper retinue, the Premier Président now fetched the late King's will from the tower in whose wall it had been immured; then, solemnly, it was opened and read. After that, it was time for speeches. With a deep bow, the Premier Président turned to the Regent: as the only grandson of France in the assembly, he had clear precedence, and as soon as he began to speak the tenor of his conversation, the previous day, with the Premier Président became clear. Not only, he said, was the government set up by the will obviously impractical, it actually contradicted the late King's stated intentions. During that whispered farewell, Orléans explained, the dying man had told him: "Nephew, I have preserved for you the rights your birth gives you. I think I have arranged everything for the best, but since one cannot foresee everything, you will make whatever alterations or additions you think fit. I ask that you relieve the State [from excessive spending]." And, the Regent added, "he also said several things so flattering to myself that I cannot repeat them."[5] It followed, the Regent continued, that his request for the annulment of the will was not only sensible: he was, in fact, following the King's dying instructions. At that, the duc du Maine, who had been fidgeting nervously, tried to interrupt. Turning to him, the Regent told him, in an imperious voice, that he would speak in his turn and not before. Then, resuming his speech, he demanded a full, unrestricted Regency, with the right to govern as he saw fit, to make appointments and order punishment, and the disposition of the Household troops, adding magnanimously: "I want to be free to do good, and consent to be so tied that I cannot treat anyone badly."[6]

After this, it was for the duc de Bourbon to opine. When he supported the Regent, everyone present understood where the real power lay; by the time the duc du Maine tried to defend the will, the hostile whispers were so loud that he turned deathly pale and sank back down into his seat. Within minutes, the Parlement followed the lead given by the Premier Président: the duc d'Orléans had just been made Regent in fact as well as name. There was nothing left now but for the duc du Maine to announce sulkily that he must decline to guaranty the King's safety since the Household troops

---

* The Peers claimed that the members of Parlement should take their hats off when addressing them, while the Parlement claimed the right to retain their hats except when addressing a Prince of the Blood.

were no longer under his command. With an ironic bow, the Regent said he would willingly shoulder the responsibility the duc du Maine could no longer assume.

It had been quick and effective: in a move that was, to all intents and purposes a nonviolent coup d'état, the Regent had taken onto himself the full powers of the monarch; but, having thus triumphed, he promptly demonstrated the kind of moderation that was as typical of him as it was unusual in France. To be sure, the duc du Maine had lost the government, but he remained Superintendent of the King's Education and a Prince of the Blood. Not one of the duc d'Orléans's former enemies was punished in any way. Even old Mme de Maintenon, who had worked so hard to deny him his rights, was confirmed in the legacy left her by Louis XIV: better yet, it was the Regent in person who brought the first month of her pension to Saint Cyr, where she had retired, and assured her that she had nothing to fear. A new era had indeed dawned. The late King had kept order by terrorizing any possible opponent. The new Regent obviously intended to kill them with kindness.

There still remained a promise to fulfill, however. First, on September 12 the Regent, Peers and Parlement met again, but this time it was for a lit de justice presided over by the little King, who, according to an eyewitness, behaved beautifully: "The King went up the great staircase on foot; M. le duc de La Trémoille, First Gentleman of the Bedchamber, carried the train of his cloak . . . Once everyone was in place, the King said very graciously: 'Gentlemen, I have come here to assure you of my affection for you. My Chancellor will tell you what I have decided' . . . During this sitting, which lasted for a full hour, the young King did not look embarrassed; he was quiet and firm in his place, only he was terribly hot and wiped his face now and again with a handkerchief which Mme de Ventadour gave him and which he returned to her while apparently paying attention to what was being said and done."[7] There, as he watched, the new form of government was solemnly confirmed. Two days later, the Regency's first edict was sent in to be registered. It gave the Parlement, once again, the right to present remonstrances to the King. The Regent's rule was under way.

Even if his great-uncle ruled, however, Louis XV remained all-important: everything depended on his remaining alive, besides which he was just as much the elect of God as if he had been twenty years older. Miraculously, given the usual paucity of good looks among European royalty, the young King actually looked the part. He was a handsome child, we are told (and his portraits confirm it), with delicate features, dark hair, big black eyes and a perfect complexion. All who saw him admired him and said so: more than a little boy, he was a kind of icon whom people came to worship, and, though uneasily aware of it, he behaved with preternatural dignity. At least he still had his governess, the duchesse de Ventadour. Only a year earlier she had nursed him through the illness which had killed his parents and elder brother, and ever since then the child called her "Maman."

In fact, the name was appropriate: Mme de Ventadour had given the little duc de Bretagne, as he was then called, his life just as surely as if she had borne him in her womb. Although the deadly illness which afflicted the entire family was nothing more than measles, the deplorable medical practices of the times, an alternation of bleedings and purges, had so weakened the three other patients as literally to kill them.

Mme de Ventadour, who understood what was happening, realized that the only way to save the child was to hide him from the doctors, so she actually kidnapped him, taking him to a remote room within the palace of Versailles and nursing him until he recovered. Now, still in charge, she saw to it that her ward ate the right food, wore the right clothes, rested and exercised. More important still, she gave him the affection he craved. Unfortunately, as everyone except the child knew, it was not to last: in February 1717, when the King turned seven, the Governess must be replaced by a Governor. Of all the King's entourage, there was only one person whose daily presence would remain constant, the child's only living relative, the duc d'Orléans.

Luckily, far from being the ogre depicted by the duchesse du Maine, the Regent was an honorable man, devoted to his new King, a kind and considerate master and friend. In 1715 Philippe, duc d'Orléans, was forty-one years old. Conveniently for those who want to know what he was like, we can go straight to the source: with admirable (if, for him, exceptional) impartiality, that memorialist of genius, the duc de Saint-Simon, has left us a full description of the man and the ruler. "M. le duc d'Orléans," he wrote, "was of only ordinary tallness at most, quite fleshy without being fat; he had an easy expression and way of carrying himself; his face was wide, pleasant, quite ruddy, his hair black as was his wig . . . His face, his gestures, all his manners were imbued with the most perfect graciousness, and it came to him so naturally that it adorned even the least and most common of his actions. With great ease of manner, when not feeling constrained, he was kind, open, welcoming, easily accessible and charming, with a pleasant tone of voice and a gift for words which was particular to him . . . marked by an ease and simplicity not to be excelled by anyone . . . The great figures of history and their lives were familiar to him, and so were the intrigues of earlier courts and of the one he lived in. To listen to him, one would have thought he was very well read, but nothing could be further from the truth. He skimmed rapidly but his memory was extraordinary, so that he forgot neither the incidents nor the names nor the dates . . . He was extremely witty, and in several ways . . . His unusual perspicacity was coupled with such judgment that he never would have taken the wrong course in any of the world's affairs if he had only followed his first impulse . . . With all this, no presumption . . . Nothing imposing or constraining in society even though he was well aware of his rank . . . He put everyone at their ease . . . No one had a more respectful look or air when he was with the Royal Family or the King, and yet this was blended with great dignity. He was naturally kind, humane and accessible to pity . . . He loved freedom as much for others as for himself."[8] Quite an encomium, and yet it was fully deserved. Few princes have been given a worse reputation; none has deserved it less. This enormously talented man was a highly competent chemist, a gifted and successful general and, as he began now to demonstrate, a daring and effective statesman. After the rigid intolerance which had marred the last reign, the Regency proved itself open, flexible, tolerant. More unusual still for his time, the duc d'Orléans was a good and loving father who single-handedly saved his daughter Elisabeth when she caught smallpox and was given up by the doctors. Now he proceeded to show the same affection—marked, however, by a strong tinge of respect—for the young King.

Why, then, the bad reputation? Partly because of those whispered campaigns of the duchesse du Maine's; partly because Louis XIV, who always feared that his relatives would set up competing power centers, practically ostracized him; partly because he had the startling habit of saying what he really thought in a world where deceit and flattery were the rule, and thus made himself many unnecessary enemies; and mostly because he had no use for either the Catholic Church or sexual hypocrisy.

The Church, at best, was a worldly institution. In France, for instance, the King appointed the bishops whom the Pope then routinely confirmed. That meant that the sees with large incomes were kept as plums for the great noble families, so there was very little question of religious merit and, indeed, many bishops spent their lives at Versailles instead of tending to the faithful. Even those people who really cared about religion were engaged in complex and obscure disputes, the only result of which was to awaken fanaticism and create warring, irreconcilable sects. All this was bad enough, even if you believed in the Church's every dogma; but the duc d'Orléans had developed healthy doubts about such stories as the Immaculate Conception, the Garden of Eden or the existence of purgatory, partly because of their sheer improbability, partly because his scientific studies had made him aware that the Church held as truth many fables. In a society where, for a short moment still, religion seemed important, this open agnosticism was enormously shocking. A man who didn't believe in the Gospels, people said, must be in league with the devil, so much so that Saint-Simon felt compelled to set down his certainty that the Regent had never met Satan at all.

Then there was the matter of his debauchery. That anyone should have blamed him for getting drunk and having mistresses seems a little surprising considering how everybody else behaved. Louis XIV, after all, though not given to drink, had had many openly declared mistresses and acknowledged an impressive number of bastards; in all his court, there cannot have been more than a dozen faithful couples. Perhaps it was because the duc d'Orléans made what others considered a weakness into a rule of life, perhaps it was because he organized his pleasures in so sensible— and so daily—a manner: the fact remains that the pots called the kettle black because every evening he would shut himself up with a group of pretty, easy women and amusing men, get drunk, and end the night with whoever took his fancy, so that his mistresses were legion. It seems no great crime today, especially since these orgies never prevented him, once he was Regent, from attending to business at eight every morning. It should also be said that the duc's spectacular misbehavior developed early as a reaction to Louis XIV's refusal to give his nephew any significant work. Eventually the King, who had been shocked at first, caught on: his nephew, he said, made himself look much worse than he actually was. He was right: Orléans was taking the only revenge he could on a frequently sanctimonious court. "The more one was schooled, obstinate and excessive in lack of religion and in debauchery, the more [the duc d'Orléans] respected one," Saint-Simon wrote disapprovingly. "I have always seen him display admiration tending to actual veneration for the Grand Prior [de Vendôme, the son of one of Henri IV's légitimés and a notorious reveler] because for forty years he had gone to bed drunk every night, and never ceased keeping mistresses publicly or making impious and irreligious speeches."9

Still, even these apparent faults had a happy result: a skeptic is not usually given to persecution or a dictatorial way of ruling, and is far less likely to be taken in by zealous frauds than most. In fact, Orléans had seen enough of the ways which prevailed at Court, that jungle peopled with selfish, ferocious predators, to take no one at his word. "His lack of trust was without exception,"[10] Saint-Simon noted sadly; as it turned out, that, too, was a useful characteristic in the new ruler of France.

That the Regent faced enormous problems was clear from the beginning; but before the debt could be tackled or the government reformed, there was one piece of business that would brook no delay: the little King must have proper care. Shortly before his death, Louis XIV had given instructions for moving the Dauphin to Vincennes as soon as he became King. The air there was supposed to be healthier than that of Versailles, so on September 5 the Regent called a meeting of the Court doctors. After much discussion about the comparative merit of the air in the various royal palaces, they agreed that Vincennes was indeed best. On September 9, therefore, the King, dressed in purple* velvet, "left Versailles at two in the afternoon and arrived at Vincennes in excellent health. With him in his carriage were M. le duc d'Orléans and Mme la duchesse de Ventadour sitting with him in the backseat, M. le duc du Maine and M. le maréchal de Villeroy [the King's Governor] in the front seat, with M. le comte de Toulouse at the door . . . All along the road and especially near the walls [of Paris], there was an infinity of carriages and people. One could hear people shouting 'Long live the King' even in the streets on the other side of the walls,"[11] Dangeau noted, and on October 1 he added: "The King is getting stronger and enjoys the best of health, but since the bad weather will soon be here, it is thought that he will be more comfortable in the [Palace of the] Tuileries for the winter."[12] In fact, while Vincennes would indeed have been a little sad in the winter, the truth was that it suited the Regent far better to have the King in town, thus avoiding the daily ninety-minute drive to the suburban fortress.

Even so, he had to proceed with great care. There were far too many people who believed that the Regent meant to ensure the King's death; so, on November 15 "there was a great consultation of doctors to decide when the King could be taken to Paris. All agreed that it was best to wait until after the first freeze."[13] Evidently, for once, they did no harm. On December 30 Louis XV was installed at the Tuileries, and on December 31 Dangeau noted: "The King is in the best of health and shows much pleasure at being in Paris."[14] It is easy to see why. The Tuileries was a much more cheerful residence than Vincennes, that medieval stronghold; it was an open palace looking out onto a handsome, if public, park and had been sumptuously redecorated in the 1660s. As for the Regent, who had always preferred to reside in Paris, the Tuileries was just around the corner from his own palace, the Palais Royal. More than all this, however, what really mattered was the visible break with the world of the Sun King.

Versailles, its palace and its park, had been more for Louis XIV than an architectural and horticultural triumph. For the first time in French history, all the great nobles, along with the ministers, actually lived in the King's own house and were thus

---

* Kings wore purple for mourning, queens white, and the rest of the Court black.

able to attend him from morning to night. In centralizing and reinforcing the powers of the monarchy, in stressing the semidivine nature of the ruler, Versailles had played a key part. It had also precluded yet another repetition of that old Parisian custom, an assault on the royal palace. Within sixty years two kings, Henri III and the child Louis XIV, had been trapped by a mob and, ultimately, forced to flee. There was no possibility of the King's being besieged in Versailles, where there was no population to speak of, and where troops could easily be maneuvered to stop any foray from Paris. Now, after all those years away, the monarchy was back in the often unruly capital. Even more than a proof of trust, it was a clear indication of the new government's tendencies: the sort of high-handed autocracy practiced by Louis XIV was evidently a thing of the past.

There were many other changes as well, and all in the same vein. Not only was the Parlement authorized to offer remonstrances once more, it was actually allowed to do so before registering the edicts, which gave it, at the very least, a temporary veto. There was a time limit, to be sure: the Regent had specified, on September 15, that the remonstrances must be made "within a week at most for the courts which are located in the place of our residence"[15]; but there was no sure way to force registration anymore, except through the spectacular, and therefore seldom used, procedure of the lit de justice. Clearly, the new government intended to allot the Parlement a considerable role.

Even more spectacular was the reorganization of the actual structure of the government. Under Louis XIV there had been five or six ministers who reported directly to the King. While they provided information and advice, it was the King alone who made the decisions which the ministers were then bound to carry out. Now the ministries were abolished and replaced by a series of councils, each staffed not by the kind of competent, middle-class professionals (Colbert, Louvois) that Louis XIV had wisely chosen, but by a motley group of aristocrats whose understanding of the processes of government was, in most cases, extremely slight, and who, besides, had better things to do than work. This bizarre idea was not the duc d'Orléans's at all but rather the result of conferences between the duc de Bourgogne, the new King's late father, and Fénelon, his tutor. Since the two men attributed all the troubles of France to the despotic government set up by Louis XIV, they thought to improve the situation by reviving a blend of monarchy and oligarchy which had, in fact, never existed. It was a proof of the Regent's open-mindedness and of his respect for the duc de Bourgogne's memory that he now set to carry out that peculiar scheme.

Thus, councils for the War, Navy, Finances, Interior and Church Affairs were set up, and they all reported to a Council of Regency. Each council met once a week (unless prevented from doing so by disputes over sticky points of etiquette) and supposedly produced both accounts and suggestions. In fact, as the Regent soon found out, either decisions were taken by the professional clerk in attendance because he was the only one who knew anything, or, most often, the members of the Council were far too busy squabbling to bother with actual governing. Since, in theory, the Council of Regency only acted on reports sent to it by the other councils, it soon became obvious that the system wouldn't work. Then, too, the Regent was only supposed to implement the decisions reached in the Council; but since everyone knew that his was the real authority, few in the Council were apt to disagree with him when it really came to an important question. That the whole system was unwieldy and doomed to failure should have been plain from the start, especially since each council was presided over by a Prince of the Blood or a duke whose competence was not necessarily as imposing as his lineage. That the system lasted some four years is nothing short of amazing; the answer to that riddle, of course, is that within a very few months the Regent was unofficially bypassing the councils and dealing directly with the professional civil servants.

Strange as it might seem, however, the new system was received with enormous enthusiasm. There were several reasons for this. The first, of course, was that it represented exactly the reverse of what had been done before. After the unhappy years at the end of the last reign, any change looked like an improvement. Then, it seemed like democracy of a kind. No one yet thought the people competent to rule, but a blend of the nobility and the Parlement came as close to a representative system as anyone could imagine. Finally, the fact that the Regent was carrying out the duc de Bourgogne's system was widely admired as proof that the new ruler was free from any temptation at governing like the late King.

Altogether, these changes apparently amounted to nothing less than a revolution. The sudden emptiness of the great hive at Versailles symbolized it quickly. Now that the monarchy was back in its ancient residence and once again shared its power with its traditional rivals, the Court, which had been a center of power, vanished utterly. The King retained a Household, of course, but it was relatively small and the Regent cared nothing for etiquette or display. The great mansions of Paris, until now deserted, were full of life again, and soon more began to rise.

As a result of all this, and of the Regent's leniency, the atmosphere was utterly changed. Freed from their constant attendance on the King, the nobles proceeded to have fun instead. Etiquette gave way to pleasure. The Regent and his nightly orgies made everything permissible, and so all through the capital there was an enormous explosion of drinking, gambling, party-giving and luxury. It was a little like the twenties of our own century: after a period of war and repression, the only thing that mattered was having fun. Fashion changed radically. The straight lines and stiff brocades typical of the court gowns worn at Versailles were replaced by light silks, pastel colors and soft, ballooning skirts. The tall, stiff coiffure held up by wire vanished in favor of short, curly, lightly powdered hair. Ease and enjoyment were the order of the day, so there was a revival of the theater and of the dance, while a wave of redecorating swept over Paris. And along with this went a new spirit of intellectual inquiry, of freedom. Censorship was virtually abolished; talent was encouraged even if irreverence went with it. After the sullen magnificence of the "grand siècle," the eighteenth century, with its grace, its charms and its pleasures, was born.

In the center of this whirlwind, however, there was an island of quiet where an all-important little boy lived. Only his presence made the good life possible, and everyone knew it. "The King might well die, but it would be a terrible misfortune, even for us," the Regent's mother wrote, mindful that her son was the Heir Presumptive, "for

I think there would then be a terrible war."[16] Naturally, the King's popularity soared; every day his attendants told him that he was beloved of his people. For the icon in the Tuileries, surrounded by bowing elders, there could be no doubt: in him, and him alone, France's welfare was incarnate.

Chapter Two

The Wise Uncle

AN orphan's life can never be easy, and just because Louis XV was King of France, it did not follow that his childhood was made any happier. To be sure, he lived in a palace and was surrounded by swarms of servants. His governess loved him; his great-uncle visited him every day and treated him with a particularly tactful blend of respect and affection; but, still, the child was never allowed to forget that he was unlike any other child in the realm. Time after time, on ceremonial occasions as well as in the course of his ordinary life, the adults surrounding him demanded that he behave with a maturity well beyond his years.

"Our young King is at the Tuileries and, thank God, in good health; he hasn't been sick for a moment," the Regent's mother noted with satisfaction, but then went on: "He is allowed to do anything he wants lest a refusal make him ill. I am sure that if he were punished, he would be less passionate . . . but everyone wants to remain in the King's good graces, no matter how young he may be."[1] The old duchesse d'Orléans loved to complain so much that she apparently forgot she was referring to a six-year-old child. In fact, given his age, the King was already demonstrating the most startling sense of decorum. Even though, before 1717, his public appearances were still relatively rare, he had been taught that he must display the same kind of majestic politeness for which his great-grandfather had been famous; and that meant remembering the names and faces of a bewildering array of people while always concealing any manifestation of personal feeling. There was the time, for instance, when the little boy, who had been desperately suppressing a natural and imperious need because he was on show, simply fainted dead away: hardly the behavior of a spoilt child.

The King was taught this hieratic manner by the duchesse de Ventadour, who was still faithfully following the instructions given her by the late King. She looked after the child's health with great zeal, of course, made sure he ate the right food, wore the right clothes for the season and exercised enough but not too much. She gave him as much affection as she could, but above all she taught him three great principles: he must always serve God; he must always remember who he was and behave accordingly; and he must learn not just to keep a secret but also never to let the outer world know about his true feelings. The child listened carefully, and at about the time when he began to write in a clear, tall hand he showed he had learned his lesson well: by the time he was seven, no one really knew what he actually thought or felt. Of course, the governess was merely trying to mold her charge so that he would become a great king, but what she actually did was to create a split between the child's two personalities, the public and the private, while instilling in him an absolute lack of trust in anyone he did not know very well indeed. Soon Louis XV became convinced that everyone, without exception, wanted something from him, and the behavior of his courtiers only reinforced that conviction. Unfortunately, he was considered far too grand to play with other children; at least with them he would have dealt with equals in age who would seek no favors, and who, in a fight, would give as good as they got. Instead, the King had servants but no companions. Very infrequently another child was brought in for the afternoon after having been properly indoctrinated, but even then Louis could only relate to them as he did to everyone else: he gave them presents, going so far, one day, as to hand his own watch over. It was generous, it was kind; but it was not the way one child should treat another. And when, on occasion, he misbehaved, he was not punished. No one wanted to take the chance of being remembered one day by His Majesty as the person who had sent him to bed without supper. Far worse, he was made to feel guilty instead. A King of France, his attendants explained gravely, should know better and remember that he was at all times responsible for his actions. Because the child was lively and intelligent, he took it all in and did his best, but he was left in no doubt that his was a very heavy burden indeed.

It is sometimes a little difficult to remember, as we look at this living icon, that all these solemn demands were made of a six-year-old child. At an age when little boys are expected to do little more than run, play and have fun, Louis XV was already treated as an adult in every way except the one that really mattered. He had no control over his own life, so that while he was fully aware of his responsibilities, he also knew that he was utterly powerless. Forced to play a role he hadn't chosen, he had none of the compensating freedom. The world of the King, in 1716, was one in which he was endlessly expected to behave well by much older people who obviously knew better than he did but still treated him, outwardly, as if he actually ruled them all. It hardly needs saying that this must have been the most uncomfortable of situations.

In February 1717 this already trying world suddenly became more difficult still. Tradition demanded that all royal princes be put in the care of men as soon as they reached the age of seven; so one cold morning the little boy was stripped naked in front of a gathering of courtiers and doctors presided over by the Regent, pronounced healthy, and delivered into the hands of the man Louis XIV had chosen to raise him, the old maréchal de Villeroy. It was a dreadful wrench: the only person in all the world Louis really loved, the only one whom he trusted completely, his governess, was taken away from him, so he sobbed throughout the day, refusing to eat and calling for Mme de Ventadour, all, of course, to no avail. The next day he was handed a casket of jewels—a necklace of large pearls, a diamond cross—to give the duchesse as her reward; and as he gave it, he remarked sadly that the present was as nothing compared to the gratitude he owed her.

Unfortunately, the new Governor had none of Mme de Ventadour's qualities. Although he was probably fond of his charge, he was also too experienced a courtier not to take advantage of his position. He flattered the King, whose education he neglected utterly, and displayed him constantly, much the way one would show off a tame monkey or a trained dog, all the while constantly reminding the boy that he was the absolute ruler of the greatest kingdom on earth. Louis XIV could hardly have chosen a worse governor.

"The maréchal de Villeroy," Saint-Simon wrote, "was tall and well built, with a very pleasant face. He was strong, robustly healthy, and could do anything he wanted to his body without fear. He had no difficulty in spending fifteen or sixteen hours on horseback and stayed up all night. All his life he lived and prospered in the highest society. The son of [Louis XIV's] Governor, he was brought up with the King and was his familiar friend from his earliest youth. A lady's man by profession, he knew all about all the love affairs of both Court and town, with which he used to entertain the King, whom he knew thoroughly and whose foibles he was able to exploit . . . He lived in great style and had very noble manners . . . was never gratuitously nasty . . . excessively proud by nature, but also humble to excess whenever it could do him any good . . .

"He had the kind of wit one learns at Court and in society and spoke the fashionable jargon . . . He was a man born to preside over a ball . . . He understood neither people nor events . . . [was] incapable of giving good advice . . . incapable also of attending to business of any kind, or even of understanding anything in depth, stopping always at the surface . . . He was personally brave; as for his lack of military capacities, it was all too dreadfully obvious [Villeroy had been a remarkably incompetent general, and was responsible for a number of defeats] . . . He was the least liked of anyone at Court because people found in him only a mass of fatuousness, of self-interest and smugness, of boasting about the King's favor and about his great successes . . . He had read nothing, knew nothing, was completely ignorant in every field, given to shallow jokes, much wind and all completely empty."[2] A harsh description, but one which Villeroy's behavior as Governor thoroughly justified.

It was bad enough that the maréchal, who constantly gloated about his unique proximity to his pupil, also tried to set himself up as the Regent's successor; but, worse still, he also tried his best to mold his pupil into a monster of vanity and ignorance, a king whose defects would make him easier to control by the likes of Villeroy.

There was the time, for instance, on August 25, 1717, when a huge crowd gathered in the Tuileries Gardens to celebrate the King's name day. Naturally, the maréchal urged the boy to appear at the window so that he could be shown off. Louis, who was rapidly developing an almost torturing shyness, tried to refuse, but to no avail. "The maréchal de Villeroy," Saint-Simon noted, "convinced the King, with great difficulty, to acknowledge the crowd . . . and as soon as he appeared, the shouts of 'Long live the King' were doubled and redoubled. The maréchal de Villeroy, repeatedly pointing out this prodigious multitude to the King, said sententiously to him: 'See, my master, see all these people, this great crowd, these immense numbers; all that is yours, you are their master,' and ceaselessly he repeated this lesson to make sure the King had understood it."[3] It should have been enough to spoil anyone;

and yet the child—he was only seven—managed, even then, to discount the old man's flattery.

Unfortunately, Villeroy, in one respect at least, turned out to be highly effective. He had received an open, friendly, lively child from Mme de Ventadour; within weeks he transformed his charge into a withdrawn, suspicious and agonizingly shy little boy. It is no wonder: by constantly reminding the King that he was the master of all, by displaying him as often as possible after having carefully coached him, by multiplying the occasions on which the monarch could be paraded in public amid awesome ceremonial, the maréchal insured that Louis would see the world as a stage on which he, the principal figure, must never falter. And to make it all more harrowing still, the full range of ceremonial activities set up by Louis XIV was now imposed on his great-grandson, so that his *lever* and *coucher* were performed every day in front of crowds, while the elaborate ritual of dressing and undressing was followed to the letter.

The results of this treatment were soon noticed. By November 1717, the old duchesse d'Orléans could write: "The young King is good-looking and very intelligent, but he is not a nice child. He loves no one in the world except his former governess; he takes a dislike to people for no reason and is already fond of making sharp criticisms."[4] As usual, the duchesse was exaggerating, but she is a useful witness all the same, precisely because she spent very little time at Court. We can see through her eyes what the public watched: an appearance radically divorced from reality. In October 1718, for instance, she commented: "The King . . . loves ceremonies. The lit de justice bored him a lot less than the [Parlement's] remonstrances . . . He would really be nice if only he spoke a little oftener, but one really has trouble getting him to say a few words."[5] Obviously, Villeroy's method had worked: although, then as later, Louix XV loathed official ceremonies, he managed, at the age of eight, to look as if he enjoyed them, but the silence the duchesse noticed was the consequence of the enormous effort the King was making in order to behave properly.

At least there were two men in his entourage who showed the child kindness and understanding: the Regent himself and the tutor who was actually in charge of the King's education, André-Hercule de Fleury, Bishop of Fréjus. That the duc d'Orléans, however, did not have much time for Louis is easy to understand: he did, after all, have a government to run, so his daily visits lasted between fifteen and forty-five minutes; besides, he had no power, as Villeroy would have been quick to remind him, over the way the King was brought up; that was the sole and exclusive province of the Governor. Luckily, though, Villeroy cared nothing for learning, and little for the details of the King's life when he was not on display, so soon the boy was spending most of his time with Fréjus.* As it turned out, this last-minute choice—Louis XIV appointed him tutor in a codicil to his will dated August 23, 1715—proved to be just the sort of man to offset, inasmuch as it could be done, Villeroy's pernicious methods.

Fréjus, in fact, was a curious choice. For many years he had been refused a

---

* It was customary to call a bishop not by his family name but by the city of his bishopric: the Archbishop of Paris, for instance, became M. de Paris, and Fleury, M. de Fréjus.

bishopric by Louis XIV, who thought him too worldly. Finally, in 1698, after much begging from his protectors at Court, Fleury, at the comparatively advanced age of forty-five, was appointed Bishop of Fréjus and, to everyone's surprise, proved to be a model pastor. That, in itself, was exceptional enough to bring him to the King's notice, favorably this time. Rarer still was Fleury's exemplary conduct when it came to women and high living. In a time when well-born bishops openly kept mistresses, drank, gambled and vied with each other in luxury, Fleury was chaste, sober, modest. As it turned out, he also had another unusual quality: he liked children; so, from the moment he took on the King's education in February 1717, the Bishop provided an essential counterpoise to the vain and selfish Villeroy.

It took M. de Fréjus very little time to realize that the King would not obey someone he disliked, so if he was to be effective he must gain the child's affection. It was not a difficult task. The master of the greatest country in Europe was a sad and lonely boy who responded immediately to warmth, care and affection. Now that Mme de Ventadour was gone, Louis needed someone to love: Fleury made sure he would be that person. His method was simple enough: first, utterly shunning rank and honors for himself, he spent every possible moment with his pupil. In itself that was the very reverse of what everyone else did; then, he made sure that the child's studies were presented to him in a lively and amusing manner, a highly unconventional notion at a time when education consisted mostly of learning by rote. Finally, he arranged the day's program so that his pupil would have a sufficient amount of physical exercise, first in order to keep him healthy, but also as part of the overall learning process. As a result, Louis XV soon became a superb horseman, one whose endurance kept surprising everyone who hunted or rode with him.

Still, every day there were lessons. Aside from grammar and spelling (it is startling to see how few spelling mistakes Louis XV made, especially since most of his contemporaries misspelled constantly), the boy was taught geography and mathematics, history, Latin and the ways in which justice could miscarry. Just how conscious Fleury was of raising a king we can see clearly in the phrases he used in 1718 as examples of good grammar:

"O my subjects, pray to God that I never use my power except for the good of the people."

"Although the King has promised to control his anger, it still often rules him to the point where he sometimes strikes those he loves because they are most faithful to him and serve him best."

"Disorders dishonor a king."

"No one is greater than a kind and hardworking king; no one, on the other hand, is more despicable than a lazy and cowardly king."

All these admirable precepts were obviously chosen by Fleury to counteract Villeroy's example. Even more important, however, was the emphasis on religion. Serving God, Fleury repeated tirelessly, was the most important thing in life. Since the King was God's representative on earth, he must be even more pious than other men. "The King should govern wisely," ran one of Fleury's maxims, "but it is even more necessary for him to govern in a Christian manner."[6] It wasn't merely that being a good Christian was the be-all and end-all of life on this earth either: Fleury made it very plain to his pupil that he risked an eternity in hell if he failed in his duty. For a child to whom untimely death was so very familiar, this was indeed food for thought.

Almost as often as he talked about God, Fleury warned his pupil of the dangers to which kings were exposed, the worst of which was flattery; and while he readily praised the boy when he did well, he was equally prompt to criticize him when he misbehaved or lagged behind in his studies. Nor, legend to the contrary, was the King's curriculum a mere pretense. By 1720 the ten-year-old boy was studying, with numerous specialized teachers, history, geography, Latin, astronomy, drawing, the natural sciences, mathematics, the art of war and dance and deportment. This was a daily routine. The King never had a single day off and was expected to work even when all others rested. Luckily, it was no hardship: Louis XV was intelligent, quick to understand and remember, and full of curiosity. Soon he was drawing his own maps of France, working a little printing press and engraving semiprecious stones.

It was so obvious to the Regent that Fleury was doing a good job that on May 14, 1717, the Bishop was granted the rare privilege of riding in the King's carriages— something which was usually reserved for grandees—and was told that this was not due to his status as a bishop, or to his being the King's tutor, but solely to his personal achievements. While Villeroy still pranced and strutted, it was becoming obvious to a few discerning men, the Regent among them, that Fleury had earned the young King's love.

Fleury's curriculum notwithstanding, Louis's life was not all study. He rode, and soon he hunted in the forests surrounding Paris. He had pets, mostly dogs, but also a little doe who often followed his carriage; and, to break the routine, there were occasional extraordinary events like the visit to Paris of Tsar Peter the Great.

"The Tsar," Saint-Simon noted, "was a very tall man, very well built, rather thin, with a rather round face, a large forehead and fine eyebrows. His nose was rather short, though not to excess . . . his lips were thick, his complexion tanned and ruddy. His eyes were black, large, piercing, wide open, and his glance was majestic yet gracious when he was watching himself, at other times severe and a little wild . . . On Monday, May 10, [1717], the King went to see the Tsar . . . All present were surprised to see the Tsar take hold of the King under the arms, raise him to his own height, kiss him thus in the air, and the King, in spite of his youth, and of the fact that he had not been prepared for this, showed no fear at all. We were all struck by [Peter's] graceful way of treating the King, by his look of tenderness, by his politeness, which seemed completely unconstrained and yet was marked by a blend of grandeur due to their equality of rank and slight superiority due to age, for it was all distinctly felt. He praised the King greatly and seemed very taken by him . . . kissing him several times. The King delivered his short speech beautifully."[7] All in all, it must have been a memorable experience.

Louis XV's early childhood, in fact, can fairly be described as monotony relieved by unexpected events, like the Tsar's visit, and interrupted by sudden change. There had been the switch from Mme de Ventadour to Villeroy in February 1717; a year and a half later, on August 25, 1718, the King's close entourage went through yet another major upheaval. Although, in September 1715, the duc du Maine's wings had been severely clipped, he was allowed to remain Superintendent of the King's

Education. This was in many ways an empty title since Villeroy did all the showing off and Fleury all the actual work, but it still meant that the duc visited the King every morning and told him amusing stories.[8] In all probability, the boy was actually fond of him: whatever his other shortcomings may have been, du Maine had lost none of his considerable charm. Unfortunately, ever since 1715 he had also been plotting against the Regent; his castle at Sceaux, just outside Paris, was a center for all the new regime's opponents, and it began to look as if all the talk was about to be translated into action. As a result, the duc d'Orléans, who until then had deliberately closed his eyes to all the goings-on at Sceaux, decided that it was time to strike a blow. He arranged for a sudden lit de justice and surrounded the palace with an awesome display of troops, all without announcing the purpose of the solemn meeting. Still, it was reasonably obvious that it somehow involved the légitimés, and the terrified duc du Maine, walking up to his friend the maréchal de Villars just before the beginning of the lit de justice, whispered, "Something violent is going to happen to my brother and myself."[9] He was only partly right. The Regent was too great a skeptic to believe in repression: the duc du Maine simply lost his capacity to succeed to the throne, his exalted rank (no longer a Prince of the Blood, he now took precedence from the date of his peerage, just like any other duc), and his Superintendence of the King's Education, this last simply because the ambitious and greedy duc de Bourbon wanted the sinecure and had exchanged his support of the other changes for the appointment.

As usual, Louis XV kept his feelings to himself. "I had watched the King carefully when the question of his education came up [at the lit de justice]," Saint-Simon wrote, "and I saw no alteration, no change, no constraint, even . . . He only mentioned the duc du Maine's name once, after his dinner on that same day, and then he asked where he was going in the most indifferent way."[10] No matter how he felt about losing the duc du Maine, the young King must have soon realized that the new Superintendent was no improvement. The duc de Bourbon, or M. le Duc, as he was generally called, was the head of the Condé branch of the Bourbons, and thus, for the moment, the First Prince of the Blood Royal. That is about the only neutral thing that can be said about him, for M. le Duc was unquestionably one of the most unpleasant, greedy and dishonorable men of his time. Tall, thin, ugly, one-eyed as the result of a hunting accident, this young man—he was in his mid-twenties—did not feel that it was enough to be the third person in the realm (after the King and the Regent) and enormously wealthy to boot: he always wanted more, more honors (hence the Superintendence), more power (but the Regent was in the way), more money. He demanded and received several enormous pensions which, together with his extensive estates, gave him the huge income of 1,800,000 livres*; he made himself thoroughly unpleasant in the two councils he belonged to, and terrorized his entourage by the violence and frequency of his rages.

Naturally, there could be no question of rages when it came to dealing with the King: there, M. le Duc was all amiability, but, unlike the duc du Maine's, his visits were relatively rare; still, the change in superintendents only caused the King to rely

---

* Although it is very difficult to equate money in the preindustrial era with our own, the best possible equivalence would be about $4.50 to the livre.

on Fleury the more. As for the tutor, who realized full well that he had his pupil's love and confidence, he made very sure not to rock the boat. He carefully avoided all political discussions and asked for no favors, in itself an act of extraordinary self-denial. Moreover, when, in 1721, he was offered the Archbishopric of Reims by the Regent, he actually refused it. By the standards of the time, this appeared absolutely incomprehensible. Not only was Reims one of the richest sees in the kingdom (and Fleury was poor) but its archbishopric automatically conferred a dukedom; and, finally, the coronation was approaching. It was the Archbishop-Duke of Reims who actually crowned the King. What better consecration of his services, Fleury was told, than to have the glory of placing the crown on his pupil's head?

A lesser man might well have been taken in. Social distinctions counted for a great deal in the eighteenth century, but Fleury saw the offer for what it was: an attempt to get him out of the way; and he had no doubt about the real identity of its author—not the Regent, as it appeared, but the Regent's most trusted advisor, the enormously ambitious abbé Dubois. More than anyone, Dubois, himself a clever man, realized what was happening, since he himself had attained power by relying on just the same relationship to the duc d'Orléans, whose tutor he had been, as the one Fleury was establishing with the King. "The abbé Dubois was a little thin man, sharp, hypocritical, with a blond wig, the face of a weasel and a look of wit . . . All the vices fought within him . . . Avarice, debauchery, ambition, these were his gods . . . He excelled at low intrigues . . . but always had a goal to which all his stratagems were directed, and this with a patience whose only bound was success,"[11] wrote Saint-Simon, who obviously didn't like him. In fact, the abbé Dubois, who was no cleric,* had early recognized the duc d'Orléans's intelligence and encouraged his intellectual development; but then, in order to keep his hold on his pupil, he had taught him how to lead a life of debauchery, introduced him to the brothels in Paris, and still participated in his orgies.

It was only when the duc became Regent that Dubois's full scope became apparent: as a kind of secret prime minister, he did much to determine the government's foreign policy, went off on secret missions and, in one case at least, managed to provide France with a major alliance: that was Dubois's good side. The other, even if one ignores his pimping, whoring and drinking, was a growing ambition. He wanted to be appointed prime minister instead of just playing the part behind the scenes, he wanted money, and he was determined to become a cardinal. The Regent was far too easygoing ever to become an obstacle; the one man who could stand in his way, however, was the modest, almost invisible M. de Fréjus. After all, the King's minority would soon end, since kings of France came of age at thirteen, and then Dubois assumed that Fleury, who must have the same ambitions as himself, would so maneuver as to become prime minister himself.

Of course, Fleury understood all this; he realized, too, that his future depended entirely on his pupil's future backing: if he were to move to Reims and away from the King, he would soon be forgotten. If, on the other hand, he declined the plum proffered by the Regent, he would earn Louis's gratitude, since he would appear to

---

* It was quite possible for a layman to be given an abbey; he then enjoyed its income and received either minor orders or, as in Dubois's case, none at all.

be sacrificing the most brilliant promotion to his affection for the boy; and so, with many expressions of gratitude, he declined the offer, saying that his only desire was to stay near the King, finish his education and remain in obscurity. Of course, it was a smart move, but, to be fair, it was a kind one as well. The King, who was deeply attached to Fleury, would have been devastated by a separation. As for the Regent, who was surprised at first, he didn't really worry about Fleury's real motivation: after all, the Bishop was already sixty-seven. At that age, he obviously couldn't be expected to live much longer.

Fleury's refusal, in fact, turned out to be even better politics than anyone could have imagined. The King was very fond of the Regent, who was not only respectful and attentive but kind. In August 1719, for instance, the duc offered the boy a little hunting lodge at La Muette, just outside Paris. "The King was delighted. He thought something at last belonged to him personally, took great pleasure in going there, obtained bread, milk, fruit and vegetables from its kitchen and garden and indulged in all the games which amuse one at that age."[12] But Dubois was altogether another matter. The King had learned to dislike him and was naturally encouraged to do so by both Fleury and Villeroy. "No one is more spontaneously proud than children," Saint-Simon wrote, "and most especially a crowned and spoilt child! The King was, in fact, very aware of his position, very sensitive and easily offended, and noticed everything without showing it. Dubois never worked with him, but attended him and spoke to him with a kind of familiarity and informality which upset him . . . [Villeroy and Fleury] took care to point out to the King the disrespectful and improper behavior of the abbé Dubois."[13] It is perhaps a little difficult for us today to realize that a child of nine or ten might be shocked by the breeziness of an elder, but, more perhaps than any other King of France, Louis XV cared about etiquette. Unlike Louis XIV, who had codified it, he had lived with it from birth, and it determined the way his environment functioned. Louis XIV considered etiquette as a useful tool in his effort to cow the nobility; Louis XVI eventually thought of it as a nuisance which had to be endured; for Louis XV, it was the very air he breathed, and he was therefore especially sensitive to any break in the accepted code. Besides that, he had early learned to think of himself not as a child but as the King. By treating him as if he were of no consequence, Dubois offended him gravely. Even more remarkable, however, than this early identification of the person with the function is the ability of a very young child to conceal his displeasure. It boded ill for Dubois's future; at the same time, Louis XV clearly held a high regard for the dignity of a king: he would not manifest his displeasure until he was in a position to do something about it, since otherwise he would show the world the exact limit of his power.

The Regent, on the other hand, did everything he could, within reason, to please the King. There were the daily visits, there was La Muette, there was also the King's own little army over which he had already begun to rule. "The King has created a regiment of all the young noblemen who surround him," an observer noted in July 1720. "It is divided into companies which practice the changing of the guard every night after His Majesty's studies on the terrace of the Tuileries. The King has given it the name of Royal Terrace . . . [It] practices regularly and observes a very exact discipline."[14] More important still, the duc d'Orléans was sensitive enough to understand the strain inherent in having the appearance of power without the reality, and he treated the King accordingly. Saint-Simon, who was in a position to watch all this, saw clearly "the King's liking for M. le duc d'Orléans . . . who always approached him in public, but also in the most private situations, with the same respectful manner which he had used to the late King. He never took the slightest liberty, even less any familiarities, but all this with grace, and without any of the imposing air to be expected from someone his age and who occupied so important a function. His conversation was tailored to [the King] both when he spoke to him and when he spoke in front of him, with a little gaiety, but in a very measured way, and which merely banished overseriousness while taming the child. When he worked with [the King], he did so in a relaxed way, but so as to show him that he did nothing without accounting to him for it, while keeping it short, easy to understand for a child of the King's age. He always behaved as if he were merely the King's minister. As for the things to be given [i.e., promotions, titles, offices, pensions, etc.], he would propose recipients . . . but never failed to add that he was merely giving his opinion as he was in duty bound to do, but that it was not for him to make the gift, that the King was the master, and that it was up to him to choose and decide. Sometimes, even when it was a matter of little consequence, he urged the King to decide himself; and if, on rare occasions, the King seemed inclined to someone, for he was too proud and too shy to make his wishes plain, M. le duc d'Orléans always paid this desire great attention and told the King gracefully that he could guess his preference and then immediately added: 'But aren't you the master? I am here only to inform you, to propose solutions, to receive and carry out your orders'; and on the instant the favor was easily granted, without any emphasis on it at all, and [the Regent] immediately went on to something else. This behavior in public and in private, and especially that way of working with the King, charmed the little monarch. He felt himself a man, it was as if he were ruling, and he was grateful to the person who thus enabled him to reign." And Saint-Simon, who was nobody's fool, goes on to say: "The Regent was hardly taking a great risk: the King seldom cared much."[15]

This last is not surprising: Louis XV, at the time, was nine years old. Still, since his entourage kept expecting him to behave as an adult, it was all the more praiseworthy of the Regent that he, almost alone, managed to separate the function and the person. Further, even as he pleased the boy, he was also, by degrees, teaching him the business of government and that, in itself, was no mean achievement.

All through the years 1720 and 1721 Fleury continued to mold the King in much the same spirit: he was to be made fit to rule. As the boy grew familiar with Latin, he was made to translate dicta from the *Imitation of Jesus Christ,* phrases like this, the very first in his exercise book: "Vanity of vanities, all is vanity except the love and service of God"; or, a little further on, "The most important and useful lesson is the true knowledge and contempt of oneself"; or, again, "He who knows himself well sees with his own eyes and has no taste for the praise of other men"; or even, "Jesus Christ chose to suffer and be held in contempt and you dare to complain?" Not the kind of ideas likely to appeal in a post-Freudian world: we are hardly encouraged, these days, to think of ourselves as vile; but for a child almost smothered in flattery, for the man whom all would worship as semidivine, these stark reminders of his fallibility provided a useful balance. There were sentences from Proverbs as well: "The fear of the Lord is the beginning of wisdom"; "If wisdom enter into your heart, and science please your soul, wisdom will defend you and prudence keep you"; and, no doubt with an eye on Louis XIV's numerous mistresses, "He who is adulterous will lose his soul through the folly of his heart. He will be covered with infamy and ignominy and his opprobrium will never cease."[16]

These maxims were intermixed with the teaching, in great detail, of the precepts of the Roman Catholic Church as they were then understood. The emphasis was on orthodox practices rather than dogma, a matter which was considered best left to the professionals; so the young King was taught to believe that he could save his soul by attending Mass every day—he was, after all, Eldest Son of the Church and the Most Christian King—and by adhering to a number of accepted rules which ran all the way from the sanctity of the sale of indulgences to the taking of communion in one kind only, except for priests. This emphasis on rigid but thoughtless orthodoxy had, at that very moment, an important political meaning. One of the senseless religious disputes of which the French were then so fond had been raging since 1712. While this controversy concerning the papal bull *Unigenitus* will be discussed a little later, it remains that Fleury had chosen to obey the bull at the earliest opportunity, thus separating himself from a number of other bishops. Now he was teaching his pupil that obedience to God, in religious matters, meant obedience to the Pope.

All through this period, Villeroy continued to display the King as often as he could. There was, for instance, early in 1721 the episode of the ballet. "The maréchal de Villeroy, who was incapable of teaching the King anything solid, who adored the late King almost as if he had been a god, and who was full of wind and frivolity, decided that, like the late King in his youth, the King would dance a ballet," Saint-Simon recorded dourly. "It was too soon to think about it: this was too strenuous a pleasure considering the King's age [he was not quite eleven] and it would have been better to overcome his shyness little by little, letting him grow used to the world he feared rather than convincing him to show himself off in public and dance on a stage . . . The King grew so bored and so tired with having to learn, rehearse and dance a ballet that he developed an aversion for all these festivities and for spectacles of all kinds."[17] In fact, Louis XV needed no such nuisance to make him dislike this kind of show, but it is obvious that Villeroy's insistence, far from curing the child's shyness, could only make him feel more inadequate. A diarist who was allowed into the hall at the Tuileries during one of the performances noted: "[The King] did not dance with any vivacity; he looked serious."[18] No wonder: for him the amusement was just a chore.

At least another ballet gave the young monarch a chance to show what he could do. On January 10, 1721, Marais, that busy observer, recorded: "The King attended the play *Dom Japhet* by Scarron, which is very amusing and made him laugh. There has been a quarrel about it which the King resolved like a second Solomon. The duc d'Aumont, First Gentleman of the Bedchamber, whose year is ending* and who had ordered that Cardenio's new ballet be performed, claimed that if it was still being

---

* There were four First Gentlemen, all dukes. They were the most important of the King's attendants, and each served a year at a time.

danced, he must oversee the performances even though his year was over. The duc de Mortemart, whose period of office began with the year 1721, said on the contrary that it was his duty to oversee them, and that no one would usurp any part of his year. The Regent told them to settle the dispute themselves, and that he had more important business to attend than their ballet. They went to see the King, who told them that in order to solve their problem, he no longer wanted to see the ballet, which had bored him, and that he wanted performances of *Dom Japhet,* which had made him laugh. And so this frivolous dispute has been solved by a child."[19]

Marais, who recorded this incident, was no courtier, indeed, he wasn't even noble, but the attention he paid the King is characteristic. The child was enormously popular because it was generally assumed, as was always the case in France during minorities, that once he was old enough to rule, he would bring forth a new golden age; and, no doubt, the fact that he was, as the old duchesse d'Orléans put it, "the handsomest child anyone has ever seen"[20] could only help. At eleven, in fact, Louis XV was tall for his age, slender yet quite strong, with abundant black hair, huge black eyes, a delicately curved nose, a generous mouth and a dazzling complexion. And then, much to everyone's surprise, a mere six days after his eleventh birthday, he entered puberty. "The King has had a very pleasing illness, and one which he hadn't yet endured: he suddenly became a man. He thought he was ill and confided in one of his valets, who told him that this particular disease was a sign of health. He then decided to talk about it to Maréchal, his First Surgeon, who told him that this disease would worry no one, and that, at his age, he had no reason to complain. People call it laughingly the King's disease,"[21] Marais noted. That a Parisian lawyer should have known this kind of intimate detail is typical of the atmosphere in which the King was being raised, although it is only fair to add that sexual matters were not then considered taboo.

Five months later, another royal disease made the news, but this time it was no joke. On July 31, 1721, Louis XV became seriously ill. "He was seized by a fever as he attended the Mass and was forced to leave it," Barbier, another lawyer-diarist noted. "He has been bled from the arm." Immediately the Court and town panicked, and with good reason. Doctors were notoriously incompetent and given to despatching their patients to the next world with great speed. Everyone remembered that the King's father, mother and brother had died in just a few days after being bled and purged repeatedly. Now it looked as if history was about to be repeated, and, in fact, the next day the King got worse. On August 1 "[his] fever doubled and even made him delirious, so the doctors have had great disagreements about bleeding him from the foot . . . The King . . . almost fainted at the end of the bleeding. All the Court was in a great fright, but he soon regained consciousness, and then he slept for eight hours." Clearly, more remedies were needed; so, having bled their patient, the doctors now purged him. "On Saturday morning [August 2] the King was given twice two grains of emetic"[22] which brought about, another observer noted, "a charming evacuation."[23] The peril was over, the fever broke, the King slept. By the following day he was able to get up again and was greeted by an explosion of joy. "Paris has learned the good news about the King's health with extraordinary joy. Nothing could be added to the demonstrations of love from people of all classes and conditions.

Prayers, Te Deums, bonfires, illuminations, danses, songs, cavalcades, celebrations
are given by the bourgeois as well as the people, in a word, all one can imagine by
way of excessive pleasure . . . has kept Paris busy for several days. The fishwives
took an eight-foot sturgeon to the Louvre, the butchers an ox and a sheep, everyone
has brought his offering . . . and the streets echo night and day with shouts of
'Long live the King' . . . The nobility has spent a prodigious amount on fireworks."[24]

For weeks the rejoicings continued. On August 12, Louis XV appeared in public
for the first time in order to attend a thanksgiving service at Notre-Dame. "He looked
very pale in his carriage," Marais noted. "The people, showing its joy anew, shouted
more than ever. It is impossible to describe the full extent of their celebrations."[25]
Indeed, the King was passionately loved; but there is some truth in a dry little
sentence jotted down by the often dour Barbier: "One can tell how much we need
him to live, and how deeply the Regent is hated, by the way everyone worries about
his health, for, as to himself, we have yet no reason to love or hate him."[26]

By the summer of 1721 the Regent, who had now been in power for six years, had
become enormously—and unjustly—unpopular. The King's life was therefore all the
more precious because at his death it was the Regent who would become King.

Few French rulers have been more attacked than the duc d'Orléans. He has been
accused of ruining the State and the country, of giving in to France's enemies while
deserting its friends. He was, people said, too kind, too harsh, too blunt, too subtle,
too simple, too calculating, too lax, too authoritarian. He had refused to make war
when France's honor was at stake and attacked instead the King's own uncle, the
only living grandson of Louis XIV. And, of course, people blamed him for his orgies,
his mistresses, and his tolerance of the equally spectacular deportment of his daughter Elisabeth, the widowed duchesse de Berry.

In fact, with the exception of the orgies, the mistresses and the daughter, none of
the accusations were true; and even then it should be noted that the numerous ladies
who succeeded one another in the Regent's bed had very little to show for their
efforts except, one hopes, pleasure and a certain notoriety. Unlike Louis XIV, who
had enriched his mistresses, the Regent was sparing with the State's money, and he
was well known for his constant refusal to speak about politics with his paramours,
but even this was used against him. Every night, at eight o'clock, the doors of the
Regent's apartments in the Palais Royal were closed to all except servants, and no
politics was ever allowed to distract him from his orgy. Of course, that was de-
nounced as the worse scandal of all, although it is perhaps a little hard to see why.
Would the critics, one cannot help wondering, have preferred it if the Regent had
conducted the business of the State in the midst of drunken revelry? These complaints were all the more unfair in that the Regent gave government an even greater
number of hours, every day, than Louis XIV. If, instead of spending his mornings out
hunting, he chose to spend his evenings closeted with a group of pretty women and
cheerful young men, surely that was his privilege; but the truth of the matter was
that for the first time in half a century, censorship was virtually abolished, and the

explosion of criticism that resulted was directed at the Regent's way of life simply because it was so very visible and convenient a target.

These violent attacks, in turn, made the duc d'Orléans more and more unpopular, but he cared so little about them that he allowed them to multiply; only in one case did he take offense. In a pamphlet published in 1719—and, naturally, unsigned—the author, a fifth-rate writer called Lagrange-Chancel, warned: "Nocher des ondes infernales / Prépares-toi sans t'effrayer / A passer les ombres royales / Que Philippe va t'envoyer." ("Boatman of Hell's river / Prepare without trembling / To carry the royal shades / Which Philippe will soon send you.") The Regent didn't mind if he was represented as a besotted and corrupt debauchee, but that one accusation rankled, perhaps because it was so generally whispered, more probably because it reminded the duc d'Orléans of the duchesse du Maine's calumnies of 1714. As for the accusation itself, of course, it needs no disproving. The King not only survived the Regency, he was transformed from a fragile, sickly boy into a remarkably healthy adolescent during the years of his uncle's power.

Accusing the Regent of wanting to do away with the King was an easy way out for his enemies: the (predicted) murder of a child makes for better polemics than arguments on the deficit or the conduct of foreign policy; but it was because of his new system of alliances that the Regent was hated by all those who still yearned for Louis XIV's policies while, on the other hand, those who had resented them now blamed the government for its revolutionary fiscal and monetary solutions.

As the result of the Treaty of Utrecht, which ended the War of the Spanish Succession, Europe had been left divided into two uneasy halves. On one side were France and Spain, now ruled by a grandson of Louis XIV; on the other, Austria and England were supported by smaller countries like Holland and Piedmont. It was a dangerous situation at best, and soon it became even more tense. Philip V of Spain had been forced at Utrecht to buy peace with the cession of a few fragments of the widespread Spanish Empire—Flanders, Milan, Naples and Sicily in particular. Now, instead of being satisfied with Spain and its immense colonies, he longed to recover his lost possessions, even if that meant starting the European conflict anew. Considering that the late war had very nearly ruined France, Spain's only ally, and left its government saddled with a crushing burden of debt, it hardly seemed like a good idea to start fighting all over again, this time for the sake of a few far-flung provinces.

An alliance with England made perfect sense for France, however, since it would ipso facto dismantle the anti-French coalition. By 1715 the two countries were anxious to preserve the peace, France because it was exhausted, England because it had just installed a new dynasty, the Hanoverians, whose throne was hardly solid yet. So, after much hesitation, and on the advice of the abbé Dubois, the Regent started negotiating with King George I. This, in itself, was a revolutionary gesture, because France had supported the Stuart Pretender, a Catholic, whose place the Protestant George I had now taken. After much secret negotiation, a treaty linking the two nations was signed at The Hague on January 4, 1717.

This was a most unpopular move in France. England was the hereditary enemy, had just fought a long, hard war against France and was thought to be a greedy, predatory power. The "old Court," that is, the ministers of the last reign, the courtiers who had been close to the late King (like the maréchal de Villeroy) and, of course, the group of opponents around the duc and duchesse du Maine were all fiercely opposed to the new policy. Their discontent turned even more vocal when it became apparent that France was also drifting into a war with Spain.

That the state of tension between the two countries was due to the incredible foolishness of the Spanish Government naturally made very little difference: bad faith and politics are often bedfellows. And, naturally, the Spanish party in France carefully refrained from acknowledging that they were merely serving the greed of Philip's wife, Queen Isabella.

The Queen's demands were logical enough. Because she was Philip's second wife, and because he had a son by his first wife, her own son, Don Carlos, was unlikely to succeed to the throne, so she set about finding another state for him to rule. An Italian herself (she was a Farnese), she plumped for Naples and Sicily. Only, at Utrecht, Naples had been given to Austria, and Sicily to Piedmont, so it followed that a war with Austria was the next step. As for the King, who might be expected to have had more sense than to listen to a plan that would pit his enfeebled nation against most of Europe, he, too, had a problem. Not only was he, at best, weak-willed and not very bright, he was also beset by ferocious sexual appetites. Having intercourse only once a day struck him as extreme deprivation, while total abstinence caused him to sink into a deep, pathological depression; and since he was far too bigoted to take a mistress, he had to rely exclusively on his wife for relief. Whenever, therefore, the Queen wanted anything, she simply refused to have sex until her husband yielded. It did not take much of this sort of treatment before Philip informed his cousin, the Regent, that he had decided to demand the return of Naples and Sicily.

He didn't have long to wait for an answer. France, the duc d'Orléans pointed out, was in no state to fight anyone, and, in any event, would hardly be disposed to take on the rest of Europe just to please Queen Isabella. Still, fearing that war might erupt even if they remained neutral, the two new allies, France and England, came up with a compromise solution: both Parma, where the last of the Farnese would leave Queen Isabella as his heir, and Tuscany, whose grand duke was childless, would go to Don Carlos whenever their current rulers died. Austria would keep Naples; the Duke of Savoy, who had become King of Sicily at Utrecht, would give it to Austria and receive Sardinia in exchange. It was a reasonable arrangement, one which Austria was prepared to accept. Philip V, however, who listened not only to his wife but also to an Italian adventurer, the abbé Alberoni, whom the Queen had just made Prime Minister, was convinced that Spain could defeat the rest of Europe. He therefore rejected the compromise and refused all further talks.

In those leisurely days, even declarations of war came slowly. Great Britain warned Spain that if it persisted for a few months longer, it would be forced to come to Austria's help; and since France was committed by treaty to act in accord with England to preserve the status quo, it also prepared to let Philip know that it might eventually have to think about taking steps.

Needless to say, the impending conflict with Spain gave the opposition to the Regent all the ammunition it needed. It could now point out that after a ruinous but successful war France had finally made sure that Spain could never again be a danger by placing one of its own princes on that throne. Now, eight years later, the Regent was allied with France's traditional foes and getting ready to fight this very King, Louis XIV's grandson and Louis XV's uncle. Obviously, it could be made to look very like treason.

As a result, it was with great and unusual difficulty that the Regent convinced the Council of Regency to approve the agreement with England concerning the proposed anti-Spanish intervention, but he carried the day. An ultimatum was sent off to Madrid: if, by November 2, 1718, Spain did not desist, France (and England) would join Austria.

The full extent of the Queen's foolishness now became apparent. Having, single-handedly and without allies, started the hostilities, the Spanish Government sat and waited while its only fleet was literally annihilated at the Battle of Passaro, off the coast of Sicily, on August 11, 1718. Without a fleet, there was obviously no longer any chance of conquering either Sicily (an island, after all), or Naples. Alberoni and Isabella, however, were not so easily discouraged: if Spain could not fight alone, they reasoned, then France would have to help; and since the Regent was so blind as to refuse assistance, he would have to be deposed. The Spanish Ambassador, therefore, was instructed to encourage a plot, to be led by the duc du Maine, so as to seize the duc d'Orléans, imprison him and proclaim the King of Spain Regent in his stead. The duc du Maine would then rule for the King, and all would be well. None of the plotters seems to have realized that this was a direct violation of the Treaty of Utrecht, and that therefore the whole of Europe would promptly declare war on France; or perhaps they did, assuming that France could resist a united continent. In any event, Spain proved as incompetent at plotting as it was at fighting. On December 5, two Spanish envoys who had been shadowed all along were finally arrested. They carried with them the full outline of the plot, the names of the plotters and the date of the proposed coup d'état. On December 13, the Prince of Cellamare, the Spanish Ambassador, was seized and sent back to Spain; and on December 28, the duc and duchesse du Maine were also arrested. After that, there was nothing left for the Regent to do but declare war on Spain, and this he proceeded to do in January 1719.

There are wars and wars, however. It cannot be said that the French Army tried very hard to invade Spain, but the state of that country's defenses was so grotesquely inadequate that, with the best will in the world, the French could not help but progress. On April 20, they seized the harbor of Los Pasajes, just across the border, and burned the ships being built to replace the defunct Spanish fleet, thus neatly settling the issue; but still Philip would not give up, so the Army moved forward, still as slowly as possible, and settled down before Fuenterrabia, which it proceeded to besiege with a marked lack of zeal. Finally, after offering the duc d'Orléans half of France if he, Philip, could have the other half, the King did what he should have done in the first place: he fired Alberoni, spoke forcefully to Isabella and, on January 6, 1720, at long last sued for peace. The final settlement, generously enough, followed exactly the same line as the compromise offered two years earlier.

At least this fiasco gave birth to a new alliance linking France, Spain and Great Britain; and its first manifestation was matrimonial. Princely marriages were the normal way of confirming political settlements; in this case, one of the Regent's daughters was sent off to marry the Prince of Asturias, the Spanish Heir Apparent, while an infanta came to Paris as Louis XV's affianced bride. Only this time the tradition misfired: the little fiancée was only three and a half years old. Considering that the King had already entered puberty, and that an heir to the throne was a crying necessity, it seemed shortsighted, at the very least, to postpone by some twelve years the moment when Louis XV might hope to have children. Indeed, this one time it seems that the Regent let personal ambition sway his policy since, after all, his daughter would one day be Queen of Spain, and his grandson, therefore, a king.

This marriage excepted, however, the Regent's policy had clearly been wise. His giving in to Spanish ambitions would have had catastrophic consequences, while, in the end, the King of Spain lost little more than his fleet, and France nothing, from the Franco-British alliance, but that hardly swayed those people in France who were determined to criticize the government no matter what it did. And by the time Louis XV became ill, there was yet another good reason, or so the opposition thought, to hate Orléans.

Galloping inflation and collapsing stock market bubbles are never pleasant things for the speculators who are caught in the debacle. In 1721, in fact, these phenomena were just occurring as the result of a bold experiment with that novel commodity, paper money.

On May 26, 1716, John Law, a Scottish adventurer who had fled England, opened a banking house in Paris and immediately began to demonstrate the wonders of credit. He could hardly have chosen a better time to do so. Like much of Europe, France was suffering from a severe shortage of currency. Today we are accustomed to watching governments print whatever quantity of money they need: paper is cheap and the printing press works fast; but in 1716 money consisted of gold and silver coins, and there was nothing anyone could do to create more. When the amount of precious metals in circulation rose, as it had in the sixteenth and early seventeenth centuries thanks to the production of mines in Spanish America, prices tended to go up as well, but slowly, and prosperity resulted from the overall stimulation of the economy. When, however, populations grew larger but the quantity of money remained stable, as it had been for some decades, then a severe economic contraction followed. The value of gold went up, that of agricultural and manufacturing products down, incomes shrank, commerce slowed and poverty worsened.

That kind of economic downturn was bad enough. In France, to make matters even worse, the enormously costly War of the Spanish Succession had speeded up the process: as it kept taxing and spending, the government withdrew money from general circulation and either sent it abroad to pay its troups there or turned it over to a few financiers who hoarded it in the confident expectation it would soon be worth more. Then, because it was forced to borrow heavily, it naturally paid ever higher rates of interest—a situation with which we are not unfamiliar—so that by 1715 a handful of Paris financiers had become enormously, unprecedentedly rich while everyone else, including the Treasury, experienced a severe liquidity crisis.

In that atmosphere, the replacement of gold by paper made eminent (but not yet obvious) sense; and that is just what Law began doing, privately and in moderation.

By issuing notes backed only partly by gold, the Banque générale was already behaving like its modern successors and creating credit. Success was immediate, and the stock of the Banque, another innovation, began to rise. At the same time, the Regent was struggling with the crushing debt bequeathed by Louis XIV. Unlike modern national debts, the French Debt in 1715 was unfunded: there was neither any surety of its being repaid—since it was, in theory, the King's personal liability, which he could repudiate if he so chose—nor any schedule of repayment, nor even any regularity in the payment of interest. As a result, the Debt tended to absorb whatever the taxes produced, without, however, shrinking visibly.

At first the Regent tried the old-fashioned method of prosecuting the holders of state paper. Unlike today, when government bonds are widely held, state notes in 1715 were the property of some fifty financiers, most of whom had acquired them at a scandalous discount; in order to get one hundred thousand livres in cash, for instance, the Comptroller General of the Finances often found himself forced to give out half a million in paper, all of which was due, and on which interest had to be paid. Since that paper then had a tendency to depreciate (no one knew when, if ever, it would be redeemed), it was sometimes possible to buy that half-million note for as little as a tenth of its value; so, for an investment of fifty thousand livres you would own a theoretical capital of half a million while collecting interest often superior to your total outlay. All this was well known, and slowly people realized that the King (and therefore the taxpayers) was the victim of an enormous swindle.

Because of this, and because the splashy nouveau riche were extremely unpopular, the prosecutions were widely praised. They reduced the Debt a little, produced some ready cash—only a few million—but all that was still insufficient. Of course, economies, as budget-cutting was then called, were also tried. The Regent reduced the strength of the Army, virtually closed the Navy down and even thought for a while of razing the palace of Marly (Saint-Simon talked him out of it) just to save the upkeep. Still, none of these measures came even close to balancing the budget, besides which the liquidity crisis continued unabated. That was when the Regent heard about Law.

What followed was the first experiment in controlled inflation; only economic theory was primitive or nonexistent, and the notion of paper money revolutionary, so no one ever quite understood just what was happening—except poor John Law, who watched as his sound, indeed inspired, idea was slowly ruined. First, the Banque purchased the West Indies Company. With its hints at mythical Mississippi gold and quite real Colonial produce, the Compagnie instantly became a popular investment and its stock went up. Then, the credit mechanism of the bank was used by the State, which had allowed the Banque to buy the Compagnie and given it a trade monopoly, and all the most important people—Princes of the Blood, dukes—showed everyone the way by purchasing bank or West Indies stock. As the value of the stock rose, more stock was sold to the public, and the Treasury borrowed more heavily from the Banque. Soon dividends began to rise because both bank and company were, in fact, doing excellent business. And then people everywhere caught on: Law was a genius who, with a touch of his magic wand, was creating wealth where before there had been poverty.

The next step was obvious. Money was needed to finance the campaign against

Spain, and there was only one place where it could be found, so, against Law's repeated objections, on December 4, 1718, the Regent made the bank the sole receiving and paying agent of the Treasury. This was no nationalization: the stock of both bank and company was left in private hands and was freely traded; only now the Banque used its notes to pay the State's creditors, in effect assuming the burden of both current expenditure and the Debt.

That, in itself, only made the Banque's paper more desirable, since it was so clearly preferable to the old Treasury notes. All through the year 1719, the Banque's shares kept rising. The French had discovered speculation and everyone took part. Footmen became millionaires and turned into magnates, water carriers were covered with gold and jewels, while the aristocracy also participated in the great boom. The immediate effect of all this increase in the quantity of money was a return to prosperity. As the new rich spent, built and consumed, employment and profits rose. The depression was over.

The only problem was that no one knew when to stop. By July 1719, the Banque's shares, originally sold at par for five hundred livres, had risen to eight thousand livres. The Regent, who was as dazzled as everyone else, now turned over the rest of the State's financial operations to the Banque: it collected taxes and even ran the mint. Still the fever grew, still the price of a share of stock rose. By December 1719, it was over eighteen thousand livres, or thirty-six times the original par value. Even then, collapse could have been avoided: the Banque was making money and so was the West Indies Company, but it was dealt its first major blow by a few greedy men. In late November, the ever predatory duc de Bourbon, along with his cousin the prince de Conti and four or five great noblemen began to sell their stock. Still, the prices continued rising for a while, but then, in January, the break came. On January 5 the Regent, who was beginning to get worried, appointed Law Comptroller General (i.e., minister) of the Finances, but that move failed to stem the rapid drop in share value. On January 28, the value of the shares was set by law, but their price fell anyway, so, in what turned out to be a fatal mistake, all shares of stock became convertible into bank notes. You could take your share of stock, now worth thirteen thousand livres, go to the Banque and receive bank notes, redeemable in gold, for that amount: obviously, this saddled the bank with an impossibly high debt.

Any hope that the System, as it was called, might still survive was then ended by two men. On March 2, the prince de Conti drove into the Banque's courtyard with several large carts behind his carriage and left again, a few hours later, with the enormous sum of fourteen million livres in gold. The very next day, the duc de Bourbon did even better: he took over twenty-five million livres' worth of bullion. After that, obviously, everyone realized the Banque would soon run out of gold, so the Regent gave out an edict ruling that henceforth gold was demonetized: bank notes were to be the only legal currency. Soon it was even against the law to hold precious metals in the form of jewelry or plate.

The immediate result, of course, was panic. Anyone who held metallic money promptly hid it, while the value of the bank notes crashed. Since, by now, the once popular Law had become the most hated man in the country, the ever loyal Regent, in late April, revived for him the extinct title of Superintendent of the Finances, but in vain: shares and notes continued their fall. On May 21, a new edict was published to try and regulate the crash: each share of stock, which at this point was still worth 8,500 livres was to come down to 5,000 livres by December 1, and the value of the notes was halved. By July, there were riots as the downward trend continued. Law still tried to stem the panic, but it was too late. On October 10, the bank was forced to close. On November 1, as Law fled to Italy, gold was once again declared the only legal currency.

On the face of it, the System had been a spectacular failure, and the Regent's popularity, never great, dropped with the rate of the bank notes. In fact, in spite of the crash the experiment had revived trade and manufacturing while allowing the government, in effect, to cancel most of the huge debt left by Louis XIV. In 1715 the State was, to all intents and purposes, bankrupt; in 1721, the budget was very nearly balanced thanks to the enormous reduction in interest charges, the debt was all but gone and a foundation had been laid for what proved to be a remarkably long period of fiscal and monetary stability.

At the moment, however, people saw only what looked like an unprecedented debacle; but while the losers cursed, quite a number of rich men were openly rejoicing. Among their numbers were the financiers whose profitable relationship with the Treasury had been interrupted by Law, profiteers like the duc de Bourbon, who, having milked the System, were now anxious for the fuss to stop; and, fully revived, the Parlement, as ready to make trouble as ever.

That the duc d'Orléans had made a terrible mistake in giving the Parlement, once again, the right to remonstrate before registering had become all too clear. Of course, he had had little choice since that was the price he had had to pay in order to receive the unrestricted powers he sought; but just how high a price that was he soon found out. The rich men who made up the membership of the Parlement were, by nature, conservative. They resisted all change, so of course they opposed the System and its newfangled ideas. Worse, in their eyes Law was threatening the very basis of their own prosperity: after land, government notes were their preferred form of investment. As the Regent published edict after edict, therefore, the Parlement remonstrated with increasing animus until, in July 1720, it flatly refused to register the edicts which were supposed to shore up the collapsing System. Since this was the last in a long series of refusals, the Regent struck back and exiled the members to Pontoise, outside Paris, from whence, in December, they were recalled because there was no longer any System to oppose. Clearly, the docile assemblage of judges left by Louis XIV had become a politically ambitious body whose claim to power rested on its carefully nurtured popularity.

In fact, the Parlement did not even wait for the advent of the Banque to make trouble but seized the chance given it by a complex, unnecessary religious dispute. Louis XIV, after having expelled the Protestants from his kingdom, had gone on to tackle a small sect of Catholics, the Jansenists, who, while accepting the Church's dogma, had nonetheless developed an attitude to the worship of saints, the exact role of divine grace and the importance of acts versus faith which was not unrelated to Protestantism. The King, intent on perfect conformity, tackled the Jansenists in three stages. First, he closed and razed the convent at Port Royal, where the doctrine was taught; then, he appointed only anti-Jansenist bishops; and, finally, he forced Pope Clement XI into issuing a bull entitled, according to the first word of its text, *Unigenitus,* which listed and condemned a certain number of Jansenist tenets. The bull was signed by the Pope on September 8, 1713; on February 15, 1714, at the King's express command, it was registered by the Parlement.

As it happened, the Jansenists preached so austere a doctrine that they had extremely few followers, so with the promulgation of the bull *Unigenitus* the little sect should have simply expired. In fact, though Jansenist numbers did shrink, a controversy of mammoth proportions was started. There were several reasons for this: opposing the bull in the name of one's faith was easier than opposing the government in the name of politics; the Jesuits, who were widely feared as a wily and powerful order, were the enemies of the Jansenists, so backing the Jansenists meant fighting the Jesuits; there are few things more likely to revive any sect than persecution; and, finally, France had a long tradition of Gallicanism. For centuries, the French Church had been practically free from papal interference. The Pope's bulls and letters could, according to custom, only be published with the King's permission, and any attempt by a bishop to appeal directly to the Pope could result in the seizure of his temporalities. Now, by asking Clement XI to decide single-handedly a question relating to the French Church, Louis XIV had gone against the old Gallican tradition. In 1714, there was nothing the Parlement could do about it. In September 1715, it rushed with enthusiasm where it had hitherto been forbidden to tread. With the Regent's full agreement, it proclaimed that the Pope could not impose on the Gallican Church a series of tenets, or constitution, unless he had first consulted with and obtained the agreement of a majority of the French bishops. One article in particular, Article 91, seemed altogether unacceptable. It stated that a papal excommunication must be fully enforced even if it were unjust. In other words, the Pope would have the power to cut anyone off from all religious (and, in theory, civil) life without any valid motive, simply on his own authority. So, in 1715 the Parlement amended its earlier registration: Article 91, being accepted only with reservations, was, in effect, canceled.

The Regent, so far, agreed with the Parlement. He, too, disliked the Jesuits and thought Louis XIV had gone too far; but he cared not a fig for this or that religious principle and only wanted to end the whole controversy. Besides, he had quite enough to do without being forced to listen to bickering bishops. Still, when, in March 1717, seventeen of the prelates, including the Archbishop of Paris, formally made an appeal to a future council (i.e., refused to accept the Constitution until that hypothetical council had confirmed it), the Regent supported them, largely because it was less trouble to do so. And the Parlement, which was naturally delighted, published a ruling forbidding the publication of any pontifical act, bull or letter unless it had first been authorized by the government. In doing so, it was merely forestalling the inevitable reaction from Rome: popes had always claimed to be the font of doctrine and superior to any council's authority. It was a safe bet, therefore, that the appeal would not go unanswered, and, indeed, in March 1718 the Holy Inquisition formally condemned it. As expected, the Regent then forbade publication of the condemnation and, at his request, the Parlement made obedience to the "illegal" decree a crime.

The Pope then went one step further. On September 4, 1718, he issued letters entitled *Pastoralis Officii* forbidding all priests to administer either communion or the last rites to anyone who refused obedience to the Constitution. This was strong medicine, so once again the bishops appealed the Pope's decision and the Parlement condemned the letters as abusive of the liberties of the Gallican Church. A deadlock had clearly been reached.

So far, at least, the Parlement and the Regent had been on the same side of the issue; now they began to drift apart. The Parlement opposed the Constitution with ever growing fervor. The Regent, on the other hand, found himself faced with angry bishops of both parties—seventeen were against the Constitution, twelve for it and the others were undecided—a war of pamphlets, and fiery sermons, so he decided that what he wanted above all was peace. The imbroglio with Spain and the financial crisis were quite enough to deal with, especially since the new councils made the government function so very slowly; on October 17, 1717, therefore, he issued a declaration ordering both parties to remain silent. Not very surprisingly, no one paid any attention to this, so on June 5, 1719, the Regent reiterated his orders in even stronger terms. The second attempt seemed more likely to succeed: in September 1718, after three unsuccessful years, the councils were abolished, the ministries reestablished and the Regent's grasp on the machinery of government strengthened.

The new declaration did, in fact, have a marked effect, though not the one the Regent had expected. The Parlement, which knew a good issue when it saw it, now condemned and banned any text favorable to the Constitution on the grounds that it was following the Regent's orders, but it somehow forgot to proceed against publications attacking the bull. And while it was at it, it also suppressed (or tried to) the letters written to their flocks by pro-*Unigenitus* bishops, who naturally complained that the Parlement had no right to do this, defended their position and appealed to the Regent. Worse, they soon went a step further and excommunicated anyone within their sees who had appealed to the future council. The Gallican Church was split right down the middle.

Naturally, the anti-Constitutionalists weren't about to accept their excommunication. They promptly appealed to the Parlement, stressing that the bishops had exceeded their powers, and, naturally, the Parlement agreed. This led to a number of impossible situations. In Reims, for instance, the Archbishop excommunicated the Cathedral Chapter, who then sued him and obtained an order from the Parlement forbidding the Archbishop to use his powers of excommunication; so the indignant Archbishop promptly re-excommunicated the Chapter, only to have his order burned at the stake. Clearly, something had to be done, so in August 1720, right in the middle of the System's collapse, and while the Parlement was exiled in Pontoise, the Regent promulgated a compromise, the so-called Body of Doctrine. This took the form of a royal declaration (signed, of course, by the ten-year-old Louis XV) enforcing the observation of the Constitution as interpreted in the Body of Doctrine (i.e., without the controversial Article 91), ordering the end of all written and oral disputes and canceling all previous appeals to the Parlement. It all seems fair enough when viewed in hindsight, but contemporaries on both sides of the issue naturally felt it was too favorable to the other side.

No such declaration, furthermore, was valid until it had been registered. The Parlement, away in Pontoise and busily refusing to register the Regent's financial edicts, was not about to oblige him on the Body of Doctrine, so, to no one's surprise, it refused registration. At that point, the maddened Regent turned to a seldom used judicial body, the Grand Conseil, and ordered it to register the Declaration. The Grand Conseil, whose members sat on cases too urgent to await the exceedingly slow Parlement procedure, complied all the more willingly in that its judges sat at the King's pleasure; and, of course, no one paid it the slightest attention. There was nothing left for the Regent, therefore, but to start negotiating with the Parlement; and since the System was collapsing anyway, he traded it for a partial acceptance of the Declaration. On December 4, 1720, a month after Law's flight, the Body of Doctrine was finally registered, but with a clause restoring the right of anti-Constitutionalists to appeal from any episcopal abuse of power. The Regent's victory was decidedly ambiguous, and it took no great wisdom to predict that the controversy would flare up again.

Still, the Regent had achieved a sensible compromise over this maddening problem which, furthermore, was not of his own making, while at the same time avoiding a European crisis and restoring the national finances. Not a bad record, really, but appearances were against him. He had tried having councils instead of ministers, people said, then gone back to the old system; he had opposed the Constitution, then favored it, and then, in essence, washed his hands of it; he had promoted the System only to watch it self-destruct; he had fought an unnecessary war with France's closest ally: it needed very little to make this look like incompetence; and while the King did not have the power to discharge the Regent so long as he was still a minor, he would reach his majority in February 1723 and be able to appoint anyone he chose as prime minister. By 1721, the contenders were already positioning themselves for the succession.

This hardly worried the Regent, who was nothing if not tolerant; but since he had every intention of staying in power after 1723, he now began to take sharper notice of one man in particular who was in a position to do him a great deal of harm: the maréchal de Villeroy. When, in July 1721, Louis XV was so ill, the maréchal made it very plain that, in his view, there had been foul play. As it turned out, the King recovered, but Villeroy continued his campaign, using his proximity to the King to court popularity and thus appear as a possible successor to the Regent. Quite openly he opposed the System, sided with the Parlement, and generally presented himself as the man who could bring back the good old days. At the same time, his vanity was beginning to irritate people, especially since it might be contagious. When, for instance, in March 1722 Louis XV first met the little Infanta, his future bride, Marais noted: "People are displeased with the way the maréchal de Villeroy is teaching the King to be haughty: he now only salutes the ducs and will not take his hat off to other noblemen."[27] And, of course, whenever possible the Governor reminded the Regent of his own power over the King. Already in September 1720 Marais had noted one such confrontation: "The Regent sometimes spends the night at the Louvre. The maréchal de Villeroy had gone to pay court to him one morning, and the Regent seemed very pleased with the King and the fact that he seemed to have a more mature mind than most children his age. 'But,' he said, 'I would like to know whether he can keep a secret.' The maréchal answered that he could indeed, and that he already used certain very clever tricks to confuse people who wanted to know what he really thought. 'In that case,' the Regent said, 'I want to speak to him in secret of a number of matters which he should know.' Upon which the maréchal answered: 'Monseigneur, I must tell Your Royal Highness about something which happened to my late father when he was governor to King Louis XIV . . . The Queen Mother, then Regent, came one day to see the King; she took him into a corner and was speaking to him in a low voice. My father withdrew out of respect and so as not to overhear the conversation. The Queen said to him: "M. le maréchal, I must teach you your duty. The King's Governor must never allow anyone to speak to him in private, and that rule even applies to me, his mother. Come closer, you belong right here." ' The Regent said the story was interesting and that he was glad to have heard it."[28] Since direct access to the King would soon be the source of all power, the Regent had good reason to find the story riveting. If Villeroy were allowed his way, he might well convince a young and easily influenced child to make changes at the top when the time came.

At first, there was very little the Regent could actually do. Since people still suspected him of longing for the throne, any attempt at removing Villeroy would meet with the stiffest opposition: everyone would assume that it was only a first step, to be followed by the elimination of the King himself. Still, Villeroy was managing to make himself unpopular at Court without any help from the Regent. It is quite probable, therefore, that when, to everyone's surprise, the duc d'Orléans decided to move the Court back to Versailles, it was in part to remove Villeroy from his Parisian supporters. That the King could have better riding, better hunting and fresher air than in Paris, as the Regent announced officially, was also undoubtedly a motive for his startling decision. In the long run, it turned out to have been a major turning point inasmuch as it removed, once and for all, the monarchy from Paris.

The move back to the great palace took place on June 15, 1722; already on the sixteenth Marais commented: "The King is very fond of Versailles, so fond, in fact, that it has been decided to leave him there all winter,"[29] adding, some three weeks later, "The King is in splendid health; he goes up, he comes down, he runs, he walks and is becoming healthier-looking and stronger."[30] A week later, the old duchesse d'Orléans could write: "Our King is a very handsome and very pleasant young man, but he is too silent. When he doesn't know people intimately, one can get nothing out of him."[31] She was right. As he grew, the King became a strikingly handsome, tall, well-built adolescent, but his well-founded distrust for the courtiers who surrounded him and his shyness had in no way abated. Still, he could be amused, as the duchesse herself tells us. "I am on pretty good terms with the King," she wrote proudly. "Yesterday I played a trick on his governors [Villeroy and Fleury] which really entertained me. They are so jealous of the King that they always think we must be telling him something against them; I really caught them out. The day before yesterday, the King had a gassy colic, and yesterday I walked up to him with the most serious expression and slipped a note into his hand. The maréchal de Villeroy, who was terribly embarrassed, asked me very seriously: 'What is this note you are giving the

King?' So I answered him just as seriously: 'It is a remedy against gassy colics.' The maréchal: 'Only the King's First Physician may give him remedies.' To which I answered, 'As for this one, I am sure that M. Dodart will approve of it; it is even written out in rhyme and can be sung.' The King, who was also embarrassed, opened it, read it and immediately burst into laughter. The maréchal said: 'May one see it?' 'Oh, yes,' I answered, 'there is nothing secret about it.' This is what he read: 'Vous qui dans le mésentère / Avez vents impétueux / Ils sont dangereux / Et pour vous en défaire / Pétez, pétez.' ('You who, in your intestine / Feel some impetuous winds / They are dangerous / And to expel them / Just fart, just fart.')"[32] It is not hard to imagine the look on Villeroy's face.

Pompous or not, however, the maréchal remained in place. Once before, according to Saint-Simon, the Regent had decided to dismiss him, but had been talked out of it; but then, at the end of July 1722, with the King's majority a mere six months away, a scandal in the King's entourage gave Villeroy's enemies their chance. It started with the Governor's granddaughter. "They live in the most open debauchery at Versailles," Marais recorded. "The princes have declared mistresses, politeness, manners and good order are a thing of the past . . . The maréchal de Villeroy has been pained to learn that the duchesse de Retz, his granddaughter, has had lovers of every social condition since she's been at Versailles . . . She tried to seduce the King himself . . . and attempted to handle him in a very hidden place. Upon which the maréchal exploded with anger against the duchesse and sent her away from Court on the spot." Even worse was to come, however. "There are also orgies of young gentlemen together which they don't bother to conceal. The young duc de Boufflers, the marquis de Rambure and the marquis d'Alincourt [Villeroy's grandson] having walked to a secluded wood, the duc de Boufflers decided to rape Rambure but couldn't manage it. D'Alincourt said he wanted to carry out his brother-in-law's attempt. Rambure agreed to it and went through with it"[33]. These were grave matters. The King might have reached puberty but he was still too young, it was thought, to have sex; and the influence a group of homosexual courtiers might have on the adolescent didn't even bear thinking about: if they converted Louis XV to their own tastes and thus rendered him unlikely to procreate, France would be in grave danger. That both the chief culprits were grandchildren of Villeroy's, however, must have seemed almost too good to be true: the Regent at last held his pretext.

Villeroy himself promptly made everything worse. Instead of trying to handle the whole business quietly and tactfully, he panicked. "The orgies of the men and the women have been made even more public by the *lettres de cachet** . . . which the maréchal de Villeroy has requested against his own family. M. d'Alincourt, his grandson, has been sent in exile to Joigny . . . the duchesse de Retz was sent away from Court . . . the duc de Boufflers has been exiled to Picardy . . . the marquis de Rambure, passive in every way, has been imprisoned in the Bastille. When the King asked why all these young noblemen had been exiled, he was told that they had torn down some railings in the park, so that today they are called only destroyers of railings . . . The maréchal is blamed by everybody."[34] Indeed he was: that, as governor, he should have allowed the King to be surrounded by loose women and overt

---

* These were letters, signed by the King, which ordered people into exile or prison.

homosexuals hardly redounded to his credit; still, no one expected that within ten days he would be joining the exiles.

It was, in fact, Villeroy himself who gave the Regent a perfect pretext. On the morning of August 10, 1722, the Regent walked into the King's apartment and told the maréchal to withdraw because he wanted to speak privately with His Majesty. Villeroy refused but agreed to talk it over with the Regent during the afternoon. Before the appointed hour, however, the Captain of the Guard came in to the King's room and asked the maréchal to follow him into the antechamber. There he showed him an order for his arrest. Villeroy asked to speak to the King and was told it was not possible. Within five minutes he had been bundled into a waiting carriage and was on his way to Lyon. Naturally, everybody was stunned. "Paris is appalled by the maréchal's arrest because he is much loved by the people,"[35] Marais noted on August 11, adding, on the twelfth: "The King seems quite cheerful in public, but in private he is sad, complains and cries at night. People think well of his heart and sensitiveness."[36]

Marais was quite right. Saint-Simon, who was present, confirms it. "As soon as he heard [about the dismissal], the King blushed; his eyes grew moist; he hid his face against the back of an armchair, without saying a word, and would neither go out nor play. He barely ate a few mouthfuls at supper, cried and stayed awake all night. The next morning, and dinnertime that day, were hardly marked by any improvements . . . The King's tears had been much increased by the absence of M. de Fréjus, who had disappeared."[37] It was obviously too much: the twelve-year-old Louis had lost at a blow the two people closest to him. He was, as we know, enormously fond of Fleury, and even Villeroy, with all his faults, had won the boy's affection by his constant presence. Even in this painful situation, however, it is typical of the King's exact understanding of reality—he was worshiped but powerless—that he never once asked to have Villeroy called back. As for Fleury, within twenty-four hours he had returned. Immediately the King stopped crying: the Bishop was incomparably dearer to him than the maréchal.

Fréjus' retreat had really been a sham. In a rash moment, some years earlier, he had said publicly that he would go if ever Villeroy were dismissed. Now, embarrassingly, he had to redeem his pledge but was only too glad to obey the King's plea that he return posthaste, for it was becoming apparent that this sixty-nine-year-old cleric, a Methuselah by the standards of the age, was developing political ambitions. And since Villeroy had been replaced by the honest but weak duc de Charost, Fleury and the Regent were the only two persons who could command Louis's affection. Indeed, his position was reinforced still further when his great rival, the abbé Dubois, was created a cardinal and then appointed Prime Minister: the more the King disliked the Cardinal, the more he turned to his tutor.

Of course, the Bishop was also continuing the King's education. By 1722, he had switched to Latin fables, duly translated into French by his pupil, to communicate sound moral principles. Like his father, the duc de Bourgogne, the young King often let his anger get the better of him, so he was given the story of the young lion to ponder. It started, sententiously enough, by stating: "Nothing is more dangerous than to acquire bad habits," and then went on to the demonstration. "A young lion," we read in the King's tall, careful handwriting, "the scion of a long line of kings, ruled in one of Africa's forests. His methods of government, at first, gave rise to many hopes, but then his subjects noted with affliction that he was given to bursts of anger which he could not master and which often caused him to strike anyone who opposed the least of his desires. At first, these little explosions were thought to be the signs of his vivaciousness, which age would soon cool down, so no great opposition was made to his proud and fiery temper. After reigning for a while, the lion, as he was hunting one day, was wounded by a splinter which he was unable to remove from his paw; and although he asked his courtiers, and then everyone he saw, for help, no one dared come close enough because they feared his temper, and what he might do to them if they hurt him as they took the splinter out. Unable to hunt, the lion starved and realized he would soon die: he 'understood, but too late, how important it is for a King to be loved by his subjects.' A wise old snake, from a careful distance, then told him: 'If you had paid more attention to the good advice you were given in your youth, you would not find yourself in this pitiful condition.' "[38] The conclusion was obvious: Louis must control his temper (by year's end, and for the rest of his life, he did), and rule so as to be loved by his people.

There were also axioms: "A King who is feared by his subjects instead of being their defender and father is more unhappy than the vilest of beasts." There were warnings that being handsome wasn't enough: "Good looks, a scepter, a crown are the least important attributes of a King, who only deserves to be what he is through his justice, strength, kindness and affability"; or, again: "It is only the attributes of royalty that are honored in an unworthy King." There were also definitions of the monarch's role: "A King would be nothing without his subjects, and he must be careful to treat them well; but, then, the subjects without their King would fall into anarchy and would soon be the prey of their enemies . . . There is no King absolute enough not to be bound by an infinite number of dependencies, and [monarchs] are almost *always* more to be pitied than their subjects."[39] Strong words; but the King's majority loomed ever closer and he was being prepared to reign.

Already, every day, he listened to an account of the way the government actually functioned. "Cardinal Dubois," the duc de Villars noted, "had become accustomed [early in 1723] to coming in with the Regent at the end of the King's morning study period and, in the presence of M. le Duc, M. de Charost and the Bishop of Fréjus, he would bring in a memorandum which it would only take him a little over fifteen minutes to read. These memoranda contained brief instructions to start informing the King of several details regarding the Army, the finances, the current negotiations. From the beginning of the year, the Regent, after the evening study period, would come in alone. Everyone withdrew and he gave the King information without any witnesses."[40] Little by little, the thirteen-year-old boy was learning how to rule, but he showed no sign, as yet, of wanting to do so himself.

Still, people began to wonder. On October 25, 1722, Louis XV was crowned in the great Gothic cathedral of Reims with Fleury, who was standing in for the Bishop of Noyon, carrying his sword belt. The ceremony was grand, but confused and disorganized: there had, after all, not been a coronation for three quarters of a century. In the event, however, what mattered was that the shy, insecure boy was anointed with the holy chrism supposedly brought down from heaven by an angel, and then crowned: it was the most striking confirmation of what he had always been told, made manifest to all in the most solemn of ceremonies. And the effect was soon visible. "The King talks a lot since his coronation. He says, 'I want,' and that the King's will is the law,"[41] Marais reported at the end of November. Indeed, Louis XV could now be absolutely sure of his status: he alone in France was the chosen of God.

Soon afterwards, on February 16, 1723, yet another solemn ceremony took place: in a lit de justice, before the assembled Parlement, the King was solemnly declared to be of age. The Regency was at an end, and henceforth the mention "on the advice of our uncle the Regent" was dropped from all official acts. Of course, no one expected the thirteen-year-old monarch actually to start ruling himself, so nothing was really changed. The Council of Regency simply became the King's Council, which was dominated by the duc d'Orléans while Dubois remained Prime Minister; but the composition of the Council gave hints about the future: it consisted, naturally, of the duc d'Orléans; of the duc de Chartres, his son; of the duc de Bourbon as First Prince of the Blood (but under Louis XIV no prince had ever been admitted to the Council; now it was clear that the duc d'Orléans needed his backing); then came Cardinal Dubois and, a major innovation, Fleury. That the King's tutor should be a member of the Council was unprecedented, and showed that the duc d'Orléans was relying on the Bishop's influence with the King. It also allowed Fréjus, who became acquainted with all the great questions of state, to move yet another step closer to his still distant goal.

This carefully balanced arrangement, however, was soon disrupted. On August 10, Dubois died of a syphilitic infection, and the duc d'Orléans, who was well aware of M. le Duc's ambitions, went straight into the King and asked to be appointed prime minister himself. Without a moment's hesitation, the King gave him the office, but this apparent triumph merely proved that the former Regent was feeling insecure: until then, members of the Royal Family had thought themselves far too grand to be prime minister. They might appoint one of their underlings to do the job, but never took it upon themselves. That the duc d'Orléans felt the need to do so, and in such haste, is the best indication of what he feared: his replacement by the ever greedy M. le Duc.

As it turned out, he needn't have worried. Four months later, on December 1, 1723, the duc d'Orléans was sitting by the fireplace of his drawing room at Versailles. He seemed depressed somehow, so he asked his favorite of the moment, the duchesse de Falaris, to tell him some amusing gossip. She had no sooner started on a story when, to her horror, the duc suddenly tipped forward. Shrieking with anguish, she rushed out of the room, desperately calling for help. It only took a few minutes for the doctors to arrive, but it was already too late. Felled by a massive stroke at the age of forty-nine, Philippe, duc d'Orléans and former Regent of France, was stretched out on the floor before the fireplace as he lay dying; and with him an age was also drawing to an end.

Chapter Three

The Wise Old Man

AT Versailles, that most ferocious of jungles, the duc d'Orléans's death was hardly reason for sadness. As the greatest office in the State became vacant, and new preferments opened, it was simply a question of sharing out the plums. And since the King was obviously still too young to rule by himself, it was clear that whoever became prime minister would control the forthcoming distribution. There was not a moment to be lost, therefore: the ambitious and greedy M. le Duc was no sooner told of the former Regent's death that he literally ran all the way to Louis XV's bedroom and there, still out of breath, he asked to be appointed prime minister. Louis was thirteen, M. le Duc (who was only twenty-one himself) was the First Prince of the Blood after the notoriously incapable duc de Chartres (now duc d'Orléans). Within an hour of the duchesse de Falaris' first cry for help, France had a new government.

That the King should have agreed so quickly to M. le Duc's promotion was hardly surprising: he was deeply shocked by his uncle's death. Unlike his courtiers, Louis had really cared about the man. "The King, who felt deeply his unchanging respect, his attempts to please him, his manner of speaking to him and working with him, mourned him and was truly moved by his loss, so much so that he has only spoken of him since then . . . with esteem, affection and regret."[1] It must have seemed to him as if once again his main prop had suddenly been withdrawn. After his great-grandfather, after Mme de Ventadour, after Villeroy, the Regent was gone. The duc de Bourbon, whatever his other shortcomings, was at least a familiar figure. Besides, within the small circle around the King, there really were no serious rivals. The new duc d'Orléans, once considered a possible successor to his father's office, was an overweight, slow-witted young man, proud of his birth and cousinship to the King, but quite devoid of ambition, and very clearly incapable of running the government. The more remote members of the Royal Family were not even possibilities; and the only alternative from outside that golden circle was far too shrewd openly to take on M. le Duc: Fleury was content to stay in the shadows for a while longer at least. That, however, did not mean that he would be powerless. Earlier that year he had become a member of the Council; now he not only kept his place but was given a new and highly important plum by the new Prime Minister, the disposition of all French ecclesiastic preferment. Henceforth no archbishopric, bishopric or abbey could be given without Fleury's say-so. The Church still played a major role in French life; its benefices were generally used by the King to reward not only clerics but also members of the Royal Family, and even other lay personages, so at one blow the former Bishop of Fréjus had become the most important man in France after the Prime Minister. His special position was soon made even more manifest by his entry into a new, small Secret Council composed only of the King, the duc de Bourbon, Fleury and the old maréchal de Villars. Even then, all this was as nothing to the one fact that really mattered: alone, he had the King's trust; alone, he never left his side. The late duc d'Orléans had been able to see Louis alone whenever he chose. Now, as M. le Duc soon found out, whenever the Prime Minister conferred privately with the Sovereign, Fleury was also there.

Although the conciliar system of government had been abolished, so that a half dozen ministers once again administered the country, there was still no such thing, in 1723, as a cabinet. Each minister was responsible only for his particular department; he was expected to follow orders and not formulate policy. All had depended, therefore, on the duc d'Orléans, who, at least, was known to be competent. M. le Duc, on the other hand, was not only generally disliked but also inexperienced and probably incapable.

"This great and unexpected stroke," the British Ambassador wrote the Foreign Secretary on December 6, "does, I find, affect in a most sensible manner the persons of the best quality and sense here as thinking . . . His Royal Highness, considering him as to his high birth and superior talents in government, not to be replaced, besides that he had, by his capacity and indefatigable pains in business, overcome difficulties almost insurmountable, and given the nation a prospect of lasting peace, which the best patriots think absolutely necessary for France."[2] There was good reason, in fact, to doubt the new Prime Minister, since all that was known of him was very much to his detriment. In many ways, he was the very opposite of his predecessor. Where the Regent had been pleasant and easygoing, M. le Duc was proud, short and arrogant. The Regent had been uniquely disinterested; the duc de Bourbon was power mad and greedy. Finally, no matter how harshly he had been criticized, the Regent had had the good of the country at heart; M. le Duc, on the other hand, was well known to care for nothing but himself. There was one more capital contrast: the duc d'Orléans slept with women but did not listen to them; the duc de Bourbon, as everyone knew, was controlled by two equally unpopular women, his mother and his mistress.

The dowager duchesse de Bourbon was one of the légitimés, the sister of the duc du Maine, the comte de Toulouse and the now dowager duchesse d'Orléans, and like them she was enormously proud of being Louis XIV's child. Before 1715, she had been famous for her biting tongue and her drunkenness. Since her father's death, she had gone through an impressive number of lovers until, finally, she settled on the handsome M. de Lassay, for whom she proceeded to build a sumptuous house right next to her own on the bank of the Seine, right at what was then the edge of Paris.*

* The two houses, the Palais Bourbon and the Hôtel de Lassay, today house the National Assembly and its Président.

Since building two palaces required a great deal of money, the dowager's greed rivaled her son's.

This was bad enough; far worse was M. le Duc's mistress, the ambitious marquise de Prie. That Mme de Prie was remarkably pretty, sexy and intelligent no one denied. The late Regent, always tempted by beauty, had liked her; in fact, until she became M. le Duc's mistress, she had been quite popular in Paris. Of relatively humble birth—her father was a financier—she had received the best of educations. She was well read, knew how to conduct a conversation and could even run a salon. As the wife of the French Ambassador to Savoy, she had been an outstanding success; but, upon returning to Paris, she had raised her sights and become M. le Duc's official mistress, thus neatly displacing several better-born candidates who naturally resented her. Still, that would not have mattered if she had not generally appeared to be a bad influence on the already hated prince. On December 5, 1723, for instance, Morosini, the Venetian Ambassador, commented: "The duc de Bourbon has lost no time in seizing power. He has appropriated the Regent's papers and received the ambassadors' compliments, from which I came out fully satisfied by the way he greeted my and by his obliging words . . . If there is something to fear from this prince, it is his dependency on the marquise de Prie, a lady of quality but greedy and given to intrigue, who has not left his side for the last three or four days and advises him about everything."[3] In fact, Mme de Prie seems to have been greedy for her lover rather than for herself; but what really made her unpopular was her close connection to a few Paris financiers whose career she now proceeded to advance. By so doing, she managed to unite two powerful hatreds: the duc de Bourbon had first backed Law, then benefited from the System to the extent of some 40 million livres (180 million dollars) and was resented accordingly. Now, on Mme de Prie's advice, he was seen to favor Law's greedy and dishonest enemies, the Pâris brothers. Still, a few people were won over temporarily by the mistress' charm. "Nobody could be prettier," wrote that shrewd observer, the Président Hénault. "She was supple and tall, with the figure and expression of a nymph, a delicate face, pretty cheeks, a shapely nose, ash blond hair, the eyes a little Chinese-looking, but lively and gay, altogether a refined and distinguished appearance, and a voice as light as her looks."[4] And whatever her other shortcomings, Mme de Prie had at least one great merit: it was she who encouraged the duc de Bourbon to build the admirable stable block on his Chantilly estate. It is today still one of the glories of French architecture.

Of course, both Mme de Prie and M. le Duc were well aware that they were unpopular; that, in itself, need not be a major problem and they set about remedying it. First, M. le Duc announced that, like his predecessors, he wanted peace and tranquility, and that he would maintain the current alliance with England and Spain faithfully; then, he lowered the rate of a few minor taxes; and, finally, to everyone's surprise, he became positively amiable. While all this may have somewhat mitigated a few people's dislike, however, it did nothing to consolidate the Prime Minister's position in ways that really mattered; as he well knew, he had a number of powerful enemies. There was the duc d'Orléans, for instance, now First Prince of the Blood and seething with indignation at what he considered the theft of his father's position. Orléans was too stupid to matter much at the moment, but he could always provide a convenient figurehead for the anti-Bourbon party. Further away, Philip V, whose son had married the late Regent's daughter, naturally preferred the new duc d'Orléans to a man he neither knew nor trusted, so he was prepared to use his still considerable influence against the new government. Last but not least, there was Fleury. That the King's tutor didn't much like M. le Duc everyone knew; that he wanted, one day, to become Prime Minister himself, people were beginning to realize; and that he was the only man in France whom the King trusted absolutely was certain. It took almost no time for M. le Duc to realize just how unstable his own position remained: it had been the accepted privilege of the Prime Minister that he, and he alone, could speak to the King in absolute privacy, but M. le Duc, no matter how hard he tried, soon found that private access to His Majesty was not to be granted him. Already on January 13, 1724, the sharp-eyed English Ambassador reported: "The duke of Bourbon is indefatigable in his application to gain the young King's confidence; but he finds that Fréjus has the first and strongest hold there, insomuch that when His Highness sees proper opportunities to talk to His Majesty alone, as soon as he begins to be serious, the child diverts the discourse of business by idle actions and ordinary chit-chat until Fréjus, whom he never fails to call for, can have notice of time to enter the room, which goes to the duke of Bourbon's heart, as not knowing what to do, being justly apprehensive that, should he endeavour the removal of the Bishop, he would fail in the attempt."[5]

Under the circumstances, M. le Duc understandably hesitated and tried to reach a compromise with the duc d'Orléans, but the anti-Bourbon party was all the less willing to negotiate that it quickly became obvious that the King disliked Mme de Prie, whom he habitually cut dead. Finally, M. le Duc, on Mme de Prie's advice, made his decision: if he couldn't buy off his enemies, he could at least scare them. D'Argenson, the minister of Police, was dismissed, to be replaced by Ravot d'Ombreval, a relation of Mme de Prie's; this put control of all publications and a great deal of the mails in M. le Duc's hands. Then, for the first time since 1715, a new promotion of Marshals of France was announced, along with the names of new Knights of the Saint Esprit, France's highest, and most coveted, order of chivalry; and it was noticed that only M. le Duc's supporters were being rewarded. Finally, the apartments at Versailles were redistributed, with M. le Duc himself taking over the Regent's rooms just below the King's own. After that Joseph Pâris-Duverney was confirmed as Guard of the Treasury and the new regime was under way.

Just how unstable it still remained soon became clear. In March 1724, the duc d'Orléans announced that he was marrying a princess of Baden. This was a major blow for the Prime Minister. Baden, though small, was a sovereign state. If the duc d'Orléans had thus managed to bag a princess from a ruling family, it was a clear sign that no one had forgotten that he was Heir Presumptive, a position which would be further strengthened just as soon as he had children. The duc de Bourbon himself was a childless widower; by thus marrying, the duc d'Orléans was not only underlining his nearer proximity to the throne, he was also behaving as an heir should, unlike his unmarried cousin, who was living in sin. Then, too, there would now, in the normal course of affairs, have to be ceremonies celebrating the wedding, all of which would keep Orléans not only in the public eye but also in the King's company. Even worse, the increasingly eccentric Philip V chose just that moment to abdicate in favor of his son, Louis I, who was married to the duc d'Orléans's sister: it was clear, therefore, that any influence Spain could mobilize would be used on behalf of the duc d'Orléans.

M. le Duc's answer to all this was to govern as brutally as he knew how. He decided, for instance, to end the plague of beggars which, ever since the War of the Spanish Succession, had afflicted France by having the wretched creatures arrested and interned in workhouses. Since neither heat, nor food, nor even beds were provided, most of the former beggars were soon dead. After that, the Prime Minister, who was getting braver by the week, tackled another powerless minority, the Protestants, and edicted even more severe penalties than the ones already on the books against anyone not conforming to the precepts of the Catholic Church. In the same spirit, an edict of March 4, 1724, inflicted the death penalty on anyone found guilty of theft, no matter how small the sum or how worthless the object. Naturally, the censorship, so lax under the Regent, was back in full force. At the same time, and as if all that were not enough, M. le Duc greatly increased public expenditure, partly by enlarging the Court, partly by handing out pensions and offices to his supporters, but largely through sheer incompetence and carelessness; so the taxes which had been cut were raised first to their original rate and then higher still.

It is only fair to add that M. le Duc did make an attempt at governing effectively and even, sometimes, fairly. One instance of this was his reform of the prison system. The care of prisoners had, until then, been farmed out to companies who obviously cared more about their profits than the welfare of their charges. Now this system was ended and the State took over. A new canal was begun to link the Somme and Oise rivers. A stock market was founded in Paris; and, along with this, the Prime Minister actually tried to streamline the government. Under the late King, a plethora of unnecessary offices had been created just so that they could be sold. The advantage of this method was to provide the Treasury with fresh cash; its disadvantage was that it saddled the King with yet more salaries while hopelessly complicating the administrative structure; so, in September 1724 the office of Governor was abolished for all except a dozen major cities, along with a large number of unnecessary municipal offices and a hundred (theoretical) secretaries to the King, while at the same time most cities were given back the right to elect their own mayors and municipal councils.

All this was clearly an improvement, albeit a small one. Since M. le Duc fully realized that he was in no position to modify his predecessor's foreign policy, and since he was not about to embark on a reform of the unfair, antiquated and inefficient tax system, this was about the best he could do. Both he and Mme de Prie, however, were aware that a modicum of reform would make them neither much more popular nor much more powerful, so, in what seemed to be a clever move, they recalled the old maréchal de Villeroy to Court as a counterpoise to Fleury, who was still their most dangerous enemy. Unfortunately for them, the move failed dismally. Fleury took it for what it was, namely, an attempt to evict him, and was confirmed in his opposition, while the King, warned probably by the Bishop, simply ignored the returning maréchal, who, after two days of humiliating silence, simply withdrew from the Court for good.

In itself, this was a small incident, but a revealing one. As long as he was Prime

Minister, M. le Duc remained all-powerful, but then the King could dismiss him at any time, and only Fleury had the King's ear. M. le Duc may have been ruthless but he was not stupid, so he decided that if he couldn't eliminate Fleury, he must at least gain Louis XV's confidence. Since private talks between the King and the Prime Minister were ruled out, then, clearly, it was a question of indulging the adolescent. The duc de Bourbon set about doing just that in the ways he understood best: he decided to provide his master with the most exciting hunting in France and a group of pretty, willing young women, all in the splendid setting of his Chantilly estate. The only problem was that since everyone knew the King loved hunting, and since providing him with a mistress was a widespread ambition, M. le Duc's maneuver was perfectly transparent.

Hunting was a family passion. Henri IV, Louis XIII and Louis XIV all had been fanatic hunters; and when Louis XV was still a child, Fleury, with the Regent's agreement, had encouraged him to imitate his ancestors because hunting was the best of exercises. In this, as in so many endeavors, Fleury was fully successful: Louis XV not only liked to hunt, he actually needed to do so. When the ground was so frozen in winter that riding was impossible, he rode indoors, but ride he must. "The King had greatly strengthened himself by strong exercise," the maréchal de Villars wrote in 1724, "and it became obvious that while his health had seemed very fragile at first, it had now become very robust. But the hunts and the excessive distance he had to ride to get to them having become a great fatigue for himself and his suite . . . I took the liberty of proposing to him that he also take up other amusements. 'I wish,' I said to him, 'that Your Majesty would try those of Paris in the winter, and especially that you might live in the midst of the people who have given you so many proofs of their love.' I also talked to him about a King's common misfortune in being always surrounded with flatterers . . . who conceal important truths when they are unpleasant to hear about. I added: 'The only way, Sire, to recognize a true friendship is to see whether, at the risk of displeasing you, that person tells you useful but unflattering truths.' The King listened to me with an expression of satisfaction; but the occasions of speaking to him are rare."[6] It was all very well for Villars, a spectacularly successful general, to tell the King he was hunting too much, but Bourbon, who cared about nothing except his own position, did the very reverse: he encouraged Louis to hunt as often as he could, and since Chantilly, surrounded then as now by great forests, had superb hunting, it made perfect sense to move the Court there for a month.

Naturally enough, the King, when asked whether he would agree to stay with M. le Duc, answered that he would be delighted; but Mme de Prie was still not reassured: by now everyone knew that the young man was highly secretive, and that even if he were displeased, he was not likely to show it. Hunting was all very well, but obviously a love affair would be much better. The King would confide in his first mistress; she, in turn, would influence him. Under the guise of a hunting party, therefore, the seduction of Louis XV was the real purpose of the trip. Mme de Prie's plot might conceivably have succeeded if it had not been so obvious; but in the streets of Paris they were singing: "Margot la ravaudeuse / disait à son ami / Que fait-on de ces gueuses / qu'on mène à Chantilly? / Quoi, pour un pucelage / faut-il mener

le train / de dix-sept catins?" ("Margot the seamstress / said to her lover / What's the
use of these strumpets / they take to Chantilly? / What, for one virgin / must they
send a whole troupe / of seventeen whores?")[7] Not a very flattering description,
perhaps, of the high-born ladies who had been invited to accompany the King; but
accurate all the same, and Louis XV understood just what was being planned; so, by
the end of August Villars could add: "The King has not yet turned his young and
beautiful eyes on any woman. The ladies are ready, and one cannot say that the King
isn't since, at the age of fourteen and a half, he is stronger and more mature than
most young men of eighteen."[8] And, away in Paris, Barbier noted: "The main purpose of the trip to Chantilly has apparently failed. The King does nothing but hunt
and does not want to try . . . I must admit that it is a shame, for he is well built and
handsome; but if that is his taste there is nothing to be done."[9] In fact, the King's
abstinence was not surprising. Although strong and healthy, he was also extremely
shy, and he knew full well that every detail of his sex life, should he have one, would
instantly become a universal topic of conversation, besides which there was M. le
Duc's obvious design: it was more than enough to discourage a fourteen-year-old who
still listened to his tutor; and there cannot be much doubt as to just what advice
Fleury must have been giving his pupil.

As it turned out, in spite of the hunts, the banquets, the varied entertainments and
the fireworks provided by M. le Duc, Chantilly failed to please the King. The more
clearly he realized he was to be seduced, the angrier he became, so when the young
duc de Châtillon was killed by an enraged stag, Louis took it as a pretext for returning to Versailles ahead of schedule, and Mme de Prie's latest scheme was undone. This was all the more worrying to her in that, aside from all M. le Duc's
enemies and her own, she was also faced with a formidable rival in the person of the
dowager duchesse de Bourbon. The duc, the English Ambassador noted shrewdly in
November, was "encompassed with a mother and a mistress who had both their
private views and interests; who heartily hated one another, but lived well enough in
appearance; each apprehending who should get the better in case of a rupture and
both of them daily suggesting, by their creatures, some project that might flatter the
duke's particular interests and ambition."[10] Now Mme de Prie attacked on two
fronts. First, in October and November she convinced M. le Duc to move the Court
to Fontainebleau. It had the best hunting of all the royal domains; in a desperate, and
briefly successful, effort to please the King, she saw to it that there was music and
gambling but almost no balls: ever since that episode of the ballet back in 1721, Louis
XV had disliked dancing. Much to his entourage's surprise, he now became positively
pleasant to the marquise, and M. le Duc breathed a sigh of relief.

Still, even a successful stay at Fontainebleau was only a palliative. Already in the
summer, Mme de Prie had come up with a revolutionary, and far more effective,
idea: if the King wouldn't take a mistress, then the duc de Bourbon must give him a
wife who would show her gratitude by consolidating her power. At first sight, this
was nothing short of an inspiration. Mistresses came and went, after all, but a queen
was a permanent fixture, and if she were chosen with care, and made fully aware
that she owed her elevation solely to M. le Duc, then, obviously, she would back him
to the full extent of her influence. It might even be possible, Mme de Prie suggested,

to be doubly certain. Let M. le Duc offer one of his three sisters to the King. As His Majesty's brother-in-law, he would be virtually unassailable.

Brilliant though this notion might be, however, it had one very serious drawback. At the moment the King was formally engaged to a seven-year-old Spanish infanta residing in Paris, and all through the summer of 1724, in fact, the King of Spain had been exerting strong pressure on M. le Duc to have the marriage formally declared. It was thus quite obvious that breaking the engagement would provoke a major crisis with Spain; on the other hand, there were many people in France who did not especially like the Prime Minister but were anxious to see the King married and able to beget heirs. The government could thus count on real support if it chose to break the engagement. Then, too, M. le Duc had another powerful incentive. As things now stood, if the King were to die, the duc d'Orléans would succeed to the throne and the whole Bourbon party could count on spending many years in exile. If, on the other hand, the King had a son, and died, there would be another Regency and M. le Duc could look forward to remaining in power practically forever.

All through the fall, the burning topic was discussed by the Council, but no definite conclusion was reached. If the Infanta were to be sent home, it would only be because a replacement had been found. Unfortunately, while candidates were not lacking, no such person was in sight. There was, for instance, Mlle de Vermandois, one of M. le Duc's sisters, who was being educated in a convent and could therefore be presumed to lead a blameless life; but Mme de Prie quickly found out that she was devoted to her mother, and therefore vetoed her. After that, M. le Duc's other sisters came into consideration, but they all had tarnished reputations and, besides, Fleury put his foot down and let it be known that he would never agree to let his pupil marry into the Bourbon-Condé branch of the Royal Family. And while Fleury, by 1725, had ceased functioning as the King's tutor, he was still the only man Louis trusted, so there was no getting around his veto. In a moment of despair Mme de Prie, who could see that her idea would not easily come to pass, even put forward the candidacy of the Grand Duchess Elizabeth of Russia, and the Russians let it be known that they would say yes if presented with a formal request for her hand, but she was rejected as being of exceedingly low birth: her father may have been Peter the Great, but her mother, the Empress Catherine, had begun life as a prostitute. For a while it looked as if a deadlock had been reached. Then, briefly but spectacularly, the sky of M. le Duc's particular world caved in.

In mid-February 1725, the King suddenly came down with one of the severe attacks of indigestion to which he was sometimes prey, "and even though the illness was not serious, and was cured within a few days, M. le Duc was so frightened by it that one night [thinking he heard more noise than usual in the King's rooms] he got up, quite naked under his robe, and walked up to the King's first antechamber . . . He was alone, and held a candle in his hand. He saw Maréchal [the King's First Physician], who, astounded by this apparition, went to him and asked him why he had come. He found himself face-to-face with a man beside himself, in a panic, and who . . . finally said, 'What would happen to me?,' answering himself in a low voice and as if talking to his nightcap: 'I won't be caught again; if he survives, I'll see him married,' "[11] upon which the search was resumed with a new vigor. A vast number of princesses was now considered; but some were Protestant, like George I's daughter; another, the duc de Lorraine's daughter was a close relative of the duc d'Orléans and therefore could be expected to back him instead of M. le Duc; a princess of Savoy, who happened to be Louis XV's first cousin, was rejected because of her father's close alliance with the Habsburgs; the Princess of Hesse-Rheinfels, a strong possibility for a while, was disqualified when it was discovered that her mother gave birth, alternately, to a child and a hare *[sic]*; and then Mme de Prie had another inspiration.

Throughout this period, she had also been looking for a princess to marry M. le Duc; but since the marquise obviously had no intention of giving up her lover, the lady in question would have to be meek and mild in the extreme, and not too bright either. Such a princess had, in fact, been located, and she was all the stronger a candidate in that she was already living in exile near Strasbourg: this was Marie Leczinska, the daughter of Stanislas, dethroned King of Poland. At twenty-one, she was just the right age for M. le Duc; she was known to be pious, moral and kind, if a little slow; and, most important, she was both dowdy and plain. As for her eventual gratitude, Mme de Prie knew that she could count on it: the Leczinskis were desperately poor, so they would be utterly thrilled if their daughter became duchesse de Bourbon. At the same time, the former King came from one of the best families in Poland. He was related to the Sobieskis, who had often occupied the throne. He had filled the office of voivode of Posnania at the turn of the century, and then had been elected King in 1704: in Poland alone Kings received their crown as the result of an election in which only the nobility voted. Thus, the Leczinskis' status was markedly ambiguous: in one sense, they could be said to belong to the golden circle of ruling families while, at the same time, they could be viewed as little more than jumped-up nobles.

One thing, however, was certain. Stanislas was dethroned for good. The creature of Charles XII of Sweden, he had ruled over precisely the territory—quite extensive, for a while—occupied by the Swedish Army; but after Charles's defeat at Poltava, the Poles had risen, thrown Stanislas out, and elected another king in the person of the Elector of Saxony; so in 1712, with his family and a few followers, Stanislas moved first to Germany, settling in Zweibrücken in 1714; then, at the Regent's urging, he moved once again, this time to Wissembourg, in French Alsace. There he lived on a small, irregularly paid French pension of some fifty thousand livres a year, most of which went to pay the substantial debt he owed Pâris-Duverney. It was, in fact, through Pâris that Mme de Prie had heard about Stanislas and his daughter.

Now it came to her in a flash: Marie Leczinska would have been grateful enough to find herself married to M. le Duc, but if she were to become Queen of France through the good offices of Mme de Prie, she would be even more in the lady's debt. At the same time, the marriage would achieve two vital objects: it would consolidate M. le Duc's position, since Marie would have been his invention; it would ensure Mme de Prie's continued hold on M. le Duc's affection since she would, in effect, have saved him. And, finally, if, as was to be hoped, the royal couple proved fertile, there would be no more fear of the duc d'Orléans's possible succession. It was all a stroke of genius, M. le Duc agreed. On March 31, 1725, the Council met, selected Marie as the King's bride-to-be, and ordered messengers sent off to Wissembourg.

On May 27, the name of the lucky young woman was made public. At the beginning of June, the ladies of the Queen's Household were named. That particular list surprised no one. It was headed by Mlle de Clermont, M. le Duc's sister, who became *surintendante;* the duchesse de Boufflers, notorious for the number of her lovers and her loyalty to the Bourbon party, was made *dame d'honneur.* For ladies in waiting, Marie was given Mme de Prie and her closest friends, the duchesse de Villars, the marquises de Nesle, de Ruppelmonde and de Matignon, and the comtesse d'Egmont. To top it all off, Joseph Pâris-Duverney became her private secretary.

It was a clever plan, and there was no one to stop it. Fleury was bought off when the cardinal de Rohan, a potential rival, was appointed Ambassador to the Holy See, and thus neatly removed from the Court. As for both the aristocracy and the people, they were horrified by M. le Duc's choice, but they could only talk. That the King of the most powerful country in Europe should marry a penniless Polish demiprincess seemed almost beyond belief, but once he had made the leap, M. le Duc brooked no opposition. The wedding, he announced, would take place on September 5.

Of course, away in Wissembourg, the marriage looked like a miracle. When Stanislas was told by Mme de Prie's messenger that his daughter would become Queen of France, he fell on his knees and thanked God; then, tears running down his cheeks, he rushed into the next room where his wife and his daughter were sitting. It was an act of God, he said. After all their sufferings, they were being rewarded at last; their troubles were over. And having thanked the deity, the ex-King remembered that, in this case, God spoke with the voice of Mme de Prie, so he proceeded to thank her even more fervently.

Within a few days, the Leczinskis were moved to Strasbourg. There, Cinderella-like, Marie watched, wide-eyed, as box after box of silk, velvet and brocade dresses arrived, all complete with lace, furs and even jewels. As a sop to the angry duc d'Orléans, who had not been consulted, it was arranged that he would go to Strasbourg as well and stand in for the King in the marriage by procuration which was to precede the actual ceremony at Fontainebleau. So off he went, with the military escort proper to a First Prince of the Blood Royal (M. le Duc had tried to send him away without one), leading a dozen golden carriages. As for Mme de Prie, she had not waited for the official cortege.

Although Pâris had made it quite clear to Stanislas Leczinski that his daughter owed her new position exclusively to Mme de Prie, the lady felt that some jobs simply couldn't be delegated, so in May she had gone off to Wissembourg, carrying with her the King's presents to his future bride, and there she stayed, superintending the laying in of Marie's trousseau, teaching the young woman how to behave at Court, arranging every detail of her life, and making very sure that the simple, kindhearted princess felt properly grateful. She needn't have worried. Marie may not have been pretty, elegant or intelligent, but she was loyal and dutiful. From the first, her father had emphasized the fact that they owed everything to Mme de Prie. Marie now proceeded to behave accordingly.

By the time the duc d'Orléans arrived, Marie must have felt that her life had indeed become a fairy story. In a sparkle of gold and diamonds, she saw a bevy of city officials, courtiers and grands seigneurs bowing low before her. Ceremony followed

upon ceremony. There was the marriage by procuration in the sumptuously decorated cathedral; and then the trip in a great golden carriage, with stops at every town
for welcoming speeches, banquets and fireworks. And when, finally, she arrived at
the Palace of Fontainebleau, it was to be greeted by the most splendid court in
Europe at the head of which stood a tall, remarkably handsome young man. It must
have seemed too good to be true, especially since the fairy tale went right on. At the
Strasbourg ceremony, Marie had been dressed in a *grand habit de cérémonie* made of
silver brocade and embroidered with precious stones. For the wedding itself, she
wore an even more sumptuous ensemble, "a royal cape of purple velvet, held by gold
fleur-de-lys, bordered and lined with ermine; her skirt was of the same material, with
the bodice and the front of the skirt covered with precious stones and clasps made of
the rarest diamonds . . . On her head she carried a diamond crown . . . The King
was in gold brocade enriched with diamonds and precious stones, a cloak covered
with gold embroidery, a white plume and a huge diamond in his hat."[12]

After the ceremony, the royal couple dined in public, then watched an elaborate
display of fireworks. There were triumphal arches, porticoes adorned with suns and
diverse lights and an infinite number of multicolored flying rockets, and then it was
time for bed. The King and Queen retired and everyone wondered what would
happen next: after all, Louis hadn't shown much interest in the opposite sex until
then; but by the next morning, the duc de Bourbon and Mme de Prie could breathe a
sigh of relief. Their scheme had succeeded, the marriage had been well and truly
consummated by the fifteen-and-a-half-year-old groom; and since, in 1725, people
felt no compunction about discussing anyone's sex life, there was an immediate
plethora of accounts. As always in such cases, it is a little difficult to sort out fact,
fiction and mere exaggeration. Did the King really say that he had honored his bride
with seven repeated proofs of his love? It is difficult to decide today. One thing, at
any rate, is certain. Having now discovered women, Louis found that their attractions
were not to be denied. However Marie may have felt about her wedding night—
probably just resigned acceptance—there could be no doubt that her husband had
experienced what turned out to be one of the chief pleasures of his life.

All through that fall and winter, the King spent every night faithfully with the
Queen while everyone waited for her first pregnancy; but by day he soon discovered
that M. le Duc and Mme de Prie had joined him to an overly pious and extremely
dull stay-at-home who never seemed to have much fun, who liked neither the hunt
nor the theater, and would not have dreamt of spending the evening at an entertaining supper party. Marie's main pleasures, in fact, seemed to consist in sitting at
home, chatting with her ladies, dispensing charity and playing a variety of musical
instruments excruciatingly badly, sometimes interrupting the cacophony for a game
of cards. It was hardly enough to attract the handsomest young man in France, so
any worries Fleury may have felt about the influence of the new Queen were soon
dispelled.

The Bishop, in fact, had been playing a difficult game. The King's education was
now officially completed, so he no longer needed a tutor, but Fleury remained as
close to Louis—and, therefore, as influential—as ever. He had, as we have seen,
agreed to the marriage with Marie Leczinska, so M. le Duc offered him one of the

great Court appointments, that of Almoner to the Queen. Always wary, and obviously thinking that this was a repetition of the Regent's maneuver with the Archbishopric of Reims, Fleury promptly refused. M. le Duc pressed him to reconsider and, no doubt after consulting the King, Fleury finally accepted while making it plain that he was opposed to virtually every other appointment to Marie's Household. Mme de Prie in particular, he said, was not fit to attend Her Majesty. M. le Duc, however, felt he had done quite enough for Fleury by making him almoner, and, besides, he was grateful to Mme de Prie and did not even consider the possibility of doing something unpleasant to her, so Fleury's objurgations were simply ignored. The Bishop was far too clever to show his anger, of course; he simply took his revenge by making sure that his former pupil was turned, slowly but surely, against the Prime Minister.

That task, in any event, was not a difficult one. In spite of his age, Louis XV was fully aware that, as King, he was responsible for his people's welfare. Of course, since he was only fifteen, there could be no question of his running the government himself, but M. le Duc could still always be replaced. The possibility must have occurred to the King as early as June 1725: on the eighth he found himself holding a lit de justice to impose registration of a new 2 percent tax on most incomes (not those of the Clergy, however, or about three quarters of the Nobility). Then, following a disastrous crop in July, there were widespread riots which were brutally repressed while vast numbers of peasants again sank into dire misery, so much so, in fact, that on October 25 an Assembly of the Clergy asked the King to revoke the tax. True to his taste for brutal repression, M. le Duc ordered the dissolution of the Assembly on the twenty-seventh while forbidding publication of the strongly worded letter the bishops had sent the King. As was fast becoming his habit, Louis XV said nothing to anyone except Fleury; but no doubt he gave Bourbon another bad mark.

That Fleury now represented the main opposition to the ministry had, in fact, become perfectly clear. Walpole, the English Ambassador, began to treat him as an emerging power, much to M. le Duc's annoyance; but when the Bishop went on to reiterate his demand for Mme de Prie's dismissal, this time adding Pâris-Duverney for good measure, M. le Duc felt that he had gone too far. Quite aside from any struggle for power, however, Fleury had a good point: Mme de Prie was universally loathed. People were singing: "De Prie est habile / La reine docile / Le roi trop facile / Le Duc imbécile." ("De Prie is clever / the Queen docile / the King too easygoing / the Duke an imbecile.") As for Pâris-Duverney, there was an obvious impropriety in keeping a financier notorious for his speculations as the Queen's private secretary. Still, M. le Duc saw, correctly, that Fleury's attack was also directed against himself; so, refusing the Bishop's request with haughty, angry words, he went straight to Mme de Prie and settled down with her to plot a new scheme. This time the Queen was to be used to vanquish Fleury.

The first step, obviously, was to make sure that henceforth M. le Duc was allowed to see the King alone: until now, whenever the Prime Minister worked with Louis, the Bishop was also present; and since Bourbon realized that alone he didn't stand a chance of changing the situation, he talked Marie Leczinska into doing the asking for him. He hardly wasted time, either: on September 17, a mere twelve days after the wedding, the plot was set in motion. "On Monday, in the evening," the English

Ambassador reported, "as soon as her Majesty had notice of the king's return from hunting, she quitted her cards and desired to speak to him in the closet [i.e., her private study] . . . The Queen took that opportunity, in the presence of M. le Duc, to press him most earnestly, and in the most insinuating and flattering ways possible, to do business with M. le Duc alone, that night; which he would by no means consent to, notwithstanding her repeated instances for above an hour, when his majesty said he must go to the Bishop."[13] In fact, the King had not only refused to work alone with his Prime Minister: he had stood silent, embarrassed and furious while the Queen praised M. le Duc and attacked Fleury, unwilling to give in but unable to assert himself sufficiently to stop the scene. As a number of other ministers were eventually to discover, this was exactly the worst way to go about convincing Louis. Indeed, having left Marie's closet, the King went straight to Fleury, told him all about the scene and added that he not only would never work alone with the duc de Bourbon but, worse, would never see the Queen again. It was as complete a fiasco for M. le Duc as could be imagined.

Given the circumstances, Fleury could no doubt have had the post of Prime Minister for the asking; but, ever the man to shrink from sudden and violent resolutions, and hampered also by the fact that he didn't feel quite ready to take office, he convinced Louis to return to the Queen and retain his Prime Minister; but then, overnight, he decided the time had come to demonstrate his power, so while the King was out hunting the next morning, he wrote him a letter saying he had decided to retire from the Court so as to avoid further conflict and, the English Ambassador noted, "notwithstanding that he had invited some company to dine with him, and notwithstanding the most tempestuous weather of wind and rain that was ever known, [Fleury] went early in the morning to his country house at Issy [just outside Paris]."[14] Back at Versailles, M. le Duc gloated: he had triumphed at last. Walpole, who was a good deal smarter, appraised the situation more wisely: he ordered his carriage and promptly set off for Issy, where, as it turned out, he was the Bishop's only visitor—a courtesy that Fleury never forgot.

Upstairs from M. le Duc's apartment, however, gloom descended on the royal entourage. As soon as he returned from the hunt, Louis XV was given Fleury's letter. Paling visibly, he retired, first to his bedroom, then to the small room where his *chaise percée* was kept; and there, to the courtiers' growing dismay, he remained for over an hour: it was the only way he could be sure of privacy. At that point, the duc de Mortemart, who was First Gentleman of the Bedchamber for that year, intervened. Boldly opening the door, he said to the King: "M. de Fréjus has left for the country. So much the worse for the State and for you," and then went on to urge that he order M. le Duc to recall Fleury. Looking a little less desperate, Louis asked the duc whether he would take that message to the Prime Minister. That very night, a note from M. le Duc went off to Issy: "Your letter, Monsieur, has surprised me to a degree I can hardly express. The King desires your return and orders me to tell you that he wants you back. Having no time to say any more, I will wait until the first time we meet again and limit myself to carrying out His Majesty's orders."[15] The plot had failed doubly: Fleury was now more powerful than ever.

At first M. le Duc tried to pass off the incident as a silly misunderstanding. When

Walpole visited him, he reported: "He very obligingly said, 'to you I will speak plainly on this matter, which is the most ridiculous thing that ever happened; and my friend the bishop, had he been a child, deserved to be whipped. Had he said the least word to me, nothing of this nature would have been; for he had no reason in the world to go away. Mr. Fréjus and I, continued he, have always been very good friends. I do not doubt but we shall always continue so; though I am very sensible of the endeavours of some to divide us if possible; but they will not be able to gain their end.' "[16] Clearly, M. le Duc was trying very hard to save face; in fact, the situation was mortifying, especially since Fleury naturally continued to attend the King every time Bourbon worked with him. By December, he was admitting as much to his friend the maréchal de Villars: "M. le Duc [told me] that he could no longer stand his inability to obtain a private audience with the King and that he would not remain in a situation which was truly shameful for a prime minister.

" 'I must admit,' I answered, 'that it is so; but since you have put up with it for two years, you must continue to be patient . . . Besides . . . , all those who surround the King will follow influence, and if that of M. de Fréjus is the strongest, the very same people whom you believe to be most faithful to you will assuredly change; take care, therefore, not to give your trust lightly."[17] Villars was perfectly right. As soon as the whole story of Fleury's departure and return became known, most courtiers began to change course: Fleury was now clearly the rising sun. Only Marie Leczinska was too obtuse—or, perhaps, too loyal—to understand. "The Queen told me about her sufferings, which were caused by M. le Duc's, and about her desire to end them . . . No matter how hard she tried she could never convince [Fréjus] to arrange a private audience for M. le Duc; and the Prime Minister, who administered the entire kingdom, did not have the liberty to tell the King alone about it for a single moment."[18] Failing to understand where she owed her primary loyalty, blind even to her self-interest, poor Marie, already dull and dowdy enough, was managing to alienate her husband even further. Worse, from her point of view, her efforts only angered the King more against M. le Duc, since the Prime Minister had now caused discord in the royal couple.

Naturally, Bourbon's pretense of friendship did not last. Soon he was openly ridiculing him, and his every sarcasm was repeated to the Bishop. The situation, people began to realize, was not likely to last; and while most everyone was prepared to see M. le Duc dismissed—indeed, it seemed a consummation devoutly to be wished—back at the hôtel de Condé his family, which understandably took a different view, now started a plot of its own. Having concluded that much of M. le Duc's unpopularity could be laid at Mme de Prie's door, the dowager duchesse de Bourbon decided that her son could still be saved if only the lady were sent away, along with her faithful ally Pâris-Duverney. With the tenacity for which she was famous, she tried to press this view on M. le Duc; and since she realized that he required a mistress, she offered up the comtesse d'Egmont as the perfect substitute. Just at this point, to everyone's stupefaction, Mme de Prie did, in fact, retire. Unfortunately for the plot, hers was only a strategic move aimed at proving that she was indispensable after all. Within the month, to the dowager's fury, she was back, to be greeted by M.

le Duc's rejoicings and the King's obdurate snubs. It began to look as if nothing would ever be resolved.

Not surprisingly, the entire Leczinski family, which had yet to learn that discretion was the better part of valor, had publicly committed itself to the endangered party. "There isn't a man alive who approves M. de Fréjus' efforts at damaging the honor of M. le Duc and the authority of the King,"[19] the ex-King Stanislas wrote a friend, the maréchal de Bourg, on January 1, 1726, adding on the twenty-fifth: "Mme de Prie wrote me a letter which is making my heart bleed. What is the remedy? I care too much about their happiness to find anyone safe enough to confide in, and have no resource in my reason, which is overcome with chagrin."[20] Praiseworthy loyalty, perhaps; but a wiser man, aware that, in the end, all depended on the King, might have made his feelings a little less conspicuous. The key to Stanislas' position, although never openly stated, probably lies in his expectation that M. le Duc's dismissal would be promptly followed by Marie's repudiation; and given her inability to please the King, he did have some reason to worry.

Stanislas did his letter writing in Paris: the King had made it plain that he did not expect to see much of his kind but dull and verbose father-in-law. At Versailles Marie fought on. "The Queen told me with much pain about the change she had noticed in the King's affection for her," Villars noted in mid-January 1726. "Her tears came pouring out. I answered: 'I believe, Madame, that the King's heart is indeed remote from what is usually called love; you don't feel the same about him; but don't let your passion be seen too plainly . . . Besides, a natural coolness is not as cruel as unfaithfulness' . . . She blamed M. de Fréjus for this change."[21] In fact, she should have blamed herself. Quite single-handedly she had managed to do the two things the King resented most: she had embarrassed him by making a scene in front of M. le Duc, and she had tried to force him into giving his confidence to someone he distrusted. Even some three months after the event, she still failed to perceive her mistakes, and loyalty to the wrong person was not likely to earn her any rewards.

Since she wasn't getting on with the King, Marie, at the end of the month, bravely tackled the man she considered her chief enemy. "The Queen," Villars noted, "had a long conversation with the Bishop of Fréjus . . . There was much discussion of a dismissal of Mme de Prie and Pâris-Duverney. 'But what hatred,' asked the Queen, 'can you feel against them to keep demanding that they be sent away?'

" 'I have no ill will toward them,' he answered, 'and if I keep pressing M. le Duc, it is only because of the wrong they do him.'

" 'I must admit that the disgrace of those people with whom I am so pleased would give me pain,' she said. To that the Bishop answered not a word. She also talked to him of the diminution she felt in the King's affection. He answered rather drily: 'That is not my fault.' Then she talked to him again of M. le Duc's chagrin in regard to the private audiences, but it did her no good."[22] In fact, though Marie had signally failed to carry her points, the conversation may have done her more good than she knew. She had revealed her basic kindness, her complete lack of political understanding and, above all, confirmed her absolute inability to influence the King, thus proving to Fleury that he need not worry about her. She was not worth propitiating, but then, by the same token, she was not worth repudiating either.

All through this, the life of the Court continued as if nothing had happened. The King hunted with ever greater zeal, the usual festivities took place at their appointed dates, and, more and more, the old ways of the last reign were reasserting themselves. Gambling, for instance, once again became a major pastime. In February, Villars recorded that the King and Queen had lost 200,000 livres ($900,000) over a two-month period. The other change was that, more and more, Marie Leczinska found herself excluded from her husband's life. Even when she didn't irritate him, she bored him, so she ate alone in public while Louis went straight from the hunt to supper parties, often at La Muette, with two of M. le Duc's sisters and a little group of cheerful but decorous young people. In one respect, however, he did not neglect his wife. Fully aware that an heir was necessary, he made sure to sleep with her almost every night—so far without visible consequences. And, of course, throughout it all M. le Duc continued to govern France with Fleury's consent.

All through that spring, however, his position grew increasingly more fragile. Since Mme de Prie was thought to rule him, the King ignored her completely. That made her life so unpleasant that whenever her duties as a lady-in-waiting allowed, she would return to Paris, much to M. le Duc and the Queen's distress. By June it was so clear that Louis XV could no longer stand his Prime Minister that on the eighth M. le Duc offered his resignation. The King refused it and added, amiably, that he couldn't think of doing without his cousin's services.

It was even noticed, for the next two days, that the King was unusually amiable to his Prime Minister. On the tenth, before leaving for Rambouillet, the residence of the comtesse de Toulouse, where he was to hunt and have supper while the Queen remained at Versailles, Louis XV even made a point of giving M. le Duc a loaf of a special bread made with orange water, an obvious mark of favor. Better still, as he walked out he asked his cousin whether he, too, was coming to Rambouillet. Not immediately, M. le Duc answered; he had work to do. "Hurry up and finish your business, then," the King continued, "and come early to Rambouillet, as I intend to have supper at eight-thirty." As he entered his carriage, he turned back and said again: "Don't keep me waiting at supper."[23] Thoroughly reassured, M. le Duc bowed deeply and retreated to his apartment.

Just before eight o'clock that same day, he was preparing to follow the King when the duc de Charost, who was Captain (i.e., Commander) of the Guard, asked to see him. As the highest ranking court official, Charost could hardly be denied, so in he came and, walking over to the Prime Minister, was seen to whisper in his ear and hand him a letter. Looking utterly stunned, M. le Duc bowed deeply and said aloud: "Accustomed as I am to command everyone's obedience to the King, I will now offer up myself as an example of this same obedience," asked for permission to burn a few papers, and within minutes was seen to enter his carriage under guard. The letter he had been handed by M. de Charost was simple to the point of harshness. "Mon cousin,"* it said, "as I desire to govern by myself in the future, I am abolishing the post of Prime Minister; I thank you for the care you have taken of my affairs and order you, on pains of disobedience, to go to Chantilly and stay there until I com-

---

* It was proper etiquette for the King to address all members of his nonimmediate family, all cardinals, dukes and marshals of France, as "my cousin."

mand you otherwise. I forbid you to see the Queen."[24] That, in fact, was the duc de Charost's doing. He had been given two letters by the King, one amiable, one not. If M. le Duc obeyed promptly, he was to be given the pleasanter of the two; if not, the other; Charost thoroughly disliked M. le Duc, so he simply tore up the first letter and, in spite of the Prime Minister's immediate compliance, handed him the second.

It took a few hours for the great change to become known, but even while M. le Duc was setting off in his carriage, another scene was being enacted, this time in Marie Leczinska's apartment. There, Fleury, who, as her Almoner, had constant access to the Queen, walked in as she sat down to supper and handed her a letter from the King ordering her to heed the Bishop. Then, as the tears started pouring down Marie's face, he informed her of M. le Duc's disgrace and forbade her to communicate further with him. There was nothing the Queen could say except that, of course, she would obey her husband's orders. Still, as soon as Fleury was gone, she called in Mme de Prie and gave her the bad news. For the next three days, keeping to her study, she cried incessantly; as was now his wont, Louis stayed away. For the ex-Polish princess, married less than a year and still childless, the situation hardly looked promising. "The Queen told me with many tears about M. le Duc's departure," Villars recorded on the twelfth. "She was touched by his disgrace, but felt even more strongly about a letter which M. de Fréjus had given her. She showed it to me. It said exactly this: 'I ask you and, if necessary, I order you, Madame, to do everything M. de Fréjus will tell you as if I were speaking to you in person.' She read me these words with sobs."[25] That day, she also learned that Mme de Prie, who had been forbidden to stay at Versailles, would not even be allowed to keep M. le Duc company in his exile; instead, she was sent off to Courbépine, a castle she owned in Normandy. The defeat of the former ruling party was complete.

Luckily for the Queen, she was as obedient as she had been loyal; besides, M. le Duc's fate, enraging as it no doubt appeared to him, was still not such as to provoke undue pity. Chantilly was one of the most splendid estates in the kingdom. Indeed, in one respect exile proved a great boon for the ex-Prime Minister: he now had time to carry out improvements which survive to this day and have unquestionably done more for his memory than the dubious achievements of his two years in power.

As for the King's extraordinary secrecy, after the event it surprised no one. Already in 1718 the maréchal de Villeroy had commented on Louis's ability to hide how he felt, and amiability to ministers who had ceased to please was an old monarchical tradition. When the young Louis XIV had dismissed Fouquet, his Superintendent of Finances and the most powerful of his ministers, for instance, he had used almost exactly the same tactics. The rationale for this was simple enough: a minister who knew that he was about to be dismissed might make trouble. Better to lull him into a feeling of false security until it was too late for him to do harm. As for exile, though a singularly golden one in the case of M. le Duc, it was also a perfectly rational move. Many historians have assumed it was all timidity on the King's part, that he wasn't up to facing a dismissed minister. In fact, since the Court was a seething mass of contending factions, keeping an ex-minister at Versailles would have allowed the formation of an opposition cabal before the new ministry could prove itself. When the former minister was sent away, however, his supporters, realizing they needed a new patron, either supported the new men or, at least, were so dispersed as to be harmless.

Obviously, the sixteen-year-old Louis had played his part to perfection, but the parallel with Louis XIV and Fouquet, which undoubtedly occurred to him, should not be carried too far. When the great-grandfather had imprisoned his Superintendent, it was so that he could start running the government himself. Now, in 1726, the great-grandson had neither the capacity—he was still learning—nor the desire to do so himself. And just in case there was any doubt that the revolution, as it was called, had been engineered by Fleury, we have his letter to the British Ambassador, dated June 11 at five o'clock, three hours before Charost handed M. le Duc his letter of dismissal. "I have often been tempted to reveal to your Excellency what has just happened," he wrote Walpole, knowing that the letter would be delivered later in the evening, "but I was not master of the King's secret and my orders were too positive to be disobeyed. His Majesty suppresses the office of first minister and the duke of Bourbon is commanded to retire to Chantilly. I have no doubt that he will obey and I have the honour to write this to you before hand because I shall have no time after."[26] [Walpole's translation] Six days later Walpole commented: "Without the title of Prime Minister, [Fleury] will have the power in a more absolute manner than it was ever enjoyed by Cardinal Richelieu or Mazarin."[27] The Ambassador couldn't have been more right. Ever since that visit to Issy the preceding September, Fleury and he had become the closest of friends, so he perceived early what soon became visible to all. The King was still too young and too fond of amusement to take on the tasks of government. He loved and trusted his former tutor: clearly there would be no limits to the Bishop's power.

Still, appearances were kept up. On June 13 Louis XV wrote an autograph letter, the first of many, to his cousin* and ally, the Elector of Bavaria. "Having decided to take the government of my realm in hand, I have abolished the post of Prime Minister, while at the same time admitting to the knowledge of the most particular business and to my most intimate confidence the former Bishop of Fréjus, who, ever since my earliest youth, has given me proof of his zeal and attachment to my person . . . This new disposition will entail no change in the general conduct of business."[28] And later that day, the King told his Council: "It was time I took over the government of my State . . . I want to follow the example of the late King, my great-grandfather, in every way."[29] Here, indeed, was the rationale. Only Louis XIV had set policy and merely allowed his ministers to carry out his orders. There was no question of this in 1726. Fleury, and Fleury alone, was at the helm.

It was, once again, the British Ambassador who made it all clear. On September 28, after a new ministry had been brought in,** and the maréchaux d'Huxelles and de Tallard were admitted to the Council, Walpole wrote the Duke of Newcastle: "As [Fleury] certainly has the best intentions, as well as perseverance to do what is right, so he is likewise desirous that the voice of the nation should accompany his good actions. This love of popularity, joined with the natural mildness of his temper, is

---

* Louis's grandmother was the Elector's aunt.
** Chancellor: d'Aguesseau; Comptroller General of the Finances: Le Péletier des Forts; War: Le Blanc; Navy and Royal Household: Saint-Florentin (who kept the Household until 1774); Church affairs: Maurepas. Fleury was Minister of State without portfolio.

sometimes a restraint upon him . . . but as it never makes him swerve or deviate, in the least, from pursuing the point he has in view, he has steadiness, and with it dexterity enough to encompass what he designs without the displeasure or resentment of any body . . . The preserving of a strict union between his [Britannic] majesty and France . . . is the foundation of his present thoughts and system."[30] It was an accurate description. The only thing Walpole doesn't mention is that in 1726 Fleury had reached the Methuselah-like age of seventy-three; it was clear to everyone that, no matter how well preserved he might be, he was unlikely to live longer than two or three years: his would be a ministry of transition during which the King would learn enough about the government to be able to run it himself once his old tutor was gone.

Partly for that reason, and partly because M. le Duc was so universally loathed, the new minister of State (Fleury's official title) was popular at home. "The people have been so delighted with the change that it has been necessary to stop them from lighting bonfires in the streets, as it would have been too great an insult to a Prince of the Blood Royal,"[31] Barbier noted, continuing, a few days later: "The King, like the man he is, has made a speech at the first council held since the exile of M. le Duc. He declared that what he had done in no way lessened the friendship he felt for his cousin, but that he was pleased to put things back in the same condition as during the reign of Louis XIV . . . that people should now speak to him directly about any favor and that his ministers would work with him according to a regular schedule, in the presence of the former Bishop of Fréjus, who will be there for everything. Thus, the Bishop of Fréjus, though he doesn't have the title of Prime Minister, will have almost the power of that position."[32] A clear appreciation of the situation had now seeped all the way down from an ambassador's dispatch to become the talk of Paris.

Although Fleury remained a minister without portfolio in theory, he was soon given the postal service. This wasn't due to any desire he may have felt to improve the mails, rather, it ensured the secrecy of his own correspondence while giving him the *cabinet noir,* the secret police which opened and copied all interesting letters. It was a necessary perquisite for the principal minister since it allowed him to know just what plots and intrigues were taking place. When, moreover, the former Bishop was created a Cardinal on September 11, the situation became crystal clear. By then, His Eminence had moved into a much larger apartment within Versailles—always the sure accompaniment of power—and taken to having a public *coucher* just like the King, which, indeed, was rather better attended than the Sovereign's. As for Louis XV, he now faithfully sat through all Council meetings, though he often remained silent, and was seen to closet himself frequently with Fleury. He might not be governing yet, but he was obviously learning.

It quickly became evident that he could hardly have a better master. What France still needed was peace; Fleury thought virtually no war was worth its ultimate cost. The State needed a balanced budget, the economy a stable currency: ever since the collapse of the System, the value of the livre had wavered back and forth, thereby gravely hampering trade and industry. Finally, the cost of the Court, brought down by the Regent, had been allowed to soar under M. le Duc; now it must be reduced.

Fleury promptly set to work, and within a remarkably short time he carried through a whole series of reforms.

Some were more spectacular than others. Pâris-Duverney, the very symbol of speculation and peculation, was sent to the Bastille for a short stay. The 2 percent tax was abolished. This was a popular move, even if it came at the behest of the small part of the nobility that had been taxed. The currency was redefined: a standard gold coin, the louis, was henceforth worth twenty-four livres; the silver écu, three livres. Since the livre itself was an accounting convenience—there was no such thing as a one-livre coin—earlier ministers, when fiddling with the value of gold, had taken the louis all the way from fifteen to thirty livres. Now it would be stable, the Cardinal announced, for a renewable six-month period; at the end of the first semester, nothing changed, and the arrangement continued for the next twelve years until 1738, when it was finally defined as permanent. In fact, it lasted as long as the ancien régime itself—no mean achievement in a country where manipulating the currency had been a standard expedient for raising the King's income. And with the new, stable louis, a marked expansion of trade began.

Of course, the continued solidity of the currency depended on a balanced budget, something which hadn't been seen since the 1680s. Clearly, a dual approach was needed: unnecessary expense must be cut drastically and the tax revenue must be significantly increased without, however, raising the tax rate. This last was not quite as impossible as it might seem. About half of the government's income came from consumer taxes, the equivalent of our sales taxes, which were collected by the *fermiers généraux,* rich financiers who, at the beginning of every year, would bid for the total amount to be paid into the Treasury. The highest bid won, but it usually remained well under the amount actually collected; "rich as a fermier général" was a current and fully justified saying. Clearly, the thing to do was to apply pressure so that the fermiers généraux would raise their bids; this Fleury, through the agency of the Comptroller General, proceeded to do. On August 19, 1726, the fermiers généraux undertook to pay the Treasury eighty million livres, the highest sum yet, and larger by four million than that of the previous year. By 1732, this figure had risen to eighty-four million.

Still, even though 4 million livres was a significant figure in an overall budget of some 150 million, it would hardly do the trick; so Fleury set an example by living modestly. Although he cost the King virtually nothing—most of his 86,000 livres ($387,000) income came from two abbeys—Fleury made it a point to eschew the kind of conspicuous consumption for which his predecessors had been famous. While making sure that great ceremonies retained all their accustomed splendor, he cut down ruthlessly on unnecessary expense, even going so far as to order the demolition of the artificial cascade at Marly because it cost too much to run. Best of all, however, for the first time in a century all the powers in the State—the King, Fleury, the Comptroller General—agreed that finance must be put on a sound footing. Until then, the hapless Comptroller General would protest while the monarch went on spending. Now, two competent men in succession—first, Le Péletier des Forts; then, after 1730, Orry—were able to keep expenditure down, safe in the knowledge that their decisions would be upheld at the highest level.

It is, in fact, not the least curious characteristic of Fleury as principal minister that he launched himself into a series of economic reforms. His training, after all, had been that of a priest and an educator; but then, during his tenure at distant, backwards Fréjus—so far away from Versailles that, apart from the acceptance of the *Unigenitus* bull, no one cared much what happened—he had learned just how a community functioned, what taxes meant, why roads were important; and he had also discovered that government by consent works more smoothly and more efficaciously than even the best organized tyranny. Now that his field of activity had broadened from a small, impoverished bishopric to the entire kingdom, he proceeded to apply his earlier discoveries.

First, he freed all political prisoners and declined to use the Bastille. Censorship, tightened under M. le Duc, was relaxed again. Then, he turned his attention to the highways: ever since the beginning of the War of the Spanish Succession, some quarter of a century earlier, they had been allowed to deteriorate. Travel for both persons and goods had become excruciatingly slow and difficult, with obviously deleterious consequences for the expansion of trade. Now the Cardinal gave orders that the old roads be made passable again and construction on new ones begun. Since there were many toll roads, the owners of which often took gross advantage of their users, he instituted uniform, fair tolls and in many cases abolished them altogether.

Aside from the Court, the main expense borne by the State was for the military. Fleury was no soldier, but one thing was quite clear to him: in its present state, France could not afford a first-rate Army *and* a first-rate Navy, so the Navy was deliberately starved while commercial shipping was encouraged. Within a few years, the merchant marine grew from 300 to 1,800 ships and since the movement of goods was taxed, the combination of better roads and increased shipping swelled the Treasury's receipts. As for the Army, while it obviously must be maintained, Fleury saw no reason to keep its numbers up to those required in times of grave international tension. With the English alliance steady, France was not at risk from anyone, so the Army was reduced by a third, from 150,000 to 100,000 men. This was still more than adequate and made for substantial savings.

There are times, in human history, when nothing succeeds like good sense. Fleury had the luck of being in power during one of those times and, as a result, his popularity endured. Even at Court, where intrigue was the stuff of life, it soon became obvious that there was no unseating the new minister. Indeed, it was extremely hard to find anything, except parsimony, with which to reproach him; and while that characteristic might fail to please the denizens of Versailles, it earned everyone else's approval. The only problem was that it was all unlikely to last. By 1727, Fleury was seventy-four, an age reached by exceedingly few people during the eighteenth century. Clearly, he would soon be dead, and no one could tell what would happen to his reforms then. With that very important caveat, however, France was in the best of hands; and while he lived the Cardinal could count on the King's support. In November 1727, Walpole reported to his brother: "The Cardinal's . . . loyalty and natural affection for the king, whom he looks upon in a manner as his own child, and his majesty's reciprocal love and confidence in him only, will never let him quit his majesty's service, much less suffer any sharer in his administration and authority, of which, although he is perhaps the mildest man being, no minister of state was ever so jealous, or ever kept the other ministers at so great a distance or in so much awe . . .

"He expressed himself to me, as indeed he does to others on proper occasions, in such a manner of the present administration of England with regard to their integrity and abilities, that I am persuaded that no condition or consideration could tempt him to contribute to their removal [i.e., by encouraging the Jacobites] upon whose continuation . . . he thinks the present peace and tranquility of Europe depends."[33] Walpole was right. The new order born of the Utrecht settlement and the Franco-English alliance was now proving remarkably stable. To the south, Spain, enfeebled by its recent war, was forced to depend on France for support. To the east, Prussia, allied to France and Great Britain, kept Germany stable by providing a threat to Austria's flank, while Leopold I of Habsburg was too deep in debt to start a war without British subsidies. Italy, it seemed, had been carved up to everyone's satisfaction. Sweden, having lost its long war with Russia, asked for nothing better than peace, while Russia itself was not yet powerful enough to intervene in the affairs of Europe.

It was one thing for the Continent to be quiet, but, far more difficult, the Cardinal even managed to keep everyone at Versailles contented. M. le Duc, it is true, remained in exile, but no one missed him. The King was leading the best of lives, hunting almost every day, visiting the witty, charming and kind comtesse de Toulouse at Rambouillet, and holding lively yet decorous supper parties in his hunting boxes at La Muette or Choisy. Even better, Fleury's parsimony failed to hamper the explosion of artistic creativity which was just beginning and which Louis XV, in spite of his youth, was enthusiastically supporting. Already under Louis XIV, new standards in architecture, decor and painting had been set in France. Now, artisans of genius went to work, and, like all people of taste everywhere, Louis XV patronized them. In 1728, for instance, he ordered a medal chest from Gaudreaux. It was to be placed in his study, where he kept his collection, and it is still there today. A prime example of the new curving, graceful rococo style, its magnificence is only eclipsed by the perfection of its detail. Inlaid woods, sculpted gilt bronzes and complexity of design all combines to make it one of the most beautiful pieces of furniture ever crafted. And, of course, the King watched the work of the new painters. Because Oudry was so adept at painting animals and the hunt, he soon became Louis XV's favorite painter, but others, like Lancret and Pater, who worked in the manner of the recently deceased Watteau, also enjoyed their share of royal favor.

Finally, in the one quarter where, perhaps, it mattered most, Fleury was able to make peace. He convinced Louis to forgive the Queen for her overenthusiastic support of M. le Duc. There could be no question of a perfect marriage, of course—Marie was too dull and dowdy for that—but the King now took pride in being a good husband and the reconciliation bore fruit: at the very beginning of 1727, the Queen's doctors informed the King that Her Majesty was undoubtedly pregnant.

Chapter Four

Coming of Age

WITH the Queen's pregnancy, Louis XV settled into what seemed to be a long-lasting pattern. Although he was still barely seventeen, he had reached a level of maturity, in his personal and public lives, which apparently did not admit of change. While not exactly in love with Marie Leczinska, he now felt tied to her by more than just protocol. This orphan, this adolescent whose closest relatives were the unappealing ducs d'Orléans and de Bourbon, wanted a family of his own more than anything in the world. As soon as the Queen showed signs of providing him with children, she earned his deep and lasting affection. In spite of countless offers, of endless temptation, the strong and virile young man remained absolutely faithful to his wife: it never ceased to astonish the Court.

Even when he left the Queen behind, as he still often did, Louis relied on family members for entertainment. The stars of his suppers were the comtesse de Toulouse and Mlle de Clermont, both relatives, though in different degrees. Mlle de Clermont was a sister of M. le Duc, while the comtesse de Toulouse, who was born a Noailles, was married to the youngest of Louis XIV's légitimés. Like the duc du Maine, the comte de Toulouse was Mme de Montespan's child, but he was his brother's opposite in every way. He lacked ambition, guile and the ability to charm the people he needed; but, on the other hand, he was modest, competent (as Grand Admiral of France), hardworking and reliable. As for his wife, unlike the ferociously ambitious duchesse du Maine, she was quite content not to be a Princess of the Blood, and much preferred a quiet life at Rambouillet to the traps and allurements of the Court. As a result, while the duc du Maine schemed, plotted, was discovered, went to jail, and was stripped of his semiroyal rank, the Toulouses were so popular with everyone, including, most importantly, the Regent, that they were allowed to keep the rank and precedence lost by the du Maines. And since the comtesse made up in wit and liveliness for the seriousness of her husband, they formed a most amiable couple. It was no wonder the King often sought their company.

Still, virtually in secret Louis XV also worked hard. Because Fleury was so obviously in charge, people assumed the King did nothing but hunt. In fact, he not only met almost daily with his Minister, he also began his lifelong habit of checking for himself, directly, the actual functioning of his government. This took a number of forms. First, the King read, and often initialed, most of the flood of documents which came across his desk every day and which ranged all the way from instructions for the repair of a bridge to major foreign policy documents. Then, he insisted on writing out, and often drafting, all the important letters sent to foreign rulers. Finally, he kept a close check on all the money which was spent in his name. This meant he was aware not only of the larger budget outlays but also of the daily expenses of his Court. No sum was paid, in that department, unless it bore the King's autograph *bon* ("all right") in the margin.

Indeed, leafing through the accounting books provided him with a remarkably clear idea of how the Court functioned. In 1731, for instance, he authorized a special bonus of 11,000 livres ($49,500) to the duc d'Humières, his Captain of the Guard, for expenses connected with a trip to Compiègne; he ordered that the duc de La Rochefoucauld, that year's First Gentleman of the Bedchamber, be given 50,269 livres ($226,210) to pay the expenses of the Grand Master of Wardrobe (i.e., all the King's clothes, shoes, hats, gloves, etc., for the year). Then there were large sums, all broken down to their smallest components: 294,863 livres for the King's horses; 48,039 livres for the October quarter (i.e., three months starting then) for the royal hunting equipage—a hefty 192,156 livres ($864,702) a year, the clearest indication of Louis's ruling passion, especially since outlays increased to 67,566 livres in the January quarter. There was also money for building: the hunting box at La Muette was ideally located, but it was too small, so the King was having it enlarged. For the quarter beginning January 1732, the work there cost him 27,420 livres, which rose to 33,717 by the end of the year. And, finally, there was a miscellany of very small sums which bore the royal *bon* just like all the others: 1,260 to feed the wild boars in Saint Germain from January to August; 5,221 livres for the embroidered purses which the King gave out to the Royal Family and the principal dignitaries of State on January 1; or even 559 livres for the illumination of the village of Sèvres on June 12.

At the same time, not content with merely controlling and authorizing expenditure, Louis XV insisted on knowing how much had actually been paid out, and how much was still due. Since, most years, the Treasury was at least six months—and, more often, a year or two—late in meeting outstanding bills, this was an important element of the financial situation. Even in February 1733, for instance, at a time when the budget was nearly balanced and the country prosperous, the Treasury still owed 54,434 livres for the July quarter of the Queen's Household and, more shocking still, 14,000 livres for the year 1730.[1]

None of this prevented the King from behaving with royal magnificence. In 1731, for instance, he gave the comte de Toulouse 120,000 livres ($540,000) to compensate him for the expenses caused by the royal stay at Rambouillet; and the great Court festivities were as splendid as ever. Nothing, in fact, was ever meant to change the high standards set by Louis XIV. Brought up in a world where etiquette was all-important, Louis XV paid even more attention to it than his great-grandfather. He usually knew, better than anyone at Court, what the rules demanded and made very sure that they were followed. When, for instance, he noticed that the ducs, when attending mass, knelt on velvet cushions, he promptly reprimanded them: only those ducs in attendance on his person (e.g., the Captain of the Guard, the First Gentleman of the Bedchamber, or the Grand Master of the Wardrobe) were entitled to the cushions; but then, since he was kind, he added that as long as he couldn't *see* the cushions, he would consider them nonexistent; so any duc who liked to be comfortable made sure he wasn't placed next to the aisle. In the same way, Louis XV maintained the elaborate ceremonial used when the Sovereign ate in public; but since, unlike his great-grandfather, he was shy, he felt most uncomfortable and ate very little, catching up later in private. Still, the elegance with which he knocked the top off his boiled egg was famous, and people came from Paris just to watch it. Again, although styles had changed, he refrained, at first, from making any alterations in the decor of Versailles and even went so far as to use the splendid but drafty bedroom in which the Sun King had died.

Besides the usual yearly occasions—January 1, Carnival, the King's Birthday, etc. —the first of the great Court spectacles came in August 1727: on the fourteenth the Queen had gone into labor and been delivered of twin daughters, Mesdames Elisabeth and Henriette. While they were a bit of a disappointment—everyone had hoped for a son and heir—still, there was much rejoicing: the royal couple was young, they would obviously have more children, so this was only a first installment. People were right. Between August 14, 1727, and July 15, 1737, the Queen gave birth to a total of ten children, although it took her a little while to produce a son. Soon after the birth of the twins, she became pregnant again; but, on July 28, 1728, in spite of everyone's hopes, she gave birth to another daughter: the throne was still without a direct heir. Nothing loath, she became pregnant a third time almost as rapidly as the second, and on September 4, 1729, to the King's immense joy and amid great celebrations, a Dauphin was born.

No sooner did the baby appear, under the watchful eyes of the King, the Princes of the Blood, Fleury, and assorted dignitaries, but Louis, bending over, kissed the Queen and thanked her; then the Cardinal de Rohan, Grand Almoner of France, put a dab of holy water on the newborn's forehead; the Dauphin was given the blue sash of the Saint Esprit; and, finally, the duchesse de Ventadour, the King's old Governess, took over. In Paris, for three days there was a succession of fireworks and bonfires, while at Versailles Louis XV received the official congratulations of the ambassadors and the rest of the Court. There, too, fireworks dazzled the onlookers on the evenings of the fourth and fifth. And just under a year later, on August 30, 1730, the Queen gave birth to yet another boy who was created duc d'Anjou.* The succession was safe.

In this politically stable world, however, much was changing. By 1730, the last traces of the old Court had vanished along with the old fashions. The young King might not be very well known yet outside his immediate entourage, but no one doubted that he was now presiding over the century of Louis XV. It wasn't only that the decor, with its rococo curves and light, cheerful colors, had been transformed; the way people understood life was now radically different. Gone were the universal pomp and display of the old reign, with its huge, splendid but drafty rooms. Now, comfort and convenience were given priority, and elegance was prized far above grandeur. New necessities became pressing: in 1700, ladies still received guests fully dressed, but lying on top of their (fully made-up) beds. By 1730, there was a whole

* He died before his fifth birthday.

range of possibilities: intimates were invited into the boudoir, a small, often circular or oval room, while larger, grander salons were used for more formal occasions. More and more, a special room was set aside for that new highlight of the evening, the supper. Less official than the dinner (which was usually eaten around four o'clock), the supper usually began a little before nine and gathered carefully selected guests, a mixture of wits and pretty women. More than any other social activity, it represented the prevalent sophisticated atmosphere of both Court and Town. And the people who chatted, ate, drank and laughed sported a completely new look. Gone, for instance, was the immense leonine wig favored by Louis XIV. Instead, men wore their hair flat on top, curled at the sides, and gathered at the back in a queue tied with a wide ribbon. Even more important, powder, either white or gray, was in general use, and its effect, especially on young people, could be immensely flattering: there is nothing like the contrast of a sparkling glance and fresh complexion with the snows of one's coiffure to produce an enticing look. The women, who also wore powder, kept their hair short and gently curled. There were other changes as well. Men's coats were shorter, fuller, more graceful, with far more flowing lace at cravat and cuffs; stockings, once colored, were almost invariably white. But what people really marveled at, mocked and celebrated, what the preachers in church thundered at was that startling new invention the *panier*.

Under Louis XIV, women's dresses had followed straight lines; then, around 1716, the hoop, called panier in France, made its appearance. Unlike the later crinoline, it expanded mostly sideways, so that skirts grew wider and wider; quite often the overskirt was split in front so as to reveal a contrasting or matching underskirt, but in every case it was lavishly adorned with embroidery, lace, artificial flowers and ribbons. Clearly, the preachers said, these new fashions were an invention of the devil, especially since the wide skirts were combined with tightly corseted bodices cut so as to reveal plunging necklines. And, as always at Court, the innovation produced a problem of etiquette. "It is hard to believe, but true, that the Cardinal has been embarrassed by the paniers that women wear under their skirts to make them wider," Barbier reported in March 1728. "They are so ample that when women sit down the stays are pushed out and take an amazing amount of space, so that now they have to make special armchairs. Only three women can fit in the boxes at the theaters . . . This fashion has become so exaggerated . . . that the princesses who sit next to the Queen were covering her skirt with their own. This seemed impertinent, but it was difficult to find a remedy, so the Cardinal, after much pondering, decided that there would always be an empty chair on either side of the Queen to prevent her from being bothered; and the pretext is that the two chairs are being kept for Mesdames de France, her daughters."[2] Fashion, however, is not as easily manipulated as politics. Excellent minister though he was, Fleury was hardly up to solving this sort of problem. "The story about the paniers at court has had consequences," Barbier noted a month later. "Since there is now a space between the Queen and the Princesses of the Blood Royal, these last have demanded that the same sort of distance be established between them and the duchesses and, in fact, their request has been granted . . . That has greatly annoyed the ducs. A manuscript is circulating throughout the court. It attacks the Princes of the Blood Royal and is both clever and strongly worded, so that it has been burned by the executioner."[3] At first glance, the whole incident seems simply funny: in our more egalitarian age, it is difficult to take this kind of seating dispute seriously. In fact, it was enormously important at the time. Precedence was the lifeblood of the court the ultimate status symbol, and no one was more conscious of it than the King. He did not hesitate to reprimand cardinal de Tencin in public, thus humiliating him deeply, because at the reception of the papal nuncio the Cardinal had stationed himself *inside* the balustrade dividing the King's bedroom simply because cardinal de Rohan was there already. As Grand Almoner of France, Rohan had a right to be there; that had nothing to do with his also being a cardinal, and therefore his presence gave no right to Tencin. Because precedence defined you so clearly, it was a subject that all European nobles had thoroughly mastered, and the disputes which often took place could be quite violent. In April 1731, for instance, the Queen suddenly found herself in the middle of a real brawl.

"There has been a great fight at Court between the duchesses and the other ladies of the nobility," Barbier recorded. "During a ceremony, Madame la duchesse de Gontaut-Biron, who is a very pretty woman, tried, in the most marked manner, to pass before Madame de Ruppelmonde. Madame de Ruppelmonde, seizing her arm, pulled her to a stop. The dispute went so far that they called each other strumpet and each literally told the other to go f—— herself. The fact is clearly established and it is agreed that they knew perfectly well what the words meant.

"The ducs have complained about this . . . [but the other nobles] claim that the duchesses have no prerogative other than sitting on a stool in the Queen's apartment* . . . M. le cardinal de Fleury has settled the dispute by deciding in favor of the duchesses, to whom he has given precedence for three occasions."[4] This was only one of many such disputes, although it was, perhaps, a little more spectacular than most.

The importance and frequency of these drawn-out battles are in themselves a clue in the Court's real nature: it had become a special world where different standards obtained—*ce pays-ci* ("this country"), as its own denizens called it—a place where people spoke, walked (they glided instead) and behaved in ways utterly different from those of the rest of France. You could tell at a glance whether someone belonged to the Court, and that particular, artificial and glittering world was the environment within which, day in, day out, the King must function.

Given the size of the Court—at least two thousand people, sometimes as many as four thousand—it was also everything Louis XV most disliked. All through his late teens and early twenties, he continued to be agonizingly shy while being forced to cope with people he knew little or not at all. It was no wonder he was often described as cold or haughty, or simply blank. Like most shy people, he froze when faced with strangers, and so instead of saying just the right few words to every person presented to him—the brief but apposite remark had been one of Louis XIV's specialties—he simply stared in silence. Nor was he happier during most Court ceremonies, whether it was receiving the courtiers whose birth gave them a right to be at Versailles, eating in public, or performing half a dozen other well-attended rituals. It was at this time,

---

* All the other ladies stood.

in fact, that a few intimates began to realize that the King had two radically different personalities, one distant and majestic, the other warm, lively and friendly. As a result, he was scarcely known at all by anyone except a few close courtiers and attendants, and this distance from ordinary people was made even greater by the fact that the King never resided in Paris. Indeed, it was not until October 1728, some three years after her marriage, that the Queen visited Paris for the first time, and even then she was incognito—that is, her cortege consisted only of four golden carriages, each drawn by eight horses and surrounded by twenty horse guards, twelve footmen and a number of pages. She didn't much care for the city and, as it turned out, the Parisians weren't impressed either. "She is small, thin, not pretty without being ugly, with a kind, sweet expression which does not give her the majesty required of a Queen,"[5] Barbier noted dourly.

Still, the people were proud of their King. He was good, he was handsome, and he was still very young. A German nobleman, the Baron von Pollnitz, who visited France in 1732, described it all: "[The King] is one of the handsomest princes in Europe. One can say of Louis XV that he was born without vices, and free of that pride which is usually felt by monarchs. He is friendly with his court, reserved with people he doesn't know, and most particularly with ambassadors; he is more circumspect and secretive than other people his age. His habits, his behavior and his feelings are those of a virtuous man . . .

"The Queen is a princess of exemplary virtue whose only care is to do her duty to God, the King and her children. She is very gracious and polite and expresses herself very easily in French, German and Polish . . . She likes to read. Always in agreement with the King's ideas, she takes no part in the government. She likes neither splendor nor ceremony."[6] As is so often the case, the foreign visitor's eyes were more observant than those of many Frenchmen. At just about the same time, the lawyer Barbier, who, through his clients, had connections with the Court, decided to find out more about his sovereign. The results of his inquiries quite surprised him. "The King's personality is not known among the public," he wrote in August 1732. "The professional Jansenists [naturally at odds with the government] describe him as a young man unable to talk or listen. They are very much mistaken. I have informed myself, in confidence, from people who are close to him. The King is kind, has an excellent memory, knows mathematics perfectly and reasons well; and it is no small merit for a young man [Louis was twenty-two] who is King to be taking an interest in these kinds of sciences, and he also tells stories better than anyone; but, for that, he must be among his private circle. They say that the suppers he hosts at the Bois de Boulogne with M. le duc de Noailles, M. le duc d'Antin, M. le marquis de Pezé, who are all witty men, are very lively. The King is very shy and does not like to be on show. His discretion is carried so far that it is actually secrecy . . . [He has] a blind attachment for the Cardinal, so that it is difficult to know whether he does not fear him just as much as he loves him. But then, if once he gets over his shyness, we can expect the best from the King's many gifts."[7] Barbier was right, and so was Pollnitz: the Royal Family seemed a model of all the unfashionable virtues. Fewer than a dozen of all the husbands and wives at court, probably, were faithful to each other and, with the exception of the Cardinal, no one worked so hard or relaxed in so decorous a manner. France, everyone agreed, was lucky.

Most surprising of all, however, was the Cardinal's continuing popularity. The French had, until then, made a habit of hating the ministers. In their time, Richelieu, Mazarin, Colbert and Louvois had been just as unpopular as the Regent or M. le Duc. Now, for the first time, the principal minister was widely considered as a statesman whose government could hardly be improved. "The Cardinal de Fleury," Pollnitz wrote, "in spite of his extreme old age [he was now seventy-nine], displays the most admirable physical and mental strength. He is rather tall; his face is pleasant . . . He is humble, easy and polite . . . No one can accuse him of enriching himself or thinking about the aggrandizement of his family. The Cardinal spends as little money as his rank will allow. He is very regular in his habits and in his way of life; his extreme sobriety is, no doubt, the reason why he has retained such strength. He works with much application"[8]; after which Pollnitz goes on to extol the efficacity and success of his ministry.

This praise was fully justified. While, popular belief to the contrary notwithstanding, the King paid close attention to the workings of his government, attended Council meetings Mondays, Wednesdays, Thursdays and Fridays, met with the Cardinal every morning and with the other ministers at least once a week, it was nevertheless Fleury who set policy and oversaw the functioning of the complex, already highly centralized machinery of government. By 1732, he had been in power for six years— far longer than expected, considering his age—and he could begin to list a number of substantial achievements. First and foremost, of course, he had maintained the peace. When, in 1727, Spain and Great Britain once more drifted to the brink of war —Spain wanted the return of Gibraltar; England had promised it, then reneged on its promise—the King of Spain asked for the assistance of French troops to recapture the citadel. Carefully, the Cardinal avoided saying yes or no, letting time pass until, in May, he was able to convince Philip V that a congress, to be held at Aachen, would be the easiest way out of the dispute. Then he talked both parties into moving the Congress to Soissons, in northern France, so he could attend it. That, of course, automatically gave him the chair; he then proceeded to let the Congress waste time until it ended, no one quite knew how. At the same time, Spain, which had been aiming at an alliance with the Emperor Charles VI, broke the talks off. Fleury saw his chance and tightened the Franco-Spanish understanding. In the Treaty of Seville, Philip V agreed, in November 1729, to give France and Great Britain commercial rights; in exchange, he was allowed to garrison Parma and Tuscany even though their rulers were still alive, so that there could be no question about their eventual reversion to Spain. It was a sensible compromise and everyone was satisfied. Then, in 1731, Charles VI set up a trading and shipping enterprise at Ostend which was a clear menace for French, English and Spanish commerce. Fleury convinced him to suppress it in exchange for a guaranty of the Pragmatic Sanction: this was an act stating that in the absence of male heirs (which Charles VI could no longer expect) his hereditary possessions would all go to his daughter Maria Theresa. Obviously, once again this was a fruitful compromise. France, Spain and Britain were free of a dangerous commercial rival, while their accession to the Pragmatic Sanction made a War of the Austrian Succession unlikely: once again peace was consolidated.

At the same time, within France itself improvements were proceeding apace. New canals were started—a major step, since road transport, even under the best conditions, was slow and expensive, whereas a network of linked rivers made trade easier and shipping cheaper. Marshes in the center of the country and on the coasts were drained. Ports were enlarged and improved, thus expanding overseas commerce: Law's old India Company, for one, was beginning to show substantial yearly profits. These were all the kind of sound, sensible policies which, though useful, were nothing new: Colbert had taken much the same kinds of measures in the third quarter of the seventeenth century; but now Fleury proceeded to take a revolutionary decision. With the help of the great engineer Daniel Charles Trudaine, he created a new administration for roads and bridges—the corps des Ponts et Chaussées—staffed by competent professionals so that communications would continue to improve no matter what the government's other preoccupations might be. This was followed by a Bureau of Maps, again a bold departure since until then maps were generally inaccurate and incomplete; and by a Bureau of Mines, also staffed by specialists, while a new State-sponsored system of mining concessions was promulgated. All this work soon bore fruit: the sixty-year period separating 1730 from the onset of the Revolution witnessed a growing, sustained, unprecedented prosperity at just about every level of the economy.

All this still wasn't enough to satisfy Fleury's yearning for ease and order. The legal system, in 1730, consisted of a haphazard, often contradictory amalgam of laws and regulations which made everyday life immensely complicated while giving rise to endless lawsuits. Since, moreover, the Parlements, where those suits were tried, saw to it that the various procedures dragged on as long as possible (there was a fee attached to every legal document), these suits often continued for years, even extending to a decade or two. This was obviously intolerable; but since the Parlements defended their every perquisite with tooth and nail, the reform, if any, must come from elsewhere. If the courts could not be improved, at least the laws could be streamlined; and so, under the direction of the chancelier d'Aguesseau, then of Chauvelin, the Keeper of the Seals, a new code was gradually promulgated in the form of ordinances regulating donations, wills, civil and criminal suits, the wardship of minor children and even, miracle of miracles, the amount of the fees to be paid for specific legal processes. Except for a few selfish Parlement men, these reforms were greeted with widespread approval. Once again, the Cardinal was making it easier and cheaper to carry on one's business.

In spite of the repeated successes of Fleury's policies, however, there was, as always, an opposition party composed largely of men who wanted office. Since it did no good to complain about what were, obviously, improvements, they decided to fight on a more convenient ground, that of the Cardinal's vanity (always good for a little sharp satire) and the King's enslavement. Because Louis XV said so little in public, and because Fleury was so clearly in charge, it was assumed that the ministry governed while the Sovereign hunted. In fact, this was a wholly inaccurate picture. The King still worked hard; he was fully aware of the measures being implemented in his name. What, apparently, occurred to almost no one was that, quite simply, he approved of what was going on, realized that no other minister would be as competent, faithful and selfless as Fleury, and that when you get excellent advice you do well to take it. Still, people tried hard to discredit the Cardinal, but even the poisonous marquis d'Argenson, whose ambition it was to be Prime Minister someday, and who, in the meantime, was enraged at not being offered even a minor ministry, still found it nearly impossible to justify his attacks; so he contented himself with mocking the old man.

"One of the most ridiculous spectacles of this time," he wrote in December 1731, "is the *petit coucher* of M. le cardinal de Fleury. I don't know where the old man has discovered that prerogative of his office, or why he thinks it belongs to his post, since, although in truth he has full authority, he is after all only a minister of State . . . All of France, all of the Court, therefore, wait outside his door. His Eminence comes in, goes into his study, then has the door opened, and you see that old priest take off his breeches, which he then folds neatly; his servants give him a rather mediocre robe, they put his nightshirt on him; he spends much time combing his four white hairs, he reasons, he chats, he repeats himself, he makes a few bad jokes . . . The old man apparently thinks this is a consolation for the rest of us."[9] No doubt the picture is exaggerated, but even if Fleury was as vain as d'Argenson would have us believe, he was fully justified. Seldom, if ever, had France been better governed.

When all else was going so well, however, the Parlement de Paris could always be counted on to provide some complications. Apparently forgetting his usual tolerance, Fleury gave it just the handle it needed: in that one respect, perhaps, it proved unfortunate that he was a bishop. Where a lay minister might have taken the *Unigenitus* bull as a mere encumbrance to be disregarded whenever convenient, the Cardinal unfortunately considered it as an article of faith. Then, too, he was anxious to stop the controversies which had rent the French Church, so in 1730, like so many before him, he decided to end the controversy. On the grounds that the ecclesiastics who had appealed to the Parlement were actually flouting the King's authority, he decided to make the whole sorry mess into an affair of State. On March 24, 1730, a Royal Declaration was issued, whereby the bull was declared to be the law of the land. All nonconformers lost their power to hold religious services, along with their benefices (i.e., their income, an obviously tender point); the bishops were given wide powers to punish any disobedience; none of the opponents were protected any longer while their appeal was pending; and all Jansenist publications were banned. The Declaration could hardly have been clearer or more thorough, and if obeyed it would finally end all resistance.

Naturally, the Parlement, no doubt fed up with four years of peace, jumped right into the fray: it refused to register the Declaration. Nothing loath, Fleury had the King hold a lit de justice on April 3 so as to force registration; and, well aware of the precedents, he followed this up with a whole new procedure: a lettre de cachet forbade the Parlement even to discuss the lit de justice. At that the Parlement protested, only to see the protest forbidden. Since, however, several of the principles contained in the Declaration were being ignored, the Council issued a decision confirming the bishops' jurisdiction as defined by the Declaration. In theory, the matter should have ended there, since the King in Council was considered to be the chief judge of the realm. Although he no longer performed that function in person, except on very rare occasions—perhaps once every five years or so—purely to keep his right alive, the Council was indeed considered the court of last resort. Once the Council, in its judiciary capacity, confirmed the Declaration, therefore, the Parlement lost jurisdiction.

That was the theory—and even the law—but, of course, it didn't stop the Parlement, where debate reached a new level of violence. One of the conseillers, an old man named Pucelle, staked out the now familiar position: he was not, he explained at excruciating length, opposing the King's legitimate authority; he was, in fact, supporting it, since in forcing acceptation of the bull the King was, by an unfortunate oversight, curtailing his own rights. The argument, if not new, was ingenious, and won Pucelle vast popularity. Even his fame, however, was soon eclipsed by that of a more spectacular cast of characters.

Jansenism in its prime (i.e., around 1660) had been an austere, highly intellectual doctrine professed by the likes of the great mathematician and philosopher Pascal. If anything, it was too restrained, too remote from the emotions. Now, however, a new Jansenism appeared. Far from being philosophically coherent and religiously intense, like its predecessor, it was instead a French version of the Holy Rollers. Unconnected, really, to those churchmen who refused to obey the *Unigenitus* bull on the grounds that it embodied papal usurpations, the new Jansenists were given to convulsions, faints and other similar outbursts. Pucelle naturally considered himself a Jansenist, but he limited himself to nonstop speechifying. The place to go, if you wanted to see some truly spectacular behavior, was the cemetery of Saint Médard, one of the parishes within the city of Paris, where a deacon named (by coincidence) Pâris had been buried.

In his own lifetime, François Pâris had been an obscure Jansenist with a local reputation for good works and austere living. Now that he was safely dead, he became the focus of a small, highly visible cult. Miracles supposedly took place on his grave: the lame recovered the use of their legs, the blind that of their eyes, while others simply went into convulsions as the Holy Ghost entered their bodies. By 1732 a traveler noted: "One cannot go to anyone's house without hearing some new story about the abbé *[sic]* Pâris; and yet I protest that not a single miracle has been verified . . . and I have heard M. Hérault, the lieutenant [i.e., chief] of Police say . . . that it is an obvious fraud which is only tolerated at the moment so that the authorities can investigate the origins of all this, the better to disabuse the people. I think they will not have an easy time of it, so strong do I find people's prejudices."[10] The scenes at Saint Médard soon became so much like a circus that, finally, the authorities stepped in and closed the cemetery to the public, upon which a poster went up on the gates, the work of a wit rather than a Jansenist: "De par le roi, défense à Dieu / De faire miracle en ce lieu." ("The King hereby forbids God / to create miracles here.") At the same time, of course, there were many sceptics—Voltaire was one— who thought the whole affair grotesque; and since a Jesuit, Father Girard, had just run off with a maid called Cadière, a new song, alluding to the Jesuits' supposed preference for their own sex, was also making the rounds: "Que Saint Pâris à ses malades / Fasse faire maintes gambades / Le beau miracle que voilà! / Croyons plutot à la Cadière / Qui fait sauter un Loyola / De Sodome jusqu'a Cythère." (That Saint Pâris his patients / causes to dance all around / that's not much of a miracle. / Let us rather worship Cadière / who caused a Loyola* to jump / from Sodom right to Cythera.*)[11]

Although it was obviously a little hard to take the new Jansenism seriously, all the hubbub suited the Parlement very well. On September 17, 1731, it gave out a judgment reaffirming what it considered to be sound Gallican principles. The very next day that judgment was reversed by the Council: it was back to the deadlock the Regent had faced in the early twenties. This time the Parlement tried a new move: in November a deputation of fifty présidents and conseillers went to Marly and asked for an audience with the King. Louis XV, who backed Fleury all the way, and who had also learned to distrust the Parlement, simply refused to see the delegation. At that, the Premier Président, Portail, whose high office gave him the right of access to the King's presence, made his way in alone. As soon as Louis XV saw Portail, he simply turned his back on him. Still, something had to be done, so on January 10, 1732, a delegation was indeed received by His Majesty, who, however, said not a word. Instead, the chancelier d'Aguesseau read a declaration which ordered the Parlement to submit: "The King knows the full extent of the rights of the supreme power," it said. "The most inviolable of maxims regarding his authority is that no one is ever permitted to exempt himself from the obedience which is due by all."[12] The chancelier could hardly have been clearer; as it happened, he was also expressing the King's own feelings. While Fleury was now beginning to think of trying to reach a compromise, it was Louis XV who was holding firm: he was all too familiar with the Parlement's opposition.

In the meantime, and behind the scenes, the Cardinal was doing the best he could to quiet things down. Closing the Saint Médard cemetery proved remarkably effective; and when a Paris priest refused the last rites to a dying man who was suspected of being a Jansenist, Fleury saw to it that another priest was sent for, so that there need be no further controversy. That, unfortunately, was just the moment chosen by the Archbishop of Paris for banning an especially annoying Jansenist publication (it was wickedly satirical) called *Les Nouvelles ecclésiastiques (Church News)*, thereby bringing new fuel to the fire. Without wasting a moment, twenty-one Paris priests appealed to the Parlement on the grounds that the Archbishop had overreached his authority, and the familiar confrontation was again under way. On May 14, 1732, two conseillers who had made particularly violent and offensive speeches were arrested; it was no surprise to anyone that Pucelle was one of the two. On May 16, as a protest, the Enquêtes et Requêtes chambers, comprising about half the Parlement, went on strike; on the twenty-third, the King sent Letters Patent ordering an end to the strike. The Letters were obeyed, but the returning chambers took up the Archbishop's ban as their first order of business. This was directly contrary to the King's earlier orders, and on June 12 the Parlement predictably decided to hear the twenty-one priests' appeal. This time Fleury didn't hesitate. On June 15 and 16, one président (Ogier) and three conseillers (Robert, de Vrévin and Davy de la Fautrière) were

* Loyola: an allusion to the founder of the Jesuit order; Cythera: the island of Venus.

placed under arrest. At that, all the members of the Enquêtes et Requêtes chambers resigned en masse, but the Grande Chambre, which was composed mostly of older, more moderate men, continued to function.

This gave Fleury and the King a chance of blending authority and conciliation. Louis XV now addressed the magistrates of the Grande Chambre and congratulated them on their sense of patriotism. He then went on: "I am willing to heed your request and give those who have sent me their resignations a few days in which they may return to their duty. If they don't, they have no hope of forgiveness: they will feel, to their last day, the effects of my indignation."[13] This time, the Enquêtes et Requêtes felt they had gone too far. On July 5, all the resignations were taken back. Once again, a deadlock had been reached, but this time Fleury was determined to solve the problem. On August 18, the King sent the Parlement a Declaration of Discipline modifying the entire system. Henceforth, it proclaimed, all edicts registered in the course of a lit de justice would become executory at once; remonstrances could only be made one single time; they could not thereafter be renewed without the King's express permission; and the Parlement was forbidden ever again to go on strike. It was strong, it was clear, it was everything the Parlement had been fighting against, so it naturally refused registration. It was back to business as usual. On September 3, 1732, the King held yet another lit de justice to force registration. The very next day, the Enquêtes et Requêtes were back on strike.

Once again, Fleury and the King took a firm stance. On September 6 and 7, 139 conseillers were exiled: the deadlock was again complete, as it became apparent that the Parlement was intent on arrogating to itself a whole range of powers which belonged to the King alone, while Louis XV, fully aware of his rights and prerogatives, was equally firm in resisting the Parlement's encroachment. Interestingly enough, except perhaps for the populace in Paris and the relatives of those involved, the Parlement had very few supporters. It was clearly making trouble just to benefit itself, and even a man with strong ties to the judges, like d'Argenson, felt compelled to write Fleury on September 4, 1732: "Rigor must be exercised to the greatest possible extent, and be apparent already tonight . . . The State cannot be governed thus; retrench from our midst, Monseigneur, a body which is becoming so great a subject of scandal. Three or four faithful subjects will be sufficient to propose and organize with Your Eminence the means of, once and for all, doing without this body, which has already so often attacked the authorities to which it owes its being."[14] This was a new and drastic proposal. Louis XIV had simply gagged the Parlement while still letting it operate as the chief civil and criminal court; but already in 1732 it was becoming clear to all enlightened people that, quite aside from its political claims, the Parlement as a tribunal was slow, inefficient, harsh and corrupt. There would have been a double advantage in simply abolishing it, therefore, and replacing it with a more effective and impartial court system. Unfortunately, Fleury believed too devoutly in the virtues of conciliation ever to take so radical a step; and so for a while nothing happened at all.

One immediate consequence of all the fracas, though, was a marked loss of popularity in Paris—the one place where the Parlement was always liked—for the Cardinal. As usual in France, the middle-of-the-road policy was attacked by the extremists of both parties, and some of the blame actually spilled over on the King himself. In 1732 Louis XV was twenty-two years old, and it was time, some said, for him to take over the reins of government; as for Fleury, well, he was sinking into senility and should retire. Anti-Fleury songs began to be heard: "O roi né pour la chasse au cerf / Seras-tu donc toujours le serf / d'un prélat plus qu'octogénaire?" ("O King born to hunt deer / will you always be the slave / of an octogenarian prelate?")[15] was typical of the new spate of attacks on the hitherto unassailable principal minister. At Court itself, there was a whole group of ambitious young men—d'Argenson was one of them—who thought it was high time they got their chance. Their prolonged wait was all the more frustrating in that the Cardinal should have been long dead; as it was, everyone expected him to go at any moment, but the longer he stubbornly refused to retire or expire, the more unconscionable his tenure of office seemed to be. Of course, there was a simple way to get rid of him: convince the King that enough was enough; only Louis XV was loyal to those who served him well, enormously fond of his old tutor, and quite sure that Fleury was a wise and effective statesman. There was no chance at all, therefore, that the King would send him away.

It was just at this point that trouble in Poland gave the anti-Cardinalists hope again: its elected King, Augustus II of Saxony, was obviously not long for this earth. When he died, there would have to be a new election, in which France would naturally take an interest: before Augustus II, France and Poland had traditionally been allies against the Habsburgs. Now, as before, it was in France's interest to place its own candidate on the Polish throne; and, as it happened, it had a ready-made King in the Queen's father. By the end of 1732, no one doubted that France would back the election (or reelection) of that amiable nonentity Stanislas Leczinski.

Unfortunately, a large number of powerful people were equally determined to keep Stanislas off the throne. Naturally enough, Augustus II wanted his son to inherit the crown; the Emperor Charles VI was anxious to keep the French out of Poland; and, finally, in Poland itself the nobility, which had been generously bribed, was determined to vote against Stanislas. That, however, was not as decisive as it might appear. Although, in fact, the King was elected by the assembled nobility, the tradition of anarchic rivalry and private warfare was so deeply ingrained that it was always possible to gather a dissident Diet, get one's candidate elected, and then, after having supplied him with men and money, hope that he would defeat the candidate unfailingly chosen by a rival Diet.

Nobody much doubted that France would back Stanislas, especially since it had the power to ensure his election by a group of dissident nobles. The only problem was that a war with Austria, and possibly other powers, was likely to follow. In the last year, the Franco-British alliance had become markedly brittle, partly because of commercial rivalries, partly because England was slowly returning to its traditional policy of keeping a balance between the several Continental states. Any move by France to extend its influence was quite likely to result in a British-Austrian alliance.

Within France itself and, no doubt, much to Fleury's chagrin, the impending conflict had one immediate consequence: since wars were expensive, they were always accompanied by increased taxation. In this case it would mean reviving the *vingtième,* the 5 percent income tax which Orry and Fleury together had repealed.

Like all royal edicts, new tax laws had to be registered by the Parlement; and with 139 conseillers scattered through the provinces, registration was an obvious impossibility. If the government was to prepare for war, some sort of compromise would have to be arranged. For Fleury himself, this was a consummation much to be wished since it would end an unpleasant conflict; so, on November 11 he took the first steps and recalled the conseillers back to Paris. There, after many consultations, a solution was found. On the one hand, the Declaration of Discipline would remain intact since its cancellation would be too signal a defeat for the King; but, on the other hand, it would not be enforced. On December 4, the chancelier announced that the Declaration was temporarily suspended. Naturally, everyone understood that, in this case, temporary meant permanent, and peace returned thanks, in part, to the fact that the fiery conseillers had found life in the provinces to be almost unbearably dull.

No sooner was the Parlement sitting again but the expected news came from Warsaw: early in 1733 Augustus II had finally expired. France was prepared to make a major effort; indeed, it was soon announced that it would support the candidacy of the former King. The problem now was getting him to Poland since, unfortunately, that country was ringed by anti-Stanislas powers: Russia, Prussia and Austria. So it was announced that the candidate would travel the only possible way—by sea—to a Polish port. By the late spring, amid many demonstrations of support, with flags waving, trumpets sounding and guns saluting, Stanislas Leczinski was seen to board his ship.

In fact, the splendidly dressed man who received all this encouragement was an impostor. The real Stanislas, disguised as an itinerant tradesman, was slowly making his way through Germany, where no one recognized him. That successful stratagem was all the more impressive in that secrets at Versailles almost always leaked: it says a great deal for Fleury's firm grasp of the administration that this most important maneuver remained a secret week after week. And for a short while after he reached Poland it looked as if Stanislas' presence was working wonders. On September 11, 1733, he was elected King.

That, alas, is as far as it went. No sooner was the election proclaimed but Russian and Austrian troops entered Poland, upon which a new Diet, attended by six thousand nobles, gathered and gave the crown to the Elector of Saxony, who now mounted the throne as Augustus III. Stanislas, whose small, disorganized army was no match for those of the two empires, vanished once more. In France, with the normally appalling state of communications adding to the confusion of the war, no one quite knew where Stanislas had gone. As usual, people sang: "Est-il roi, ne l'est-il pas? / Ce prince qu'on déplore / Que fait-il, va-t-il au combat? / Tout le monde l'ignore." ("Is he king, is he not? / This prince we deplore / What does he do, is he fighting? / All the world wonders.")[16] In fact, the amiable but hopelessly ineffective Stanislas, having failed to rally the nobles, had clearly decided to resort to his one talent: in disguise yet again, he was making for Danzig, where he found refuge; but by the time this news had crossed Europe, his situation was once again desperate, for Danzig was, predictably, under siege. That it would resist for a decent period of time was generally expected, but no one thought for a moment that it would hold indefinitely: sooner or later poor Stanislas must surrender.

Although these partly comical events seemed deadly serious to the Queen, no one else in France took them very seriously. Poland was far away, France itself was not under attack, and although, clearly, a war would eventually have to be fought, no one really worried about it. As for Stanislas, who was evidently lucky just as long as he didn't try to stay in Poland, he finally escaped Danzig in the spring of 1734 and made his way back to Paris. France, which now declared war on the Emperor, was ostensibly fighting for a King who was quite unable to remain in his own country. In fact, as usual, Fleury knew what he was doing.

The duchies of Lorraine and Bar, which were officially an independent state within the Holy Roman Empire, had long been ruled by a family closely allied to the French kings; at the beginning of the century, their Duke had married a daughter of the duc d'Orléans. Now that Duke was dead, the Duchies were ruled by his widow, and his son and heir, Francis, lived in Vienna, where he had long been groomed to marry Emperor Charles VI's daughter, the Archduchess Maria Theresa. This would have been a serious problem even under normal circumstances, since the Habsburgs had been France's constant, and often dangerous, enemy for over two centuries. Charles VI himself, before he succeeded to the Hereditary States, had, as Archduke, fought in Spain against Philip V. To have an Austrian Duchess of Lorraine, therefore, would entail new dangers for France, since an invading Habsburg Army could easily come through Lorraine. The proposed marriage was even more menacing, however, in that the Archduchess had officially been proclaimed heiress to all her father's realms—Austria, Bohemia (today's Czechoslovakia), Hungary (with a good piece of today's Romania), Silesia, Carniola, Istria, the Austrian Netherlands (today's Belgium), Milan and the Kingdom of the Two Sicilies. And since a woman couldn't be elected Holy Roman Emperor, it was widely assumed that this prestigious title would go to Francis, who would, of course, also be Duke of Lorraine. This was a situation France could not be expected to accept, since it would risk attacks from the north, the east and even, possibly, the south if the King of Sardinia allowed the Austrian Army in Milan passage through the Alps.

At the same time, however, Lorraine was itself highly vulnerable. As a tiny state without much of an army, it was quite incapable of resisting a determined French onslaught. It had, in fact, been occupied by France during much of the seventeenth century. If Fleury wanted to do something before it was too late, he had three choices. He could start the war by invading Lorraine; he could declare war on Charles VI with, as his goal, either the repeal of the Pragmatic Sanction or the marriage of the Archduchess to some other suitor; or he could try to reach a compromise through which, in one way or another, the danger would be averted. In essence, it was this last course he chose, but since Charles VI was obviously not going to negotiate until his troops had been defeated a few times, a war must, after all, be fought. Considering the well-known state of disarray of the Austrian Army, however, and the Emperor's chronic impecuniousness, the outcome seemed very likely to favor France. And since it is always a good idea to ask for more than you really want, Fleury announced that his aim was the conquest of the Austrian Netherlands. He had very little doubt that if Austria had to give up something, it would prefer to retain the Low Countries, which it owned, and give up Lorraine, which it didn't.

How Francis might feel about the arrangement seemed wholly unimportant: he was in no position to make his desires felt.

As it turned out, this rather minor war worked out very well for all concerned. France promptly formed an alliance with Spain, which wasn't able to do much, and Sardinia, whose King held the Alpine passes and could, therefore, make it very easy for a French army to reach Italy. This, in fact, is just what happened. By the end of the 1735 campaigning season, the two allies had taken Milan, Mantua and Parma. It was obviously time to negotiate. On November 5, an armistice was declared and the talks started. They lasted far longer than anyone expected, but, without further ado, Francis of Lorraine and the Archduchess Maria Theresa were married in Vienna on February 12, 1736. He was handsome, kind, practical and highly sexed; she was strong-minded, intelligent and very much in love. Their union proved to be remarkably happy, but what mattered at the moment was that it looked like a straight-out provocation.

Charles VI, whatever his other shortcomings may have been (and they were numerous), was smart enough to see that it would be infinitely easier to force Francis into giving up Lorraine before the wedding, so he made it quite plain that the act of renunciation must be signed before the nuptials could be announced. This Francis, with much reluctance and to his mother's fury, proceeded to do. The Austrians could now hand Lorraine over to France if they so chose, but they naturally announced, as a bargaining position, that nothing in the world could convince them to do so.

Just as things were going so well, Fleury made his first major blunder since taking office: in a letter to Charles VI which, of course, was promptly leaked in Vienna, he offered to buy Lorraine. Since proper diplomatic finesse required that you never ask for what you really wanted, but instead take it as compensation for something else you never really expected to get, Fleury had made a grave faux pas in thus revealing his true intentions. Further, the suggestion that France might be willing to pay for Lorraine, rather than taking it as compensation for, say, confirming its earlier, somewhat ambiguous, endorsement of the Pragmatic Sanction—which, moreover, had lapsed because of the war—or returning Milan to the Emperor, implied that its position was much weaker than anyone had supposed. In fact, it wasn't; but by giving the appearance of needing peace so badly, Fleury postponed it by exactly three years. The actual treaty, known as the Treaty of Vienna, which resulted from seemingly endless bargaining, wasn't signed until November 18, 1738. Its terms were almost exactly what they would have been in early 1736 had Fleury not let his dislike of war get the better of his judgment; and they were singularly favorable to France.

In exchange for an endorsement of the Pragmatic Sanction, ex-King Stanislas was given the Duchies of Lorraine and Bar (this was, after all, the War of the Polish Succession). On his death, it would go to his daughter, the Queen of France, or her heir the Dauphin; and while Stanislas was to enjoy all the perquisites of a sovereign, the actual administration of the Duchies was to be handed over to France. This, alone, was a huge achievement. For centuries, Lorraine had been a constant danger, either because it served as a convenient launching place for foreign invasions or because it joined France's enemies just when that move was likely to be most effective. For two centuries, French kings had tried to conquer Lorraine. Now, as the result of a very minor war, it was French at last. In one swoop, Fleury and Louis XV had added as much to the kingdom as Louis XIV during his long, war-ridden reign.

There were, of course, other clauses. The King of Sardinia received a piece of Milanese territory, and the Infante Don Carlos of Spain, who had just conquered the Kingdom of the Two Sicilies, was allowed to keep it in exchange for Parma, which went to Austria, and Tuscany, which compensated Francis of Lorraine for his loss; at his death, the Grand Duchy was to go to his second son so that it would always have a Habsburg ruler but never be united to the other Austrian possessions. The Austrian Netherlands, needless to say, remained Austrian. All in all, the Treaty embodied a reasonable compromise: Austria lost nothing it really owned, while France gained a most important province. And it is comforting to record that the apparent loser, Francis of Lorraine, made a very good thing out of Tuscany: by the time he died, the formerly penniless prince had become a very rich man indeed. Even the twice de-throned King of Poland ended up, unexpectedly, with a little state of his own, in which he proceeded to live for many pleasant years.

During the protracted negotiations, and in spite of the impatience he often felt, the Cardinal had come to a new understanding of Austria's position in Europe. Far from remaining France's enemy, he realized, it could become, if not quite yet an ally, at least a partner in maintaining a peaceful balance of power. That this novel idea was suggested by the increasingly obvious British aversion for France cannot be doubted. Both France and Austria were, on the whole, satisfied with the status quo; neither was looking for aggrandizement, and neither wanted to lose what it already had: together they might keep Europe quiet.

To us, with the hindsight of two and a half centuries, this notion seems perfectly obvious, but in the 1730s it was little short of revolutionary. Chauvelin, the Keeper of the Seals, who was also Foreign minister, had to be dismissed in February 1737 because he was so rabidly, blindly anti-Austrian. He was replaced by the more flexible Amelot, but the party he represented was still powerful. Most of the people who mattered in France felt about Austria very much the way American right-wingers feel about the Soviet Union: it was a dark, demonic enemy, responsible for everything that went wrong everywhere and intent on the destruction of France. Amelot, at least, signed the Treaty, but not even he was willing to contemplate a possible Franco-Austrian alliance, and the Cardinal was not powerful enough to impose his views in so delicate an area.

As the thirties wore on, and Fleury remained unchanged, he also lost most of his popularity. This was due, in part, to the length of his stay in office: more than most, the French liked a change. The longer a minister was in power, the more disliked he was likely to become. This was especially true for the Cardinal, whose great age had led everyone to expect he wouldn't last long. In 1738, after twelve years of appar-ently absolute rule, he had reached the extraordinary age of 85, and, except for occasional stomach upsets, he gave no sign at all of being ready to expire. This monstrous unwillingness to make room for younger ministers was all the more infuri-ating in that it might go on forever. If Fleury could govern France at 84, then why not 94 or, for that matter, 104? It was altogether unbearable, and this maddening persistence was made even more annoying by the fact that, apparently, the King was

The King Taking Over the Government, 1726. This engraving was a celebration of the dismissal from power of the hated M. le Duc. In fact, the government was subsequently run by the cardinal de Fleury and not the sixteen-year-old monarch.

The cardinal de Fleury was the King's trusted and much-loved tutor. He became Prime Minister in 1726 and kept that office until his death in 1743.

ANDRE HERCULES CARDINAL
DE FLEURY

LOUIS QUINZE ROI DE FRANCE ET DE NAVARRE.

Louis XV as a young man. In this portrait, probably dating from the very early 1730s, the King is seen in the full bloom of his youth: he was, everyone agreed, the handsomest man in the kingdom.

Fireworks for the wedding of Madame Infante. All the great Court events at Versailles were celebrated with fireworks, as well as balls and theatricals. This engraving depicts the structure on which the rockets were attached.

Louis XV received by the Clergy before Strasbourg Cathedral in 1744. A Te Deum was then celebrated to mark the recovery from his near fatal illness at Metz.

Marie Leczinska, the Queen of France, whose kindness and charity did nothing to make her plainness or her dullness more appealing to her husband Louis XV, or, indeed, the Court.

Mme de Pompadour. The great love
Louis XV's life is seen here as a gardene
one of the many interests she shared wi
the King.

An equestrian portrait of Louis XV as
looked at the time of Fontenoy.

as fond of his old tutor as ever. Even to observant people, it looked as if the Cardinal's power was unchanged. This, in fact, was not the case, but virtually no one realized it.

It was perfectly true that Louis XV still felt great fondness for Fleury, and that he trusted him, but more and more, as the thirties passed, he began to make decisions and appointments himself. In April 1738, Barbier noted: "The King now works every day with each of his ministers in private, and he asks about details. He also works almost every day at the Cardinal's."[17] This was a far cry from his once silent attendance at the Council. More and more, the King was taking on the tasks of government while the Cardinal, once Prime Minister in all but name, had become a combination of first assistant and special adviser who kept all the outward trappings of power. And though he was still able to grant small favors, quite often now he found himself forced to seek the King's approval for major appointments without being at all sure he would receive it. Most of this remained hidden from public view: Louis XV was still shy, still fond of his privacy. He liked to work alone in his study, so that his full contribution was underestimated. Even the usually shrewd d'Argenson, panting for office, made the usual mistake while still noticing more than most people. "The King is a man of great good sense," he wrote in September 1738, "and, although still a little lazy, he likes the work to be done well. He is secretive and discreet, as all the greatest kings have been. He is an excellent judge of men, without study or effort on his part, and that perception is what kings need the most. Even with only a few of these known abilities, it seems odd that the only man in whom the King has an absolute trust should be his valet Bachelier."[18] In fact, it wasn't strange at all. Louis had learned early to trust no one. By his very function, however, Bachelier was so close to him that he felt he really knew him. He was quite right, too: the valet never once broke his master's confidence.

This new involvement of the King's soon became better known. By March 1739, d'Argenson could add: "The King writes a lot in his own hand, whether it be letters or memoranda, and makes many a summary of what he has read . . . It is quite possible that Louis XV will surprise the world by showing himself a very great King."[19]

This wasn't as surprising as people thought. In 1738, Louis XV was still only twenty-eight years old, and many of the principles taught him by Fleury remained vivid in his mind. He knew his duty, which was to be a good ruler to his people; he remembered that a do-nothing King is a despicable creature; and he never forgot his great-grandfather's example. Every time he walked through the salons of Versailles, he could see the many painted allegories representing Louis XIV governing by himself. While Fleury had a paramount claim on his gratitude and his loyalty, Louis XV never forgot his obligation to familiarize himself with the workings of government. To that end, the first step was hard work and organization. "He already likes papers, reading and even, markedly, to write with his own hand . . . He has had cupboards made in a separate study and there his papers are carefully put away in order and all labeled in his own hand."[20] By 1738, the normally sour d'Argenson was raving about the King, and his comments are all the more noteworthy because they are the opposite of his normal vitriolic attacks. Already in January there was a hint. "It is believed

that M. le cardinal de Fleury is near death and that he is ravaged by a wasting
sickness," d'Argenson noted hopefully. "He does almost no work. In the meanwhile,
the King has begun making decisions; he shows intelligence and ability; he was aware
of a great many things even when he was still so shy."[21] As for the Cardinal, d'Argenson, who longed to take his place, was indulging in a little wishful thinking, but there
was no doubt about the King's new visibility. One thing, however, hadn't changed:
now as before the King watched people and events without ever revealing his feelings, and his reactions were all the more unexpected in that no one ever knew what
he really thought.

By March, Louis XV had progressed still further. "The King now works with the
ministers, does an excellent job of it and makes the right decisions," d'Argenson,
whose younger brother was minister of War, noted. "He has a memory well stocked
with detail . . . Better yet, he displays great humanity and justice. The other day,
M. Orry [the Comptroller General, i.e., minister of Finances] proposed paying a debt
now due for four years; His Majesty asked whether this man who had been waiting
so long had received interest. M. Orry answered he hadn't, saying that it wasn't the
custom. His Majesty answered that this was unfair, and that he no longer wanted to
see such disorders and such injustices . . . The King likes economy, and conserving
rather than acquiring . . . He is kind, he is clever, he is extraordinarily discreet
. . . He says things wittily . . . He works hard naturally and without affectation
. . . With all that, he understands and likes upright people."[22] Quite an encomium,
and fully deserved. As he emerged from the long years during which he had been
training himself, the King was proving to be something very close to a model ruler.
Somehow the people felt it: seldom had a King been so popular.

When it came to the government, the King waited until 1737–38 before he began
to assert himself visibly. In an altogether different domain, he had also broken out of
his adolescence, but that particular change had taken place in 1732. That year, tired
at last of his wife's coldness, he had taken a mistress; but unlike the Sun King, whose
paramours had ruled the court, Louis XV was extraordinarily discreet. It was several
years before even well-informed courtiers found out about the liaison, and even then
they realized that the lady in question enjoyed neither influence nor power.

It was hardly surprising that after seven years of fidelity, the young, virile and
handsome monarch should, at long last, have looked for another woman. The Queen,
never pretty, was not embellished by her well-nigh continuous state of pregnancy.
She had, as we have seen, given birth for the first time in August 1727; she did so
again in July 1728, September 1729, August 1730, March 1732, May 1733, July 1734,
May 1736, and July 1737; from which we may deduce that the King was especially
ardent in the autumn and condemned to 70 months of enforced chastity out of a
120, a pretty high proportion for a man his age. This last was because the doctors
forbade sexual intercourse as soon as pregnancy was noticed; it certainly did not
make the King's life pleasanter. Then, too, the Queen made it very plain that she
only endured her husband's lovemaking because it was her duty. By 1740, when the
King's amours had become common knowledge, the always acerbic d'Argenson
noted: "A lady-in-waiting has told me that it was all the Queen's fault if the King had
taken a mistress . . . She [i.e., the Queen] said: 'What, always in bed, always preg-

nant, always giving birth!' As a consequence, she forced the King to abstain for long periods of time, giving her poor health as a pretext, and disdained what today she bitterly regrets. One must also know that the Queen is afraid of ghosts; even when the King was lying at her side, she had to have a maid who held her hand all through the night and told her stories to make her go to sleep; and when the King wanted to use his conjugal rights, that maid barely went away. Besides, the Queen hardly sleeps at all; she gets up a hundred times a night, sometimes to piss, sometimes to look for her dog; besides, she practically puts mattresses over her because she is so afraid of being cold; so that the King died of the heat, and left in a sweat without having done anything. He would withdraw to his own bedroom . . . so as to get a good night's sleep and find a solitary relief for his sensual ardors, and this finally induced him to take a mistress."[23] D'Argenson's anonymous source ("a lady-in-waiting") hardly induces perfect belief: it seems out of character for the usually dutiful Marie Leczinska to have made that remark about her pregnancies. That the description of her bed is true, however, cannot be doubted, as it was a matter of common knowledge; and as for that final note about the King's "solitary relief," we may assume it was founded on the close daily scrutiny of the royal linen which was then the usual practice.

Whatever the Queen's feelings about sex and pregnancy, however, there can be no doubt that she was unbearably dull. A glance at the *Mémoires* of Président Hénault, one of her devoted courtiers and an ardent admirer, provides abundant proof of that. The following description of Marie's daily routine was written as an encomium. To our less complaisant eye, however, it reads like the perfect explanation of the King's infidelity.

"The Queen does not live haphazardly," Hénault wrote. "Her days are regulated and filled so that, even though she spends time alone, she is always short of time. She spends her morning praying and reading moral tales, then she visits the King, then comes a little amusement.

"That is usually painting* . . . The toilette takes place at twelve-thirty, then she goes to mass and has dinner. I have sometimes seen as many as a dozen ladies there. Not one escapes her attention. She speaks to everyone, and not about those general subjects everybody knows, but about personal things because they please the person so addressed. Once her dinner is over, I follow her into her study. There another climate reigns: it is no longer the Queen I see, but a private person. There, embroideries of all kinds are to be found, and also assorted crafts, and while she works she is kind enough to tell us about the books she has been reading . . . Sometimes she likes to play some of her instruments—a guitar, a violin, a harpsichord—and when she makes a mistake** she mocks herself with gaiety, sweetness and simplicity . . . She sends me away to my dinner around three, and then begins her reading time; she usually reads history books . . . in their original language: French, Polish, Italian or German, for she knows them all . . .

"The Court [in fact, a tiny part of it] gathers in her apartments around six to play cavagnole; she eats supper . . . then goes to visit Madame la duchesse de Luynes [her best friend] around eleven. There are only five or six persons, at the most, who

---

* The Queen's proficiency was easily that of a seven-year-old.
** She was a notoriously incompetent performer, even for an amateur.

have the honor of being allowed to join her, and at twelve-thirty she retires. The
conversations there are free of all gossip, the intrigues of the Court are never mentioned, and politics still less: this would seem to make for dullness, and yet the talk
hardly ever ceases and is ordinarily very cheerful. The Queen not only allows but
likes people to argue with her. She hates flattery, and when arguing wants *reasons* . . .

"That same princess, so good, so simple, so kind, so amiable, holds her rank with a
dignity that commands respect and which would actually frighten one if she did not
condescend to be reassuring. From one room to the next, she becomes the Queen
again . . . She in no way participates in politics . . . Her piety is of a severity all
the more necessary because of the century we live in."[24] Hardly the picture of a
lively, amusing woman. That Marie Leczinska was kind, charitable, pious, reserved
and undemanding is certain; that she was also plain, dull, dowdy and untalented is,
alas, equally sure. Louis XV, at the beginning of his marriage, had tried to spend time
with his wife, but he soon found himself forced to look elsewhere for company: it is
remarkable that even when she was still in her twenties, Marie Leczinska already led
the life of a middle-aged matron. Given the chance, the King preferred the people he
knew well; he longed for a real family; he is all the less to blame, therefore, if he
sought amusement elsewhere. Further, a strong young man of twenty-two could not
suffer from both boredom and an enforced chastity without doing something about
it; and so, with the utmost timidity at first, he began to look for distractions.

Louis XIV, in spite of his ostentatious piety, had been unfaithful to Queen Marie
Thérèse within months of their wedding. His great-grandson remembered what he
had been taught by Fleury, so at first he was content to spend his evenings with a
small circle of friends centering on the comtesse de Toulouse. Born a Noailles, the
comtesse, by virtue of her marriage to the youngest of the légitimés, was by way of
being the King's great-aunt even though she was just over forty. Dignified, handsome, kind, witty, she soon gave Louis XV just what he wanted: friends, intimacy, a
warm and pleasant circle in which he could relax and enjoy himself, whether in her
apartment on the ground floor of the Palace at Versailles or at her château of Rambouillet, where the hunting was even better than the conversation. The circle was
composed of a few grands seigneurs, all young men: the duc de Penthièvre, the
Toulouses' son; the duc de Gesvres, First Gentleman of the Bedchamber; the duc
d'Epernon; the marquis de Meuse; and of a few young women, all virtuous except for
Mlle de Charolais, M. le Duc's sister, who was notorious for her numerous affairs;
but even she always behaved properly in front of His Majesty. In 1732, she was
thirty-seven, but still handsome-looking, witty and amusing. Conveniently, her country house, the château de Madrid, was right next to the King's favorite hunting lodge
at La Muette, so supper parties often took place at Madrid.

That Mlle de Charolais longed to become the King's mistress was clear to all
concerned. Louis, however, was not only shy, he was also sensible. A Princess of the
Blood who was also his mistress would soon grow dangerously powerful; and so, late
in 1732 the King began to look toward the bottom of the supper table. There he
noticed a lady who was neither rich, nor famous, nor even very pretty. She was
young—the King's age, in fact—well born—her family, the Mailly-Nesles, could

trace their nobility all the way back to the eleventh century—but poor. She had married a distant cousin, the comte de Mailly, who was a lieutenant in the Scottish Guards, a troop belonging to the King's Household; and as a new bride, thanks to her family's influence, she had received an appointment to be lady-in-waiting to the Queen.

When, in 1732, the King first noticed her, he discovered that she attracted him in several ways. First, her lack of conspicuous beauty was reassuring to the shy young monarch: a plain woman seemed somehow less frightening, less daunting. She had "a long face, a long nose, a large and high forehead with slightly flat cheeks, a large mouth, a white complexion, rather beautiful large eyes with a lively expression, a very rough voice, ugly breasts and arms, but fine legs. [She was] tall, without grace or presence, but very elegant; amusing, cheerful, good-tempered, a good friend, generous and kind."[25] Altogether, not a bad ensemble, and, most important, she was lively and entertaining, the very reverse of the dutiful Pole.

It seems probable that the liaison started in the spring of 1733: Marie Leczinska, who was evidently among the first to know, wrote the news to her father; but the rest of the Court remained in deepest ignorance. The King was still remorseful, so he hid his transgression so thoroughly that no one guessed. Mme de Mailly, indeed, continued to be part of the little group around the King, but her place at the supper table was still close to the bottom. She received no special favors, was given no special precedence. Worse, from her point of view at least, Louis, who was pious and therefore remorseful, kept trying to break off the affair, doing so with great regularity a little before Easter, so that he might take communion in public, and falling back into Mme de Mailly's arms soon afterwards. At the same time, he made repeated efforts to be satisfied with the Queen, who gave birth to three more daughters in 1734, 1736 and 1737, respectively. Then, once more Marie became pregnant, but this time, she lost the baby early. After that, it was all over. In July 1738, Barbier remarked that Mme de Mailly's position had become common knowledge: that Easter, for the first time, the King had failed to take communion.

Of course, well-informed courtiers had found out the great news before that. Already in September 1736, d'Argenson noted: "The King . . . took as his mistress, some six months ago, Mme de Mailly, daughter of M. de Nesle. Thus, M. le Cardinal has consented to this arrangement, seeing that the King needed a mistress. He had 20,000 livres [$90,000] given to her . . . This affair is kept a strict secret"[26]; and in July 1737, he added: "When they came to tell the King about the birth of yet another daughter, they asked him whether she should be called Madame Septième [Madame the Seventh],* and he answered Madame Dernière [Madame the Last] from which people have concluded that the Queen will be neglected indeed."[27] He was right. Mme de Mailly was now the only woman Louis cared about, but, much to everyone's surprise, she received neither money, nor a higher position, nor even influence. There was no doubt, everyone agreed, that the King was a model ruler: it was unprecedented for a royal mistress not to be living in dazzling luxury. Besides, it was considered a good thing that the King had joined the rest of humanity and been

---

* Because several years often passed before the King's daughters were officially baptized, they were at first given numbers: Madame the First, Madame the Second, etc.

unfaithful to his wife. In January 1739, Barbier commented: "Mme la comtesse de Mailly is still thought to be the King's favorite. There are now many suppers, either at La Muette or at . . . Madrid; the King is beginning to have a taste for ordinary pleasures. There is nothing wrong with his being a little less passionate about hunting . . . which might have made him too somber and wild. The frequentation of women and the experience of pleasure will take him less time and improve his mind and his feelings."[28]

That point of view was widely shared. The eighteenth century, in France, was the century of women. While it was understood that they were as intelligent and as capable as men, it was clear that they were also more graceful, more sensitive, more polished: in a word, more civilized. Worldly parents counted on their son's first mistress to give him sophistication and poise, a feeling for the world and the good things of life. The King's shyness had removed him from the kind of easy social intercourse that was considered one of the chief pleasures of life. Now Mme de Mailly could do for Louis XV what Marie Leczinska had so signally failed to provide.

While the King, no doubt, soon began to feel less shy, more at ease, the improvement was extremely slow, probably because of Fleury's continued presence. As long as the ex-tutor remained principal minister, Louis XV, from sheer gratitude, failed to assert himself openly. All through the thirties, even as he was taking on more of the duties of government, he made sure that this change was shielded from the open light. In a sense, although to a lesser degree, the King was still the idolized but powerless child. In that enduring psychological state lies the explanation for those aspects of Louis XV's character which so puzzled the Court. Anyone who knew him well agreed that he was intelligent, clear-sighted, hardworking, that he knew what he wanted; but all these admirable qualities were eclipsed, and sometimes annulled, by Louis's apparent inability to assert himself: now, as in the teens and twenties, he seemed always willing to believe that the professionals knew best.

This apparent willingness to defer to another's opinion could, however, be very misleading: when it came to basic principles, the King knew exactly where he stood. There could never be any question, for instance, of his allowing the Parlement to seize the powers it claimed. The ministers might find that their advice was listened to, and often followed, but even then the King never forgot that the final decision was his, and his alone, and when he felt he was being manipulated, he didn't hesitate to come down hard; this was the case, for instance, when Chauvelin was dismissed. And as the years passed, Fleury himself found that he could no longer count on his master's automatic approval: more and more often, the men and women Fleury proposed for State or Court appointments were turned down in favor of the King's own choices. Why, then, did Louis XV allow the Cardinal to retain the appearance of untrammeled power? Laziness and force of habit, most contemporaries would have answered. In fact, and without discounting the gratitude and love Louis felt for his former tutor, the reason was both simple and sufficient. Ever since he had assumed power in 1726, Fleury had governed France with efficacity, frugality and success. His record was the best anyone could remember. He had engineered prosperity, a stable currency, a nearly—sometimes completely—balanced budget. He had allowed France to engage in just a single war, and that had resulted in the acquisition of

Lorraine at relatively little cost. Thus, Louis XV, who remembered the precepts he had copied as a child, was behaving like a good king in retaining the minister who did so much for the State and the people. And even if, as the thirties ended, he began to feel a growing need for emancipation, he was kind and patient enough to let the years do their work: whatever his other qualities, after all, and appearances to the contrary notwithstanding, Fleury was not eternal.

Without in any way underestimating Louis XV's professional conscience, his extraordinarily busy schedule also played a role in Fleury's hold on his office. Even more than his great-grandfather, Louis XV liked moving about. Already in 1730, for instance, Narbonne, the Versailles Chief of Police, noted that the King had spent 86 nights at Marly, 50 at Fontainebleau, 46 at Compiègne, 52 at La Muette, and 33 at Rambouillet, which left only 98 nights for Versailles itself, a remarkably small total. The explanation for this incessant travel is simple enough: since the King insisted on maintaining the full, incredibly demanding, etiquette first defined by his great-grandfather despite the fact that he was a shy and private man, life at Versailles quickly became unbearable for him, so he went off to other residences where he could live more like a normal man. This was true of Marly, where dazzling gardens, complete with fountains, cascades, basins, canals and sculpture, surrounded twelve small pavilions—just enough for the King's intimates—and where he could happily play cards without being watched by crowds. La Muette was a mere hunting lodge which, during the thirties, was gradually expanded until it became a small château. There, too, the King could be private, and it was also the perfect place from which to set off for Louis's favorite sport. The same was true at Compiègne, then still a small, old-fashioned castle. Rambouillet was the country residence of the comtesse de Toulouse and had some of the best hunting in France. As for Fontainebleau, it was a traditional royal residence which was conveniently surrounded by a forest rich in game. We have only to look at Louis XV's timetable to see what mattered to him: the hunt and the company of a small group of friends.

That Louis XV should have dreaded the ceremonial which surrounded his days at Versailles is hardly surprising. Quite apart from the even more complex etiquette which prevailed on special occasions, the standard ritual was quite awe-inspiring. It started with the King's lever. That in itself was a purely formal affair: unlike Louis XIV, who actually slept in the splendid but drafty State Bedroom overlooking the cour de marbre, Louis XV soon moved to another, smaller, more comfortable bedroom; so, far from being awakened in his official bed, he generally lay down in it only after he had been up for several hours already. Every evening he told his Premier Valet de Chambre the hour at which the lever would take place the next day. At the appointed moment, the First Valet opened the bed curtains and signaled the beginning of the elaborate ritual of the entrées, literally the "coming-ins." Just as precedence mattered enormously during the rest of the day and evening, so did the order in which the courtiers entered the King's bedroom in the morning: it reflected not only one's importance but, even better, allowed access to His Majesty before he was surrounded by the usual crowd. As a result, the exact order of the entrées was a matter of intense interest to everyone at Versailles, so much so that the duc de Luynes, one of the most important noblemen at Court, and the husband of the

Queen's dame d'honneur and dearest friend, felt compelled to set it all down in his diaries.

"The entrées in the King's bedroom," he wrote in 1737, "are the familières [family], the grandes entrées, the Premières entrées, and the entrées of the chamber. The entrées familières come in the moment the King is [officially] awake and while he is still in bed. All the Princes of the Blood Royal, except M. le prince de Conty, and also M. le Cardinal [de Fleury], M. le duc de Charost [who had been the King's governor], Madame de Ventadour [the King's governess] and the wet nurse are the only ones who have them. The grandes entrées, when the First Gentlemen of the Bedchamber come in, are when the King has just risen from his bed. The Premières entrées are when he is up and wearing his robe. The entrées of the chamber are when he is in his armchair in front of his toilette; and after that all the courtiers come in.

"All these entrées, in the evening, are exactly the same for the King's coucher [going to bed], which is to say that the familières, the grandes and the first entrées stay for what is called the petit coucher, that is, until the King is actually in bed. The others leave when the King's armchair is brought near the toilette. When the crowd has left, the Premier Valet de Chambre, on the King's order, gives a candlestick to whichever one of the courtiers is allowed to stay. [This was a much sought-after mark of favor and allowed the happy man to speak privately to the King while he undressed.] One keeps the candlestick until the King rises from his armchair to get into bed. Then one gives it back, but one stays on after having given it back until everyone is out. The entrées of the chamber, along with the courtiers who have no entrées at all, go out when the [First Valet] says: 'Proceed, Gentlemen,' that is to say, when the King's shoes have been entirely taken off and his armchair is brought near his toilette. In the evenings, the King, as he comes out of his study, goes over to his prayer stool within the balustrade near the bed, and then he takes off his blue ribbon [of the Order of the Saint Esprit] and his coat. That is the moment when the First Valet de Chambre holds out the candlestick and the King says the name of the person to whom it shall be given. The King takes his chemise from the hands of a Prince of the Blood, the Grand Chamberlain, the First Gentleman of the Bedchamber or the Grand Master or Master of the Wardrobe. Then he takes his robe; he sits down and his shoes are taken off; the pages of the chamber give him his slippers; then the armchair is brought near the toilette and [the Valet] says: 'Proceed, Gentlemen' and all leave the room."[29] If the duc seems somewhat unclear at first reading, it is simply because of the complexities involved; and even then, what he describes is severely pared down: added to the actual ceremonial were the burning questions of who stood where, when and how. Then, of course, people who didn't have the entrée, or who had been allowed in once, invariably claimed that they certainly did have the right to be there. Sometimes the disputes became so heated that the King would settle them for one occasion only. In the books of the Master of Ceremonies, we keep reading that such and such was allowed to be in some particular place "sans tirer à conséquence," without the creation of a precedent. In December 1736, for instance, there was a hot dispute about the King's almoners. Originally, in the 1660s, they had had the entrées of the chamber just like, say, the Captain of the Guard.

Then, sometime in the previous reign, they had lost them; but now they were allowed the entrée in the morning so that they could be present for the King's prayers. Having been given the morning entrée, they naturally claimed the same privilege for the evening; but this time they were refused.

These complexities made for endless, tedious, often embittered disputes which the King had to settle. Of course, there was also the rare act of politeness. On one occasion when the King was dining with the Queen, for instance, he found that the sun was shining right into his eyes, so he asked that the curtains be drawn. Since he was in the Queen's apartment, it was for the dame d'honneur, the duchesse de Luynes, to give the actual order; but thinking that the King's command should be relayed by the First Gentleman of the Bedchamber, she failed to do so. At that point, in what one can only call a miracle of selflessness, the First Gentleman in question, the duc de Gesvres, said to the attendants: "Gentlemen, Mme de Luynes says that the curtains must be shut."[30] By so phrasing his command when, in fact, the duchesse hadn't said a thing, M. de Gesvres made it plain that he gave the order *as if* it had come from the dame d'honneur, thus preserving her right to do so on all future occasions. This kind of behavior, however, was exceedingly rare; perhaps the duc de Gesvres, who was notoriously impotent, felt he owed the ladies a little extra courtesy.

Most of the time disputes raged; and just to make things more difficult, the etiquette regulating the Queen's lever was fully as complex as that affecting her husband. There was, for instance, the touchy question of when the Governor of a Prince of the Blood was to have the entrée; and the duc de Luynes, who tells the story, promptly comes to his own conclusion. "Today Madame de Luynes, who was going to the Queen's at noon according to her custom, found at the door to her bedroom M. le duc de Chartres [the duc d'Orléans's son], M. de Balleroy, his Governor, and Mme la duchesse d'Alincourt," he noted in January 1737. "Since it was at the time when the grandes entrées go in to the Queen, and since also Mme d'Alincourt had those entrées, Mme de Luynes could not understand why Mme d'Alincourt had stayed outside or why M. le duc de Chartres hadn't gone in. Mme de Luynes immediately went in to the Queen, who told her that M. le duc de Chartres was waiting at the door, that she had given orders to let him in, but that M. de Balleroy had wanted to come in as well; that she had no intention of treating M. de Balleroy the way she treats M. de Châtillon [the Dauphin's governor], but that she would be delighted to see M. le duc de Chartres as long as he came in without his governor. Mme de Luynes went herself to the door and called M. le duc de Chartres, whom she let in. M. de Balleroy then presented himself, and she asked him to be so good as to wait for a few moments. Mme d'Alincourt, who had remained on the outside only from consideration for M. le duc de Chartres, came in with him. A few moments later, the entrées of the chamber were called in and M. de Balleroy entered. He came close to the Queen and made some representations to her; but even though they were received with a kindly manner, it was evident that they made no impression. It has only been for the last few years that the Princes of the Blood have thought they had a sort of right to the entrées; before that, they had none."[31]

What the duc means, of course, is that under Louis XIV the Princes of the Blood, as distinct from the immediate Royal Family, were often given the entrées individually, but that their status as princes gave them no special rights. As for the unfortunate M. de Balleroy, he was trying to usurp a precedence which belonged to the Dauphin's governor only.

Seen from a distance of two and a half centuries, all this has undeniably comic overtones; to the King, Queen and Court, however, it was deadly serious. Everyone was willing, indeed, eager to spend months discussing controversial points; some disputes, in fact, were never solved—that of the exact rank of the princes of the House of Lorraine, for instance—and they plagued the King until the end of his reign. For Louis XIV, it had all been a way of turning the great nobles' minds away from civil war, but by the eighteenth century, when that danger had faded, it merely entailed endless, often unpleasant, complications.

Much the same was true of the ceremonials which, at Versailles, defined the King's day. Dutiful as always, Louis XV respected them, but they made him miserable. For instance, after the lever—in itself, as we have seen, a masterpiece of intricacy—Louis XV took his breakfast (a little paté, some fruit) in public, sitting alone at a table while people stared. Then came Mass, with its own carefully worked out etiquette, after which the monarch saw the Cardinal and his ministers, one at a time. Then came one of the councils. On the two days a week without a Council, the King retired to his study and worked for the rest of the morning. Sometimes there were special ceremonies: presentations of noblemen or ladies; receptions of ambassadors or special bodies, like the Parlement; solemn taking of the oath of office for ministers and marshals of France. Then, around one o'clock, the King dined in public, surrounded by much ceremony, many attendants and very little amusement. The meal usually lasted for a little under an hour; refusing many of the proffered dishes, Louis XV usually ate soup; a little game or poultry and a roast of lamb, veal or beef; few vegetables, but occasional salads; then fruit, fresh or stewed, and often some cookies. The afternoon, however, made up for the morning's constraints: this was the time to hunt, starting a little before two and ending around six; Louis XV usually led the pack and exhausted the other hunters. After that, once again the Court took over. On Mondays and Saturdays there was a concert, on Wednesdays and Thursdays a play, on Fridays and Sundays card playing. Then came, for the King, the crowning moment of the day: unless there was a ceremony of some sort, he vanished into his private apartments or went over to the comtesse de Toulouse's: it was time for the supper, usually eaten sometime around nine, for conversation and light amusement. The King usually drank nothing but champagne, and not much of that, relaxed and, at long last, felt he could rejoin the rest of humanity.

Indeed, unlike his great-grandfather, whose indifference to most human feelings was nothing short of amazing, Louis XV behaved very much like the rest of his people. He had been a good husband for several years, and he always remained a kind and faithful friend to his wife. In a century when upper-class children were neither seen nor heard, he was a devoted father. Most amazing, perhaps, considering the almost standard monarchical tradition of hatred between the ruler and his heir, the King loved the Dauphin dearly, spent time with him, gave him numerous personal presents, took pride in his achievements, oversaw his education and watched his health with the deepest concern. In 1738, for instance, the nine-year-old boy was suffering from an abscess at the juncture of cheek and jaw which had to be incised. Anesthesia had yet to be invented, so the operation was dreadfully painful. Against all tradition, the King insisted on being present, but when he heard his son's shrieks, he began to shake and grew so pale that his attendants expected him to faint.

In one respect, however, and in spite of his obvious reluctance, he behaved like an eighteenth-century father. At Fleury's request, and for reasons of economy, it was decided that five of his seven daughters would be sent off, for a few years, to the convent of Fontevrault, thus obviating the need for costly separate households.* The two oldest girls, Mesdames Elisabeth and Henriette, who were eleven, and thus approaching marriageable age, were allowed to stay. Then, when the King announced his decision, the six-year-old Madame Adélaide burst into sobs, flung herself at her father's feet and begged not to be sent away. Unable to resist the child's tears, Louis agreed to let her stay, so in May 1738 Mesdames Victoire, Sophie, Félicité and Louise went off. Once again Fleury had placed his ex-pupil before his duty; once again that duty had prevailed.

Because he became a father at the young age of seventeen, because he had so many children so quickly, most of all because he was the King, it is far too easy to think of Louis XV, in the late thirties, as a settled, mature man. In fact, he had remained, if anything, young for his age; Fleury was largely responsible for that. And like any other grand seigneur, he had as much fun as he could, even if it meant keeping a positively hectic schedule. On a Sunday in March 1737, for instance, he drove to La Muette, where he had supper and spent the night. The next morning, he went out hunting, only returning to Versailles for supper. At midnight, he got back into his carriage, went off to Paris, spent several hours at a masked ball being given at the Opéra, left it at four, arrived back at Versailles at six, heard an early mass; then, having slept a few hours, he was on his horse again at eleven and spent the afternoon hunting. Once back at the Palace, he retired to his private apartments, where he had thirty guests for supper and stayed up very nearly until dawn. If nothing else, this kind of schedule reflects a remarkably high level of energy. Louis XV was not only the handsomest man in France, he was also one of the strongest.

All those pleasures were well organized. Louis XV, like the gourmet he was, liked his champagne properly iced, so he owned ten underground icehouses which, together, contained some four hundred cubic feet of ice. They cost him 4,000 livres ($18,000) most years, but when the winter was warm or the summer torrid, that sum could rise all the way to 40,000 livres.[32] There was an extensive hunting equipage so that the King could hunt every day if, as was often the case, he so chose: that cost some 250,000 livres ($1,100,000) a year.[33] There was Mme de Mailly, of course, who often received a sum not much larger than that spent on the year's provision of ice. And, finally, there were the King's *cabinets*. These were a suite of relatively small rooms, on the floor above the official apartments, where only a very few of the King's friends had access and from which all ceremony was banished. There, Louis XV had his library, a study, a workroom in which he sometimes turned out ivory pieces, a

---

* Levron, in his biography, suggests that another reason may have been the King's desire to keep his now open liaison with Mme de Mailly from his daughters' eyes; given the standards of the time and the fact that the three eldest girls remained, however, that explanation does not seem convincing.

summer dining room and a winter dining room. From 1738 on, Mme de Mailly was also given a suite of two rooms, one a bedroom, the other a study in which the King often liked to work. It was in these cabinets that the suppers took place, at least once a week and with people gathering between seven and eight. "Those who wish to present themselves for the honor of taking supper with His Majesty come into the King's [official] study, if they have the entrée, or, if not, they stay in the bedroom at the door of the study," the duc de Luynes noted. "The King comes out of his study for a moment, looks at those who present themselves and immediately goes back in to make out his list. The doorkeeper calls out those whose names are on the list; they go in as soon as they are called and sit themselves at table immediately. These suppers usually last until about midnight."[34] This was in January 1737. By July, when Louis XV was getting over one of his occasional gastric attacks—like all the Bourbons, he ate too much, but exercise kept him slim—he was holding his suppers at least twice a week but no longer drank champagne (he soon started again) and went to bed earlier. This relative abstinence, however, in no way damaged the young monarch's high spirits. "For some time now," the duc de Luynes wrote on the fifth, "he has been going up after supper onto the roofs of the castle, takes walks with those who have the honor of being invited to sup with him, sometimes all the way to the end of the new wing, and from there to the end of the wing of the Princes. Several times he went into Mme de Chalais's apartment for a chat, entering through her window, which looks out onto the roof, and to Mme de Tallard's, down the chimney. There was even a rather pleasant conversation at Mme de Tallard's . . . The King spoke quite naturally about his tastes and his character as they relate to life in society."[35] Any of Louis XV's friends, in fact, could now expect this kind of flattering but surprising visit. On August 4, for instance, Luynes recorded with undisguised satisfaction: "The King . . . after supper came for a walk in the gallery and the corridor which run around my apartment; he had someone scratch* at one of the back doors and had me called. Mme de Luynes also came to the door, the King came in and played cavagnole until almost three in the morning."[36] It is pleasant to record that even in the huge, solemn Palace of Versailles, the young King could still behave very much the way one would in a large country house where, after the day's activities, the host drops in on one or another of the guests.

With all that, however, Louis XV was no philistine. Although he played no instrument, he liked and understood music: most of Rameau's works, for instance, were given their premieres at Versailles. He also understood painting. When, in 1738, he visited the yearly Salon, he promptly noticed the works of a new artist, Chardin. That he should have done so was proof of unusual discernment on his part, since the artist's middle-class subjects were generally disliked by the aristocracy. Louis XV expressed his enthusiasm in so warm a manner that Chardin promptly gave him the two paintings in question, which today hang in the Louvre. Then, too, there were orders to Oudry, who started working on the great Royal Hunts series in 1736; to Boucher, to Van Loo; to Desportes, whose splendid still lifes combined lushness and order; to Pierre, that minor but highly attractive practitioner of the currently fashionable rococo style. Constant orders for new, splendid pieces of furniture were given;

* At Court, you never knocked on a door; you scratched instead.

but of all the arts, architecture was the one closest to Louis XV's heart. "Apparently the King continues in his taste for building," Luynes noted in 1737. "I learned today from M. Gabriel that the ordinary appropriation for building is 2 million livres (9 million dollars) a year . . . People had said that the King's cabinets at Versailles would cost 150,000 or 160,000 livres. M. Gabriel told me that from 1722, when modifications were begun, until today, the total expenditure . . . comes to only 580,000 livres."[37] Although none of the early buildings of the reign have survived the Revolution, the ground was clearly being prepared for its later achievements; and it is characteristic that when Louis XV came to choosing an architect, he picked Jacques Ange Gabriel, unquestionably one of the greatest who ever lived.

Most of the King's activities were known only to a very small circle. To people outside the Court, he remained a distant deity, majestic but mysterious, much loved, but in an almost impersonal way. By the late thirties, though, one begins to note a pervasive feeling that the monarch was too shy, too withdrawn, and far too willing to let Fleury run the government. By 1741, songs were, as usual, expressing the people's gripes: "Un prince mineur à trente ans / Un prêtre régent en enfance / Des conseils sans expérience / Et des généraux sans talent" ("A king still a minor at thirty / a senile priest to govern us / councillors without experience / and generals without talent")[38] was a typical theme which was soon elaborated in even stronger terms: "Malheureux peuple d'un enfant / D'un roi qui ne voit ni n'entend / Qui laisse flotter mollement / Le timon du gouvernement" ("Pitiful subjects of a child / of a King both blind and deaf / who allows softly to sway / the rudder of the ship of state")[39]: it seemed all too true to the uninitiated. At Court, of course, people were beginning to notice that appearances were deceptive; and among the French at large, Louis XV had only to show himself and resonant shouts of "Long live the King" filled the air: when they actually saw him, his subjects knew, somehow, that he cared. Indeed, he seems now and again to have been in contact with very ordinary people. In April 1740, for instance, d'Argenson noted: "During his last stay at Choisy, His Majesty spent his days in a pavilion close to the ferry, watching the bargemen conveying wine and fish as they passed by, asking them questions and talking to them simply and easily . . . He stayed there so long that he was exhausted in the evenings."[40] That was hardly the act of a lazy or uncaring ruler, and many of his subjects sensed that he was neither.

The few courtiers who knew him well were, of course, quite aware of this: they saw him every day, set down the details of his life and behavior and came up with a singularly attractive picture, that of a conscientious, hardworking king and a kind, sensitive person. In May 1740, for instance, Luynes recorded the King's extraordinary indulgence to the people who served him, his patience when his shirt failed to appear, when his coffee was served without sugar, when he was given two left boots; and while these are small incidents, they took place in a milieu where perfect service was the norm, and where servants could expect severe reprimands if they failed to provide it. And yet, already in 1737, the duc had noted with wonder that the King was willing to be thoroughly uncomfortable just to spare his servants.

"A few days ago, the King, who was talking of the extreme coldness of his bedroom here [at Versailles], said that it sometimes actually forces him to move to his study when he gets up in the morning before he has anyone come in to him. I had the honor of answering him that if he found his study warmer, it seemed to me he could use it more often; and that is when he replied to me: 'When I get up before anyone has come in, I light my fire myself and need call no one. If I went into my study, I would have to call a [servant]; I would rather let the poor people sleep, I keep them awake often enough.' "⁴¹ This may, at first, not seem like much; but anyone who has spent time in a country house without central heating will know just how painful it is to get up in an unheated room in winter; besides, this kind of consideration for one's servants was almost unheard of in the eighteenth century. Nor was the King's kindness reserved for his attendants: anyone involved with Louis XV felt it. There was the episode of the chevau-légers (a cavalry regiment) in July 1737, for instance. In amazement, Luynes noted that "the King refuses to keep the chevau-légers in Versailles after the end of the quarter so that they could escort him to Paris if the Queen gives birth to [a son]. After he listened to representations from the duc de Chaulnes, the King told him: 'It would actually be better [to have them stay] but it would make them remain here another eight days and that would cost them too much money; I won't have it.' The chevau-légers, when they heard about the King's act of kindness, all said they wished they could stay."⁴² Indeed, this kind of consideration for others marked most of Louis XV's life. In one day, June 28, 1737, Luynes jotted down several little incidents which are typical of the King's behavior.

"I have heard today," he noted, "three facts which are unimportant in themselves but are good examples of the King's kindness. Yesterday, M. le duc de Béthune, who was hunting with the King, had heard that Mme la duchesse de Béthune was spitting up blood and pus and was in a state of extreme affliction. The King, who knew nothing of this, asked him for news of Mme de Béthune. M. de Béthune was unable to answer and simply burst into tears. The King, when he came in from the hunt, said to M. de Charost: 'I thought your son was going to make me faint,' and told him the state in which he had seen M. de Béthune."

Soon afterwards, when the ducs de Villeroy and de Béthune asked to exchange apartments in the Palace, they were allowed to do so: this was most unusual. Because lodgings in the Palace itself were so scarce and so desirable, exchanges had long ago been ruled out: it was just like Louis XV to bend those rules in an effort to oblige. Then, Luynes goes on, "the King was working on the [distribution of] apartments at Fontainebleau. M. de Chalais asked that his daughter, who is eight, be given a room next to him. The King said to him at first: 'Talk about it to the comte de la Suze.' M. de la Suze told M. de Chalais about a convenient apartment, and M. de Chalais reported to the King. His Majesty answered: 'That one would not be convenient enough; I want to give you a better one.' "⁴³

This wasn't just personal kindness, a fondness for friends. Louis XV felt a strong sense of obligation to all those who served him well. Fleury, of course, was living proof of this, and so is a conversation the duc de Luynes jotted down in April 1737. "We were speaking of Philippe de Commines, who had left the service of the Duke of Burgundy [in the fifteenth century] because that prince, to whom . . . he had rendered an important service, had not rewarded him adequately . . . At that, the King said, 'They were both wrong.' " In the same way, Louis XV felt himself accountable for the welfare of the people entrusted to him by God. In the course of the same conversation, he looked at a map showing the battles of Louis XIV and listing the reasons for the Sun King's wars. "About that," Luynes goes on, "His Majesty said: 'Some of these reasons are indeed light; that is our affair; we are responsible for the blood that is shed.' "[44] No wonder the duc rushed to his diary: this was a most unusual position in an era when war was still regarded as a glorious game, the best occupations for monarchs and nobles, and when conquest of foreign territory was the end-all of a successful policy. We, in the twentieth century, have learned that the gains of war are often bought too dearly, but in the eighteenth century the opposite held true. Frederick II's conquest of Silesia in 1740 and the later partition of Poland are cases in point. Louis XV, on the other hand, understood perfectly the cost of war. Perhaps he remembered his great-grandfather's dying admonition; but, in any event, he deserves credit for despising false pride and sympathizing with the sufferings not only of his soldiers but also of the peasants whose crops were ravaged, whose cattle were stolen and whose houses were burned to the ground.

At the same time, these admirable feelings were not often, if ever, expressed in public. A casual conversation within the King's intimate circle was one thing, official statements quite another. When, however, Louis XV felt free to talk, he sometimes said things which, for a King of France, were positively startling. "We were talking during supper of the difficulty we all naturally have in admitting to a mistake. The King . . . said: 'As for me, if I had made one, I would admit it.' This is all the more remarkable in that it is, in fact, accurate."[45] Surprising, coming from a living icon. More down to earth still was a conversation about death. "We were talking during the King's dinner about the custom of temporarily depositing in the local parish the corpse which is to be buried elsewhere. The King did me the honor of telling me: 'We [Kings] are exempt from that ceremony.' I thought it right to answer that only His Majesty could suggest the possibility of such an event [i.e., the King's death] and that we could never contemplate it. 'And why not?' the King retorted. 'Must it not happen someday?' "[46] People are seldom willing to face their own death, especially if they are twenty-seven and in the pink: once again, Fleury's precepts had sunk in.

Unfortunately, all these admirable qualities remained hidden to the world at large. It was not just that the King was so grand, so distant: he was also paralyzingly shy, so that people who only came to Versailles occasionally left it with the image of a cold, unfeeling monarch. An incident which took place in October 1742, is absolutely typical of this problem.

The maréchal de Belle-Isle had been representing France in Frankfurt during the election of the Emperor, and had helped engineer the French candidate's success. It was to be expected, therefore, that when his wife the maréchale came to Court, she would be singled out for a few special words of praise. Indeed, "Mme de Mailly, who is very fond of the márechal de Belle-Isle, expected the King to speak to Mme de Belle-Isle for quite a long time; but the King did not say a single word to her, which surprised all those who take an interest in her. Mme de Mailly talked to the King about it and told him how hurt she was, all the more in that she had believed him to be pleased with M. de Belle-Isle. The King, speaking to her in confidence, said: 'You know how embarrassed, how shy I become. I am just desperate about it; ten times I opened my mouth to speak to her.'

" 'But,' said Mme de Mailly, 'even without talking to her about M. de Belle-Isle, you could have mentioned Frankfurt to her.'

" 'It is precisely about the maréchal that I wanted to talk to her,' the King answered."[47] Anyone who has ever been shy knows just how Louis XV felt. It is much to Mme de Mailly's credit that she at least made it possible for the King to discuss his affliction; still, the effect of that kind of silence on the outside world was obviously deplorable.

It was certainly one of Mme de Mailly's chief merits that she tried to help the King grow up in a variety of ways. In choosing her, Louis XV proved that, although he might be afraid to speak, he was quite able to judge character. Not only did the mistress behave well and modestly, she managed to provide the King with just the sort of family milieu he had always sought. That paralyzing shyness of his dated all the way back to his orphaned childhood; now she was helping him create an environment in which he might gain the kind of self-confidence which he lacked, and d'Argenson, that shrewd observer, soon noticed it. In September 1738, he noted about Mme de Mailly: "The King finds in her the help he needs to surmount the obstacle of his shyness; then, too, she amuses him and no affair has ever been conducted with more mystery and less scandal."[48] For the first time, Louis XV felt like an ordinary man: only then, when he measured himself against others as if he were their equal, could he see that he was indeed as good as they. It was an important discovery. Soon he was showing his gratitude. "Mme de Mailly," d'Argenson recorded in June 1739, "is behaving as if she were enormously important, like a maîtresse déclarée [official mistress], in fact, and everyone can see that she is of great consequence, but she hasn't any money at all."[49] It is easy to see why she was acting that way: her therapy was beginning to work and her lover was grateful. "The King seems more and more cheerful and affable with his courtiers; he speaks to them with the most adorable familiarity," d'Argenson noted that same month.[50]

That the King was more pleased than ever with her seemed certain to the Court. In fact, there was another woman lurking in the background with whom Louis was falling in love, and poor Mme de Mailly knew it; hence, no doubt, her attempt at affirming her position more and more publicly. One sign of the King's waning interest was her constant, severe lack of money, but no one saw it as such because the monarch was well known to be very careful about what he spent. In January 1739, for instance, we hear of him adding up his card losses for the preceding year: they came to the reasonable sum of 24,336 livres—not much for a King of France at a time when great nobles sometimes lost (or won) as much as half a million livres. And in July of that year, d'Argenson spitefully noted: "Mme de Mailly is poorer than ever . . . Her chemises are worn out and full of holes, and her lady's maid badly dressed, which is a sign of true poverty. Just the other day, she didn't have 5 écus [15 livres, some $65] to pay up when she lost at quadrille. She is as disinterested as possible, she renders her friends services but understands nothing about money and won't even listen to offers [to use her influence for a fee]."[51] In fact, she knew better than to ask: the King was willing to let her have the appearance of power, and she was still actually his mistress, but already his interest and gifts went to his new love. For anyone who knew how badly Louis XV had always wanted a family, the choice was logical; to the rest of the world it seemed, when eventually it became known, particularly shocking; and for Mme de Mailly herself it was especially galling. In turning to another woman the King hadn't gone very far: his choice had settled on none other than Pauline-Félicité de Nesle, marquise de Vintimille, and Mme de Mailly's own sister.

Louis XV's new love for Mme de Vintimille corresponded to a change in the royal circle. As Mlle de Charolais receded into the background, new friends began to appear. There was the duc de Richelieu, that perfect example of the eighteenth-century man. The great-grandnephew of the famous Cardinal, Richelieu was a small, lively, attractive man who seems to have easily surpassed Don Giovanni's famous two-thousand-plus conquests during the course of a long and remarkably active life. Well introduced at the Court of Louis XIV—his parents were Mme de Maintenon's close friends—he had early distinguished himself by carrying out an attempted seduction of the duchesse de Bourgogne* so far that the Sun King, who didn't trifle with such matters, promptly put him in the Bastille. Within some four years of his release from that less than fearful prison—noblemen lived in comfortable, airy apartments—he was back; this time he had combined scurrilous opposition to the Regent with the successful and public seduction of one of his daughters. Since then, apparently, he had become irresistible to women: he had only to look at them and they headed straight for the nearest bed. With all that, Richelieu was intelligent, if frivolous, witty, well read (Voltaire was a close and valued friend), altogether a delightful companion, and the King found that his presence much enlivened his suppers.

Another addition to that small cast of characters was the duc d'Ayen, the eldest son of the maréchal de Noailles, a small man "of much wit who is lively, amusing, a welcome guest anywhere people like to laugh about their friends,"[52] a competent if uninspired general, and a polished conversationalist with links to the Royal Family through his aunt, the comtesse de Toulouse. While Richelieu represented no one but himself, however, Ayen stood for the entire powerful Noailles family: this proved particularly handy when his father, the maréchal, wanted something made known, discreetly, to the King.

On the fringes of this circle—briefly in, mostly out, sometimes hovering so close that people thought he might succeed Fleury—was the King's distant cousin, the prince de Conti. Born in 1717, this young man was tall, handsome, well built. "He had wit, an amiable character and has not disappointed, as he grows more mature, the hopes he had created," a contemporary account noted. "He is brave, he likes the military, is lively, touchy about his rank, but too careless about spending."[53] In fact, although a civilized and polished guest, he turned out to be that most difficult of advisers, a man with his own ambitions (if he couldn't be Prime Minister, he wanted to be King of Poland), a man who is offended whenever someone else is listened to, who demands great rewards and takes them as a matter of course when they are given. Still, the star of the suppers was naturally Mme de Vintimille. Taller than her sister, and just as plain, she was remarkably witty, able to converse with dazzling ease

---

* Louis XV's mother.

and elegance, full of animation and fun, just the sort of woman, in fact, to draw the King out. And in case there was any doubt about his feelings, it was noticed that on January 1, 1740, the only person, outside his immediate family, to whom he gave a present was Mme de Vintimille, who received a gold box set with diamonds. It was plain to all, then, that she was the King's new mistress.

She was, however, remarkably willing to share: Mme de Vintimille might be the rising, or risen, star, but Mme de Mailly remained in place. There were even rumors, quite unverifiable, that the King sometimes spent the night with the two sisters together. In any event, Mme de Vintimille soon found that, like Mme de Mailly, she was given neither much money nor much influence. As usual, the King was being cautious. He had allotted himself a total of 105,000 livres a month for his privy purse and never overspent. On the other hand, he didn't hesitate to indulge his passion for building: in November 1739, he bought the little château of Choisy, just outside Paris, for 300,000 livres ($1,350,000). Luynes reported: "The King is very pleased with his new acquisition. The furniture is handsome, the dining room very pretty and the view admirable."[54] Indeed, Choisy immediately became one of his favorite houses, on a par with La Muette. A year later, Luynes could add: "The King continues to enjoy [Choisy] greatly. On the days he doesn't go hunting, he takes walks there, after mass, in his garden and in the house itself, for which he has several building projects, one of which will be carried out this year . . . His Majesty then goes and visits the ladies."[55] Like everything else, the estimates for the new additions had to be approved by the King: it is instructive to note that, from the late twenties on, every Court and State expense of any magnitude invariably bear the King's bon. Like Louis XIV, he knew at all times the state of his treasury.

Careful though he was, the King was fully aware that magnificence was part of the office. Mme de Mailly might have holes in her chemises, but Louis himself always looked appropriately elegant; occasionally he was actually dazzling. At a ball in 1739, for instance, he was dressed in cut blue velvet lined with white satin; his coat and waistcoat were adorned with diamond buttons, and he wore more diamonds on his hat and shoe buckles. He also made sure that his environment was as splendid as possible. In his bedroom at Versailles, the duc de Luynes reported, there were hangings of "a gold and crimson fabric on which they have been working in Lyon for five or six years. The taste, the design and the texture of this fabric are admirable. The furniture is covered with crimson velvet enriched by a very wide, very thick gold embroidery in a superb pattern of flowers and green-gold ornaments."[56] Clearly, there was no stinting here.

The same was true of the splendid festivities given in August 1739 to celebrate the engagement of Madame Elisabeth. After much negotiating, the King's daughter was marrying Don Philip of Spain, Philip V's youngest son. There were balls, banquets and fireworks both in the park of Versailles and in Paris, where a special island, laden with allegories, was built in the middle of the Seine. It was noticed that for the wedding ceremony Madame Infante, as she was known henceforth, was wearing a gown of cloth of silver, liberally sprinkled with diamonds, while the entire Court tried to rival the Royal Family's glorious display.

It looked very much, at that point, as if nothing was likely to change. The Queen had lost all importance; the King, in spite of his new mistress, was still keeping Mme de Mailly; the country was at peace; and the seemingly eternal Fleury ruled with as firm a hand as ever. Even taking the squabbles with the Parlement into account, there was apparently no reason why earlier, successful policies shouldn't be continued for a long time. To ambitious men like d'Argenson, it was unbearable. To generals like the maréchal de Noailles or the comte de Belle-Isle, spoiling as they were for at least a few battles, it was dreadfully dull, but they were all resigned to an apparently endless continuation of the status quo. In fact, they needn't have despaired. Suddenly, in 1740, the world changed. Louis XV became, apparently, a new man. Within a few years, the government of France was deeply modified, the map of Europe was redrawn to make room for a major new power, and a different cast of characters appeared. Together they made history for the next forty years.

Chapter Five

King at Last

FRANCE, in 1740, was unquestionably an absolute monarchy. The King held all the powers: executive; legislative, subject to registration, but that could be imposed on the Parlement; even judicial, since the Council acted as a court of last resort, able to confirm or annul the Parlements' decisions. He was able to tax pretty much as he liked, and to spend the State's revenue exactly as he saw fit. He declared war, negotiated and ratified all treaties, whether of peace or commerce. He could raise troops or disband them. He could govern with the help of one minister, or several, or none. He could, and did, order censorship of all printed matter, whether books or periodicals. He appointed bishops and abbots, as well as all civil servants and military officers. He gave patents of nobility, titles, honors of all kinds. No one could stop him or bring him to account. And yet, both the King and his minister that year adopted a policy they disliked—even sometimes feared—solely because of the pressure of public opinion, all because on October 30 the Emperor Charles VI died.

In hindsight, it seems as if no question should have arisen at all. The treaty which closed the War of the Polish Succession had stipulated that France endorsed the Pragmatic Sanction. When the Emperor died, therefore, his hereditary lands were to pass directly to his daughter, the Archduchess Maria Theresa, and it was generally understood that her husband, Francis of Lorraine, would be elected Emperor and succeed his father-in-law. Along with France, most of the other European countries had acceded to the Pragmatic Sanction; there was thus no reason why the peace which had lasted since November 1738 should be troubled. In fact, as so often before or since, a mere signature suddenly became very unimportant compared to the possibilities for gain resulting from a general attack on the Archduchess. And while in France the Cardinal might have scruples, the new King of Prussia, Frederick II, had none at all. He promptly claimed Silesia, a large, wealthy province and, without further ado, proceeded to invade it.

Prussia and France were friends; still, just because Frederick chose to rape and pillage Silesia did not mean that France had to imitate him, and the two men who mattered most at Versailles, the King and the Cardinal, were both averse to war,

Louis XV because he believed in keeping his word and wanted to avoid the sufferings inherent to war, Fleury because his last experience of a limited conflict had been harrowing enough to exclude any desire for a repetition. Unfortunately for both, however, neither was prepared to make his will prevail. The King was still shy and uncertain of himself; he was quite able to analyze the situation, weigh his options and come to a sensible conclusion, but he lacked sufficient confidence in himself to impose his views on a virtually unanimous people. Always willing to think that others knew better, since it had been the case all through his childhood and adolescence, he was all too ready to let himself be forced into a policy which he believed to be foolish and wrong. As for the Cardinal, in 1740 he was eighty-seven. Even in our century, that is considered the extremity of old age; in the eighteenth century, it was the equivalent of being a hundred.

For most of his long tenure of office (fourteen years so far), age had seemed completely irrelevant to the Cardinal's ability to rule and, indeed, its only visible effect had been to keep up his enemies' hopes: surely, they thought, the old man must die sometime soon. By 1740, even that piece of common sense was beginning to look singularly unconvincing. Clearly, he was exempt from the usual ravages of senescence. Nor could illness make a difference. In 1737–38, for instance, the duc de Luynes recorded in his journal that Fleury was constantly suffering from severe digestive troubles. He vomited frequently, could scarcely eat anything at all and, even then, was forced to resort to his chaise percée as often as twenty-five times a day. That alone would normally have been enough to kill a younger man; but after a few days' rest, the Cardinal reappeared as pink-cheeked and masterful as ever. Poor d'Argenson nearly went mad. He recorded Fleury's symptoms time and again, each time with greater hope, only to find out that the old man was indestructible. By 1740, his fantasies took over: "The rumor is spreading," he wrote, "that M. le cardinal de Fleury may well be elected Pope; Spain would join France in arranging this so as to be rid of him."[1] It would have been the most spectacular kick upstairs ever; unfortunately for d'Argenson, however, the rumor was completely unfounded. Soon he was back to denigrating the unbudgeable minister: "Something I noticed, more than four years ago, about the cardinal de Fleury, at the time when I was on the best of terms with him, is that he is a great admirer of Cardinal Mazarin and his ministry, and has nothing but contempt for the Cardinal de Richelieu."[2] This time, d'Argenson was right on the mark: Fleury, like Mazarin, believed in the virtues of conciliation; only, while it is relatively easy to impose one's will endlessly, compromise requires a fine sense of where to stop, and when a man ages or becomes tired, he is apt to give away far more than he should.

Briefly, at the end of March 1740, it had looked as if Fleury was losing ground after all. The prince de Conti, as everyone realized, wanted power. He had been a frequent guest at the King's suppers, had obvious abilities, and was young besides. Unfortunately for him, he tended to let his ambition show a little too clearly, along with his contempt for those he considered his inferiors. D'Argenson was quick to notice his shortcomings. "M. le prince de Conti is basically intelligent; but he makes the great mistake of indulging in a quantity of affectations; he exaggerates what he is, plays at being a debauchee, which he actually is, at being unkind and mocking, which he is also, and if he goes on like this, he will end up sick and hated."[3] The King, who was shrewder than his cousin thought, was noticing much the same thing. In spite of repeated hints on the prince's part, it soon became clear that Fleury would not be replaced after all.

What no one did notice was that, at long last, age was beginning to alter Fleury; no one, that is, except his former pupil. When d'Argenson noted, in July 1740, "People say that the King is obstinate instead of firm but, in fact, he now keeps certain matters for his own decision and makes the right choices,"[4] he was beginning to catch on. Louis XV knew that the Cardinal could no longer bear the same kind of burden, and he was also growing increasingly impatient with Fleury's methods: deliberation had turned into procrastination, moderation into indecisiveness. Besides, he was no longer a child who needed a tutor: in 1740 he had reached his thirtieth year, and Fleury's old maxims about the King governing by himself were actually beginning to work against their originator. Still, Louis felt much too grateful simply to fire the old man; and he also realized that, in truth, the Cardinal was not likely to live all that much longer. So, at first he simply compromised. Fleury's power remained unchanged in appearance, but the King took many more matters into his own hands: at best, the minister could only govern in tandem with him.

The immediate consequence of the King's assertiveness, however, was weakness at the top. Partly because of his age, partly because of his diminished power, the Cardinal no longer felt up to braving public opinion, no matter how wrong it might be, so he no longer gave the King the kind of clear, decisive advice which might have convinced him to stand fast. When, therefore, the Court and people alike clamored for an anti-Austrian offensive in the last months of 1740, the weight of that demand soon became overwhelming.

At first, Fleury made it plain that he intended to do nothing at all. France had endorsed the Pragmatic Sanction, and that was that. He was all the more determined to avoid war in that, for the first time, he was having trouble with his domestic policy. The crops had been insufficient, there was a shortage of food compounded by a very steep price rise provoked by scarcity, and the usual consequence inevitably followed: there were riots, first in the provinces, then in Paris. "In the middle of September," an observer wrote, "bread became very dear, rising to five sols a pound [about a dollar] and that caused a small uprising among the people. When His Majesty drove through Paris, the crowds shouted: 'Misery!' instead of 'Long live the King,' and when M. le Cardinal crossed the Place Maubert to go to the Collège de Navarre, the women stopped him amid much tumult, which frightened him extremely . . . [Because of floods] the end of the year was as lamentable as its beginning."[5] Not only had Fleury actually been frightened—a new experience for him—he also realized this was no time for a war.

As for the King, he fully agreed. Quite aside from any attack on the Habsburg hereditary lands, he was not even inclined to worry about the forthcoming Imperial election: unlike most other thrones, the Emperor's could be won only by election; but one Habsburg after another had been elected without interruption since the fifteenth century. Now it was all up to the kings of Bohemia (Maria Theresa herself) and Prussia, the electors of Bavaria, Saxony and Hanover (George II of England), and four prince-bishops to decide who the new Emperor would be.

Maria Theresa, of course, hoped that her husband would succeed her father, but many people in France thought that this was the perfect time to break Austria's ancient hold on the Imperial Crown. Early in December, Barbier recorded a story which showed where everybody stood. " 'Souvré,' the King asked, 'who do you think is likely to become Emperor?'

" 'Well, Sire, I don't worry about it, but if Your Majesty wanted, you could tell us what will happen better than anyone.'

" 'No,' said the King, 'I'll have nothing to do with it; I look at it all from the Mont Pagnote.'*

" 'Ah, Sire, Your Majesty will be cold and uncomfortable there.'

" 'Why?' the King asked.

" 'Because, Sire, your ancestors have never built a house in that place.' "[6] This was no isolated incident. Along with England, the House of Austria was the hereditary enemy. Now, at last, it was led by a well-nigh defenseless young woman: the time had surely come to encompass its fall.

It was a while, however, before the King and the Cardinal gave in. Besides all their other reasons for preferring peace, they were well aware that a war would require new taxes, which, in turn, meant having to rely on the ever fractious Parlement. Just a year before, when, as usual, it was being difficult, d'Argenson, even though he came from a Parlement family, wrote: "Today France moans . . . under an *odious aristocracy,* not of the nobility, for it would think more generously; but a *satrapy of commoners* which has shaped everything according to bad rules, wrong principles and will bring about our ruin. The parvenus of the law and of finance have so arranged the government that, today, any new remedy becomes a new evil."[7] He was exaggerating, of course, but he had a point and the King knew it.

At first, Fleury tried to work out a compromise policy. Maria Theresa would be left in full possession of her hereditary states, but, on the other hand, France would support the election of a non-Habsburg Emperor, in this case the Elector of Bavaria, who was an ally and related to the King.** Even if he had been able to stop there, however, Fleury would already have gone too far: that move alone was bound to entail war with Austria; it did, however, have the advantage of respecting France's endorsement of the Pragmatic Sanction since the Imperial Crown had never been part of the deal.

Unfortunately, people underestimated Austria's power in thinking that victory would be easy, while overrating it in supposing that if Francis of Lorraine was elected Emperor, his first move would be to engage in a reconquest of Lorraine. As so often happens when chauvinism takes over, no one perceived that the two assumptions were contradictory, so everyone united in clamoring for war. Even then, the King did his best to keep procrastinating. On January 15, 1741, Louis XV, normally the most diligent of correspondents, sat down after a delay of over two months to answer a message from the Elector of Bavaria which asked him for his support in the coming election. "I have seen with pleasure, in the letter you sent me on October 24," he wrote in his own hand, "the entire confidence you have in my friendship for you and

---

* A tall hill in the forest of Chantilly where hunters who left the hunt would retire to rest; the King meant he intended to remain uninvolved.

** Louis XV's grandfather, the Grand Dauphin, had married a Bavarian princess.

in the faithfulness with which I intend to discharge my obligations. I will do so with all my power and with all the means which the situation and the state of my kingdom will allow me. I ask you only to remember the immense expenditures which I am forced to make because of the current calamities [i.e., the floods and food shortages] . . . You may be sure that in an occurrence as important as the vacancy of the Imperial Throne, I will neglect no way of giving you new proofs of my affection."[8] Louis XV could hardly have been more ambiguous, especially since Charles Albert of Bavaria's only chance of success depended on the purchase of the ecclesiastical electors.

That, in itself, was nothing new. Bribes formed as ancient and as generally accepted a part of the election as if they, too, had been specified in the Golden Bull*; only, Charles Albert was notoriously poor. The money to buy his election, therefore, could only come from France; and by saying that he was faced with unusually heavy expenditures, Louis XV was, in effect, warning his cousin not to expect too much. Within days, however, he began to reverse himself. Reports from the French envoy at Frankfurt, the free city where elections and coronations were held, now strongly urged support of Charles Albert, arguing that his election was a foregone conclusion if only France was willing to bribe an elector or two, and went on to say that all Germany would rejoice in having a non-Habsburg Emperor. No sooner had those dispatches arrived but Fleury found the same arguments coming from the newly appointed Ambassador to the Electors, the maréchal de Belle-Isle.

It was probably when he appointed Belle-Isle as Ambassador Extraordinary that Fleury made his greatest mistake. The grandson of Fouquet, the Superintendent of Finances disgraced and imprisoned by Louis XIV, Belle-Isle had worked especially hard to overcome his family's disgrace. He was brave, bold, good at intrigue, and utterly devoid of scruples. His ambition was immense, but he was also a competent general, hardworking and eloquent. During the War of the Polish Succession, he had worked out a plan for the invasion of Bohemia, but had been foiled by the advent of peace. He was then made Governor of Metz, one of the main French fortresses, and, being just a few miles from the border with Germany, had kept up a busy correspondence with several of the rulers who were now supposedly ready to side with Bavaria. He thus appeared as the ideal man to send to Frankfurt; only, since he could only reap major rewards by winning a war, it was a foregone conclusion that, from his vantage point, he would be the chief spokesman for the war party.

The first consequence of his appointment came swiftly: distress or no, Fleury decided to start the campaign by buying the Bishop-Elector of Mainz, who was also the Dean of the Electoral College. At this point, Blondel, the previous French envoy who was still in place, began to see the light and wrote to Versailles, pointing out that a campaign to elect Charles Albert would certainly result in war; that there was really no telling how such a conflict would end, the Austrians being stronger and the Bavarians weaker than most people supposed; and that, therefore, Francis of Lorraine should be allowed to gain the crown. Unfortunately, it was too late. Belle-Isle had arrived in Frankfurt and was already sending optimistic reports. He had good reason to feel happy: because it was impossible, for reasons of precedence, to have a

* A papal bull, given in the Middle Ages, which regulated the Imperial election.

mere count as the French Ambassador, and also because, in case of war, he was slated for an important command, in January Belle-Isle was created a Marshal of France.

From then on, there was no stopping him. The Cardinal had little resistance left, and the King followed public opinion. By the spring, Belle-Isle had already pressured the French Government into signing a treaty in which Louis XV undertook to subsidize Charles Albert, then another one in which France and Prussia became allies. Belle-Isle was then given command of the French Army, which was sent into Germany, and another seasoned veteran, Maillebois, was placed under him. All this was done in the name of the Elector of Bavaria, however, so that officially France and Austria were still not at war. By November 1741, the French Army, having crossed the Empire from west to east, had reached Prague, the capital of Bohemia; only, Belle-Isle was not leading it. Far too ill to campaign—he had a very severe case of gout—the maréchal was replaced by a younger man, a bastard son of the late Elector of Saxony, now in the French service, whose taste for strong liquor and loose women was equaled only by his military genius: Maurice, comte de Saxe. In a typically bold move, Saxe led the French Army as it scaled the walls of Prague and, once in control of the city, he had Charles Albert crowned King of Bohemia. In the meantime, back at Frankfurt, Blondel convinced the electors to postpone their decision until January 16, 1742. Since delay worked against Francis of Lorraine, this, too, was a great victory. The anti-Austrian party in France was now able to point out, with considerable jubilation, that its policy was succeeding beyond all expectations.

There were, however, three major flaws in the French position: first, the old hero everyone counted on, the maréchal de Belle-Isle, was now so ill and, in consequence, so senescent as to have become incapable of leading an army; second, England promptly sided with Austria, thus ensuring a long, costly war; and, third, France's main ally, the King of Prussia, while undoubtedly an inspired general, was also a man who would not hesitate to stab a friend in the back or betray an ally if it should become convenient.

All these problems soon became manifest. Not only was France now fighting a (still undeclared) naval war as well as a Continental one, but Belle-Isle's continued ill health led to his being teamed with another experienced general, the maréchal de Noailles,* the duc d'Ayen's father. The two men loathed one another, and so instead of fighting the Austrians they sniped each at the other, thus ensuring a total paralysis of the French command. To make everything worse still, suddenly, in June 1742, Frederick II reneged on his commitments and, in exchange for Silesia, made peace with Maria Theresa. Finally, and predictably, in January 1743, after a long siege, the Austrians retook Prague and it was the Archduchess's turn to be crowned Queen of Bohemia. Belle-Isle, who for once proved equal to his reputation, managed to bring the bulk of the French Army—fourteen thousand men and thirty cannons—back to the Rhine in spite of the appalling cold. And to add to all these disasters, on July 10, 1742, Fleury made a serious mistake: he wrote Koningseck, Maria Theresa's chief minister, and explained that while the French as a whole clamored for war, he

---

* The duc de Noailles, on being created a marshal of France, automatically became known as the maréchal de Noailles.

personally wanted peace, and that it was up to the Austrians to come up with a proposal. Maria Theresa vengefully published the letter, thus making the Cardinal look like a fool, and not even a stiff answer from the embarrassed Fleury could undo the damage.

At least there was one major success to gloat about, or so it seemed at first: on January 24, 1742, Charles Albert of Bavaria was elected Emperor under the name of Charles VII. Belle-Isle, as a reward, was created a duc by Louis XV, a Prince of the Holy Roman Empire by Charles VII and a Knight of the Golden Fleece by the King of Spain. Drunk with pride, the new maréchal-duc returned to Versailles, confidently expecting to replace Fleury; instead, he managed to affront the King, the ministers and the Court by his demands and his insolence, so back he went to Germany, just in time to learn that the new Emperor's troops had been crushed by an Austrian army. Bavaria was now in enemy hands and Charles VII no longer had even an acre of ground to call his own. France had indeed elected an Emperor, but her protégé was utterly bereft: he had neither a country, nor money, nor even an army. Far from being a valuable ally, he had, in a few weeks, sunk to the sad condition of a mere encumbrance.

All these events, of course, had their repercussions at Versailles, but somehow they seemed less important when seen from a distance of several hundred miles. The war, even at its worst, was being fought outside the French borders, and so, for a while at least, it seemed as if the increasingly limping combination of King and Cardinal would continue as before. Louis's love life, however, was quite a different story. Mme de Vintimille, who became pregnant at the beginning of 1741, was now clearly the King's favorite. At the same time, Mme de Mailly remained in place, thus giving rise to a great deal of speculation about the eventual winner. Then, on September 10, Mme de Vintimille died in childbirth. The King felt her death deeply. Prostrate at first, in his need for comfort he then turned to Mme de Mailly. The rapprochement was short-lived, however. By the spring of 1742, Louis had begun to notice the youngest of the Nesle sisters, the widowed marquise de La Tournelle.

Marie-Anne de Nesle had been born in October 1717, and was thus only twenty-five in 1742, seven years younger than the King. She had married the marquis de La Tournelle in 1734 and had lost him six years later; now she was free, ambitious and highly capable. "Tall and imposing, with strong regular features . . . her large blue eyes had an enchanting expression and she moved with infinite grace . . . Her mind was . . . sometimes as majestic as her appearance, as tender as her heart and as proud as her name . . . Everything about her seemed natural, so she made no effort to charm or please people. If she didn't win one right away, then one never liked her."[9] She was also witty and amusing, so her sister counted on her to entertain the King; soon she was a guest at all his suppers and began to outshine every other woman.

In one respect she differed greatly from Mmes de Mailly and de Vintimille. While the two had been perfectly content to share the King, Mme de La Tournelle was far more ambitious. She wanted to be the sole recipient of Louis XV's favors, a *maîtresse déclarée* kept on the same scale as Mme de Montespan: she was not about to put up with torn chemises, cheap liveries and no special precedence. There is very little doubt that she was genuinely in love with the King, but she was determined not to give in to his advances before she received what she considered her due, and she was encouraged in this by her closest friend, the duc de Richelieu. Of course, Mme de La Tournelle had her own good reasons for holding out—she wanted position and fortune—but she soon realized that, alone, she was all too likely to slip up, and either give in too soon or wait so long that the King would become attracted to another woman. With the aid of so experienced an amorist as the duc, however, she was far more likely to succeed. No one knew more about love and sex than Richelieu; besides, he was part of the little circle around the King and had thus been able to get to know him quite well.

Naturally, Richelieu had his own special aim. He had recently decided that womanizing was no longer enough to occupy him fully; now he wanted to emulate his great uncle the Cardinal and become Prime Minister. If Mme de La Tournelle owed him her position, then she would press the King at least to let Richelieu into the Council and perhaps even give him a ministry; that no one was more unsuited than the duc to run a government apparently never bothered the two allies. In a sense, therefore, Louis XV was the victim of a conspiracy; instead of having another mistress like Mme de Mailly, who cost him practically nothing and had no political influence at all, he would be faced with creating a new power center; but since, as it turned out, Mme de La Tournelle really loved him, and since she kept reassuring him about his own capacities while urging him to assert himself, the bargain, on the whole, seems to have been fair.

By the autumn of 1742, the King's passion had become visible. "For the last eight or ten days, we have noticed . . . that the King no longer feels the same about Mme de Mailly, and that this change comes from a new and very decided attraction for Mme de La Tournelle," the duc de Luynes noted. "Still, the dinners and suppers go on as ever, but very sadly, and Mme de Mailly sheds many tears. They have apparently touched the King little or not at all. Nothing is yet apparent on the outside between the King and Mme de La Tournelle, however. She goes out very little and one hardly ever sees her . . . It seems certain, because of several talks between Mme de La Tournelle and M. de Richelieu, and because of a conversation he had when hunting with the King two or three days before his departure for Flanders [where he was joining the Army], that he is to carry out the negotiation. Mme de Mailly, who was still sleeping in her little apartment next to the King's cabinets . . . yesterday had to move back to her old apartment. She deserves pity all the more in that she truly loves the King . . . She has many friends . . . having never done anyone harm, and having, on the contrary, tried to be of service to people." And on the next day, November 3, 1742, Luynes added: "Mme de Mailly left [Versailles] yesterday at seven and moved to Paris,"[10] going on, a little later, "They say that already several days ago [the King] told Mme de Mailly: 'I promised I would tell you the truth: I am madly in love with Mme de La Tournelle. I haven't had her yet, but I will' . . . It seems certain that the King sees her every night."[11] In fact, Louis XV was merely granting one of Mme de La Tournelle's demands: not only did she want place and position, she had said, but her sister must also be sent away. She had no

intention of sharing the King with another woman; and so Mme de Mailly's departure turned out to be the end of her life at Court.

Still, the other conditions remained unfulfilled, so night after night, on Richelieu's
advice, Mme de La Tournelle refused the King's pleas. When to stop resisting required a delicate judgment, as already noted: now that dilemma was acute. Naturally,
the Court watched with bated breath. On November 6, Luynes wrote: "Nothing new
. . . The King is still spending every night at Mme de La Tournelle's; he goes, I am
told, alone, wearing a big wig over his own hair and a cape. I am assured that nothing
has happened yet . . . that she is demanding to be fully declared, which goes
against the King's inclination, but he is very much in love."[12] All through November
the situation remained unchanged, and towards the end of the month Mme de La
Tournelle was writing her mentor, still away in Flanders: "I am not surprised about
your anger, I expected it; but I cannot say I think it reasonable, I cannot see how I
erred in refusing the little visit [i.e., she was still holding out and Richelieu was afraid
the King would give up] . . . It will only make him want it more . . . The letter
you have sent me [to copy and give the King] is beautiful, too much so in fact, I will
not write it; then, too, it would look like a great eagerness on my part, which in truth
I want to avoid. Try to come and see me, it is absolutely necessary . . . Do not look
as if you know anything, for he has asked me to keep everything a deep secret."[13] By
the end of December, the bargain had been struck. On the twenty-eighth, Mme de
La Tournelle wrote Richelieu: "I find myself very comfortable in my new apartment
and spend very pleasant days there . . . No matter what happens, you may count
on my tender and sincere friendship."[14] In fact, there is every reason to think that
the crucial day when the King's flame was crowned at last is December 17. On that
date Richelieu, back temporarily from Flanders, had supper with the King and Mme
de La Tournelle at Choisy; then, at the end of the meal, he disappeared. A carriage
drove up to the front door. The duc reappeared, wearing a nightgown and robe, and
got in: it was that new invention, a *dormeuse* (sleeper): the seats unfolded to become a
bed, and thus comfortably was Richelieu off to the wars. One can only presume that
he slept soundly but that Louis XV and Mme de La Tournelle didn't. They had, after
all, better things to do.

The advent of a maîtresse déclarée, and one, furthermore, who made it plain that
she was interested in politics, was one major change. The other was Fleury's visible,
unmistakable decline. Already late in July 1742, he was writing his protégé, the
cardinal de Tencin, "My health grows weaker every day; my stomach hardly functions anymore."[15] Seeing clearly that his end was approaching, he tried to bequeath
the King another principal minister in the person of Tencin. As a first step, he
secured his entrance into the Council, but there the ascension stopped: Louis XV
didn't like Tencin and detested his sister, an ambitious and intriguing woman who
was known to control her brother. Besides, he had had enough of prime ministers.
He wouldn't dismiss Fleury, but after him he was determined to emulate his great-
grandfather.

In August 1742, during a four-hour conversation with the King, Fleury, in all
likelihood, gave him advice for the future; but then he rallied, and all through the
early autumn he seemed almost like his old self. This time it didn't last. By Decem-

ber, he was clearly beyond recovery. On January 16, 1743, the King went to see him at Issy and the Cardinal gave him all his papers. Thirteen days later, on the twenty-ninth, one of the greatest ministers ever to rule France was dead at last. Almost everyone rejoiced.

"M. le cardinal de Fleury died yesterday at noon," d'Argenson noted. "Never has there been such a comic end because of all the songs, epigrams and demonstrations."[16] Nor was this only the nastiness of an ambitious man long held back. Maurepas, the minister of the Navy, who was given to writing satirical songs— perhaps as a compensation for his impotence—promptly produced a few lines: "Ci-gît qui loin du faste et de l'éclat / se bornant au pouvoir suprême / n'ayant vécu que pour lui-même / mourut pour le bien de l'état." ("Here lies one who, far from pomp and dazzle / contented himself with the supreme power / and having lived to please himself / died for the good of the State.")[17] It was wildly unfair, but then attacking dead or disgraced ministers was an old habit and the Cardinal had lasted far too long for most people's taste.

One man, at least, realized his true worth. Shortly after Fleury's death, Louis XV wrote his uncle, Philip V of Spain: "I may say that I owe everything to him, that, having had the misfortune of losing my father and my mother when I was too young to know them, I always considered him a parent, which makes his loss even more painful,"[18] and he ordered a solemn funeral service at Notre Dame which he paid for out of the privy purse. When, a few months later, the Cardinal's estate was settled, it was found that it only amounted to 80,000 livres ($360,000), a pittance compared to the wealth usually enjoyed by important ministers.

Now that Fleury was gone, everyone wondered who would succeed him. They didn't have to puzzle for long. The very day of the Cardinal's death, according to d'Argenson, the King exclaimed: "Gentlemen, I have just become Prime Minister,"[19] and he then proceeded to make good on his claim. On February 22, d'Argenson noted: "The King works a great deal and cares about governing; apparently the ministers do not control him yet . . . He is firmly determined to prosecute the war with as much vigor as possible, and more."[20] By April, the King's takeover had become even more obvious: "My brother [the comte d'Argenson, minister of War] told me that when a minister talks to the King about anything outside his department, His Majesty remains as silent as a fish, a sort of behavior which upsets them, so that one doesn't know what will happen to the people called the Cardinal's ministers."[21] Louis XV was resurrecting the Sun King's methods. Each minister was to run his department, none would have an overall competence. The King alone would make policy; he was strongly encouraged in his determination by Mme de La Tournelle, whose notion of her role was perfectly clear: she would consolidate her position, and deserve it besides, if she helped her lover become a great king.

There were, in fact, a few changes after the Cardinal's death. Amelot, a second-rate man, had been a perfect Foreign minister as long as Fleury made policy; now he remained on sufferance only; the cardinal de Tencin lost what little importance he had enjoyed; and the maréchal de Noailles was called to the Council.

Not only was the sixty-four-year-old maréchal-duc de Noailles the head of that powerful family, the father of the duc d'Ayen, one of the King's close friends, and the brother of the comtesse de Toulouse, he was also gifted with a remarkably intelligent and quick mind. Married, early in life, to one of Mme de Maintenon's nieces, he had enjoyed great favor in Louis XIV's last years. Under the Regency, he had become Président of the Council of Finances and, at a time when the State was virtually bankrupt, carried through a number of praiseworthy but insufficient reforms. When Law and his System appeared, however, the duc de Noailles opposed them both and, as a result, found himself out of the government; it had been one of his goals ever since to regain power, and he had used all the resources of a great family and a brilliant but unscrupulous disposition in vain. A brave, competent but uninspired general, he had earned his creation as Marshal of France by the services he rendered; and now he began to look like that ever appealing combination, a soldier-statesman.

When Fleury began to decline in the autumn of 1742, Noailles saw his chance and sent the King a very clever letter. "However great the zeal and the desire to serve which fill a heart given over completely to the love and respect it feels for Your Majesty, an infinity of reasons which your understanding will quickly discover holds back even those whose intentions are the very best and who might best be able to serve you. Thus, until it pleases Your Majesty to let me know your will and your intentions, limiting myself solely to that which concerns the border I am watching . . . I will remain silent about all the rest . . . If, Sire, you want that silence broken, it is for Your Majesty to command me accordingly."[22] Behind the flattery and the twisted, courtly phrasing, the meaning is crystal clear: were it not for his fear of offending Fleury, Noailles would be able to give the King the best of advice; and so Louis XV understood. By return post an autograph letter from the King was on its way to the maréchal. "The late King, my great-grandfather, whom I want to imitate as far as possible, advised me, on his deathbed, to take advice and seek to know the best possible policy so as always to implement it; I will therefore be delighted if you give it [i.e., advice] to me . . . You may tell me whatever your zeal and care for myself and my kingdom will suggest to you. I have known you long enough, and well enough, not to doubt the sincerity of your feelings or your attachment to my person."[23] It was everything Noailles had sought: anyone who could keep up a secret correspondence with the King obviously occupied a position of enormous influence. In fact, the maréchal de Noailles had acted just in time. The comtesse de Toulouse had been very much on Mme de Mailly's side, but any danger to the Noailles from the change in favorites was neatly obviated by the maréchal's move; and he wasted no time in making it plain to the new mistress that she could count on him absolutely.

Like the good courtier he was, Noailles read Louis XV's letter carefully and realized it gave him just the opening he needed. As long as he could be sure that the King really admired his great-grandfather, and with the Cardinal on his deathbed, Noailles had a trump card. Naturally enough, he proceeded to play it.

"I make bold to give myself the honor," he wrote in early January 1743, "of presenting to Your Majesty the instructions which the late King, your august great-grandfather, gave in person, after having written them in his own hand, to the King of Spain when he set off [in 1701] to take possession of his crown . . . I would reproach myself with having waited too long had not one of the principal maxims of these instructions seemed to me directly opposed to the kind of government which

Your Majesty, because of your extreme youth when you succeeded to the throne, found already established and which your modesty, Sire, and the natural kindness of your heart has not, heretofore, allowed you to change . . .

1. Do all your duty, especially to God.
2. Make sure God is worshiped everywhere your power extends . . .
4. Always openly take the side of virtue against vice.
5. Never allow yourself to become fond of anyone.
6. Love your wife; remain on good terms with her . . .
8. Make your subjects happy, and in that purpose, only go to war when you are forced to do so, and only after you have fully considered and weighed its causes in your Council.
9. Try to balance the budget.
10. If you must make war, lead your armies in person . . .
12. Never leave business for pleasure, but organize your life so as to have time for amusements and freedom from your obligations.
13. No [pleasure] is more innocent than the hunt, and a taste for a few country houses as long as you don't spend too much money on them.
14. Pay great attention when people talk to you about business; at first, listen to a great deal before deciding.
15. Once you know more, remember that you must make the decisions yourself; but, no matter how experienced you may be, always listen to the advice and reasoning of your Council before you decide.
16. Do everything you can to know all the most important people so that you may make the very best use of them.
. . . .
25. Treat your household well, but do not allow them too much familiarity or influence . . .
. . . .
32. Get a strongbox to which you alone will have the key, and keep all your most important papers there.
33. I end with some of the most important advice I can give you. Never allow anyone to rule you or be the master. Never have a favorite or Prime Minister. Listen to and consult your Council, but decide alone. God, who has made you a King, will give you all the understanding you may need as long as you have good intentions."[24]

It is a formidable list and, on the whole, a clever one. Not unnaturally, it confirmed the King in the trust he was beginning to feel for the maréchal de Noailles, who now entered the Council. And, knowing Louis XV's deep awareness of his royal duties, it no doubt led him to reexamine his life.

In his elaborate preamble, Noailles was, of course, alluding to the fact that, ever since 1715, there had always been a prime minister. Now Louis XIV's voice confirmed Louis XV's intentions: henceforth the government would be the King, a principle which, except for an interruption of sorts in the late sixties, prevailed until the end of the reign. What, then, about the other rules?

God-fearing Louis XV unquestionably was. So far, he had not had any temptation to take the side of vice—having a mistress was just a normal part of life. He certainly remained on good, if somewhat distant, terms with his wife. He was trying to make his subjects happy, had only gone to war with the greatest reluctance, and was now doing his best to win the conflict so as to bring it to an early end. The budget, in time of peace, had been balanced. The King had never left business for pleasure. He did love the hunt and building (small) country houses. He did listen to advice but was now making the decisions himself. He was thoroughly familiar with the most important people at Court. No one in the Household ever felt that they could presume. Better than a strongbox, he had a whole chest of drawers to which he alone had the key. He had no intention of ever having another prime minister, nor was anyone about to become a favorite in the sense that Louis XIV had meant, that is, a man who, acquiring undue influence, would run the government.

So far, therefore, the King could feel that he had lived up to his great-grandfather's precepts. There were, however, two exceptions. Louis XV was far too affectionate by nature never to allow himself a fondness for anyone. Indeed, even when he was madly in love with Mme de La Tournelle, he had resisted as long as he could her demand that he send Mme de Mailly away, had done so at last with the utmost reluctance, and missed her dreadfully. And then there was the tenth rule about leading his armies in person, something that had not, so far, occurred to the King and which, even now, seemed a possible recipe for disaster: he had, after all, no military experience. If he commanded his troops himself, he might well lead them to defeat. If, on the other hand, he merely stood by while an experienced general ran the battle, he would appear like a mere puppet. There was also the fearful possibility that he might be captured by the enemy: no one had forgotten the consequences of Francis I's captivity after the Battle of Pavia. Finally, Louis XV was a man of habits. He was quite reluctant to leave his familiar haunts, his friends and his children for the life at army headquarters.

Of course, the maréchal de Noailles had altogether another point of view on that subject. It was one thing to write the King and, occasionally, sit in the Council and quite another to have the monarch at headquarters, where, suddenly, the experienced maréchal would become adviser-in-chief, so he tirelessly urged the King to come out to the border. And from the spring of 1743 on, he had an unexpected ally in his enterprise: Mme de La Tournelle. Far from being afraid that Louis XV would forget her once he was away from Versailles, she kept urging him to go: leading the Army to victory was the fastest way of acquiring glory, and she wanted her lover to be a great king.

All this happened at a key moment in the reign. Although Louis XV refused to leave his palaces, it became obvious to all that he was indeed taking charge. His ministers noticed it, and so did the new Emperor. Until now, Charles VII, encumbrance though he had become, had received the tenderest of treatment from Fleury. In January 1743, safe in the knowledge that his plaints would be listened to, he wrote to Versailles complaining about the maréchal de Broglie, who was now in command of the French Army in Germany: very sensibly, Broglie had declined to carry out the Emperor's absurd strategy. The answer the Emperor received must have given him quite a jolt.

"I have received Your Majesty's letter of January 23," Louis XV's autograph reply runs, "and I have seen with extreme pains the reasons you think you have for being displeased with the maréchal de Broglie's behavior. Since nothing matters more to me than Your Majesty's interests, and since I have even sacrificed mine by refusing all the advantages offered me [for abandoning Charles VII's cause], if I had thought I had a better general, I would have chosen him to lead my German armies. The maréchal de Broglie's long experience, along with his zeal for Your Majesty's glory, have led me to give him my full confidence, and I could transfer it to no one else. If one had to go over in detail all the reasons for our troops' lack of success in Bohemia, as well as the lack of concerted action which ruined all our operations, it would be easy to see that it is not the maréchal de Broglie who is to blame . . . I could, with better reason, complain about the lack of help given my troops in Bavaria and about several bad maneuvers which I prefer not to mention . . . I must therefore ask Your Majesty to give less credence to the evil reports you may receive about the maréchal de Broglie, and to show him a little more confidence: that would be the best way to reinforce his zeal for Your Majesty's interests."[25] This was a sound piece of advice to the forlorn Emperor, but also an unusually harsh way of treating another crowned head, and we may be sure that both tone and contents are the King's rather than Amelot's.

All this new assertiveness, however, did not mean that the King had forgotten Fleury. In February, Chauvelin, who was still living in exile on his estate near Bourges but felt that his anti-Austrian policy was being vindicated at last, sent Louis XV a long memorandum setting forth the mistakes of the old administration. The response was clear and swift. "M. Chauvelin has received a lettre de cachet sending him from Bourges to Issoire in the Auvergne [and therefore much farther away from Paris]," Luynes recorded. "The King spoke about it at supper: 'I have been given a memorandum by M. Chauvelin which tries to attack the achievements of M. le Cardinal. I am horrified by its tone and have exiled M. Chauvelin farther away than before.' The King seemed very angry."[26] It was typical of Louis XV to go on feeling gratitude even after Fleury's death.

All through that first spring of his personal government, the King worked harder and harder. There were long letters from the maréchal de Noailles, sometimes asking for favors—a promotion for the duc d'Ayen, for instance; a long, highly technical memorandum about the reprovisioning and reorganizing of the Prague army, now back on the banks of the Rhine; constant requests for funds; a long, intricate memorandum about a proposed alliance with the King of Sardinia which, it was thought, would bring Spain into the war; and more requests for funds and provisions. All these letters were answered promptly and fully. And the wretched Emperor, who was still complaining, was once more put in his place. "I can understand Your Majesty's reluctance to renew your earlier requests for the recall of the maréchal de Broglie all the better in that you must know how I dislike the ceaseless complaints you send me,"[27] Louis XV wrote his cousin in March.

For once, the Court and the country both realized what was happening. "The King works by himself and rather despotically . . . He does not prefer any one of his ministers," the duc de Croÿ noted,[28] while in Paris Barbier wrote: "We all continue to admire the King . . . He has told his ministers that no matter where he may be, he

will always be available to them if they have urgent business . . . He is accessible
. . . and works with competence . . . The King is always hard at work."[29] Not
only that, but Louis XV was now demonstrating an appreciation for true merit
(always a rare quality at Versailles) which was little short of startling. "The conversation fell on the favors the King sometimes grants to people of lowly birth and the
King said: 'It is my pride to raise them higher.'"[30] Virtually no other European
monarch could have said the same.

At the same time, people wondered at the new mistress's modest position. Apparently, she hadn't driven so hard a bargain after all, and this also redounded to the
King's credit. The courtiers realized, of course, that Louis XV was deeply in love and
that, as a consequence, there had been some major changes in the small circle of his
friends. "Almost none of Mme de Mailly's friends are left," the duc de Luynes
commented. "M. le duc de Villeroy, M. le duc d'Ayen and M. le comte de Noailles,
who are still well liked by the King, cannot be counted among Mme de Mailly's
people . . . What one might call the new court of the cabinets is composed of M.
de Richelieu . . . M. de Guerchy, the comte de Fitz-James, the marquis de
Gontaut, M. le duc d'Aumont, all linked to Mme de La Tournelle," and he added:
"Mme de La Tournelle still persists in refusing to let the King have his dinner
brought to her apartment. She says she will be delighted to dine with him just as
soon as he gives her the means to provide that meal."[31] And the duc de Croÿ, at the
same time, noticed that Louis XV seemed quite determined to let no woman influence him.

Of course, people did find it a little shocking that the King was now the lover of
the third sister in a row. "Choisir une famille entière / Est-ce être infidèle ou constant?" ("To choose an entire family / Is that betrayal or constancy?")[32] a song asked;
but they also noticed a new aura about the monarch. "The Court was very brilliant
during this last stay in Choisy," one of the royal pages noted. "M. de Richelieu always
accompanies the King."[33] There was no doubt about it: Louis XV was enjoying his
life. He was happy in love, happy to be governing at last and, at thirty-three, in
splendid health. He had also never worked harder.

His correspondence with the maréchal de Noailles, all through the spring, testifies
to his new involvement, and it was only a small part of his task. It is worth noting
that while ministers were notoriously slow in answering their mail, Louis XV sent off
autograph replies to every one of the maréchal's letters within twenty-four hours—
and often within twelve. Even when he had not just received a letter from the Army,
he was still planning and giving orders. In mid-April 1743, for instance, he wrote the
maréchal: "I know how important it is for the safety, the good discipline, the conser-
vation and the success . . . of the Army which I have entrusted to your command
. . . that it always be ready to be reassembled, that the communications between its
various corps not be interrupted by placing them in quarters too distant from one
another. I am writing you this letter to tell you that I command you, except for the
cases where you would deem such a separation indispensable, to obey my instructions faithfully and firmly to oppose any orders [i.e., from Charles VII] to the contrary."[34] A few days later, Noailles wrote the minister of War complaining that the
Emperor was, once again, complicating his task. D'Argenson went straight to the

King with the letter. "I cannot better comply with your request than by forwarding you the letter His Majesty has written you in his own hand,"[35] he wrote on April 24, and, indeed, the King's letter could not have been clearer.

"When I entrusted you with the command of the forces I have sent to Germany," it runs, "my intention was that you have sufficient authority to direct its operations . . . If the Emperor suggested that you fight a battle in circumstances you do not think propitious, or if he orders you to make movements you think contrary to the good of my service, I allow you, better, I command you, firmly to refuse obeying these orders . . . You will, however, only make use of this power if you think it absolutely necessary to do so, you will avoid as much as possible anything which could damage the understanding between generals without which no success can be attained, and you will even try to respect the Emperor's feelings as long as they are not contrary to the good of my service."[36] It is a masterful letter, firm but flexible in all the right ways. There could no longer be any doubt about Louis XV's capacities, or the fact that he was in charge.

Controlling the Emperor was a matter of high policy, but armaments, supplies and adequate funds were also important to the Army's welfare. Far from leaving these more mundane concerns to d'Argenson's care, we find the King writing Noailles in May to tell him that the Comptroller General and the War minister are about to meet and discuss the financial side of the war; that the Army is being supplied with all possible speed ("but we are not God"), that supplies are dreadfully costly. Let the army, therefore, have all it needs, while waste is being eliminated so that total expenditure will be prevented from rising.[37] Then, a few days later, another letter came from Noailles. There had been leaks about the plan of operations, the cardinal de Tencin had blamed them on the maréchal, and Noailles now wrote to plead his innocence. What he received in return was a letter remarkable both for its grasp of reality, its broad-mindedness and its firmness.

"Since," the King wrote, "I was quite sure that the rumor [you had leaked] was false, I was hardly bothered by what they said about you. One thing which worries me a good deal more, however, is to see that you have completely discarded the plan you had when you left here. The dispatch M. d'Argenson is forwarding . . . will acquaint you fully with my decisions . . . You cannot do better than return to your original plan. I also know very well that things which ought to be kept an absolute secret are not always so; I am, and have been, very annoyed by it; but one would have to attend alone to the matters one doesn't want known, and you know this is almost always impossible . . . Envious people eventually die, but never envy, and as long as you justify it so little, you need not worry about what they may do or say. Who indeed is immune from [adverse] comment?"[38]

And the long letters continued. All through June, the two men were exchanging views about the best way of enticing the King of Sardinia into an alliance. Day after day, Louis XV corresponded with Sardinia and with Noailles, while still working with and without his ministers on a multitude of other questions. Sometimes, indeed, the days seemed too short. On June 4, for instance, the King's long letter to the maréchal ends with: "My letter is not very well planned but I am in a hurry . . . Besides, I am no more witty than this; but what is sure is that I am doing my best."[39] Here is an endearing human touch. Anyone who, although in supreme power, is willing to admit his shortcomings deserves respect and admiration.

Unfortunately, the first battle fought under the new system turned out to be a missed victory. All through June, Noailles had been maneuvering to prevent the junction of the Anglo-Hanoverian force, led by George II in person, with the Austrian Army. On the twenty-ninth, he gave battle at Dettingen, near the Main; but what should have been a major French success was marred by the incompetence of a few officers and the lack of discipline—some said cowardice—of the Household troops and, in particular, the Gardes Françaises. Noailles at least had the satisfaction of having given George II a bad scare (he fled the field of battle as fast as his horse would carry him), but his inability to crush the English meant that in order to avoid being split off from Broglie's army, he had to retreat to the border of Alsace. It was a major disappointment.

"Your Guard regiment has behaved badly," the maréchal wrote the King. "I did not want to tell M. d'Argenson the whole truth, but I owe it to Your Majesty: I entrust it to your prudence and wisdom . . . The troops have not had enough training or discipline."[40] Immediately the King replied: "I am quite convinced that it is not your fault if the battle you fought at Dettingen did not end well; everyone does you the justice of realizing it, and I more than all others . . . I am very annoyed by what you tell me of the Household troops . . . Too much complaisance must be the cause; let us behave accordingly in the future."[41] It would have been easy to blame Noailles and make him a scapegoat; many another ruler would have done it. That Louis XV, on the contrary, encouraged him gives the measure of the man.

He soon went even further. While Noailles had undoubtedly been disobeyed at Dettingen, in particular by the duc de Gramont, who wanted to earn a promotion, the other commander, the maréchal de Broglie, had simply frittered away both time and opportunity. Now he was beating a hasty retreat, thus exposing Bavaria, which the poor Emperor lost again. He had given the enemy a double advantage, strategic and political, since no one was likely to take seriously an Emperor who could not even defend his own lands. Noailles understood this, of course, and he also wanted to command both armies, so off went one more letter to the King: "M. le maréchal de Broglie is thus retreating, Sire; he abandons Bavaria and makes the Emperor a fugitive, all without losing a battle, without any specific need, without Your Majesty's order, in fact, against your express and declared command. The Emperor will not believe this was so, nor will Europe . . . and even your own subjects won't unless Your Majesty gives visible and public signs of displeasure . . .

"I cannot help saying that there is all through the administration a sort of sleepiness, of indolence, of insensitiveness which must be remedied as soon as possible . . . The Foreign Affairs ministry is badly run. Most of our ministers to foreign courts are unable to discharge their duty because of their professional incapacity and their [lack of] personal qualities. When appointments are made, favors and connections prevail instead of talent and merit."[42] That Noailles had a point is certain. During Fleury's long reign, the government had, on the whole, tried to do less rather than more; the different factions at court had been pacified by being given spoils when they should have been ignored or repressed; and with the exception of Orry,

always a model Comptroller General, the ministers tended to be mediocrities carefully picked by the Cardinal so as to protect himself from any possible rival. As long
as Fleury was there to oversee it, the system had worked well enough; now it was
slowly grinding to a halt. With characteristic exaggeration, the marquis d'Argenson,
the War minister's elder brother, noted: "A great change is certain to occur in this
State; its very foundations are collapsing."[43] This was still very far from being the
case, but new, energetic ministers were certainly needed.

The King was fully aware of this, but he also realized that none of the great
aristocrats around him was capable of running a ministry. He distrusted the prince
de Conti's ambition; and thus he hardly knew where to turn.

In one respect, at least, he could act. "Your desires are already fulfilled as to the
maréchal de Broglie," he wrote Noailles in mid-July. "Orders have been sent off; as
soon as he reaches [Bad] Wimpfen, he will turn the command over to you [and be
exiled to his country estate] . . . I know that our ministers abroad aren't much; but
where to find replacements? You know we lack suitable men for all places."[44] The
letter then goes on to analyze the financial structure inherited from Louis XIV, the
administration's inefficiency, the desirability of peace, unattainable as it is for the
moment.

All in all, the letter reads more like the communication of an elder statesman than
that of a thirty-three-year-old King who has been governing by himself for less than a
year. It is always easier to ignore these kinds of problems than to face them, and yet
Louis XV was quite ready to see things as they were. Where, unfortunately, he
wasn't qualified to remedy the problem was in his limited knowledge of the people
who could have staffed the administration. Having always led a life entirely hemmed
in by the rigors of etiquette, the King literally did not know where to find the people
he needed: he was limited to the courtiers, the civil servants already in place and
their relatives. Clearly, the administration needed an infusion of middle-class blood;
but in 1743 Louis XV had no access to the most intelligent, best educated and most
dynamic section of his subjects.

By mid-summer, the King was longing to go and lead one of the armies: Louis XV,
the maréchal de Noailles and Mme de La Tournelle formed a powerful trio; but duty
came first, and that meant staying at Versailles. When, on July 24, he received yet
another appeal from Noailles, he replied with great sense and dignity: "I am accustomed to holding myself back when I desire something which has not, until now,
been possible, or at least which has not been believed such, and I will also hold
myself back on this one, although I can assure you I have the strongest desire to
acquaint myself with a profession at which my forefathers have been so successful
and at which, until now, I have not done well by procuration."[45] By way of explanation, we should remember that thus far France was merely helping the Emperor:
officially it wasn't yet at war with anyone. It would not have looked well, therefore,
nor would it have helped whatever tiny chance of peace there might be, if the King
led his armies in person. It was all highly frustrating.

The maréchal de Noailles, however, soon found that his ally at Court was growing
more effective at just about this time, and that increased the possibility of the King's
move to headquarters. All through the spring and early summer, Mme de La

Tournelle had been impressing the King by her quick intelligence and good sense, so that the love affair was enriched by trust, shared preoccupations and friendship. A corresponding—and well-earned—rise in the mistress's status was now in the offing. Already in July 17, she wrote Richelieu: "My great business [a proposed dukedom] has gone no further . . . The King has told the Comptroller General to look for an estate with a twenty thousand livres income [as territorial support for the title]; apparently he hasn't found it yet."[46] By October the estate had been found and, on the twenty-first the marquise de La Tournelle was created duchesse de Châteauroux. Even before she received her new title, however, she had started her own correspondence with the maréchal de Noailles. In an impetuous, often ungrammatical, style, amid a welter of spectacular spelling mistakes, she made her position quite clear: "I know quite well, M. le maréchal," she wrote, "that you have better things to do than read my letters and yet I flatter myself that you will sacrifice a moment of your time both to read and answer them, it will be a proof of friendship which will mean a great deal to me, the King was kind enough to tell me about your proposal that he set off for the army soon, but don't worry, though a woman I can keep a secret, I am much your friend and think it would be glorious for him and that he alone can lead his troops the way they should be led . . . As for a desire to go, I can assure you that it is not lacking, but what I myself would like is to see it generally approved.

"If the King goes to the army, it should be very quick there is not a moment to be lost. What will I become? Would it be impossible for my sister and I to follow him? At least, if we cannot go with him to the army, could we have news of him every day?

"Please advise me for I do not want to do anything . . . for which he might be blamed and that will make him look ridiculous."[47] All in all, an impressive letter. Mme de La Tournelle (as she still was) makes no attempt at using her position to overawe the maréchal; she is clearly anxious to do whatever is best for the King; and her desire to follow him, while it can be attributed to pure self-interest, in fact most probably indicates genuine feelings of love.

In his answer, Noailles, who understood all this, spoke remarkably straightforwardly. It would be a bad idea, he wrote, for the mistress to follow the King, and he added: "You see by this frank answer that I speak to you as a true friend and not as a courtier who wants to please."[48] The maréchal had understood Mme de La Tournelle while underestimating her tenacity. By return post he received this answer: "I find your letter . . . the best possible . . . sensible throughout, even to the last; but . . . I have the colic . . . and think the waters of Plombières [near the army] would be wonderful and that they alone can cure me."[49] This little difference aside, the maréchal and the mistress together made a formidable combination. A weaker man than Louis XV might well have given in to their solicitations; instead, once again, he decided against a move to headquarters.

All through the fall and winter of 1743, the new duchesse's position grew increasingly strong, and people approved. "It will all be done in the grand style, in the style of Louis XIV," Barbier noted after Mme de Châteauroux's new title was announced. "It is much more dignified for the King and for her."[50] And in December, Richelieu got his reward: he was given the highly desirable post of First Gentleman of the Bedchamber. The King was surrounded with people he knew he could trust; but even that feeling was nicely differentiated: Richelieu was fine as a pleasure companion, but he would not do as a minister; so, in spite of his burning desire and of Mme de Châteauroux's hints, the duc was kept out of the Council.

That was typical. Already as a child, Louis XV had been able to watch at first hand the self-interested maneuvers of the people around him. The exceptions—the Regent, Fleury—were so few in number that he felt quite sure about one thing: ambition, greed and egoism formed the basis of men's characters. It was no wonder, therefore, if the monarch remained secretive: there was practically no one he could trust. In 1743, most unfortunately, the ministers were no exception. Amelot, d'Argenson, even Orry—all had their axe to grind and were tied to pushy coteries, so they were all incapable of giving disinterested advice.

It is hardly pleasant for a head of state to feel that he can count on no one except, perhaps, his mistress. When, in December 1743, Louis XV sat down and wrote a long letter in answer to Charles VII's perennial complaints, much of his bitterness suddenly made its way to the surface. This is indeed a remarkable document, showing, as it does, the King's firmness in dealing with a difficult ally, his tact, and his real feelings about the actual processes of government.

"I have felt deeply all Your Majesty's reverses," he wrote the Emperor, "and will abstain from commenting on past events—that would be too sad, and one cannot reawaken these memories without going into inopportune details about the mistakes that have been made; I think I can say that neither side has been free of blame . . .

"I am sorry that Your Majesty is displeased with some of my ministers and that you distrust them. I am well aware that kings are often unhappy enough to have in the administration of their affairs people more concerned with their own particular views and interests than with the glory and true interests of their master. I neglect nothing to protect myself against these traps and always try to discover the truth, but since this misfortune is, so to speak, tied to the fact of being a ruler, let Your Majesty allow me to ask you whether you are aware that you are not yourself exempt from this problem . . .

"I find it impossible to add to the three hundred thousand livres I now give Your Majesty for your personal expenses . . . The greatness of kings lies not so much in ostentation, and doing more than one can afford, than in knowing how to make do with what one has."[51] Once again, we might be reading the words of a very old, very disillusioned king; indeed, it seems difficult, at first, to make them fit with what we know of Louis XV: this handsome, strong young man; happy in love, hunting, building; the affectionate father of a large family, who, after a long wait, was finally ruling as he pleased. In fact, what this letter reveals is the contradiction at the center of the King's life: he was at the same time a thoroughly cynical and experienced monarch who had been on the throne for nearly thirty years, and a shy, self-conscious belated adolescent, often unwilling to assert himself against the views of supposedly competent men. Not trusting himself or others, he was naturally unwilling to reveal himself; and, like all shy people, he found it virtually impossible to criticize someone to his face. In fairly short order, his ministers began to feel the consequences of this problem: the King listened to them and often adopted their views in place of his own; but once he found out that the advice in question had been self-serving, or simply incompetent, then, without a word of warning, the offending councillor found himself removed to the outer darkness of exile.

The first instance of this process took place, suddenly, on April 23, 1744, when Amelot, the incompetent Foreign minister, was brusquely dismissed. "M. Amelot was sent away yesterday at midnight," d'Argenson noted. "The [other] ministers are trembling."[52] Unfortunately, as the King now found out, it was easier to fire a minister than to replace him: it was the curse of the forties that so few competent men seemed available. First, Louis XV turned to M. de Villeneuve, an experienced diplomat who had been Ambassador to Turkey and had negociated the Treaty of Belgrade; but Villeneuve was old, tired and unwilling to shoulder the burden. Time passed until, finally, in November, on the recommendation of the Premier Commis (permanent under secretary) of the ministry of Foreign Affairs, the King appointed our old acquaintance the marquis d'Argenson, brother of the War minister and a man of undoubted intelligence. Unfortunately, d'Argenson, who had been devoured by envy when he was out of office, became equally resentful at his lack of success once in power and turned out to be that most disastrous of all possible foreign ministers: a man with a bee in his bonnet. His dreams included an Italian federation; a European code; the abasement of Spain, for which he professed a violent and unreasonable hatred; and, generally, French preponderance. As the King eventually realized, none of these were attainable, or even desirable, goals.

Amelot's overdue dismissal, was accompanied by another, equally long-awaited change. After many arguments from Noailles and Mme de Châteauroux, Louis XV finally decided to join the army. Few doubted that he would do well. "The King . . . left yesterday at three in the morning," one of his pages reported on May 4, 1744. "There is no doubt that he will enjoy the war since he likes hard work and drives himself so hard . . . M. le Dauphin and Mesdames [i.e., the King's daughters] were much saddened by the King's departure. M. le Dauphin had tears in his eyes when he came from the King . . . He is desperate because he can't accompany his father [the Dauphin was not quite fifteen years old]."[53] Several key members of Louis XV's entourage did accompany him: Richelieu, the duc d'Ayen, the marquis de Meuse and —because even at the front etiquette survived—the duc de Gesvres, First Gentleman of the Bedchamber, and Prince Charles of Lorraine, the First Equerry. The one person who most wanted to be with him, however, found herself left behind. "How happy you are, M. le maréchal, you are with the King; how unhappy your Ritournelle* is, she is away from the King,"[54] Mme de Châteauroux moaned on May 11. Not for nothing were she and Noailles allies, though: already on the sixteenth she was thanking the maréchal for a first news bulletin, and on June 3 she was able to add: "Everything you tell me about the King delights me but does not surprise me. I was quite sure that as soon as he became better known, he would be adored: the one is the necessary consequence of the other."[55]

The King's mistress might, perhaps, be expected to sing his praises, but, as it happened, she was one voice in a universal chorus. There could be no doubt: in his first stay with the army, Louis XV was proving an enormous success. "All people talk

---

* A nickname based on a pun: a ritournelle is a catchy little tune; the duchesse had been Mme de La Tournelle.

about here is the King's actions," Barbier noted back in Paris. "He is extraordinarily cheerful, he has visited all the fortresses around Valenciennes, the hospitals, the warehouses. He has tasted the broth given to the wounded, the soldiers' bread. That should force suppliers to be honest. He wants to know all the officers and speaks to them with kindness. Apparently the King is to stay with the army until October, and there is no question of women."[56]

That, however, was one development the woman-in-chief was working hard to alter. On June 3, she already felt sure that the King would soon allow her to follow him but she worried all the same. "Does the King look as if he thinks about me?" she wrote Richelieu. "Does he speak of me often? Does he miss seeing me? You can surely tell whether he does. As for me, I couldn't be more pleased with him. It would be impossible to be a more faithful correspondent, or more trusting and friendly, but I draw no consequences from all this: the moment when one fools someone else is often that in which one makes the greatest efforts to hide it . . . In truth, I wasn't made for all this and, from time to time, I become terribly discouraged. If I didn't love the King as I do, I would be sorely tempted to drop everything. I'm telling you the truth; I couldn't love him more."[57] It was obviously in Richelieu's interest to have Mme de Châteauroux join the King, and the maréchal de Noailles, who had earlier been opposed to the move, now concurred: he hoped to succeed Amelot as Foreign Affairs minister and the duchesse, if present, would plead his cause. Faced with this consensus, the King hesitated no longer. By the end of the month, Mme de Châteauroux was within easy reach.

Of course, the public disapproved. While Louis XIV had set a precedent, he had taken not just his mistress along but the Queen as well. This time, there was no question of having Marie Leczinska leave Versailles; she was the very last person Louis XV wanted to see. As it was, Mme de Châteauroux remained commendably inconspicuous; and while she happily saw that the King loved her as much as ever, she also began to realize that he was even harder to influence than usual. Carefully, she abstained from backing Noailles's appointment as Foreign minister. As for her attempts to have Maurepas dismissed (Richelieu hated him), her failure was total: evidently the King could discriminate between good advice and selfish suggestions.

All this was apparent even from afar. "The public has not approved of Mme de Châteauroux's departure," Barbier noted, "but one must admit that there are always many people in Paris who so like always to criticize that they are angry because we have done well so far, and they no longer know what to say about the King since the marked development of all his good qualities of courage, of caring and kindness for his troops, of concern for all the details, of politeness for the officers and of hard work in all the business of war."[58] Even the marquis d'Argenson, still, at that moment, pining for office, wrote: "The King seems attentive, brave, he talks to his troops, is thoughtful, exact, hardworking and, above everything, discreet."[59] That last had always been one of Louis XV's characteristics, but his other qualities, which, until then, had had little occasion to show themselves, were at long last coming into the open. It was, after all, one thing not to spare yourself when you went hunting and quite another to be tireless when commanding an army. Similarly, the kindness known heretofore only by a few privileged courtiers was at last experienced by officers and men alike. Indeed, Mme de Châteauroux was right: to know him was to love him.

If anything, the King seemed too courageous, too forgetful of danger. "God grant that he no longer expose himself [to enemy fire] as he has done until now," one of his pages wrote before going on to tell a typical story. "The King just made a fine answer to M. de Chevreuse. He had just received a letter from M. de Fouzy, commander of the deer-hunting equipage, telling him about the latest hunt which they had in order to stay in shape. It ended by saying that they had missed their deer. M. de Chevreuse told the King he wasn't doing the same with the army. The King answered: 'With the equipage I have here, I may not miss.' "[60] The King was referring to the war, naturally, and it was typical of him thus to praise his troops.

During the year and a half stretching from Fleury's death to that day in July, Louis XV had, after a long wait, truly become king. Free at last of the most enduring of his mentors, with no one to whom he felt the need to defer, the monarch, at the age of thirty-three, had begun to exercise his craft and had learned much in doing so. Many problems now faced him. The ministers (Orry excepted) were incompetent, lazy or frivolous. The machinery of government, sluggish at best, sometimes seemed altogether paralyzed. It now looked as if France itself might soon be attacked. Still, no one was very worried. The two main armies, one with the King in Flanders, the other in Alsace, were strong, well supplied and adequately led. The King's very presence, by spurring officers and men to greater efforts, was a real asset. It was possible to expect victories, therefore, and perhaps a relatively early end to the war. Clearly Louis XV's personal reign was beginning under favorable auspices. Always popular, the King was now literally beloved by all the French. Of his two predecessors, one had been called "the Just," and the other "the Great." Now Louis XV had become *le bien-aimé,* "the Beloved." He could have had no finer title.

Chapter Six

The World Upside Down

POPULAR and conscientious though he might be in the early summer of 1744, the King had few illusions about his need for competent generals and ministers. At least when it came to the war, all the signs were promising: not only were the troops fired by the monarch's presence, but France had at least two exceptional commanders, the maréchal de Saxe, unquestionably a military genius, and the maréchal de Noailles, whose experience—he had first led troops in the War of the Spanish Succession some forty years earlier—and natural caution seemed the perfect complement for Saxe's ardor. Seen at close range, however, the situation became distinctly less rosy. It was fast becoming evident that Noailles understood Court intrigues better than military maneuvers—even his own son, the duc d'Ayen, had begun to criticize him— while the maréchal de Saxe let everyone know that he loathed his fellow commander. Since France had a long history of battles lost because its generals failed to work together, it was now clear that it was all up to the King. Only he could make decisions that both generals would respect.

It was precisely at this juncture that the character of the war suddenly changed. So far, the French had been cheerfully, if slowly, taking a few towns in the Austrian Netherlands; now, suddenly, an Austrian army under Francis of Lorraine's brother began to move towards the eastern borders of France. Since Noailles's army was too small to offer more than token resistance, it became necessary to shift both men and headquarters to the crucial provinces of Alsace and Lorraine. In late July, the King moved to Metz, while finding himself faced with an increasing amount of work. It wasn't just that he had to run the war, control his Foreign minister, settle the endless disputes between Argenson and Noailles, make sure that finances and supplies were in order and attend to such ceremonial duties as the reception of a loyal deputation from the Parlement; even the smallest matters were routinely referred to him. In early July, for instance, an anxious query reached him: a few ladies were entitled to be presented at Court, but they had, in fact, not yet been through the ceremony. Might they eat with the Queen and ride in her carriages nonetheless? And might Mme de La Guiche, who had been presented to the King years ago, but not to the

Queen, behave as if she had been? In this case, the carefully thought out answers were a no and a yes: no to the ladies as yet unpresented to His Majesty—they would have to wait; yes to Mme de La Guiche—she could be presented to the Queen even though the King was away.[1]

That the King found it increasingly easy to deal with this was obvious to all present. He had never seemed so interested or so cheerful and, aside from the undoubted exhilaration of ruling by himself at last, much of this was due to the presence of Mme de Châteauroux. She was cheerful, optimistic, helpful, sensible, and while she never forgot that she was, first, Louis XV's mistress, she was also turning into something like an adviser. She had become so necessary, in fact, that when headquarters moved to Metz, the King ordered a special wooden gallery built over the street which separated their two houses so that the duchesse could go back and forth without being gawked at. Of course, some people objected: it seemed neither dignified nor moral to have the King's mistress thus enthroned in the middle of the army. But when, at 5 A.M. on August 8, Louis XV woke up with a badly upset stomach, a headache and a fever, the gallery proved a great convenience: the mistress became a nurse and was able to visit the King frequently and easily.

At first, it seemed to be just another of the King's indigestion attacks, so he was given the standard remedy—repeated enemas—which resulted in "great evacuations"[2]; but since by the early afternoon his headache was, if anything, worse, and the fever remained unabated, the next step was taken. The doctors ordered a bleeding and Mme de Châteauroux spent the afternoon and evening at his bedside, chattering gaily: there was obviously nothing to worry about. That night, however, the King slept very badly. Something more was obviously needed, so, as usual, that meant yet another enema, which, we are told, had a great effect and after which he was able to sleep for two hours. When he woke up, the doctors, who knew when they were onto a good thing, decided to vary their basic treatment: this time the King was given emetic and made to vomit. That, according to medical theory, should have completed his cure, but, to his attendants' growing dismay, Louis XV complained that his headache was now much more painful. That night, as his fever rose, it became clear that he was getting worse, not better. At 1 A.M. on the tenth, therefore, the physicians decided on a second bleeding, which seemed to help a little; this was followed, at six, by a strong laxative.

The King's fever kept rising rapidly, however, so on the eleventh he was purged repeatedly and bled once again. This time, apparently, the treatment had some effect. On the twelfth, both headache and fever seemed a little improved, but the doctors, who were all the more worried in that they were accustomed to see their patients drop like flies, called in two local experts, Drs. Maugin and Castera, who predictably recommended more bleedings and purgings.

All this would have been serious enough if the King had been an ordinary patient; now the situation was considerably worsened by two related problems. The first was that, sick though the monarch might be, the sacrosanct etiquette still applied; the second, that if he came close enough to dying, the King would probably dismiss Mme de Châteauroux, thus dramatically changing the balance of power at Court. Naturally, both factions, pro and anti Châteauroux, were fully aware of this. "From the beginning of the King's illness until the twelfth," the duc de Luynes noted, "the two sisters [Mmes de Châteauroux and de Lauraguais], M. de Richelieu (who was alone present for the doctors' consultations) and the lower servants were the only people allowed into the King's bedroom. The Princes of the Blood Royal [the duc de Chartres and the comte de Clermont, M. le Duc's brother] and the great officers* were upset by this. The King's aides-de-camp formed still another party: they were for M. de Richelieu, and among them was the duc d'Aumont. The great officers were M. de Bouillon, the First Equerry, M. de La Rochefoucauld, M. de Villeroy and some others who thought they had reason to complain, especially since they were deprived of the right [of access to the royal bedroom] inherent to their offices. Both parties met in the room preceding the King's bedroom without speaking to each other. Finally, the matter was brought to Mme de Châteauroux's attention and she was reminded both of the rules and of the importance of keeping up appearances. She merely answered that if the rules were to be followed, she would be barred from the King's bedroom. Under these circumstances, the comte de Clermont took it upon himself to go in; he told His Majesty that he could not believe that his [i.e., the King's] intention was that the Princes of the Blood and the great officers . . . be deprived of the satisfaction of seeing how he was with their own eyes; that they had no wish to be importunate but merely wanted to come in for a moment now and again; and that, in order to prove that he himself had no other aim, he would withdraw immediately. The King, far from appearing offended by this speech, told M. le comte de Clermont that he could stay, and the usual order was reinstated."[3]

This was a clear victory for the anti-Châteauroux party, and a wholly predictable one: the King was much too dutiful to escape even the most distasteful of obligations. The next step was now perfectly obvious. If the King's life was in danger, then he must confess and receive the last rites, and that, in turn, must be preceded by the dismissal of his mistress. Already on the twelfth, therefore, the Bishop of Soissons, the First Almoner,** told the King in no uncertain terms that it was time to repent. At this point, although he was undoubtedly feeling very ill, the King did not think that his life was in danger, and he was quite shrewd enough to see what M. de Soissons was up to, so he answered that he was weak, that his head hurt dreadfully, and that a full confession would be too taxing. Nothing loath, the Bishop suggested that the King could start now and finish the next day. Still, he was rebutted, but later that afternoon, as Mme de Châteauroux sat by his bed, the King took her hand, kissed it and said: "I think I may be doing wrong, Princess"; and when the duchesse tried to kiss him, he pushed her away, adding: "We may have to separate."[4] The Church was well on its way to victory.

Of course, some people believed that the Bishop of Soissons was merely doing what he saw as his duty: after all, the King, by taking on a concubine, had placed himself in a state of sin and thereby removed himself from taking communion. Were he to die suddenly, and unshriven, he would be damned (which would be unpleasant for him) and become a subject of scandal at a time when the most enlightened people in France were busy deriding the very notion that there was a hell. There can be very little doubt, on the other hand, that the Bishop, who, by virtue of his office, spent most of his time at Court, could see a radically different kind of government in the

* I.e., the Captain of the Guard, the Chamberlain, the First Gentlemen of the Bedchamber et al.
** The Grand Almoner, the cardinal de Rohan, was away in Strasbourg.

middle distance, one in which the Church would be very powerful indeed, the
Queen influential, and some lucky cleric Prime Minister; so he pressured a very sick
man quite remorselessly. Since the King was still under the influence of Fleury's
precepts, he was more ready to listen than most people thought.

One thing, at any rate, was certain. He must not, he could not die without the last
rites. During the night of the twelfth to the thirteenth, his fever rose so rapidly that
he was bled again. Three bleedings were thought to denote a very serious illness, and
this was already the fifth. Without further ado, therefore, Louis XV sent for his
confessor. While he was waiting, he fainted repeatedly: there was obviously no time
to be lost. As soon as he revived, he confessed and gave the expected orders: Mmes
de Châteauroux and de Lauraguais were to leave Metz. It was then arranged that the
last rites be administered that evening, but when the time came, M. de Soissons,
having ascertained that the duchesse was still in town, refused to administer them.
Instead, he went back to the King's bedroom and told him that "all the laws of the
Church and all the canons explicitly forbade the last rites being administered while
the concubine was still within the city."[5] He therefore demanded of the dying man
that he give new orders. Of course, the King complied; but for good measure the
Bishop warned Mme de Châteauroux that he would let the people know that she
alone was keeping the King in a state of sin. It was as good as telling her that she
would be torn limb from limb if she delayed another moment; even as it was, the
poor woman had to borrow a carriage and flee in disguise so as not to be recognized.

At this point, M. de Soissons's real purpose became blindingly clear. That line
about canon law was, of course, unadulterated bilge: the King, having renounced his
concubine, had done all that was required of him; as for the message sent to Mme de
Châteauroux, it speaks for itself. And just in case all this hadn't been unchristian
enough, the Bishop now proceeded to organize a shameful charade designed to
smooth the Church's political path. Not only was the King forced to give new orders
for the duchesse's departure, he was also made to speak a declaration of repentance
without which, he was told, he need not expect the last rites. In front of all his court,
therefore, Louis XV was made to beg forgiveness for his scandalous behavior and the
bad example he had set, to recognize that he was unworthy of being called the Most
Christian King and the Eldest Son of the Church, and, finally, to reiterate his order
that Mme de Châteauroux stay away from Metz. An *amende honorable,*[6]* Barbier
called it, and he was right. The scandal of this forced and public confession was far
greater than that of the original transgression, and it showed the Church in the worst
possible light. Away in Paris, Barbier went on to record the general opinion: "I think
[M. de Soissons's] behavior was highly indecent," he wrote late in August, "and
consider this sudden and public repentance as a scandal in itself. The good name of a
King must be respected and he must be allowed to die, not only religiously but also
with dignity and majesty. What use is this clerical show? It was enough for the King
to feel, inside, sincerely repentant . . . I do not know what may happen after three
months of perfect health, but I find this behavior thoughtless and imprudent; it gives
too much power to the Church over a ruler in that critical moment."[7] Barbier was

* An amende honorable was the speech of public repentance demanded of criminals before their execution.

perfectly right, of course. The Bishop of Soissons, with the help of his colleague of Metz, had taken shameful advantage of a very sick man.

Far from beginning to feel better after he had received the last rites, the King now began to sink further. For the next two weeks he remained at death's door; it was August 26 before a very slight improvement was noticed. That day, for the first time, the King was well enough to be shaved; and he began to remember and resent, in particular, the Dauphin's appearance at his bedside against his express orders. Once again, the intrigue was all too clear: if a shamed, broken monarch slipped between the Church's hands, at least his heir was young enough to learn his lesson by witnessing his father's humiliation.

Still, there were two consolations for the King as, slowly, he began to convalesce: the Austrian army was beaten before it could cross the French border, and the people, throughout his illness, had demonstrated their love for him in the most visible ways. "It is impossible adequately to depict the agitation, the worry, the affliction of the people," the duc de Luynes noted. "In Paris, as in the provinces, the couriers are stopped and not allowed to proceed until they have given their news; they are kissed when it is good . . . Never has a people shown more affection for its master."[8] And Barbier described "an alarm and consternation beyond all expression, and that in all classes, the great, the bourgeoisie, the people. All through the fifteenth and the sixteenth, the post office was surrounded with people and carriages who were waiting for the couriers . . . Everyone had tears in their eyes . . . Never will the King have a more evident and more dazzling proof of the love and attachment of his people."[9]

As soon as Louis XV was known to be out of danger, there was an explosion of joy throughout the kingdom. Everywhere the streets were filled with people laughing and rejoicing. On September 10, for instance, a leaflet printed in Paris informs us: "A Te Deum was celebrated [at Notre Dame] in honor of the King's recovery and fireworks were shown in the Place de l'Hôtel de Ville which were superior to anything yet seen in this city. The same evening . . . all the houses were illuminated . . . The words 'Long live Louis the Beloved' were written everywhere in letters of fire and announced that the nation was conferring on its monarch a title which is above all others and contains them all. All through the night, the streets were filled not only with the people, who were shouting for joy, but with the nobility and bourgeoisie, who wanted to share in the public rejoicing . . . The foreigners who saw how much the French love their King must have thought that France would be a fearful enemy indeed."[10] And later that month, Barbier wrote: "In this city of Paris it goes on and on. There is no body or community whatsoever that does not order a Te Deum . . . and the day it is celebrated all the windows of the private houses are illuminated; this is true even of the carriers of the Pont Saint Bernard . . . The goldsmiths and jewelers gave a splendid celebration on the fourteenth of this month. The Place Dauphine was beautifully adorned and illuminated, and all along the quays and the rue de Harlay there were chandeliers instead of streetlights, and in the middle of the square a building was put up where they gave a concert around ten at night."[11] In November, when Louis XV made his official entry into Paris, the ceremonies started all over again. "We entered Paris by torchlight in the midst of an amazingly large crowd that was cheering everywhere," one of the King's pages recorded tersely. "The King went to Notre Dame, preceded by the four red companies [of musketeers] and followed by the Queen, M. le Dauphin and Mesdames de France."[12] Once again there were fireworks, balls, speeches and endless shouts of "Long live the King." Whatever the Bishop of Soissons may have been feeling at that moment (probably acute disappointment), there could be no doubt that the French loved their monarch passionately.

Very naturally, Louis XV resented the public apology forced on him when he was more than half dead, and M. de Soissons's career suffered accordingly, as did that of the Dauphin's governor, the duc de Châtillon. Blithely disregarding an order to stop at Châlons, he had brought his charge to Metz and then compounded his disobedience by hiding the Dauphin's presence from the King, who, some three or four days later, discovered, quite by accident, that his son was in the same house; so, early in November the duc found himself exiled to his country estate. Then there was the Queen, who had been repeatedly asking for permission to join her husband: it was finally granted, but then, during the King's convalescence, a plot to reunite the royal couple became a topic of gossip at Court. The King heard all about it and when Marie Leczinska was seen to wear pink ribbons and blush heavily whenever she approached her spouse, that disgusted monarch reacted by treating her with particular coolness. "The Queen tried again for the King's permission to accompany him to Strasbourg. The King answered as coldly as before: 'It isn't worth it, I will only stay there a short time.' She then asked whether at least she could stay on here [at her father's castle of Lunéville] and he answered in the same voice: 'You will leave three or four days after I do.' The Queen is . . . very upset by so harsh a response."[13] Finally, there was the maréchal de Noailles. At first he seemed to be as much in favor as ever, the King even writing him on August 30, only four days after his recovery had begun; but then he found out that, as he lay half dead, Noailles had been feuding with the ministers and mismanaging his army. By September 26 Louis XV had become fully aware of all this and he snubbed the maréchal accordingly: as he prepared to leave Metz for Lunéville, and then Strasbourg, Noailles came up to him and asked for permission to go along. "Do as you please," the King said coldly and turned away.

More astonishing, perhaps, was the fact that despite the Bishop's behavior, the King remained as pious as ever. In that August 30 letter to the maréchal de Noailles, for instance, he wrote: "You will find me struggling to come back; it is very true that it is from death's door. It was not without regret that I heard about the Battle of the Rhine; but God did not want me to be there and I have obeyed Him willingly, for it is very true that He is the master of all things, but a good master."[14] That this deeply felt faith would stop at chastity, however, soon become reasonably clear. By November, the King was not only fully recovered, he was also back at Versailles: would he now call Mme de Châteauroux back to him? It was, not unnaturally, the question asked by everyone at Court; as for the duchesse herself, she was not in much doubt. Already on September 13 she was writing the duc de Richelieu: "Don't worry, my dear uncle, you are about to see some events highly pleasing to us. We have had some very difficult times, but they are over. I do not know the King when he is pious, but I

The comte d'Argenson, Louis XV's long-lasting minister of War, was an accomplished courtier who made the great mistake of thinking he could vanquish Mme de Pompadour.

〜〜　〜〜

The maréchal de Saxe, under whose inspired leadership the French Army went from triumph to triumph. The King, besides admiring him, was also very fond of him.

MARIE THERESE
Reine de Hongrie,&c.
Née le 13 Mai 1717

The Empress Maria Theresa, whose letter to Louis XV started the great reversal of alliances and who was wise enough to trust Mme de Pompadour as the most effective and discreet of go-betweens.

The Yew Tree Ball. The King, seen at the right as one of the topiary yew trees, left the ball

Rameau, the great composer whose music the King loved, worked, time and again, for the Court; many of his operas received their first performance at Versailles.

RAMEAU.

hat night with Mme d'Etioles. From then on,
he new favorite never looked back.

The cardinal de Bernis, the frivolous
abbé who, in a surprising transformation, became first a competent ambassador and then the Foreign minister who
negotiated the new Austrian alliance.

Voltaire, the most brilliant and most
famous of French intellectuals, soon
fell from favor after his introduction at
Court by Mme de Pompadour.

VOLTAIRE

Decoration of the theater set up for the celebration of the Dauphin's wedding in 1745.

Ceremonie du Mariage de Louis Dauphin de France avec Marie Therese Infante d'Espagne. à Versailles le XXIII Fevrier MDCCXLV.

The Dauphin's Wedding. The Dauphin is seen here marrying the short-lived Marie Thérèse of Spain with all the customary pomp.

Louis Auguste
Dauphin de France,
né à Versailles 23 Août 1754.

Louis Auguste, Dauphin of France.
Louis XV's only son who, despite
a little shyness, greatly loved
his father. His death was a great
blow to the King.

AUTRE VUE DU CHATE
DU BORD DE LA RIVIERE
Présentée à Madame

The château of Bellevue, one of
Mme de Pompadour's favorite houses, was
a showplace for all the arts.

Jean Benjamin DE LABORDE
Premier Valet de Chambre
du Roi, et Gouvᵉʳ du Louvre

Laborde, First Valet de Chambre
to the King and, as such, one
of the men closest to him.

The duc de Choiseul. He was Mme de Pompadour's greatest gift to Louis XV. An exceptionally talented minister at first, he was subsequently corrupted by his own ambition and had to be dismissed in December 1770.

ETIENNE-FRANÇOIS   DUC DE CHOISEUL.

DE BELLE-VUE, PRISE -
PROCHE LE PONT DE SEVE.
la Marquise de Pompadour

After the marquise's death, it reverted to the Crown and was eventually given to Mesdames.

Soldier presenting arms according to the new rules edicted by Choiseul and approved by the King.

Equestrian statue of Louis XV erected in the center of the Place de la Concorde to celebrate both the King's reign and the completion of the buildings by Jacques Ange Gabriel.

do know that he is kind and very well able to feel friendship. No matter what his thought may be, I suspect, without flattering myself, that they will redound to my advantage; he knows that he can count on me, and is very sure that I love him for himself, and he is quite right, too, for I realized that I love him passionately, but what matters is that he knows it . . . Until now, I alone have understood his heart, and I can assure you that it is both kind and feeling."[15]

In fact, at that date the King was still hardly strong enough to think about his mistress: it was not until two days later that he walked out of his room for the first time. Throughout October and early November, he was clearly undecided. Although he obviously realized that adultery wasn't much of a sin, still, he seemed unwilling to sin at all. Even after the Queen's ridiculous display at Metz, Louis XV made an attempt at reconciliation. "Last night," Luynes recorded on November 15, "someone came three times to scratch at the door between the Queen's apartment and the King's. The Queen's ladies warned her about this, but she answered that they were mistaken, and that the noise they heard was due to the wind. That noise having occurred a third time, the Queen, after waiting for a while, ordered the door opened, but no one was there."[16] One can hardly blame the King for having given up; and the consequences were immediate. On November 18, the duchesse de Brancas, one of Mme de Châteauroux's best friends, was appointed dame d'honneur to the future Dauphine: it was a pretty broad hint, and the Court realized that the favorite would soon be back in place. By the twenty-sixth, everyone knew that the duchesse was returning to Versailles and that her office as Superintendent of the Dauphine's Household, which she had lost at Metz, would be given back to her. On the twenty-seventh, the King, as a clear mark of her return to power, sent her Maurepas with the message that her apartment at Versailles was awaiting her. This was a particularly significant choice. Maurepas had opposed Mme de Châteauroux from the start. Now he was sent on what was, for him, the most humiliating mission possible. Just what happened next we hear from the ever curious duc de Luynes, who had it directly from Maurepas himself. "When [Maurepas] arrived at the door of the duchesse's house in Paris, he asked whether she was at home. He was told that she wasn't. He then named himself and was told again that no one was at home. Finally, he said that he had been sent by the King, and the doors were then opened to him . . . [When he came in to Mme de Châteauroux's room, he talked] about the bad opinion of him she might have been given, and of the embarrassment he felt in appearing before her for that very reason, and then he asked to kiss her hand. When she heard the word 'embarrassment,' Mme de Châteauroux answered that it was no wonder; then she gave him her hand to kiss and said: 'This hasn't cost you much.' "[17] What she meant, of course, was that a little humiliation was nothing compared to dismissal and exile, a fate which he might well have expected.

Obviously, the reversal was now complete. The favorite was about to be more powerful than ever, but while she rejoiced, her pleasure was sharply curtailed: for the past few days she had been feeling very unwell. During the next three days, she grew steadily worse, was racked by a high fever and symptoms not unlike the King's five months earlier. By December 1, it was obvious that she was very ill indeed, and, away in Versailles, Louis XV began to look both sad and concerned. On the fifth, the

King was too worried to go hunting or even to hold court. Except for Mass, he never once appeared in public, but stayed in his private apartments, anxiously waiting for the news brought to him hourly by the duc d'Ayen, the maréchal de Luxembourg and the marquis de Gontaut. By the sixth, it became clear that no recovery was possible; the duchesse was now tortured by dreadful stomach pains and a burning thirst; on the seventh, she went into convulsions; at 10 A.M. on December 10 she expired.

Louis XV was devastated. Unable to face anyone, he promptly left Versailles for La Muette, where he could weep in private. "The King is in a state of sorrow which makes one feel compassion" Luynes noted on the tenth, and on the eleventh: "The King is staying at La Muette . . . . He hardly eats anything and spends his days shut in with only four or five people who were close to Mme de Châteauroux; they are M. d'Ayen, M. de Gontaut, M. de Luxembourg and M. de La Vallière."[18] On the twelfth; "The King's sorrow [was] even worse than before."[19] By December 18, Louis XV, still avoiding the Court, moved to Trianon; he was not back at Versailles until the twenty-second.

Once again, power had shifted, only this time no one knew whither; the only certainty was that all was uncertain. On the one hand, it was clear that the King would not return to the Queen, that he would not look to the Church for a Prime Minister, and that Mme de Châteauroux's friends, for the moment at least, remained in the ascendant; but, on the other hand, it seemed probable that the Royal Family, and especially the Dauphin, would begin to matter more. Louis XV had always been an affectionate father: might he not relieve his loneliness by spending time with his son and daughters? If he did, it would mean a revival of the Church party after all. Keen observers thought this outcome all the more likely when, on December 28, the King presented the Dauphin with a diamond plaque of the Saint Esprit. The Dauphin, whose love for his father was mixed with fear, blushed visibly, at which the King asked him why he was blushing and went on to say that he must get used to relaxing in his father's company.

Even external events seemed to partake of the overall uncertainty. Early in January, the maréchal de Belle-Isle was captured by a flying party of Hanoverian troops, thus removing a gifted but impossible general; then, on January 20, the Emperor Charles VII died: with the Imperial Crown once more available, there was clearly the possibility of a compromise; but, then again, England, which had only entered the war officially in 1744, was not much inclined to peace, while the French still hoped for a decisive victory. Here, too, no one could tell what the future might bring.

At least there was a great celebration in the offing: the Dauphin was marrying a Spanish princess, who was to arrive in mid-February. Elaborate preparations were made; there were to be balls, fireworks, displays of all kinds, and people ordered themselves the most dazzling new clothes. "Some men's suits," Barbier reported, "cost up to 15,000 livres [$67,500]; they will need three, one for each day [of the festivities]. M. de Mirepoix . . . has rented three suits that he will only wear one day each and then return to the tailor for 6,000 livres [$27,000]. M. le marquis de Stainville has a suit of cloth of silver embroidered in gold and lined with marten. The lining alone is said to cost 25,000 livres [$112,500]."[20]

When the new Dauphine, Marie Thérèse of Spain, did arrive, she was found satisfactory by the King and Court; as for the Dauphin, he instantly fell headlong in love. Better still, when supper succeeded supper, she was seen to talk well and cheerfully, to hold her place with unassuming dignity and to reciprocate the Dauphin's looks of adoration. Together the Royal Family left Etampes, where they had met the princess, for Sceaux, then on to Versailles, where, after a morning wedding ceremony, there was a play, a ballet and a public supper before the newlyweds were put to bed. The next evening there was a *bal paré,* the grandest of Court balls, in the Hall of Mirrors, and the evening after that a masked ball, which the Queen attended dressed as a shepherdess but covered with large diamonds. Throughout it all, the King, it was noticed, was in the best of humor; but only the uninformed (that is to say, most everybody) thought that his obvious contentment was caused solely by his son's marriage.

For those who watched that masked ball carefully, however, there were clues too obvious to be ignored. While the Queen and her daughters had made no attempt at hiding their real identity, the King, on the other hand, was determined to remain anonymous; so, in mid-evening one of the glass doors of the Hall of Mirrors opened and out filed twelve identical figures dressed to look exactly like the topiary yew trees which adorned the park outside. One of these walking hedges was obviously Louis XV, but which? In short order, the yews went their separate ways, and that night eleven ladies found out—too late—that their particular tree, while undoubtedly noble, was, alas, not royal. The twelfth yew, however, was seen to spend time with a pretty young woman from Paris, one Mme d'Etioles. When the couple walked out, the people closest to them saw the yew's headdress come off: it was Louis XV, and he was obviously about to spend the night with the pretty Parisian.

Of course, the news spread very quickly. People, Luynes noted, "have been speaking of the King's new love affair, and mostly about a Mme d'Etioles, who is young and pretty. Her mother was called Mme Poisson.* They say that she has lately been spending much time in *ce pays-ci*** and that she is the King's new choice; if that is true, she will probably be just a passing fancy and not a proper mistress."[21] The duc's attitude was reasonable: while it was well understood that kings might go to bed with pretty young women of the lower or middle classes, the latter were obviously debarred, by their lack of pedigree and their ignorance of Court manners, from ever occupying the position of a maîtresse déclarée. Even Louis XIV, who was well known to attack every pretty chambermaid in sight, had limited himself to ladies of the Court when it came to picking a proper mistress. Louis XV, up to this point, had not only stayed within the circle of the ladies presented at Court but had actually chosen all his mistresses within a single family, the Mailly-Nesles. Still, there was something about the young woman which struck people. "I have met one of the prettiest young women I have ever laid eyes on," the Président Hénault, a connoisseur, wrote Mme du Deffand. "Her name is Mme d'Etioles. She knows music to perfection, she sings with all the cheerfulness and taste imaginable, knows a hundred songs and acts in plays at Etioles in a theater as handsome as that of the Opéra."[22] Clearly, the lady was no ordinary amour.

* Mrs. Fish, a very plebian name.
** This country, i.e., the Court.

That she belonged to the middle class, however, was undeniable. Her father, M. Poisson, had been a financier who eventually went bankrupt. Her mother, also a remarkably pretty woman, became the mistress of another, more successful banker, M. Lenormant; in due time, with M. Lenormant's enthusiastic concurrence, she married her daughter Antoinette (who was born in 1721) to M. Lenormant's nephew and heir, M. d'Etioles. The young couple moved out to their château of Etioles, some ten miles outside the city, and proceeded to make it one of the very best houses in or around Paris. Money was no object and Mme d'Etioles, as people quickly realized, understood just how to make life pleasant. The rooms in which she moved were beautifully appointed, the food she served was superb, her gardens were enchanting, and she understood how best to entertain her visitors. In an age when everyone was mad for the theater, she was a gifted amateur actress, sang beautifully and played several musical instruments. Besides all that, she had charm, wit, dazzling beauty and an obviously sweet disposition. It was no wonder that all the upper crust of the middle class flocked to her parties, especially since she realized that having the leading Paris intellectuals as her guests added something rare and inimitable to her entertainments. In no time at all, Voltaire was making his way to Etioles.

That kind of success would have been enough for almost everyone; Mme d'Etioles, however, had something very different in mind. When, some years earlier, Mme Poisson understood what a treasure she had in her daughter, she promptly decided that only one man in France was good enough for her. Soon her nickname was, eloquently enough, Reinette ("Queenie"), and M. d'Etioles, although convenient, was obviously only temporary. Soon after her wedding, in fact, Antoinette made her first attempt: when Louis XV went hunting in the forest of Sénart, near Etioles, he sometimes found that his path crossed that of a most elegant young woman. At times she wore a blue dress and rode in a pink carriage; sometimes it was the carriage that was blue and the dress pink; in any event, it would have been quite difficult not to notice her. Soon, this interesting development was reported to Mme de Châteauroux, who caused a few hints to be dropped; after that, Mme d'Etioles decided that she didn't like the forest of Sénart after all.

The death of the favorite naturally changed everything. Binet, one of the King's valets de chambre, was distantly related to Mme d'Etioles, so he told his master about her, arranged to have her stand in the crowd which always gathered in the Hall of Mirrors to see the King walk by, and eventually, in great secrecy, brought her to the King's private apartments. Then the impossible happened: the lonely monarch and the ambitious bourgeoise fell well and truly in love—and it is easy to see why. Louis XV, in 1745, was thirty-five years old, extraordinarily handsome, strong and athletic; he was the King; and, as Mme d'Etioles quickly discovered, he was also kind, considerate, intelligent and open-minded. No doubt she also discovered that he was also insecure and easily depressed, but she had exactly the right combination of talents to reassure and amuse. For the first time in his life, the King found himself the lover of a great beauty who was also kind—not one of Mme de Châteauroux's characteristics—good-tempered, amusing, intelligent, cultivated and sensible. Then, too, in an age when the couture house had yet to be invented, and when women largely designed their own clothes, Mme d'Etioles was utterly, splendidly elegant.

By the end of February 1745, people began to see that this might be more than just a casual affair; after the Yew Tree Ball, there had been another masked ball given by the City of Paris, where the King—who, as everyone knew, didn't like to dance—was seen to spend a great deal of time on the floor with Mme d'Etioles. Still, the consensus ran, she could never become a maitresse déclarée: her low birth disbarred her absolutely from a position where she would rule over all the titled ladies at Versailles. When the news came in April that Mme de Mailly's apartment was being redecorated, people began to catch on, and they were horrified. Since, presumably, Mme d'Etioles could hardly live in seclusion, the King must intend to have her officially presented. Of course, she could not prove the required four hundred years of nobility, but then again, the King could exempt her from the usual rule and, once presented, there was no doubt that the proudest duchesses would have to kowtow to her. As this unpleasant truth began to sink in, a number of people, who had good reasons not to want Mme d'Etioles at Versailles, began to react. They commissioned songs and pamphlets which began to flood Paris and the provinces.

These kinds of libels were nothing new, of course. In their turn, the Regent, M. le Duc and Fleury all had had to put up with similar attacks; but now there was a difference: it was the King, along with his new love, who was being personally ridiculed: "Une petite bourgeoise / Elevée à la grivoise / Et mesurant tout à sa toise / Fait de la Cour un taudis. / Le Roi malgré son scrupule / Pour elle follement brûle / Cette flamme ridicule / excite dans tout Paris, ris, ris. / Cette catin subalterne / Insolemment le gouverne . . ." ("A little bourgeoise / raised as a choice piece / who brings all down to her level / has turned the Court into a slum. / The King despite his scruples / for her madly burns / this ridiculous ardor / makes all Paris laugh, laugh. / That cheap whore / insolently rules him.")[23] For the moment it didn't matter much: the King's popularity was such that nothing could harm him, but a dangerous precedent was being set: if Louis XV was to be thus attacked every time one of the factions at Court was displeased with him, then eventually some of the mud was bound to stick.

Although, by their very nature, these libels were anonymous, it is possible to make informed guesses as to their authors and patrons. Maurepas, for instance, who was still minister of the Navy, was known for his acerbic pen and his dislike of almost everybody; the duc de Richelieu, who felt that he had lost everything with Mme de Châteauroux's death, was now busy trying to procure a new mistress for the King, so Mme d'Etioles represented an obvious menace; every great lady who had cast longing looks at the King now felt spurned and humiliated: it was a sizable cast. Still, as people met Mme d'Etioles, they began to be charmed. Georges Leroy, the *lieutenant des chasses* (head huntsman) of Versailles, for instance, stared, sat down and recorded what he had seen: "[Mme d'Etioles] was a little taller than most, slim, graceful, supple, elegant; her face was well assorted to her height, a perfect oval, beautiful hair, closer to light brown than blonde, rather large eyes with fine eyelashes of the same color, a perfectly shaped nose, a charming mouth, very beautiful teeth and the most delicious smile; the most beautiful skin in the world gave her a dazzling look. Her eyes had a peculiar charm which they may have owed to the uncertainty of their color; they did not have the lively sparkle of black eyes, the tender languor of blue eyes, the subtlety which belongs to gray eyes; their indeterminate color seemed to render them able to seduce in every possible way and to express all the feelings of a rapidly changing mood; thus her face reflected all sorts of looks, but always without any discordance between her features . . . The ensemble of her person seemed to bridge the fine line between the last degree of elegance and the first of nobility."[24] Leroy was a great womanizer, so perhaps he looked unusually hard, but everybody who met Mme d'Etioles was beginning to say very much the same thing.

Late in March, there was new proof of Mme d'Etioles's power. The King, until then, had patronized painters, sculptors, architects and composers, but he was not known to be fond of writers, especially those who were inclined to disrespect towards Church or State; suddenly, he awarded Voltaire a pension of two thousand livres a year, the office of Royal Historiographer and, far more satisfying for the socially ambitious poet, the title of Gentleman of the Bedchamber in Ordinary, which carried with it a patent of nobility.

Still, few people thought it would last: as soon as Mme d'Etioles appeared at Court, she would look so grotesquely out of place that the King would fall out of love: after all, she would not know how to walk (with a glide), talk (in a special accent with a special vocabulary), curtsy (more or less deeply), or behave politely to her fellow courtiers (she knew no one, so how could she realize that she must give precedence to the lady next to her, who happened to be a duchesse?). She would be seen for what she was: a coarse, common upstart. She might do very well in bed, but once she tried to make her way in the sophisticated world of Versailles, the King would realize he had made a mistake. Even the people who, without knowing her, sympathized with her thought that she was in well beyond her depth. Barbier, noting that she was talented and beautiful, went on: "She was adored by her uncle [M. Lenormant], and was absolute mistress in the house: I wonder whether that kind of life wasn't preferable for a bourgeoise of her sort to the position of mistress to the King. It is very satisfying to one's vanity to live at Court, but also very apt to have great drawbacks."[25]

Important though this new topic had become, however, the King, the Court and the rest of France now found they must turn their attention elsewhere. The war had been sputtering along, but it was still not over, and the fighting season was drawing near. Once more, Louis XV decided to join his army; on May 6 he set off, this time with the Dauphin, the ducs d'Ayen and de Richelieu and the marquis de Meuse; as for Mme d'Etioles, whose husband had been conveniently sent away on a business trip by M. Lenormant, she resettled herself at Etioles, called in Voltaire for company, thus making sure that she could never be bored, invited two courtiers, the marquis de Gontaut and the abbé de Bernis, to stay and proceeded to learn exactly how it was that people behaved at Versailles. It must have been a delight to teach her. She was also comforted by the arrival of long, loving letters from the King. They were, of course, addressed to Mme d'Etioles; but then, one day, as she was about to break open the seal, she noticed a difference: the envelope was addressed "A Madame la marquise de Pompadour," and it enclosed a patent for the new marquessate. The bourgeoise had just joined the ranks of the aristocracy.

Marquise though she had now become, the new Mme de Pompadour stayed home.

There could be no question of attending the Court before the King's return since, in any event, she still needed special permission to break the four-hundred-year rule; and, away in Flanders, Louis XV had resumed his occupations of the previous years. Once again, he went around the army, inspecting, encouraging, praising, rewarding; only now he found himself dealing mostly with the maréchal de Saxe, who was almost as gruff as he was competent. It must have been a pleasant change from the intrigue-prone maréchal de Noailles, especially since it seemed very likely that this year the war would take on a decisive character. Opposite the French, this time, there was an English army under the orders of the Duke of Cumberland. If it was decisively beaten, peace talks might follow. If it was victorious, France would be invaded. Throughout the first days of May, the two armies maneuvered, staying close to each other; then, on the eleventh, they finally met near Fontenoy.

"The battle began with the two armies so close to each other that the English officers, as they were about to stop their men, saluted us, their hats in their hands," one of the French officers wrote. "Our people having reciprocated this courteous gesture, Charles Hay, a Captain of the English Guards, came out of his place and moved forwards. The comte d'Auteroche, a lieutenant of grenadiers, advanced to meet him. 'Sir,' said the Captain, 'tell your people to shoot.'

" 'No, sir,' M. d'Auteroche answered, 'we never shoot first.' Having bowed to one another, each regained his place. The English began to fire immediately and with such accuracy that we lost more than a thousand men."[26] Polite as it may seem, that little exchange is, in fact, misleading: whoever shot second had a considerable advantage because weapons took so long to reload. Having fired, they could then safely rush forward. M. d'Auteroche was being practical, not chivalrous. As for the thousand casualties, it is a case of battle exaggeration.

At first it looked as if the French had the advantage; then, as the King, surrounded by a few officers, watched from the top of a hill, an English counterattack began pushing the French army back. Far from flinching, Louis XV ordered the duc de Richelieu, who was next to him, to lead a cavalry charge; then, refusing to heed the maréchal de Saxe's pleas, he advanced himself until, finally, Saxe pointed out to the King that this was the best way to lose the battle since he must now concentrate on protecting the royal person instead of beating the enemy. This time Louis XV listened but, as the Dauphin wrote that night in a letter to Marie Leczinska, his father "had truly shown himself to be a King at all times, and especially when victory did not seem to favor him. For then, without appearing to be surprised by the confusion which gripped everyone, he himself gave the wisest of orders with a presence of mind and courage which people couldn't help admiring"[27]; and, away in Paris, Barbier noted that, according to his correspondents, "the presence of the King, who went among the ranks with astonishing calmness in order to cheer the troops, was a great contribution towards the gain of this battle which is a very important one, and infinitely glorious for the King."[28] Barbier was right; not only did the King's presence stop the retreat, the attack headed by the duc de Richelieu actually forced the enemy back, thus enabling the turning movement planned by the maréchal de Saxe to complete the victory. That the happy outcome was due to the maréchal's superior talents cannot be doubted; but, then again, the King played a crucial part, first in resisting the onset of panic as the troops fell back, then in so inspiring the men and their officers that Saxe was able fully to show what he could do.

No sooner did the battle cease but a bulletin went off to the Queen. Dated "From the battlefield of Fontenoy, May 11, at 2:30" and written in the King's hand, it said: "The enemy attacked us at five this morning. They have been soundly beaten. I am well; so is my son. I have no time to tell you more, since I think it useful to reassure Versailles and Paris. I will send you a detailed account as soon as I can."[29] This was no mere excuse: there was much to be done. Courageous though he was, Louis XV hated bloodshed and felt personally responsible for the carnage taking place around him. When the marquis d'Harcourt, who had just watched the English army crumble, came to announce the victory, the King, without even stopping to rejoice, simply said "Let the men be spared"[30] and gave orders to stop fighting immediately. "There is much talk about [the King's] kindness; he was moved by his losses, made sure that the wounded were in good hands, both his own and those of the enemy. He has told the officers who behaved well how pleased he was with them. He gave the Household troops the praise they had deserved."[31] As for the maréchal de Saxe, he was immediately given a pension of 40,000 livres ($180,000) as a first sign of royal gratitude; this was eventually followed by the gift of Chambord, that magical Renaissance château now thought to have been designed by Leonardo da Vinci, and the creation of a new rank that placed him above all the other Marshals of France.

All these rewards were fully justified. After Fontenoy, the French army was unquestionably the main force in Flanders. Eleven days later, it went on to take the city of Tournai; then Bruges, Ghent, Audenarde and Ostend fell, that is to say, most of the Austrian Netherlands, while, far to the east, Frederick of Prussia, now back in the war, was, as usual, beating the Austrian army. For Louis XV personally, who stayed with the army until September, the campaign was rich in lessons: for the first time he had seen the horrors of war, and they had confirmed his scruples; he had found out that his army was far stronger than he had been told, better trained, armed and supplied, and all without bankrupting the Treasury. Finally, he had seen the impact made by his presence. He had done well on the battlefield, which gave a great boost to his self-confidence.

Any last remaining doubts Louis XV might have had about the magnitude of his achievements were soon dispelled by the frenzied manifestations of love which greeted him everywhere: the best of kings had won the greatest of victories. "Everybody agrees that the Fontenoy campaign is the best ever made by any King of France,"[32] Barbier noted in September, and the public agreed: the King's achievements far surpassed even those of Louis XIV. That this was an exaggerated estimate apparently occurred to no one, and, of course, the victory seemed even more splendid once it had been described (in verse) by the Historiographer of France. Without wasting a moment, Voltaire rushed to his desk and produced a "Poem on the Battle of Fontenoy" which went into many successive editions and became longer and longer as more and more people were cited in it by name. Since he was the most famous author in Europe, Voltaire's work did much to establish Fontenoy as the greatest victory ever. Of course, he hoped that the King would be pleased, but since he realized that someone else now also mattered, he made sure to circulate a few

lines at the same time. Their meaning was clear. "Quand César, ce héros charmant /
Dont tout Rome fut idolâtre / Gagnait quelque combat brillant / On en faisait son
compliment / A la divine Cléopâtre." ("When Cesar, that charming hero / Whom all
Rome adored / Won some brilliant battle / It was to the divine Cleopatra / that one
paid one's compliments.")[33] As poetry, this little piece leaves a lot to be desired; as a
tribute to the rising star, it was both apposite and appreciated.

On September 7, the King made yet another triumphant entry into Paris. "He
drove in his carriage to the Tuileries, where he met the Queen, the Dauphine and
Mesdames. The Royal Family having thus gathered, they all attended a Te Deum at
Notre Dame. That night, there were illuminations all over, and especially at the
Tuileries; the King, the Queen and the Royal Family went to the Hôtel de Ville,
watched a handsome fireworks display and had supper with forty ladies. On the
ninth, there was a royal banquet at the Tuileries and on the tenth Their Majesties
. . . arrived back at Versailles."[34] Much as Louis XV may have enjoyed all the ac-
claim, however, something more important was on his mind. Four days after his
return to Versailles, in front of the whole Court, the marquise de Pompadour was
officially presented to the King, the Queen and Mesdames. It was no surprise that
she looked ravishing, but what startled and vexed the eagerly watching ladies was
that the outsider behaved as if to the manner born: she walked, she curtsied, she
backed away from the royal presence, kicking her train all the way with perfect style,
grace and elegance. Clearly the new favorite had also had a studious summer.

In fact, that stay at Etioles, busy as it was, turned out to be the last of Mme de
Pompadour's leisure. From September on, she found herself caught in an endless
race which sped up a little every month. It wasn't just the time she spent with the
King: she must also pay court to the rest of the Royal Family, hold her own little
court, keep abreast of the many plots to unseat her, invent new ways of entertaining
her lover, all the while looking beautiful, fresh and elegant. "The Court at Fontainebleau is brilliant; Madame la marquise de Pompadour holds her rank well, to the
great regret of the ladies of the Court; they say that she behaves beautifully to the
Queen,"[35] Barbier noted as early as October, and he was right. It was Mme de
Pompadour's ambition to be kind and even, inasmuch as she could, to make people
happy. Fully aware that her position was equivocal, she did her best not only to
propitiate the Queen by being respectful and attentive but also convinced Louis XV
that it was time to treat his wife better: suddenly, to her great pleasure, Marie
Leczinska found herself invited to Choisy, where earlier she had never set foot. The
debts which she had incurred through her overgenerous charities, and which tor-
mented her greatly, were paid by the King; her apartment at Versailles, which had
grown a little shabby, was splendidly redecorated, and she knew she had Mme de
Pompadour to thank for all this: it was a most welcome change after Mme de
Châteauroux's disdain, and was appreciated at its true value.

What was obviously more important than the Queen's tolerance was the King's
favor, and there was no doubt of that. For the first time in his life Louis XV was,
people noticed with amazement, really happy. He loved his mistress, was proud of
her and trusted her, safe in the knowledge that, unlike her predecessors, she belonged to none of the little clans at Court. Mme de Châteauroux had had supporters

whom she wanted to bring into the government; Mme de Pompadour had no client but the King; and while she lead a splendidly glamorous life, it was obvious that she wasn't particularly interested in rank or money: she merely wanted to please the man she loved. This she proceeded to do in a number of ways. More than just another mistress, she also became something like the family Louis XV had never had; she introduced him to the pleasures of gardening, of decorating; she put on plays for his benefit; she arranged to be surrounded by witty, amusing people so that the King, whose private life had been aimless and sometimes sad, now found himself entertained, cheered, cosseted. And with all that, the former bourgeoise managed to behave with dignity, grace and just the right sort of amiability. The duc de Croÿ, a Belgian grandee who had been attending the Court on and off for a number of years, was struck by what he saw: "The King," he noted, "was now ordinarily freer and more talkative since the campaign and seemed to be much in love . . . with Mme de Pompadour . . . She gathered the whole Court into her apartments and almost presided over it . . . the King usually hunted three or four days a week, took supper, on those days, upstairs in her rooms and spent most of his time there . . . He worked much and assiduously with his council and each one of his ministers, most especially M. d'Argenson . . . who took precedence over all the others because of the war . . . I found out that the marquise de Pompadour was very powerful and that everyone paid court to her, so I arranged to be presented to her . . . I found her charming, both in looks and character; she was at her toilette and couldn't have been prettier; and full of amusing talents so that the King seemed to love her more than he had the others . . . She always played cards at the Queen's games, behaving with grace and dignity, and I noticed that when the time came [to join the King] in his private apartments, she asked the Queen for permission to leave the game, and the Queen would say, with a kind manner: 'Go' . . . the King seemed to me infinitely improved in his manner, in the best of health, looking cheerful and decisive, having fun, which he hadn't much seemed to do until then, speaking much and in a very obliging manner."[36] There could be no doubt: besides all the pleasures of love, the new favorite was giving the King a new, thrilling sense of self-confidence.

Because Mme de Pompadour was so new to the Court, she was slow to develop her own set of friends, and that left the King surrounded by much the same people as before. The maréchal de Noailles, it is true, was now in semidisgrace, but his son, the duc d'Ayen, was still part of the royal entourage, and so was the duc de Richelieu, who now lived in a state of barely suppressed rage. Had Mme de Châteauroux survived, he thought, he would have entered the Council and become the most important minister; now the King, instead of letting him select the duchesse's successor, had gone and unearthed a woman who suffered from two irredeemable defects: she was middle class (Richelieu was a tremendous snob) and she owed the duc nothing at all. Since, for the moment at least, she could not be dislodged, Richelieu set about making her life as unpleasant as he could. He criticized her, he made fun of her looks, her manners, her clothes, and all in such a way as to be heard by the marquise but not by the King. Still, his unpleasantness was balanced by the attentions of another grand seigneur, the prince de Soubise. A member of the large and powerful Rohan family,* he instantly took to Mme de Pompadour and she to him. He was amusing, charming, endlessly pleasant and did much to make the marquise's life easier. Then, of course, there was the marquis de Gontaut, one of the King's dearest friends and the man who had taught her the manners of the Court; he proved to be as good a friend to Mme de Pompadour as he had been to Louis XV, and was eventually rewarded by a dukedom.

All through 1746, Mme de Pompadour's position grew visibly more established. She noticed that the Dauphin was afraid of the King, so she arranged to bring them together more often, with the best results. On November 23, 1746, for instance, Croÿ noted, "the King left for Choisy . . . riding in a *vis-à-vis*** [with the Dauphin], which . . . was the work of the clever mistress who was traveling with the Queen's ladies."[37] By December, the marquise's power began extending to politics. "She managed [Court] affairs with gaiety, ease and endless grace. I saw her receiving many petitions. She lived in the upstairs apartment . . . which had been much adorned . . . Her brother, who was called the marquis de Vandières, was about twenty and handsome; he began to be in favor and attended all the parties . . . As [the marquise] had much influence, the ministers feared and respected her."[38]

The apartment in question was the first of Mme de Pompadour's decorative triumphs. Like most of her other residences, it has since been transformed, but we do know that it was both splendid and elegant. She was among the first to use the new lacquer, the vernis Martin, developed by the brothers of the same name. Tapestries, carpets and brocade curtains softened the atmosphere, while the very best work of the great ébénistes, Oeben and Cressent in particular, furnished the new apartment. There were rare and precious objects everywhere—gold boxes, Chinese porcelain mounted in gilt bronze, intaglios, and, a striking novelty, masses of cut flowers. As for M. de Vandières, for whom she felt an almost maternal affection, she had brought him into the little circle around the King as a support for herself, but also in order to create that family feeling to which Louis XV was so sensitive. And since she believed that people should make full use of their time and talents, she decided to have Vandières trained in art history and appreciation so that he could, eventually, become a minister of culture.

All that was very well; but the marquise soon began to make serious enemies: the ministers now resented her as a competing power center; they suspected that the King discussed politics and the war with her, thus undercutting their own influence. In fact, they were wrong: Mme de Pompadour's power was limited to certain Court appointments, but already a cabal was forming against her. The d'Argensons were still neutral, though not for much longer: it was Maurepas who led the opposition to the new favorite, and if attacking the marquise meant slandering the King, then that was just too bad.

Still, there could be no denying that Mme de Pompadour had become one of the very few people who really mattered. It came to seem quite normal, as early as 1746, for people to include her in their rounds at Versailles. First, they attended the King,

---

* The Rohans claimed the rank of foreign princes—a vexing question—but indubitably belonged to the very first rank of the nobility.
** A carriage large enough for only two passengers sitting opposite (i.e., *vis-à-vis)* each other.

then they paid a very brief visit to the Queen; and, finally, they went on to the marquise. "She asks a thousand questions and is very amiable,"[39] the marquis de Valfons, a staff officer, noted. "I was [formally] presented to Mme de Pompadour, who already knew me, but I had never called on her . . . She was very courteous to me,"[40] one of the King's pages recorded. Most of these calls took place in the morning while the marquise sat at her toilette. Besides her hairdresser, her dressmakers and the other merchants who attended her, she found herself surrounded by men who bore the greatest names in France, by cardinals, by ambassadors. She was pleasant to all, never presuming but treating everyone with politeness and the appropriate respect: in a Court where people were always on the lookout for arrogance, she never made a slip. Of course, as time passed and she began to know ce pays-ci better, her manner changed a little. By 1747, "she had put on a little weight and was prettier than ever," the duc de Croÿ noted. "She was concerned with many things without showing it or seeming busy with them. On the contrary, either spontaneously or in order to be polite, she seemed occupied only with her little plays or other bagatelles . . . Now that she was firmly in place, and she knew people better, she was a little more decisive and less amiable, but always polite and trying to please people."[41]

It was, however, in the *petits cabinets,* the King's private apartments on the top floor of the Palace, that Mme de Pompadour's domain really lay. These small, low-ceilinged, beautifully decorated rooms sheltered the King's private library, his maps, his worktable, his hobbies (he was a competent carver of ivory). There, suppers were held almost every night that Louis XV spent at Versailles; there the marquise had a two-room suite where the King often took refuge. If one wanted to see him relaxed, free from etiquette, in a word, himself, the petits cabinets were the place; but only a very few favored courtiers were allowed up. "The King was always very amiable in these cabinets," Croÿ noted, "and yet one never felt tempted to be disrespectful to him, for there was always something majestic about him which . . . made one remember he was one's master."[42] And no matter how friendly the King might be in private, there were neither special rewards nor favors to be expected. Louis XV might have friends, but he was far too conscientious to let these friendships influence him.

Nonetheless, most courtiers longed to see their names on the list for the King's suppers. The duc de Croÿ tells us all about it. "I had been fretting for some time because, although I hunted with the King, I was almost the only one who never supped in his cabinets when I learned that practically the only way to be invited was through the marquise . . . On January 30 [1747], having hunted as usual with the King, he put me down on the list that the usher read at the door. One went in through the small staircase and walked up to the petits cabinets . . . There one waited in the small salon as His Majesty only came in time to sit down at table with the ladies. The dining room was charming, the meal most cheerful and easy. We were only served by two or three footmen of the Wardrobe* who left the room after having provided each guest with what he needed. The atmosphere was free, yet proper.

"The sovereign was cheerful, relaxed, but always with a grandeur one couldn't

---

* At normal dinners a footman stood behind each guest.

forget; he didn't seem at all shy, but a man of habit, speaking well, often and knowing how to enjoy himself. He didn't conceal the fact that he was very much in love with Mme de Pompadour . . . He knew about the smallest things, the tiniest details . . . but he would not commit himself about the business of the State; still, it was believed that in private he told his mistress everything . . . It seemed to me that he spoke very freely with her, as with a mistress whom he loved but from whom he wanted amusement . . . And she, who behaved beautifully, had much influence, but the King always wanted to be the master, and was firm about that.

"That is how it seemed to me . . . This privacy of the cabinets was not really so private, for it consisted only in a meal, followed by an hour or two at the card tables after supper, and the real privacy took place in the other petits cabinets where a very few of the old and intimate courtiers had access.

"Louis XV was . . . fond of habit, liked the people he had known a long time, had trouble letting them go, and did not look for new faces. It is, I think, to this taste for stability that several owed the long duration of their favor, for, excepting the real intimates, the others had no influence.

"We were, that evening, eighteen people crowded around the table, starting on my right: M. de Livry, Mme de Pompadour, the King, the comtesse d'Estrades, the marquise's great friend; the duc d'Ayen, the tall Mme de Brancas,* the comte de Noailles, the marquis de la Suze, the comte de Coigny, the comtesse d'Egmont, M. de Croix, the marquise de Revel, the duc de Fitz-James,** the duc de Broglie,† the prince de Turenne, M. de Crillon, M. de Voyer d'Argenson‡ and myself. The maréchal de Saxe was there, but he did not sit down at table because he only ate one meal a day, at dinner; he just picked up a few mouthfuls here and there, for he was very fond of food. The King only called him comte de Saxe [i.e., not maréchal], seemed to like and respect him greatly, and he [Saxe] behaved in response with admirable frankness and tact. Mme de Pompadour was very fond of him.

"We spent two hours at table with great freedom and without any excess; then His Majesty went into the small salon, warmed and poured his own coffee; no servant came in and we each served ourselves. The King played a game of comète with Mmes de Pompadour, de Coigny, de Brancas and the comte de Noailles; he was very fond of these simple games, but Mme de Pompadour hated them and seemed to try and wean him away from them. The rest of the company went around two card tables; the King told everybody to sit down,* even those who weren't playing. I remained standing, leaning on the fire screen, watching him play; since Mme de Pompadour was asking him to retire and was falling asleep, he stood up at once and said, in a fairly low voice and very cheerfully: 'Let's go, let's go to bed.' The ladies curtsied and left; the King bowed and went off to his petits cabinets; we all walked down the small staircase . . . and attended the King's [official] coucher as usual; it took place right away."[43]

* The same Mme de Brancas who had been appointed dame d'honneur to the Dauphine to please Mme de Châteauroux.
** The brother of the Bishop of Soissons.
† The military commander.
‡ The War minister.
* Normally no one sat down before the King, except duchesses, who were entitled to stools.

With all that, and in spite of the new amusements arranged by Mme de Pompadour, the King continued to work hard and long. There was still no prime minister, although the minister of War, the comte d'Argenson—as opposed to his brother the Foreign minister, whom the King never really trusted—seemed to have more influence than his colleagues. Still, there was no cabinet. Each minister worked alone with the King at least once a week, and sometimes oftener. Twice a week there was a Council at which pressing issues were generally discussed. So far, Louis XV was indeed keeping to the tradition established by his great-grandfather; but where the Sun King always knew better—God, he thought, inspired all conscientious monarchs —and therefore never hesitated to overrule his ministers, Louis XV still felt that others were more competent, knew better than he did, and that therefore he should follow their advice. Much of the time, in fact, his was far and away the better judgment, unclouded as it was by intrigue or ambition; but while, in private, Mme de Pompadour had given him a new self-confidence, when it came to the government his old diffidence persisted. Naturally, the ministers tended to take advantage of this to further their own policies.

This mattered less than at first it might seem to: while defeats are apt to engender many different parties, victories create an artificial unity. In 1745, it is true, the invasion of England, led by Charles Stuart, the Young Pretender, after achieving a measure of success, later proved to be a total failure. On April 16, 1746, on the field of Culloden, the Highlander army was crushed; the Prince himself escaped only after a series of wild adventures, and it became evident that the Hanoverians' hold on the throne was more solid than anyone (including themselves) had suspected. Still, that was, except for the Pretender himself, a minor skirmish compared to the land war in Europe; there victories came in rapid succession. In February 1746, a time of year when military operations were usually suspended, the maréchal de Saxe, in a lightning raid on Brussels, took the city and eighteen thousand Dutch troops which had garrisoned it for Maria Theresa. In October, moving northward, he took Namur, then, facing an Austrian army at Raucoux, he defeated it so thoroughly that its remnants fled with all possible speed. And it went right on: in July 1747, at Laufeldt, he defeated an Anglo-Dutch army; soon after that, one of the French generals, the comte de Lowendal, took the strong, fortified city of Berg-op-Zoom, while Saxe himself seized Maastricht. The next step was obviously an invasion of Holland; and that possibility nearly created a panic in the City of London, where many commercial houses relied on trade with the Netherlands. It would also have cut all links between Great Britain and the Anglo-Hanoverian forces, which would thus have been deprived of supplies and communications.

This, clearly, was the moment for a competent Foreign minister to end the war. France had the advantage, it held the Austrian Netherlands in its entirety, so that could be swapped for some other, more desirable goal, and both the Austrians and the British were tired of being defeated with clockwork regularity. Negotiations were indeed begun with Holland and Piedmont, but d'Argenson quite failed to see that this was mere window dressing: he was far more interested in setting up a complex and unrealistic anti-Spanish combination to pay attention to the job at hand, although he did manage one successful maneuver. The Dauphine had died a little more than a year after her marriage, in July 1746. By offering to put a Saxon princess on the throne of France, d'Argenson was able to gain the alliance of Saxony, which until then had been firmly tied to Austria. In December 1746, Louis XV announced that his son was to wed Marie-Josèphe of Saxony, and six months later the marriage took place. Curiously, it was a great success. The Dauphin, who had been passionately in love with his first wife and was remarrying merely because it was his duty to beget heirs, promptly discovered that his new wife was everything he could want; indeed, he was won over when, on their wedding night, after he burst into tears because the occasion reminded him of the late Dauphine, Marie-Josèphe praised him for his constancy and went on to say that she didn't expect to be loved until she had proved herself worthy. Within days, the Dauphin was passionately in love. Once again, everyone approved of the new Dauphine. Marie-Josèphe of Saxony, Croÿ noted, "has a good figure, a good complexion and charming eyes . . . Her nose and mouth are ugly. Overall, her face, without being beautiful, is infinitely pleasing . . . She has, in her expression and her gestures, endless attractions when she is animated, as well as a cheerfulness and even petulance which are completely natural. She shows an amazing desire to please . . . Madame Adélaide* . . . is charming both in looks and character, of the most charming gaiety . . . Since the character of the Dauphine and hers have much in common, it was amusing to see them laugh and joke together all through supper."[44] A charming picture, and one which reveals the state of the Royal Family. The King was the best of fathers; the Queen, though cold and grumpy, was not harmful; and the young people liked one another—a degree of unity seldom seen in ruling circles.

Gaining the alliance of Saxony, which thus became a menace on Austria's flank, was certainly a major achievement, but even that was no reason to continue the war indefinitely. It had started because France did not want Francis of Lorraine to become Emperor, and also because it looked as if their hereditary states might, with a little effort, be taken from the Habsburgs. Now, six years later, the French-backed Emperor, Charles VII, was dead; Francis of Lorraine had been elected after all, and it was obvious that Maria Theresa had a firm grip on her possessions: it was clearly time to end the costly, purposeless conflict. That would entail delicate negotiations, and d'Argenson, who loathed Austria as much as Spain, was not the man to conduct them. Listen as he might to his ministers, Louis XV could see perfectly well when they needed changing. Early in 1747, he dismissed d'Argenson, whose brother remained minister of War, and replaced him with the marquis de Puysieulx, a skillful diplomat who had been Ambassador to Naples. First announced in November 1747, the peace congress finally met at Aachen in April 1748.

Once assembled, the delegates quickly reached agreement. By late April, the peace preliminaries were signed, but it was not until October that all the treaties could be ratified. This was partly because so many countries—France, Great Britain, Holland, Prussia, Spain, Piedmont and Austria—were involved, partly because the British hoped for a last-minute victory: a Russian army had just been sent to Austria's help by the new Empress of Russia, Elizabeth. In fact, the Russians had much too far to

---

* The King's next daughter after Madame Infante.

go; they were also supposed to be subsidized by England and Holland, but these two powers were running out of money and simply refused to pay up.

In essence, the treaties of Aachen simply stipulated a return to the status quo ante. France was to recover the islands in the West Indies taken by the British, who, in turn, were given back Madras; Maria Theresa recovered the Austrian Netherlands. In Italy, the Republic of Genoa and the Duke of Modena were given back the areas occupied by Piedmont or Austria, but France and Spain registered an appreciable gain: the duchies of Parma, Piacenza and Guastalla went to Don Philip of Spain, the husband of Madame Infante. Since the new Duke was known to be ruled by his intelligent and ambitious wife, this meant that Parma would be virtually a French enclave in northern Italy. Silesia, conquered by Frederick II back in December 1740, remained his; and Francis of Lorraine was recognized as the Emperor Francis I.

In France the treaty was at first greeted with joy: a prolongation of the war would have meant fighting on land and at sea, always an impossible combination; taxes would have risen; defeats might well have occurred. When, in September 1749, Louis XV paid an official visit to Le Havre, he was received with the usual wild acclamations. Soon, however, people began to criticize. France, they said, had given up the Austrian Netherlands, which it had conquered, but received nothing in exchange; the only real victor was the King of Prussia, who had managed to keep Silesia. The maréchal de Saxe himself, who hated to give up his office of Governor General, objected to the restitution of the Netherlands; it soon became an accepted opinion that the French negotiators had given away everything the armies had fought so hard to win.

That this mistaken notion spread so quickly was, in part at least, the King's fault. Conscientious as he was, it never occurred to him that he owed anyone an explanation. When people told him they thought that France had given away too much, he replied disdainfully that, not being a merchant, he did not choose to bargain. In fact, the moderation shown by the King and Puysieulx was wisdom itself. Keeping the Austrian Netherlands was just not possible: England was then, and has been since, ready to fight so they would not be French. What other territory, then, was to be gained? An accretion in Germany would merely have made France the target of endless wars of revenge; and Parma was, after all, a solid benefit. It was no mean achievement to have found Madame Infante her own independent state, especially since it established a French foothold in Italy at no cost to France; besides, with good management the duchy might one day be expanded to take in the tiny states on its borders. By showing moderation, therefore, Louis XV, far from being careless or lax, was attempting to create a just and lasting peace. It was a noble objective when pursued, as was the case, from a position of strength. Fleury, no doubt, would have approved.

Chapter Seven

Peace and the Arts

WITH the return of peace, Louis XV, for the first time in the history of his thirty-three-year reign, found himself quite free of any serious political problems. France had just been on the winning side in the late war, the Treasury was in almost satisfactory condition, the Parlement was quiet, and while Frederick II was hardly a trustworthy ally, there was time to look around. As for his personal life, the King found himself happier than he had ever been. Mme de Pompadour was beautiful, intelligent, interesting and nice; and he loved her. She gave him, the owner of so many palaces, what he had never had: a home in which he could be at ease with his friends. Further, having perceived that he harbored hidden talents, the marquise encouraged him to patronize painters, sculptors and architects with, in due time, spectacular results.

There were special pleasures, too. In December 1748, Madame Infante, the King's eldest—and favorite—daughter came to Versaille and stayed for a year. A fond father, Louis XV was especially close to this intelligent, lively young woman; he enjoyed her company enormously and included her in many of the trips to Choisy and La Muette. Harmony, in fact, reigned throughout the Royal Family. Madame Infante, who was very ambitious, thought of Parma only as a first step; if, however, she wanted France to back her in the future, it was clear that she had better conciliate the rising power, so she was extremely amiable to Mme de Pompadour. It was hardly surprising, therefore, when, in short order, the King awarded her a pension of 200,000 livres ($900,000). The Queen, who found herself more comfortable than ever before, was determinedly polite to the favorite; and while the Dauphin disapproved of his father's behavior on religious grounds, he generally kept his feelings to himself.

That Louis XV was now, in many respects, the most powerful of European monarchs few would have doubted. Frederick II, that military genius, ruled over a tiny, backward kingdom with a population of some six million. Maria Theresa had all she could do to hold her hereditary possessions together. She was just then embarking on the course of reforms which, in time, brought her well-deserved fame, but in the late forties their effect had not yet become visible. England had, to all intents and purposes, just lost the war. Spain, declining slowly but steadily, could no longer be considered quite a first-rate power; and Italy was an ill-assorted mosaic of states. As for Russia, it was too primitive, and too distant, to matter. In terms of personal prestige, as well, Louis XV was unrivaled. Still the handsomest man in France, he looked young and vigorous even for his age. His court was, far and away, the most splendid, his palaces the envy of Europe. As for his having an official mistress, Frederick II, who preferred the ministrations of some strapping young officer, might well make fun: there was no one who doubted that the King of France had found the loveliest, brightest and most enchanting of women.

Little by little, the circle around the King solidified. The guests at Choisy and La Muette wore a green and gold uniform which, naturally, became an object of envy, and the many people who served Louis XV came to know their master better. While the great Court offices—Captain of the Guard, Grand Master of the Wardrobe, First Gentleman of the Bedchamber—were reserved for men of exalted birth and rank, minor officials generally came from the rich bourgeoisie. This was the case, for instance, of Dufort de Cheverny, who, having first bought an office in the Household, soon found himself Introductor of the Ambassadors. This smart young man who liked women, wine and gambling also kept a diary, and the little stories he set down give us quick insights into the personality of a man who was, for most of his subjects, an infinitely remote demigod.

There is, for instance, this incident which will endear Louis XV to every cat lover. "The cabinet [i.e., minor attendants] was composed almost entirely of young men, all very lively, and that pleased the King, who liked to talk to them," Dufort noted. "We were all waiting for the King's coucher, which was the occasion for those who wanted to be seen as often as possible. The King had a white Angora cat who was enormously big, very sweet and very friendly; he slept in the Council Room on a crimson damask cushion in the middle of the chimney. The King always came in from his private apartments at half past midnight; it was not yet midnight and Champcenetz told us: 'You don't know it, but I can make that cat dance for a few minutes.' We laugh; we bet him that he can't. Champcenetz then takes a vial out of his pocket, caresses the cat and pours out some *eau de mille fleurs* [a strong cologne] abundantly on his paws. The cat goes back to sleep, and we thought we had won. Suddenly, feeling the effect of the alcohol, he jumped to the ground, leaping about, then jumped onto the King's table, swearing, running, doing ballet steps. We were all laughing when, suddenly, the King came in. Everyone went back to his place with grave and decent manners. The King asked what had made us so cheerful. 'Nothing, Sire, just a story we were telling,' Champcenetz answered. At that moment the cat started dancing and running again like a mad animal. The King saw this. 'Messieurs,' he said, 'what has been going on here? Champcenetz, what have they done to my cat? I want an answer.' The question was direct; Champcenetz hesitated, then told the story quickly while the cat still leapt up and down. We all smiled as he told the story so as to see in the King's eyes how he would take it all, but his expression turned serious. 'Gentlemen,' he said, 'I leave you here; but if you look for amusement, I do not want my cat to suffer for it.' This was said so sternly that since then no one has made the cat dance anymore."[1] That the King should have resented the pain inflicted on his cat is perhaps not surprising; that his reproof should have been so firm yet so moderate is another proof of his sense of measure: he said just enough to make sure the incident would not happen again.

It was one of the major paradoxes in Louis XV's character that this man who loved animals—Oudry painted portraits of his favorite dogs—should have been such a passionate hunter: after all, the purpose of the sport is to kill, often in especially cruel ways, a variety of game. The exercise involved was certainly one of its great attractions: like all Bourbons, Louis XV liked to be physically active. Then, too, hunting was the traditional sport of kings—only, if it came to that, so was war, and Louis XV abhorred the bloodshed it entailed. Rather, it seems likely that the pursuit of game was the only balance for the extreme artificiality of the King's life at all other times. As a child he had learned to repress all his instinctual reactions; ever since the age of five, he had lived in public and behaved accordingly; in governing his realm, he carefully listened to his minister's advice, often ignoring his own feelings in the process: somewhere nature had to erupt. There can be very little doubt that hunting was the main outlet for all those repressions.

As a result, the King found that sport wholly absorbing, both as a pastime and as a subject of conversation. "Amiable in private, talking and talking well, no one did more than [the King] to animate the conversation by the variety of his questions. The role of a king is difficult; he models himself on no one but must himself be everyone; he is never asked questions unless it is on matters relating to his service; it is therefore up to him to carry the conversation in any way that he pleases. He can only talk about the arts, the sciences or the hunt, for if he were to talk about politics, or people, every word would have consequences. Not liking the sciences much, even though, by inclination or policy, he was familiar with them, he brought all the conversations back to the hunt of that or the following day. Lansmate, his first huntsman, who had earned his place by his tireless talent, was the one he [i.e., the King] treated the best, both in his cabinet and during the hunts; he spoke almost to no one else, except to the equerries who rode on either side of his horse. One day, in Fontainebleau, I witnessed a quip of Lansmate's. The hunt had been a hard one, two stags had been run down; the dogs, the horses, the men were all exhausted, and people were slowly getting back to the carriages. The King, with that hoarse voice which made him uniquely recognizable, called Lansmate.

" 'Lansmate,' he asked, 'are the dogs tired?'

" 'Yes, Sire, they are, rather.'

" 'What about the horses?'

" 'I should say they are.'

" 'And yet,' the King went on, 'I will hunt on the day after tomorrow.' Lansmate said nothing. 'Do you hear, Lansmate, I will hunt on the day after tomorrow.'

" 'Yes, Sire, I heard you the first time. But what annoys me,' he said as he walked away, 'is that I'm always asked whether the horses and the dogs are tired, but never the men.' It was said so that the King heard every word of it. The hunt took place as he had ordered it."[2] At the same time, and however passionately he loved his sport, the King never forgot who he was: at a time when it was all too common for the great nobles to ravage the fields through which they pursued the stags without compensation to the peasants whose crop they had ruined, Louis XV absolutely forbade crossing any field that had been sown or cultivated in any way, and he could be quite harsh towards those of his courtiers who rode even on the edge of these fields; but since, in the heat of the pursuit, some damage was often unavoidable, he was careful to have the peasants indemnified on the spot, even before they had asked for compensation.

Of course, the King had other amusements. There was the theater, or rather, the theaters: plays had long been part of the regular, indeed, automatic pleasures of the Court. The Comédie Française most often, sometimes the Comédie Italienne, which had preserved the tradition of the commedia del l'arte, as well as the Opéra came to the royal palaces. Their performances were part of the ritual enshrined in the inflexible etiquette. All was ordered accordingly. At Fontainebleau, for instance, where the Court invariably spent the autumn, the King's chair was placed in the middle of the orchestra; to his right were the benches reserved for the grands officiers; to the left sat the foreigners, with the ambassadors in front, the ministers behind and foreign visitors all the way in the back. Order was kept by the Bodyguard, with the Introductor of the Ambassadors bearing the task of admitting or rejecting all those who wished to attend. At Versailles there was no proper theater, but a temporary structure was put up in the riding school across from the Palace.

Thanks to Mme de Pompadour, however, the King, who was often quite bored at these official performances, discovered all the charms of that favorite eighteenth-century amusement, amateur theatricals. The marquise was herself an actress and singer of talent; she was thoroughly experienced because she had had her own theater at Etioles. Now she ordered a small theater which fit in the well of the Ambassador's staircase, and which could be taken down in less than a day. There, with the help of equally gifted courtiers, she put on all the new plays and operas. Chief among the male members of her troupe were the duc d'Orléans, who revealed hitherto hidden capacities; the duc d'Ayen, who had been close to the King for well over ten years; the duc de Nivernais, a competent diplomat, a wit, and the epitome of civilization; the duc de Duras, one of the First Gentlemen of the Bedchamber; the maréchal de Maillebois, a successful general who usually played old men's parts; and the duc de Coigny, one of the handsomest men at Court. Chief among the ladies were the duchesse de Brancas and Mme d'Estrades, who had been friends of the marquise from the first; but, of course, the star was always Mme de Pompadour herself. Since the whole idea was that these were private performances, the audience was usually limited to the King himself and half a dozen of his closest friends. The performers were talented and enthusiastic, the marquise shone, the King was delighted; but, naturally, everyone wanted to attend, and the audience soon swelled from half a dozen to as many as twenty. Perhaps Mme de Pompadour's greatest triumph came when the Queen herself let it be known that she would like to see a performance: once again, the wife was looking approvingly on the mistress. Of course, the invitation was issued, and Marie Leczinska pronounced herself entertained and impressed.

One other person, however, felt very differently: the duc de Richelieu, who loathed the marquise, quickly realized that these plays were the perfect way of getting at the favorite. Most of the time the costumes and sets came from the vast array of properties which were also used for the Court theater, and it was part of the First Gentleman of the Bedchamber's office to rule over that little domain. As it happened one year in four Richelieu was on duty, and he promptly forbade his underlings to give the marquise what she needed: if she asked for a set, it was being painted, or had been lost; if she needed a costume, it was being repaired; one way or the other, nothing was ever available. Everyone, by now, knew that Mme de Pompadour was kind, patient and tolerant, so this little game seemed safe enough; indeed, so long as the duc de Richelieu only made fun of her looks, her clothes, her manners or her intelligence, the marquise had said nothing. Now, finally, she went to the King and complained. That evening, as the duc stood behind Louis XV at his *débotter,** he heard the monarch ask him how many times he had been to the Bastille so far. "Three times, Sire," the duc answered, and took the hint: henceforth sets and costumes were readily available.

Another one of the King's amusements was moving from one of his houses to another. Aside from the yearly trip to Fontainebleau, there were excursions to Compiègne, an old château which the King soon decided to rebuild: its attraction was the huge forest filled with game. There, too, the theater followed, along with other entertainments. One year, for instance, a tent village was set up in the park; but these were no ordinary canvas structures: silks, velvets, brocades embroidered with gold or silver sheltered rare oriental carpets and precious furniture. These were fairly lengthy trips, but Louis XV often spent two or three days at Choisy, La Muette, Marly or Trianon, and he also visited the new houses that were built and decorated for Mme de Pompadour, Bellevue first and foremost.

After a sledding party in the gardens of Versailles held in January 1751, for instance, the King moved to La Muette. (It was, after all, only about an hour away.) "We lived there with much ease," the duc de Croÿ noted, "a large dinner was served, but the suppers were more important still because they were the King's favorite meals. [There] he would go for walks when the weather was nice; card games were held in the salon after dinner; after that, His Majesty worked or had a Council; at eight-thirty we met in the grand salon, to which the Master came down soon afterwards . . . That stay was very cheerful; the marquise was in especially good spirits; she didn't like cards; she played more to be in on things and sit down than because she enjoyed it. She spent much time with her followers, Mmes de Meuse, de Gontaut, etc. The King played two sets of card games after supper, for he liked high stakes and played well and rapidly. He went to bed around two."[3]

A few days later, the King was off to Choisy, where he stayed from the thirteenth to the eighteenth of January. Aside from Mme de Pompadour, there were some twenty-five guests living in the château, including, as usual, the ducs de Richelieu, d'Ayen, de Duras, de La Vallière, the prince de Soubise, the maréchal de Maillebois, Mmes d'Estrades and de Brancas; but some twenty other guests came to spend the day and, not surprisingly, they all belonged to the most glamorous part of the Court; since Mme de Pompadour always tried to make sure that the King remained on close and loving terms with his family, there was one unusual visitor: "M. le Dauphin had spent the previous night there," Croÿ noted, "and I noticed that he was trying to be cheerful. Instead of treating Mme de Pompadour coldly, as he usually did, he greeted her most amiably. One could see that, although he was still very religious and given

* The time when his boots were pulled off after the hunt.

to study, if, one day, his love for the Dauphine should cool, he might well take
mistresses who would give him the polish he still lacked. He seemed knowledgeable
and not lacking in wit . . . The next day, Mesdames and eight ladies of their suite
came for dinner and spent the night. For the last two years, the marquise had been
asking the family and treating it with much attention and respect; she had tried to
gain the confidence of its members, she was on good terms with all and even close to
the Queen, so that nothing was lacking to her glory and influence . . . The King
seemed more in love than ever and she behaved with much care and tact . . . His
Majesty seemed very much at ease, very pleased and was charmingly kind."[4]

Just how little time Louis XV actually spent at Versailles became clearer as one
reads on: after Choisy and La Muette, the King went to stay at Trianon* that
January. "That day, the King took us to see the hothouses where rare plants are kept,
the henhouse,** of which he was so fond (the marquise had introduced him to all
these little hobbies), several pretty pavilions, the herb and vegetable gardens. All was
planned with great taste and had caused a great expenditure which was all the more
unfortunate that it was repeated in every house, both of the King's and the marquise's."[5] The often censorious Croÿ exaggerates the expense which, in any event,
led to a variety of improvements in breeding and horticulture. Indeed, Louis XV soon
became a passionate gardener, arranging, planning and not unfrequently improving
the plantings with his own hands. At Choisy, where the King liked to watch his
gardeners at work, "we spent," Croÿ says, "an entire day chopping down a small
wood; he took the sickle from my hands to use it himself, which he did like the strong
and handy man that he was."[6]

Then, too, there was Bellevue. Perched on top of a hill overlooking the Seine and,
indeed, the whole panorama of Paris,† this small château was surrounded by extensive gardens sloping down to a riverside pavilion. On January 3, 1751—it was a
typically busy month—Mme de Pompadour wrote her friend Mme de Lutzelbourg:
"You can well imagine how pleased I have been to receive the King at Bellevue. His
Majesty has been there three times . . . It is a delicious place for the view; the
house, though not very large,‡ is comfortable and charming without any kind of
grandeur. We play a few comedies . . . The King wants to cut his expenditure all
over; although this one is not large, since the public believes that it is, I have decided
to follow the general opinion and set an example."[7] As always when it came to
money, the marquise, who was the least grasping of women, was also being unrealistic. Altogether, Bellevue managed to cost between four and five million livres because, although "without grandeur," its rooms were masterpieces of decor. Boucher,
Mme de Pompadour's favorite painter, provided both large paintings and smaller
works that fit in the boiseries over the doors, as well as easel paintings like the
Toilette de Vénus (today in the Metropolitan Museum of Art, New York). Verbeeckt,
the greatest of boiserie sculptors, carved the paneling, while the manufactures of
Aubusson and the Gobelins provided tapestries and carpets, and the brothers Martin
some of their famous lacquerwork. That it is always well worth creating a great work

* What is now called the Grand Trianon, that is; the Petit Trianon had not yet been built.
** Rare species of fowl, pheasant, etc., were kept there.
† Bellevue means beautiful view.
‡ It was, in fact, a medium-sized château which could sleep about thirty people plus the servants.

of art is a generally accepted principle today: it was all money well spent, especially since Mme de Pompadour's houses served as advertisements for French taste. Foreigners came from all over Europe, visited (any decently dressed person was allowed in when the owner was not in residence), went back to Paris and placed their orders; besides that, France's reputation as the most sophisticated, most civilised country in Europe, while certainly based on more than a few houses, did much to maintain its position in the world.

That the King, in 1751, should have decided to cut his expenditure wasn't surprising: once again, the Parlement was making trouble. In 1733, and then again in 1741, a new war tax, the *dixième,* was decreed. With a vast number of exceptions, it was a 10 percent income tax. In both cases, the Parlement registered the edict without one word of opposition. The War of the Austrian Succession, however, had been so expensive that Machault, Orry's successor as Contrôleur-Général, found himself forced, in May, 1749, to ask for a new tax to replace the expired *dixième.* This was a *vingtième,* or 5 percent income tax, to which, normally, the government resorted only in time of war. Machault wanted to use its proceeds to reimburse the loans that had been contracted to pay some of the costs of the war. Immediately the Parlement, arguing that France was at peace and therefore did not need a *vingtième,* refused to register it and presented remonstrances to the King. Louis XV trusted Machault as much as he disliked the Parlement, whose earlier resistance he remembered all too well. Refusing to discuss the remonstrances, he simply ordered that the edict be registered; amazingly, the next day his command was obeyed. The conflict had been brief. The Parlement normally resisted any attempt at taxing the upper classes; its lack of reaction this time may have been due to the loss of its devoted supporter in the ministry. The comte de Maurepas, who had served continuously since becoming minister of the Navy at the age of fourteen, back in 1715, was suddenly dismissed on April 24.* Because he had been in office so long, and because of his close family ties to most of the great Parlement dynasties, his position had seemed secure, all the more in that he was relatively competent and was thought to amuse the King. He had made one fatal mistake, though: it had long been his game to set himself up as the head of the anti-mistress faction, perhaps because he was impotent himself. Mme de Châteauroux, in her time, had tried unsuccessfully to have him dismissed; with Mme de Pompadour he finally went too far by writing the most insulting pamphlets about her. These circulated freely, and when the marquise complained, the King talked to the Paris lieutenant (chief) of police, only to be told that this official's jurisdiction did not include Versailles. It was perfectly clear: if the libels were to be stopped, Maurepas, who was known to be their author, would have to be dismissed.

It was shortly after both the King and the marquise read Maurepas's latest effort that she finally begged for action. It went: "Autrefois de Versailles / Nous venait le bon goût / Aujourd'hui la canaille / Règne et tient le haut bout. / Si la cour se ravale / De quoi s'étonne-t-on? / N'est-ce pas de la halle / Que nous vient le poisson?" ("Once it was from Versailles / that good taste came to us. / But today the riffraff / preens and rules over us. / If the Court is vulgar / why should that surprise us? / Isn't it from

---

* Quite often a ministry was passed from father to son; in this case, Maurepas, although titular minister, did not actually come into office for some years.

the market / that fish comes to us?")[8] The slur here rested on a pun: the marquise's name was Poisson (Fish) and the women of the halle, the central market, were renowned for their coarse and vulgar behavior. It is easy to understand why, after much more of the same, Mme de Pompadour felt that she had had enough, and this time the King agreed. On April 24, 1749, a holograph letter was delivered to Maurepas: "In keeping with the promise I made you to let you know myself if the case should occur, I am writing you this letter to ask you to give your resignation to M. d'Argenson and to leave within the week. Pontchartrain being too near Versailles, you will go to Bourges. You will see no one but your family and will not answer this letter."[9] While his Parlement relations were greatly exercised at Maurepas's sudden fall, the other ministers and the courtiers, who had felt the wind of the bullet, suddenly realized that attacking the marquise was not a good idea at all.

Writing anti-Pompadour songs, however, was too tempting an amusement to cease altogether; then, too, since France had a state censorship,* these attacks were almost the only way to express opposition or discontent. Interestingly enough, they came not, as has often been written, from a middle-class hungry for political power but from those very courtiers whose privileges depended upon a continuation of the system. That these pamphlets might eventually make the King unpopular, and with him the regime, apparently never occurred to Maurepas or his compeers: their contempt for the people was such that they forgot its very existence. To them, libelous songs were simply a part of whatever Court intrigue they were pursuing at the time, but the Parisians who read these attacks on the favorite and the King began to wonder whether they had not been wrong to call Louis XV the beloved.

The remonstrances of May 1749 were merely a first skirmish. In 1750, the dreary, endless Jansenist controversy was revived yet again by an act of ecclesiastical folly. Christophe de Beaumont, the Archbishop of Paris, was a saintly, charitable old man whose many virtues, unfortunately, included neither intelligence nor a sense of when to leave well enough alone. In December 1750 he ordered the priests of his see to refuse the last rites to dying persons unless they could produce evidence of having confessed to a non-Jansenist priest; on December 29, one Bouettin was allowed to die unshriven. According to Catholic doctrine, therefore, the wretched man's soul had been consigned to hell: it was as serious a matter as anyone could imagine, and the Parlement, which had always hated the *Unigenitus* bull, now took up the good fight again. On March 4, 1751, it presented remonstrances to the King. "Deign to remember," it said ominously, "how often we have brought before your throne the complaints which have been lodged against the rigor shown in several sees of your realm against persons of every condition and gender by pitilessly refusing them the last rites when they were about to expire."[10] Clearly, the old habit of opposition was reappearing; only this time there could be very little doubt that the Parlement was right. The Archbishop's act was so extreme as to be, in all probability, uncanonical; it was certainly unchristian; only there was very little the King could do about it.

The issue of the last rites was, wonder of wonders, clear-cut, but it became linked with another, far more complex (and far less vital) controversy, namely, that which surrounded the reform of the Hôpital Général. This refuge of last resort for the

* So did every other country in Europe, England being the sole exception.

destitute and the sick was, like every other similar institution in France, staffed by the Church, so it came under the control of the Archbishop of Paris; at the same time, it received funds from the Paris and Royal treasuries, thus giving the Parlement a handle if it should wish to interfere. Now the Archbishop decided to modify the charter of the Hôpital Général so as to exclude all possibility of the inmates being attended by Jansenist priests, but, cleverly, this new rule was only one among many others designed to improve the Hôpital's efficiency. This reform was, in fact, accepted by the unsuspecting Royal Council and promulgated in the form of several edicts. The Parlement, which was naturally anxious to hobble the Archbishop, promptly proclaimed it had a right to intervene and, without further ado, modified the edicts without the permission of the Council. This was obviously a critical precedent: if Parlement were allowed its way in this one instance, it would undoubtedly claim in the future the right to modify other, more important, edicts as it pleased; it was as bold an attack on the King's acknowledged power as had ever been made. Naturally enough, the royal reaction came swiftly. On November 21, by order, a deputation of the Parlement brought its registers to Versailles. There, in the presence of the King, the pages on which the offensive decisions had been consigned were torn out, after which Louis XV told the magistrates: "I forbid all deliberations and all gatherings on this subject, and will receive neither remonstrances nor representations about it."[11] Once again King and Parlement were at war; once again the Parlement went on strike; only, when it received a royal order to return to work, it did so: after all, the usurpation had been a little too bold.

There was another good reason to obey: although it could no longer take cognizance of the Hôpital Général statutes, the Parlement, much to its secret glee, found itself swamped with appeals from families whose relations had been refused the last rites. In a little over a year (March 1752 to May 1753) twenty suits were brought against the ecclesiastical authorities. This time, the King simply had the several *arrêts* (decisions) annulled by the Council, acting as the court of last resort, which it was entitled to do. Even a judgment seizing the temporalities of the Archbishop of Paris was thus negated. Once again the Parlement simply accepted the procedure.

Interestingly enough, when the Parlement, for once, was actually right in its position, if not in its methods, it failed to gather popular support. This was a rude shock since in its earlier periods of opposition it had always been able to win the Parisians over to its side. Even Barbier, who was, after all, a lawyer, commented gleefully on its defeat. "It is a good thing for the public that the Parlement should have decided to obey," he noted. "But, at bottom, after all the noise it had made, the number of assemblies,* the seizure of the Archbishop's temporalities, the convocation of the Peers,** the violent speeches of the deputies [to the King], one must admit that today's behavior proves their complete failure because when one knows what one must know, that the King has the right to impose silence and compliance with a single word, it would be better not to tire the Sovereign by constantly resisting his decisions and not to publicize oneself throughout Paris as a power established in the

* An Assembly was when the Grande Chambre, the Enquêtes and the Requêtes came together to discuss a point of public policy.
** The Peers, on great occasions, joined the Parlement and were entitled to vote along with the présidents and conseillers.

State to counterbalance the Sovereign's authority."[12] Barbier, who knew his law, was perfectly right: the Parlement did not have the right to oppose the King as it had tried to do; but that simple fact was hardly pleasing to the usurping judges, so in complying they were merely biding their time.

Within a few weeks, in fact, the whole process started again. Suits, assemblies, arrêts ordering that the last rites be duly administered and fining all priests who were not in compliance. On February 22, 1753, the King sent down Letters Patent forbidding the continuance of "all inquests and procedures." The response came quickly enough. On April 15, the Parlement sent the King new remonstrances that were monumental in both length and content; these opposed the order contained in the Letters Patent and the practice of withholding the last rites. Louis XV, whose first impulse was to refuse even to receive the deputation of the Parlement, was convinced by Machault, now Keeper of the Seals, at least to listen. The King, after all, would at some future date need the Parlement's registration of his financial edicts. Since, moreover, the controversy, annoying as it was, did not touch on the basic needs of the State, some sort of compromise seemed in order. What Machault failed to appreciate was that Louis XV had a long, unpleasant experience of the Parlement's opposition, and that he had just witnessed yet another attempt at usurping his power. As a result, on May 4, after due consideration, the King refused the remonstrances and ordered registration of the Letters Patent. The next day, the Enquêtes and Requêtes (but not the Grande Chambre) were back on strike. On the seventh, the King sent down *lettres de jussion* (letters bearing a direct order to obey) ordering an end to the strike. This time, in spite of a Council during which the ministers had advised the King to compromise, Louis XV, who could see that the very nature of the monarchy was at stake, insisted on being obeyed. On May 8, four of the leaders of the strike were arrested and a dozen others exiled to the provinces. On May 9, the Grande Chambre, which had continued to sit, joined the strike. On May 10, it was exiled to Pontoise, a few miles west of Paris and the very place chosen by the Regent back in 1722. Once again, with the *Unigenitus* bull at the center of the controversy, the Parlement set itself up as the King's rival; only, while in 1722 the King's name was merely a screen for the Regent, this time it was the royal person whose will was directly challenged.

All through that summer and fall, the situation remained unchanged. The Parlement stayed on strike; the weather grew too cold for outdoor pastimes, and Pontoise was both uncomfortable and dull, yet the Parlement still refused to give in, with the result that almost all judiciary activity came to a halt in Paris. Clearly, something must be done. Perhaps if the Parlement realized that the King was not about to relent, it would finally give in, so in November it was transferred to Soissons, some two hundred miles from Paris and a provincial hole. At the same time, seeing that it was fast losing ground, it began to claim that, far from opposing the King, it was merely defending his rights: it was the old argument that had first been used in the 1720s.

As well as sending the Parlement off to Soissons, the Council, with the King's full approval, took what it thought of as the sternest of measures. On September 11, a Chambre Royale was created to replace the Parlement. It looked like a bold and practical move: there would be less discontent if people could resume their normal habits, and the Parlement, when it realized that it wasn't needed after all, would inevitably submit. As an idea it made perfect sense; only there was a huge flaw. The new court, to be convincing, must be used by all those who would normally take their cases to the Parlement; but if these same people thought—and they did—that the Parlement would some day return, and that upon resuming its functions it would visit its wrath upon all who had resorted to the Chambre Royale, then, obviously, no matter how great the inconvenience, it was better for them to wait; so the Chambre Royale, duly established as it was, found itself deserted. What Machault and the Council had failed to see was that half measures wouldn't work. Only if the Parlement were to be permanently abolished would cases begin to come in to the Chambre Royale; with the older body in recess but still alive, it was clear that the new creation would shortly perish of languor, and no one, with the possible exception of the King, was ready to dissolve a four-hundred-and-fifty-year-old institution. It was thus easy to forecast a repeat of the classic solution: eventually a face-saving compromise would be reached and the Parlement would return.

That, in fact, is just what happened. The conseillers and the présidents were thoroughly tired of living in Soissons and, besides, they missed their usual fees. The government could see that the Chambre Royale was stillborn and that the Parlement was still needed; so the prince de Conti offered his services as a negotiator and reached what seemed the perfect halfway solution: the Parlement came back and accepted a severe Declaration in which its behavior was stigmatized and the King's rights reaffirmed; but the Letters Patent were never registered. Once again, behind the smoke screen of royal firmness, the Parlement had won. It was simply a question of time before it began to make trouble again.

By February 1755, the weary ministers who met in the Council were watching yet another replay of the same situation. Last rites were being refused everywhere, the families were appealing to the Parlement, the Parlement was producing a steady stream of arrêts, which, in April, went so far as to declare the *Unigenitus* bull null and void. It was back to square one. Of course, the Council overruled the Parlement, but in the meantime Louis XV saw clearly that this endless conflict was weakening his authority and making many people miserable as well: after all, it was very painful to believe that your mother or brother was now in hell because he or she had been denied the last rites; so the King tried a new method.

First, the triennial Assembly of the Clergy was made to see that the proofs of confession did more harm than good, so it declared them uncanonical, thus neatly removing the foundation of the Archbishop's order; then, a bright young man whom Mme de Pompadour had noticed in trying circumstances and whom she had convinced the King to appoint as Ambassador to the Holy See, the comte de Stainville, convinced the Pope to issue the encyclical *Ex omnibus* (October 16, 1756). This document, which Benedict XIV and Stainville had actually written together, endorsed the Assembly's stand: now that the proofs of confession had been outlawed both by the French bishops and by the Pope himself, the whole sorry mess was over. No one died unshriven, and the Parlement no longer had reason to oppose its sovereign. Or so the King naively thought. In fact, faced with this highly frustrating situation—peace and quiet was the last thing it wanted—the Parlement simply shifted its ground. Religion had just proved a disappointment, but there was always taxation.

Annoying as all this was, however, it remained no more than a minor irritation for Louis XV. Not only did he have weightier matters on his mind—the peace, fragile from the first, looked more and more uncertain—but he also had many closer satisfactions. Never, in sum, had he been so happy.

With the single exception of the death, in February 1752, of Madame Henriette, Madame Infante's twin, whom the King mourned deeply and sincerely, his family gave him nothing but happiness. On January 20, 1751, the Duchess of Parma gave birth to an heir, Don Ferdinand, who was followed, on December 9, by a daughter, Maria Luisa*; then, at the end of September 1752, she came back to Versailles for another one of the long visits which gave her father such pleasure. In addition, the daughters who, at Fleury's request, had been sent off to Fontevrault, at last came back to Versailles. They were fewer in number—Madame Sixième had died in 1745 —but the King was overjoyed to have them near him again. Madame Victoire, who arrived in the summer of 1748, was followed, in October 1750, by Mesdames Sophie and Louise. "The King went to greet them with M. le Dauphin and Madame Victoire," Mme de Pompadour wrote her brother. "I had the honor of following him. In truth, nothing is more touching than these meetings. The King's tenderness for his children is beyond anything and they respond to it wholeheartedly."[13]

As for the Dauphin, he was respectful, dutiful and good, if perhaps a little awkward. "[He] showed wit and knowledge, had a thousand good qualities, but not those needed by public figures," the duc de Croÿ noted. "He waddled when he walked and was careless about time, so that he was twice as difficult to serve as the King and one never quite knew how to treat him. He was often closeted with Madame la Dauphine, the rest of the time with his gentlemen who had taken him over; besides that, he was neither easy nor pleasant of access."[14] It is never easy being a Crown Prince, but it was doubly difficult for the Dauphin. His father was not only the King but the handsomest man in France and a notable athlete, as well as a man at ease with women. The Dauphin, on the other hand, was plain, overweight, clumsy and lacking in charm. Since he was also rather more pious than became a French prince, he was often unpleasant to people whose morals he disapproved of, which did nothing to increase his popularity. As to his preference for being alone with his wife, it was considered uncivilized, odd and ungracious. Still, the Dauphin did have positive qualities. He was serious, conscientious, always interested in new information and recent books (as long as they attacked neither the government nor the Church), a good son and husband; and he could, when he felt at ease, demonstrate a certain kind of humor, as in this New Year's greeting to his friend the comte de Tressan: "I wish you a happy New Year; dispense me from spinning you out a compliment on this novel and sublime theme; it would tell you no more and bore you a good deal longer."[15] Clearly, there was more to the young man than met the duc de Croÿ's eye.

Another observer thought so too. "Madame la Dauphine, née Saxony, was the most jealous in the kingdom; she was rather unpleasant to her attendants and not

* She married Charles IV of Spain and was frequently painted by Goya.

much liked," Dufort wrote. "The Dauphin, then very close to the Jesuits, was carefully watched by his wife; he had wanted to court the marquise de Belzunce, who was as pretty as an angel; he had noticed the marquise de Tessé, née Noailles, who was pleasing; but as soon as he made the first move he was caught by the Dauphine. I was several times introduced into his private apartments and saw the Dauphine sitting and embroidering in a small room with only one window, which the Dauphin had made into his library. His desk was covered by the best books, which were renewed every week . . . The Dauphin walked up and down or sat. I found myself several times chatting with him as if I had been in an ordinary salon . . . He had a pleasant, logical, instructive manner of conversing; nobody was better at giving audience to the ambassadors. He knew the needs of the several states, all about the ruling families of Europe and was familiar with the production of the different countries. He measured the intelligence of those with whom he spoke and had the art of keeping the conversation general without letting it become too long . . . He sang arias, played the harpsichord and loved music. I saw him very cheerful in private, but in a decent and well-bred way."[16] Whatever the marquises de Belzunce and de Tessé may have felt, it looked as if the Dauphin might make quite a good king. As for Louis XV, he felt he had a loving son and a worthy successor.

That the Dauphin and the Dauphine had at least one essential function became very clear on September 27, 1751. By his first marriage, the Dauphin had remained childless, indeed, the poor Marie Thérèse probably suffered from an advanced case of tuberculosis when she arrived at Versailles. For the first three years of his second marriage, he had failed to father the expected heir; but at last, on that September day, the Dauphine gave birth to a boy. "You can imagine my joy since you know how much I love the King," Mme de Pompadour wrote Mme de Lutzelbourg. "I was so struck that I fainted in the antechamber of Madame la Duchesse. Luckily, they pushed me behind a curtain, so only Mme de Villars and Mme d'Estrades knew what happened. Madame la Dauphine is in the best of health and so is M. le duc de Bourgogne [the new baby whose title was that of Louis XV's father]. I saw him yesterday; his eyes are just like his grandfather's, which is very clever of him."[17] The King was indeed overjoyed: not only was the succession safe for the moment, but there was every hope that the Dauphine would produce more sons in the years ahead.

Even the Queen, dowdy as ever, had subsided into a routine which, dull as it might seem to others, she found highly agreeable. "The Queen's coterie gathered at Mme de Luynes," Croÿ noted. "It was composed of the Président Hénault [a pleasant, entertaining man who loved royalty], Moncrif [the author of a lively *History of the Cat*], a lot of very pious people and all the older ladies of the Court. They played at commerce and the Queen held her game of cavagnole* from seven to nine. The Dauphin, the Dauphine and Mesdames came regularly to play for a while. All [the Court] was allowed in to this rather dreary spectacle, but except for a few old courtiers, a few officers of the Bodyguard and some of the Captains of the Guard, nobody bothered to come."[18]

The Queen's tastes seemed to have passed on to most of her daughters, but she

* simple, dull card games.

still treated them with cool, distant politeness. The two exceptions were Madame Infante and Madame Adélaide, who loved music and had a lively disposition; the latter was, however, beginning to turn sour and old maidish. Mesdames Victoire and Sophie were, to say the least, not very bright; Madame Louise was imperious, demanding and often unpleasant. As it was, they all did their best to survive the tedium of their lives. They took Italian lessons from Goldoni, the great playwright, and music lessons from Beaumarchais,* surely one of the wittiest men of his time. They had coffee every day with their father before he went hunting; and they ate almost without stop: their cupboards were full of all kinds of foods—hams, sausages, stews, pastries—which they washed down with sweet Spanish wines. Still, theirs was hardly an enviable life.

"Mesdames led the saddest, most uniform existence imaginable. Every day they put on Court dress and joined the King, with whom they went to Mass; then they came back to their apartments, where they waited for a dinner which they ate in public; then they undressed, only to put the same Court dress back on so as to attend the King's débotter and the Queen's card game."[19] This was all such a chore that they soon invented a shortcut. In private, Mesdames wore loose, comfortable dresses. When the time came to visit their father, they would tie paniers and a train over their dress, put on a loose, waist-length cape to conceal the fact that they were not wearing the stiff, uncomfortable Court bodice; then, when they returned to their rooms, off came the cape, the paniers and the train, and they were again comfortable.

"A few ladies of their suite were admitted to their private apartments during their week of duty,** like Mme la marquise de Narbonne, of whom Madame Adélaide was fond. She [Madame Adélaide] had a lively and interesting face and everything needed to make a man happy; she had talents and cultivated them, but, like her sisters, her only dissipation was a change of residence. M. le Dauphin, whose temperament was kept in check by his austere mores, watched them carefully . . . Madame Adélaide depicted her situation perfectly to a lady, on duty that week, who was complaining about dressing and undressing four times a day, and about not having a free quarter of an hour. 'Madame,' Madame Adélaide told her, 'you can at least then rest for a week; but since I have to do this work the whole year round, you will allow me to keep my pity for myself.' "[20] With all their dullness, and their increasingly crotchety dispositions, however, Louis XV loved his daughters, and whenever he could he tried to make their life pleasanter. Soon after Madame Henriette's death, for instance, he decided to give them larger apartments, so he ordered the celebrated (but unneeded) Staircase of the Ambassadors torn down and a long suite of rooms on the ground floor of the south wing of the Palace was redecorated in the newest fashion.† Still, even a fond father could only bear so much of Mesdames' company, and it was on that hard reality that a whole succession of attempts at ousting Mme de Pompadour foundered: the princesses were quite unable to provide the lively atmosphere to which the King had grown accustomed.

* The author of *The Barber of Seville* and *The Marriage of Figaro*.
** Mesdames' ladies came on duty one week in four.
† Newly restored, these rooms can once again be visited.

Like their brother, they loathed the favorite, he because he was so pious, they because they were so jealous. They objected, in the first place, to their father having a mistress,* but they also loathed everything the marquise stood for: she was worldly, intellectual, mildly anticlerical, a friend of such enemies of the Church as Voltaire. They fumed in private, therefore, and frowned in public, but they were quite unable to influence their father in this or any other respect.

More than ever, as the years passed, Louis XV depended on Mme de Pompadour. She, for her part, always managed to invent new amusements for him. In September 1751, for instance, she wrote Mme de Lutzelbourg: "On Monday I go to Crécy [one of her castles] for five days . . . I am having a wedding for the girls of the villages and will show it all to the King. They are coming tomorrow to eat and dance in the courtyard of the château."[21] It was obviously a pleasing novelty for the King suddenly to find himself playing that favorite eighteenth-century character, the kindly lord of the manor. There was the theater, of course, especially at Bellevue. There were a growing number of houses—Crécy, which was quite large, as well as a tiny pavilion near the Palace of Fontainebleau or a two-room "hovel" in the park of Versailles, all with the appropriate decors and charming gardens. It wasn't all amusement, though: Louis XV, who had noticed that his mistress often made more sense than his ministers, was beginning to ask her for advice. In 1753 the duc de Croÿ noted: "The marquise always had a great, and still growing, influence; charming in looks and character, and most amiable, she did her best to please; not only the great questions but even the details passed through her hands." And, naturally, her status rose accordingly. Croÿ continues: "I noticed the easy way in which she passed before the first duchess in the most polite way . . . but all let her go ahead and she behaved beautifully to them."[22]

All these triumphs had a price in terms of effort and fatigue. "We are so often on the road that I have given up hunting . . . I need some time to think"[23] she wrote in December 1751, and in October 1752: "I have just had a fever for ten days . . . [have been] bled and have had a terrible headache . . . I am overcome with visits, with letters and still have at least sixty more letters to write."[24] "The life I lead is terrible," she complained in another letter. "I scarcely have a minute of my own: rehearsals and performances, and twice a week a trip . . . Indispensable and considerable duties: The Queen, the Dauphin, the Dauphine, who, luckily, is consigned to her chaise longue, three daughters [Mesdames], two Infantas, see whether I can find time to breathe."[25] And gradually, to all these obligations were added the cares of State as well as occasional acute anxiety: by the early fifties, the triumphant mistress hardly ever slept with the King anymore.

Never really fond of sex, the marquise soon found herself exhausted by the King's frequent lovemaking, an obvious catastrophe for someone whose position depended on satisfying desire. At first she tried stuffing herself with such aphrodisiacs as truffles, crayfish and vanilla, but instead of becoming passionate, the marquise simply made herself sick: obviously, there would have to be another solution. It was then

* One wonders whether Madame Adélaide ever knew that her dear Mme de Narbonne had an affair with the King and bore him a son.

that, with admirable insight, she took the very step that should have resulted in her prompt dismissal: she encouraged Louis XV to take other mistresses.

The King was too fond of pleasure to settle for a semicelibate life. At the beginning, no doubt, he had been attracted to Mme d'Etioles, as she was then, because of her looks; now he was in love with her because of her other qualities: her kindness, her lively intelligence, her feeling for the arts, her common sense. Before Mme de Pompadour, a new love had meant the dismissal of the current mistress; but if Louis XV could have a succession of purely sexual affairs while his official mistress became his best friend, then she was safe. It took a stroke of genius to realize this, of course, and a woman of extraordinary talent to make it work.

More than ever, therefore, it was important that Mme de Pompadour be, at the same time, entertaining and useful; the former went almost without saying; the latter had a number of glorious consequences. There was, for instance, the establishment of the Ecole Militaire.

It had long been evident that many French officers, brave though they might be, sorely lacked training, especially in those specialized branches like the artillery, which required scientific knowledge. Even when it was just a question of performing the right maneuver, or keeping in touch with another army corps in enemy country, more than just courage was needed. If, on the other hand, a cadet school were established in which would-be officers were thoroughly trained in military matters while receiving an adequate scientific and literary education, then, obviously, the country would have a better army. At the same time, there were many impoverished noble families that could no longer afford to educate their children. In the seventeenth century, Louis XIV had created, at Mme de Maintenon's suggestion, a school at Saint Cyr for the daughters of these same families. Why not, said the marquise, emulate him and create a school for the boys?

The answer to that question was perfectly simple: it would cost a great deal of money to create, build and run the school, and so at first Machault opposed it. Mme de Pompadour, however, cared little about money as long as it was well spent, so she persisted. First she convinced the King to take a long overdue step. "The King has established a military nobility which a man can earn by serving in the Army; every general officer . . . becomes noble by right and all his descendants enjoy the rights and privileges of the nobility; every lower officer who is a knight of Saint Louis* and has served for thirty years will be exempt from paying the *taille*** even after he has left the Army,"[26] Barbier noted with approbation. It was, in fact, a major step: for the first time it was possible to enter the ranks of the nobility simply by serving in the armed forces, so that a talented or brave commoner could hope to raise his family to a new, higher rank. This gave the otherwise rigidly stratified French society a sorely needed degree of fluidity and emphasized once again the King's recognition of personal merit.

Soon after this major reform, the establishment of the Ecole Militaire was announced. "You must be thrilled with the King's edict, which ennobles the officers," Mme de Pompadour wrote a friend in January 1751. "You will be even more im-

* A decoration given to reward military merit.
** A personal, flat-rate tax paid only by commoners.

pressed with another, which will soon be published, in which His Majesty will undertake to educate five hundred noblemen in the military arts . . . That establishment is all the finer in that His Majesty has been working on it for a year, and in that his ministers have had nothing to do with it."[27] The marquise was right: it was indeed a major step forward; within a very few years the quality of the French officer corps improved markedly. It naturally took awhile for the full effect of the new education to be felt, but when the French armies swept to unprecedented triumphs at the end of the century under the leadership of a graduate of the Ecole Militaire, one Napoléon Bonaparte, it became quite clear that the institution—which, in a slightly different form, still exists today—had indeed proved a success. To make it all even better, Louis XV commissioned Jacques Ange Gabriel, unquestionably the greatest architect of his time, to design the new school buildings, which have remained one of the chief ornaments of Paris.

Indeed, it was another one of Mme de Pompadour's gifts to the King that his interest in architecture became refined and focused. By the 1750s he was able to read floor plans and draw them himself. To the duc de Croÿ's amazement, Louis XV asked to see the preliminary drawings of a house that the duc was having built, commenting on them with considerable expertise, then suggesting improvements which he traced in himself. Just as he understood the rules and practice of architecture, so the King recognized quality, and he was quick to see that Gabriel was a genius. From the forties on, the architect designed masterpiece after masterpiece all through France, like the two city squares in Rennes or, in Paris, the Ecole Militaire and the two palaces of the Place Louis XV (today the Place de la Concorde), the new palace at Compiègne and, in the park of Versailles, that pure jewel, the Petit Trianon. Interestingly enough, the King, who was fond of the rococo as a decorative style, understood the artful simplicity, classic proportions and chaste ornamentation of Gabriel's architecture. While elsewhere in Europe buildings bulged and wriggled, in France they seemed, by comparison, almost severe, but they gained in serenity what they lost in eccentricity.

Architecture was a traditional royal concern; but then, at Mme de Pompadour's instigation, Louis XV decided to champion a whole new art form. Chinese porcelain had long been admired in Europe, but the secret of its manufacture only reached the West at the beginning of the eighteenth century. The very first European porcelain was made in Saxony, where the Elector had installed artisans in the little town of Meissen. By the mid-forties, a small, privately owned and financially weak porcelain manufacture was established in the royal château of Vincennes, and it began to produce pieces of remarkable quality. Because the factory was undercapitalized, however, and because most people simply ordered directly from Meissen, the enterprise would have closed its doors if the marquise hadn't stepped in. She arranged for the King to buy out the former owners; then the works, now the Manufacture Royale, were transferred to the little village of Sèvres, outside Paris, where in 1752 a new building was erected. Sèvres porcelain was born, and it went on to astound Europe by the quality of its design, the perfection of its detail, the intensity of its color and its translucency. The greatest living artists were enlisted (Boucher was one) to produce scenes suitable for plates or vases; completely new, sometimes whimsical, forms were invented; a process was found to make the gold ornaments shinier and longer-lasting: in no time Sèvres provided the standards by which all other porcelain was judged. Glorious as all this was esthetically, however, it also made for a very expensive product: perfection does not come cheap; so Louis XV and Mme de Pompadour transformed themselves into merchants. Once a year, in January, the newest Sèvres pieces were displayed in the Hall of Mirrors, and the King made it plain that he would look with favor on those of his courtiers who did not leave empty-handed. That hint was enough, and it started a fashion which has continued to this day.

Not all Mme de Pompadour's efforts were quite this successful. When she tried to protect the intellectuals, she met with royal resistance. Although he wanted to reward achievement, and realized the luster that great writers could shed on his reign, Louis XV felt that there was not just a difference of rank but almost a difference in nature between an intellectual and himself. All familiarity was thus impossible, especially since genius tends to assume equality with other eminent personages. Writers might have their place, but it wasn't a seat at the King's suppers, and although the young Mme d'Etioles had tried to attract people like Voltaire to her salon, the marquise de Pompadour could no longer do so, especially since the King deeply resented the Enlightenment's attacks on the Church. Even Voltaire, who loved kings in general and his own in particular, never managed to behave in such a way as to please. When he tried to flatter, the King thought him merely impertinent. An ode, dated February 1748, is a perfect example of the gap which separated the Court from the rest of the world. It runs: "Ainsi donc vous réunissez / Tous les arts, tous les goûts, tous les talents de plaire; / Pompadour, vous embellissez / La cour, le Parnasse et Cythère. / Charmes de tous les coeurs, trésor d'un seul mortel / Qu'un sort si beau soit éternel! / Que vos jours precieux soient marqués par des fêtes; / Que la paix dans nos champs revienne avec Louis / Et tous deux gardez vos conquêtes." ("Thus you bring together / all the arts, all the refinements, all the ways of pleasing. / Pompadour, you embellish / the Court, Parnassus* and Cythera.** / Charm of every heart, treasure of just one man / Let so fine a life be eternal! / Let your precious days be endlessly festive / Let peace come back to us with Louis / Both be without an enemy / And both keep your conquests.")[28] At first sight, and to our less sophisticated eyes, this looks like mere flattering clichés; in fact, the King and the Court saw nothing but presumption and impertinence. What did Voltaire think he was doing when he equated the King's conquests and the sway held by his mistress? How dare he tell them to keep their conquests, as if the King were just another fallen fortress? How could he use so familiar a tone? Louis XV was furious, but not nearly so angry as when, a few months later, two more lines of doggerel became widely quoted.

Although she had adopted all the manners of ce pays-ci, the marquise, when surrounded by friends, sometimes used typically middle-class expressions which amused the King; so it happened one day that, in the presence of Voltaire, she used the slangy diminutive *grassouillette* ("fatty") about a quail she was eating. Instantly Voltaire, who frequently was carried away by his facility, improvised two lines: "Grassouillette, entre nous, me semble un peu caillette / Je vous le dis tout bas, belle

---

* Parnassus was Apollo's residence.
** The island of Venus.

Pompadourette." Since they rely on Paris slang, the two lines cannot be translated literally. A *caillette,* ("little quail"), the bird the marquise had found *grassouillette,* was also a prostitute; thus what Voltaire had said was: "Fatty, between us, sounds to me quail-like / [or: common, vulgar] I tell you this in a whisper, pretty Pompadourette." It was one thing for the marquise to use a slangy diminutive about a fat quail, quite another for the poet to do the same with her name; as for telling her that she had the manners of a caillette, it obviously needs no comment. Voltaire, who thought he had been witty, saw to it that the lines were widely repeated. The marquise, who had just been painfully reminded of the nature of her calling, was deeply insulted. After that, any courtier could have told Voltaire that he would no longer find himself welcome at Versailles.

Although, as far as the King was concerned, it was a case of once bitten by his own historiographer, twice shy, Mme de Pompadour continued, from a slightly greater distance, to protect the intellectuals; and she had a direct link to them in the person of her physician, Dr. Quesnay, whom the King also liked. It was Quesnay who introduced them to Buffon, the great naturalist, whose knowledge fascinated them. Through him, the marquise was in touch with the Encyclopédistes, those intellectuals who set about writing down, in a series of volumes, everything that was known. Since the Encyclopédie, as admirable a compendium of human knowledge as has ever been published, paid very little attentions to dogma, whether religious or political, it was soon banned for doubting that the world had indeed been created in seven days, or that kings were instituted of God. At just about this time, there was a supper party at Trianon. "The duc de La Vallière was saying that he wondered what gunpowder was made of. 'It seems so funny that we spend our time killing patridges, and being killed ourselves on the border, and really we have no idea how it happens.' Mme de Pompadour, seeing her opportunity, quickly went on: 'Yes, and face powder? What is that made of? Now, if you had not banned the Encyclopédie, Sire, we could find out in a moment.' The King sent to his library for a copy, and presently footmen staggered in under the weight of the heavy volumes; the party was kept amused for the rest of the evening looking up gunpowder, rouge and so on. After this, subscribers were allowed to have their copies, though it was still not on sale in the bookshops."[29] It is wholly characteristic of the King that he allowed continued publication because of the scientific content of the Encyclopédie; but, sadly, in an age when all Europe spoke French and looked to France for intellectual leadership, Louis XV felt thoroughly out of sympathy with the men who, like Diderot and d'Alembert, did so much to make the century glorious.

Her various triumphs notwithstanding, Mme de Pompadour found life difficult. She loved the King and he loved her, but otherwise she was engaged in a constant struggle; nor did her kindness help her. It was all very well to write her brother, in April 1751, "Poor Mme de Mailly is dead, and I'm really sorry; she was unhappy and the King feels it"[30]; if that sentiment had become widely known, people would merely have laughed at her. In fact, she was becoming cynical. "I find that Alexandrine [her daughter by M. d'Etioles] is getting much uglier; as long as she is not really hideous, I will be perfectly satisfied, for I am very far from wanting her to be a great beauty. That only makes enemies of all the female sex, which, with the friends of

said women, makes up two thirds of the world"[31]: a bitter comment from a woman
whose attractions were so splendid; and her advice to her brother confirms her
feelings. "What I advise you to do above all is to show the greatest politeness and an
equally great discretion, and to get into your head that since you are made to live in
the world and in society, you must be pleasant to everyone, for if we were nice only
to the people we respect, we would be hated by most of mankind . . . Do not think
that because I am young I cannot give good advice. I have seen so much in the four
and a half years that I have been here that I know more than most women of forty,"
and, movingly, she concludes, "love me as much as I love you."[32] The world to which
she refers, of course, is always ce pays-ci. "As for the courtiers, I must enlighten you
about them," she continued three months later. "If your birth allowed you to com-
pete with them for the offices to which they aspire, you may be sure that, secretly,
they would try to harm you; but since that is not the case, they have nothing but
indifference for you."[33] And again, two months later: "Except for the happiness of
being with the King, which, assuredly makes up for everything else, all the rest is
nothing but nastiness and platitudes, in a word, all the worst of which we poor
humans are capable."[34] These words were written in January 1756, and the marquise
knew whereof she spoke: in the preceding year, as the result of a plot against her
which involved her best friend, she had nearly lost the King.

When she had first moved to Versailles, Mme de Pompadour had brought with her
a cousin, Mme d'Estrades, who, in that new, difficult world, accompanied her everywhere and became her best friend. The King, it soon turned out, also liked her.
Although plain, she was witty, lively and amusing, qualities which counted for much.
That, very quickly, she had tried to seduce the monarch mattered very little since it
was virtually a reflex for every woman at Court. She was neither pretty enough nor
kind enough to succeed, so Mme de Pompadour never gave her attempts a second
thought. Besides, Mme d'Estrades was clearly ambitious, a characteristic Louis XV
detested. As a result, she knew the Court and its intrigues, and that, in turn, was
useful for the marquise. Soon, as a reward, she was appointed a lady-in-waiting to
Madame Adélaide, a post which gave her an income (not very large) and, far more
important, an official position. As if all this weren't enough, she soon turned into a
backstairs power by becoming the comte d'Argenson's mistress. Unlike his unpracti-
cal brother, the marquis and ex-Foreign minister, the comte had become a fixture.
The King trusted him and failed to see that he had a tendency to arrange military
affairs in such a way as to make himself look good. A master intriguer but also, to be
fair, a competent minister, he was unquestionably the most influential member of the
Council in 1752 and yearned to be Prime Minister, in name if possible, but, at any
rate, in fact.

It seems pretty certain that Mme d'Estrades actually loved d'Argenson. In any
event, whether it was sentiment, ambition or, more probably, both, she wanted to see
him succeed, especially since she herself would become immensely powerful if he
did. Unfortunately, Mme de Pompadour was in the way, so together d'Argenson and
Mme d'Estrades arranged for her to go. Having looked around carefully, they picked
a charming, ravishingly pretty, vivacious, empty-headed young woman, the comtesse
de Choiseul-Romanet. A cousin of Mme d'Estrades, the young comtesse, then still in

her late teens, was thus also, by stretching the family tree a little, a relation of the marquise's, who, kind as always, had arranged her marriage to M. de Choiseul. For the lady it was a great step up: the Choiseuls were an old and illustrious Lorraine family; for the husband it meant access to the intimate circle around the King, something of which everyone dreamed.

The plan was simple enough. Mme de Choiseul would seduce the King, carefully resisting until he had promised to send Mme de Pompadour away; thus two objects would be attained at one blow: Mme de Pompadour would be gone and the new mistress, who had neither brains nor experience, would be wholly dependent on d'Argenson and Mme d'Estrades.

At first everything went according to plan. Mme de Choiseul-Romanet made a dead set for the King, behaved as provocatively as she knew how, flaunted her eighteen-year-old charms and declared to all who would listen that, being a model wife, she would never ever leave her husband for anyone—except, of course, the King. It had been quite a while since so pretty a woman, whom the King saw so often, offered herself so openly. Louis XV, not unnaturally, was tempted. Now, in a repeat of Mme de Châteauroux's strategy some years earlier, it was a question of playing with him until she had the required guarantees. This was a delicate matter. If Mme de Choiseul succumbed too soon, he would lose interest; if she waited too long, he would grow angry and look elsewhere. The lady was not up to playing so subtle a game, but she had Mme d'Estrades to advise her—sometimes several times a day. And since Mme d'Estrades saw the King constantly and knew him very well indeed, she could appraise the situation from moment to moment.

It was during the autumn stay at Fontainebleau that the great moment finally came. The King twisted his knee on a dark staircase that led to Mme de Choiseul's room and began to feel that he had had enough. The lady, clearly about to fall, asked that the marquise be dismissed. Driven by desire, the King agreed; and not very much later the comtesse, her dress still in disarray, rushed triumphantly into d'Argenson's room, where he and Mme d'Estrades were waiting: she had won, the King loved her, the old mistress was to be sent away. Her victory, and that of the intrigue, was complete.

Or so it seemed. Mme de Pompadour, who understood what was going on, stayed most of the time in her rooms, despairing; and her great friend the marquis de Gontaut desperately tried to help. As it turned out, M. de Gontaut's brother-in-law, the comte de Stainville, was also a member of the Choiseul family—the comte's cousin, in fact. At first, all M. de Gontaut did was to share his unhappiness with Stainville without expecting to get much sympathy: although he had tried to bring them together because they were both lively, witty and civilized, Mme de Pompadour and Stainville had disliked each other on sight, and it was purely by chance that Stainville, who was pursuing a military career, was at Fontainebleau.

"M. de Stainville," Dufort noted, "was known in Paris for his wit. Although extremely ugly [he had carrot-colored hair, a turned-up nose and thick lips] he lived the life of a Don Juan and was said to be one of the most bitingly funny men in the city. His mind was subtle, delicate, amiable."[35] Of course, his cousin kept him abreast of the progress of her romance with the King. Stainville was a notable seducer and, quite possibly, Mme de Choiseul was being flirtatious while bringing her family into her new fortune. Here was the beginning of a new party at Court, in which the Choiseul family would have the first place; besides, it must have been hard for a girl of eighteen not to crow about the fact that she had seduced the King. Perhaps Stainville expressed doubt; in any event, the comtesse produced a letter from her lover which, amid the clearest expressions of endearment, promised to send Mme de Pompadour away. At that point M. de Stainville had a flash of genius: he asked whether he might keep the letter overnight. The foolish comtesse said he could.

Had Stainville been less intelligent, he would have backed his cousin on the assumption that favors would be showered on the entire family; as it was, he clearly realized that Mme de Choiseul simply didn't have what it took to keep the King for more than a few months; so, putting the letter in his pocket, he went off to see his brother-in-law, who was more distraught than ever. Mme de Pompadour, he said, was in a terrible state. Stainville, who pretended he was uninterested, remarked in the most offhand way that, by chance, it was in his power to end her troubles; but then, he went on, they were on such bad terms . . . Frantically M. de Gontaut begged him to go and see the marquise. Naturally, Stainville made it plain that he expected to be asked—and with a good deal of urgency—by the marquise herself. Off went M. de Gontaut; and after a lot of back-and-forth negotiation, he convinced Stainville to come along. By the time he walked into Mme de Pompadour's apartment, she was frantic; and that is when he produced the letter.

Instantly Mme de Pompadour's tears ceased: she knew she had just the weapon she needed. If there was anything Louis XV loathed, it was indiscretion; he was also much too kind—and much too fond of the marquise—to tell her to her face that she must go; so when he came in she cleverly brandished the letter and made a scene. On the point of losing her, the King realized how much he needed her, even if he was sexually attracted to Mme de Choiseul; besides, he could only suppose that she had been bragging about the letter—as, in fact, she had—and that was unforgivable. Within twenty-four hours the Choiseuls were ordered to leave the Court.

Mme de Pompadour had triumphed, but the limits of her power were revealed by the fact that both d'Argenson and Mme d'Estrades remained in place. Perhaps it was a compensation that the marquise now found herself with a new friend: M. de Gontaut had been right after all, it seemed, for she and Stainville discovered that they liked each other immensely. Unfortunately for Stainville, the King, who was reminded of Mme de Choiseul-Romanet every time he saw the comte, now wanted him out of the way, and so he told the marquise. Mme de Pompadour, however, was nothing if not loyal. Send him away if you want, she told the King, but make him an ambassador: within a few days M. de Stainville found himself appointed as French Ambassador to the Holy See. If he did well there, who knew where he would stop?

Both the marquise and the King had learned a lesson from all this fracas: she, that it might be well to oversee the King's pleasures so that he would no longer be tempted by the likes of Mme de Choiseul; he, that Mme de Pompadour was very much more than a mistress, an irreplaceable friend. It was, after all, easy for him to find pretty, willing young women, but no one had ever made him feel at home the way the marquise could; besides, more than ever he needed disinterested advice: the peace was unstable, the Parlement was acting up and he had only the most moderate regard for his ministers. At the same time, he decided that Mme de Pompadour was entitled to a new proof of his affection: at the end of 1752, the former Mlle Poisson became a duchess.

Her new title made the most enormous difference to Mme de Pompadour's standing at Court: an iron wall separated "titled ladies" (i.e., duchesses) from the rest. They alone were entitled to the "honors of the *tabouret,*" which gave them the right to sit on a stool in the presence of Their Majesties; they preceded all nontitled ladies; they wore a ducal coronet and mantle on their coat of arms at a time when the latter were everywhere, from one's carriages to one's bed linen; they could use sedan chairs bearing these instead of a fleur-de-lys when they were carried about the Palace of Versailles. With all that, however, Mme de Pompadour chose to go on being called Madame la marquise, as before, to show that she was above it all.

Just how truly, how deeply, the King cared for her became evident soon afterwards. In 1754 her daughter, Alexandrine, whose future she had been busily planning and whose plainness, as we have seen, she applauded, fell ill and died. The marquise, who was a very loving mother, was devastated: with her daughter, it seemed to her, her whole future was gone. In an agony of grief, unable to eat or sleep, she took to her bed, bemoaning the loss of Alexandrine. "The affliction this unhappy incident has thrown her mother in is almost indescribable," wrote Lord Albemarle, the British Ambassador. "The tender attachment His Most Christian Majesty has shown her on this occasion has plainly proved that her favor has not diminished."[36] In response, the marquise did all she could to resume a normal life and appear as gay as before—and she almost succeeded. "I saw the marquise for the first time since the death of her daughter, that dreadful blow by which I had believed her crushed," wrote the duc de Croÿ. "But too much chagrin would not have helped her looks and might even have lost her her place, so she seemed to me neither upset nor changed and, by one of those frequent miracles of the Court, I found her neither less well nor looking more serious. Still, she had been bitterly struck and was probably as unhappy inside as she seemed happy outside."[37] The duc was only partly right: while undoubtedly miserable about Alexandrine's death, the marquise could not feel altogether unhappy as long as she retained the King's love.

She also had her brother. He had just been given the marquessate of Marigny. "Poisson by birth, since then Vandières and having now taken the name of Marigny, he said himself that he had been called comte d'Avant-hier [the day before yesterday —a pun] and that he was now called marquis de Marinière [of Fishy] because his name was Poisson. He was witty, had a good memory and some learning; born to be an employee of the Ferme générale and perhaps, after rising slowly, a fermier général himself, he had felt the effect of his sister's fortune as soon as he had come out of school. Sent to Rome at the age of eighteen with Cochin [the great draftsman and engraver], he had made good use of his travels. Very selfish, rude and presumptuous, he was ready to joke about his birth as long as people admired his mind."[38] In fact, although Marigny did tend to brusqueness, he was a man of taste and culture. During his Italian trip he admired the ruins of ancient Rome and came back with countless drawings and plans; it was largely due to his efforts that the neoclassical style replaced the rococo in France as early as 1760, and the artists he protected went on to do him honor.

All through 1753, 1754 and 1755 it was obvious that the King relied more and more on Mme de Pompadour, but, even so, the Court was dumbfounded when, on Sunday, February 8, 1756, Louis XV announced that the marquise-duchesse de Pompadour had just been appointed a supernumerary dame du palais de la Reine (lady-in-waiting to the Queen). There was, of course, a precedent of sorts: Louis XIV had made Mme de Montespan, his maîtresse déclarée, Superintendent of the Queen's Household; but no one thought that Louis XV was capable of so oppressing his wife. In fact, the Queen was in full agreement because she knew something the rest of the world didn't: sometime in October 1755 Mme de Pompadour had altogether stopped being the King's mistress.

Ever since Alexandrine's death, some eighteen months earlier, the heretofore irreligious marquise had turned to the Church for consolation. Whether she found it may perhaps be questioned, but, at any rate, she did her best to behave like a good Catholic and that, of course, meant putting a stop to the double adultery in which she and the King were engaged, so she started having long conversations with a Jesuit,* Father de Sacy. When she told him she wanted to take communion, however, he answered that it was impossible because she was still living in sin. At that the marquise showed him that the secret staircase to the King's room had been blocked and announced that she was perfectly chaste. The existence of other, less convenient staircases was politely forgotten. That wasn't enough, the Jesuit answered; she must return to her husband. That, in spite of appearances, was easy to evade. M. d'Etioles, now a fermier général, was busy leading the good life with a mistress he adored. The very last thing he wanted was to have Mme de Pompadour back in his house, playing the ghost at the feast, so to his wife's request he sent a polite answer: they had been separated so long, he explained, that he really couldn't take her back. Triumphantly the marquise showed this letter to Father de Sacy, only to be told that, husband or no, she would have to leave the Court. This was obviously too much: not only did Mme de Pompadour not want to go away, she felt sure—and rightly—that the King would never allow her to do so; so she ended the discussion and found herself instead a priest who would allow her to stay at Versailles while taking communion in private. Delighted that she could thus have her cake and eat it too, Mme de Pompadour did just that, and the Queen—once she knew that the marquise no longer slept with the King, had tried to return to her husband and took communion regularly—saw no reason not to have her as a lady-in-waiting.

Aside from her official chastity, the only change in the marquise's life was that she stopped eating meat on Fridays and Saturdays and no longer received the Court at her toilette. "The following Tuesday," Croÿ noted, "she received the ambassadors [while] sitting before her tapestry frame . . . Since people always go to an extreme, they said that she would stop wearing rouge,** but, on the contrary, she was very dressed up that day and spent her tour of duty at the Queen's as if she had done it all her life."[39] It had been a brilliant, well-planned move: now that she no longer caused

---

* The Jesuits were notoriously tolerant of worldly faults among the highly placed.
** Every lady at Court, without exception, wore rouge on her face.

the King to sin, there was no conceivable reason why the Royal Family should want to remove her. Indeed, if she were replaced, the new mistress was likely to be far more objectionable. Further, now that the King and she were simply friends, there was no reason why they should ever be separated.

This dazzling promotion did, however, leave Louis XV with a problem. While Mme de Pompadour was quite content to remain celibate, he, like all the Bourbons, had a voracious sexual appetite. There could be no question of sleeping with the Queen, who was elderly by the standards of the time and unattractive into the bargain; and another maîtresse déclarée was an obvious impossibility. Having thought it over carefully, however, he reached a perfectly sensible solution. There was a little house—it had some five or six rooms—just outside the park of Versailles at a place called the Parc aux Cerfs. Louis XV bought it, staffed it with a few discreet servants and used it to keep a succession of pretty young lower-middle-class women who were told that their visitor was a foreign dignitary. Every so often a new lodger came in, while the old one was pensioned off and often found a husband as well. Just how attractive these young women could be we know from their portraits: there was Mlle Murphy, for instance, whose fresh complexion and callipygous charms Boucher lovingly painted, thus hinting heavily at the King's preferences. All in all, it was a perfectly sensible solution; and, given the standards of the time, it hardly seemed excessive for a man to take a new mistress every few months; indeed, Louis XV was behaving with more restraint than most of his courtiers.

It was just as well, really, that the King's personal life had settled down, for he was about to face the most difficult years of his reign. By 1755, the peace had broken down and France found itself in a most precarious position, lacking a single ally it could depend on. The Parlement clearly intended to take advantage of the financial stress that would be caused by any conflict. The ministry was divided, and its chief member, d'Argenson, was Mme de Pompadour's personal enemy. It is important, therefore, to know what sort of a man Louis XV had become after all the recent changes and at the start—he was forty-six—of middle age. Luckily, a number of his courtiers set down their observations. It will be seen that they are overwhelmingly favorable; but the truth is that, time after time, people who came close to Louis XV were enormously impressed. Unlike the Sun King, who awed but hardly charmed his attendants, Louis XV was sensitive, kind and ready to be amused. That Mme de Pompadour never ceased to love him for himself cannot be doubted; the surprise is that so many of his courtiers shared her feelings.

The duc de Croÿ is a good example of the way Louis XV attracted people. A Belgian grandee, he was anxious to make a career for himself in France. He served in the French armies, spent much time at Court and wanted, above all, to become a general, a French duc—so that he would have the precedence denied foreign noblemen—and a knight of the Saint Esprit. In due time he achieved all three goals, but not without much delay or anxiety. Still, although in his *Mémoires* he complains about the ministers who failed to recognize his merit, about the King's slowness in granting him favors, and about the dissolute mores of the Court—he was himself intensely religious—he can clearly be seen, as the years pass, to appreciate Louis XV more and more. There are frequent small notations like this one, dated 1753: "I was really touched to see the King, who was an excellent grandpapa and a very young one, play wholeheartedly with [his grandchildren]."[40] As for his opinion of the sovereign, here it is: "The King had the most impressive appearance, being the handsomest man of his Court; he spoke admirably well about everything and—except for the fact that he did not trust himself enough, that he had too much difficulty in making decisions, which caused him to be led too easily—he had all the qualities needed to be a great king, being intelligent, knowledgeable and having a good memory; he was brave, active, tireless, kind or firm according to the circumstance."[41] And none who knew the King would have disagreed.

Croÿ was a grand seigneur, but Dufort de Cheverny came from the upper middle class and might, therefore, have been more critical. In fact, he, too, became devoted to his master. Because he spent so much time around Louis XV, he also allows us to visualize the King's life. "I had to be present in the King's cabinet," Dufort wrote. "And I spent most of my off-duty time there. Here is the list of those who were in attendance: Bachelier, the First Valet de Chambre and his survivancier,* Lebel, who has since played a great role in his master's pleasures; the First Gentleman of the Bedchamber of that year, M. le duc d'Aumont; M. le maréchal de Richelieu; M. le duc de Duras [all three were friends as well as First Gentlemen]; M. le duc de Fleury [an amiable nonentity who was the Cardinal's nephew]; M. le marquis de Mirepoix, Captain of the Guard [whose wife had become a great friend of Mme de Pompadour]; M. le comte de Maillebois, Grand Master of the Wardrobe [a competent general and actor]; M. le Premier [the First Equerry, the marquis de Beringhen, whose father and grandfather had served Louis XIV]; M. le comte de Brionne; M. le prince de Condé and his under governor, M. du Bonset; M. de Saint-Florentin [Minister of the King's Household since the twenties]; the ministers, when they had something they needed to say; M. de Fontanieu, the father as well as the son, who were in charge of Crown furniture; M. Hébert, Treasurer of the Menus-Plaisirs,** as witty as he was subtle; Papillon de Fontpertuis, in charge of the Menus; Senac, First Physician; Quentin de Champcenetz, First Valet de chambre; Quentin de Champlost, First Valet of the Wardrobe . . . Verneuil, secretary of the cabinet; one also met there the equerries like de Briges, Tourdonnet and old man Dampierre, one of the Chief Huntsmen. I was forgetting the marquis de Marigny . . . Superintendent of Crown Buildings." It is interesting to note that there was a preponderance of middle-class men around the King, most of whom came from families that had served the monarchy for generations, so that they became quite as much a part of ce pays-ci as the ducs while still being able, because of their connections, to keep the King in touch with public opinion.

Dufort then goes on: "Every morning, when my service was over, I stayed until the King left. In the evening, I came to his débotter and stayed for the coucher. Those who were most accustomed to him had warned me that if, in the cabinet, he came close to you and, out of respect, you backed away, he had the discretion of not speaking to you. I overcame my shyness and stood still: he liked young people and I was a child in comparison to old Sainctot [the former Introductor of the Ambassa-

---

* Almost every Court function had a survivancier who inherited the position at the holder's death.
** The department in charge of Court entertainment and festivities.

dors]. I soon had my reward; he spoke to me often and I grew so used to it that, because of his kindness, I often found myself better at ease with him than with some other people.

"The first time I had to take his orders for the presentation of some foreigners . . . he was sitting down. I came close to him and told him the names of those who had applied, softening my voice, which was already all too soft. He started to smile and, turning to me, he said: 'You are an alto?'

" 'No, Sire,' I answered, 'I sing off key.'

" 'You're not alone,' he said, and he himself shouted 'Tallyho' when hunting in so hoarse a voice that you could recognize it everywhere.

"I concluded from this that I had not displeased him, and before the end of the stay [at Compiègne] I obtained that he drop the 'monsieur' before my name, which was a mark of favor."[42] Even though the normal fascination exercised by a monarch may have had something to do with Dufort's liking for the King, it is still obvious that the feeling would not have lasted if it had not been frequently reinforced.

Sometimes the kindness was blended with a little teasing. "The King, in private, was as amiable as possible. Cheerful, pleasant, he often said interesting things. One day M. le prince de Condé came in to tell him about his wife's delivery . . . I should point out that it had happened quite late [April instead of January] . . . 'M. de Condé,' said the King, 'we are accustomed to arriving later than expected in the family; you, your grandfather and your great-grandfather, you all did just the same, as I did, along with my [great-]grandfather Louis XIV,' upon which he displayed an astonishing erudition and spoke at length about the family of the King of Sardinia. He was amused because the prince was so embarrassed that he answered only in monosyllables—'Yes, Sire'—being, as usual, very shy. This conversation lasted over an hour and fascinated us." At the same time, Louis XV could seem to take a strange distance from his own government. That same day "he spoke to the maréchal de Biron . . . He said: 'Maréchal, have you seen the new uniform of the Bodyguard?'

" 'No, Sire.'

" 'Have them show it to you. Ah, it is fine, magnificent, embroidered all over. I don't know what it will cost, but they wanted it so: God knows who will pay for it all, for the Treasury is short this year.' "[43] What Dufort failed to understand—but the maréchal surely did—was that Louis XV was, in fact, manifesting his displeasure with the apparently immovable comte d'Argenson. In 1756, as before, the King kept a close watch over the Treasury's expenditures. The minister who had ordered expensive new parade uniforms when war was looming had obviously made a serious error; but, save in extreme cases, Louis XV was loath to criticize ministers to their faces, preferring the blame to come through a third party. If, as is probable, the maréchal de Biron told d'Argenson about this little scene, the minister should have begun to worry: the next step was a letter of dismissal.

It is not the least pleasing aspect of Louis XV's character that, with all his understanding of the dignity proper to a monarch, he could still be good-natured about incidents which other kings would have punished severely. "Bontemps . . . was only just sixteen and we were impatiently waiting for him to come of age so he could take up the place [First Valet de Chambre] which the King had kept open for him.

The King, who liked children, often played with him and the young man without becoming too familiar, cooperated willingly with the royal jokes, which occasionally made him cry, for the King sometimes pulled his ears hard. We who stayed in the private apartments were almost always present for this. One day, at Versailles, Ville-pail accompanied the King at his débotter; once he was through, the King stood up and . . . went downstairs to Mme de Pompadour's. As soon as he had left, the room became the scene of a rough game between Bontemps and Villepail: the latter, who still had his horsewhip, used it, and seeing Bontemps pick up the King's hunting whip, he ran down the staircase. Bontemps stationed himself behind the door of the room and hid behind the tapestry, the whip at the ready. He had not been there a quarter of an hour when the King, who had an appointment to work with M. d'Argenson, came in hurriedly. That harebrained Bontemps, who had not recognized the King's step, came out from behind the tapestry, the whip held high, and stood frozen. The King noticed him, took him by the ear, and dragged him thus two or three feet. Bontemps was shouting: 'Sire, forgive me, Villepail whipped me, I thought that you were he.' The King only left him when he became tired of shaking him and laughing."[44] It is also worth noting that Louis XV was hurrying back upstairs to work: now, as ever, he watched conscientiously over the government and was probably the best-informed man in his kingdom.

Another aspect of his character which remained unchanged was his secretiveness. As he acquired experience, he saw that, in one respect at least, the old maréchal de Villeroy had been right: everyone had an ax to grind and therefore gave flawed advice; discretion was nonexistent at Versailles; ministers and courtiers unhesitatingly leaked the gravest matters of state in order to score a point. Everyone, that is, except Mme de Pompadour. She alone could be trusted absolutely, and so it was that in the most important diplomatic negotiation of his reign, Louis XV turned to the marquise for help in carrying out the talks—she could do so in secret, while he was always surrounded by people—and for advice on the crucial decisions which had to be taken. And along with the marquise, he made use of a most peculiar but, as it turned out, effective and discreet little man, the abbé de Bernis.

Bernis was the perfect example of that odd eighteenth-century phenomenon, the *abbé de cour*. Because the King disposed freely of all ecclesiastical benefices, he could give an abbey *in commendam* to a layman if he chose. The impetrant would collect the abbey's often considerable income and appoint an ill-paid cleric to act as abbot; even the comte de Clermont, M. le Duc's younger brother, was thus the beneficiary of an abbey. In some cases, of course, the abbé intended one day to take orders, but he might not become a priest for many years. The abbé de Bernis was just such a lay abbot: having received only minor orders, he sought a career in the Church because he was the younger son of a noble but poor family. Off to Paris he went, therefore—his family came from Provence—to receive an education; only, when that was completed, and because the cardinal de Fleury disliked him, all hopes of promotion were at an end: he was called abbé purely as a matter of courtesy. Fleury wasn't totally wrong: Bernis was known for his witty conversation, his gluttony and his extreme frivolity, as well as for his light, semierotic verse. Voltaire, who rather liked him, nicknamed him Babet la bouquetière (Babet the Flower Girl)—hardly what one might expect of a pillar of the Church. Still, because he was desperately poor, Bernis persisted in begging Fleury for any odd crumb until the Cardinal, weary of his importunities, told Bernis that he would never get a benefice as long as he, Fleury, lived. "I will wait, monseigneur," Bernis replied insolently, and that was that.

If you were poor but witty in Paris, there was at least one resource open to you: you could dine out every night and repay your hostess by amusing her. This Bernis did with great success, and among the ladies whose dinners he graced was Mme d'Etioles. Then, during that last summer before she was presented, he joined M. de Gontaut in teaching her the manners of the Court. She liked him, he admired her, and so Bernis became part of her intimate entourage. At first, Louis XV ignored him even though, at the favorite's request, he had given the abbé a well-endowed canonry in the Chapter of the Lyon Cathedral. "The King," Bernis wrote in his memoirs, "whom I saw every day at the favorite's, only spoke to me after three years, so shy does this prince feel towards people to whom he is not accustomed . . . As soon as the King had taken it onto himself to speak a word to me, he no longer felt any embarrassment: he even gave me a great mark of favor by leading me himself to the theater of the petits cabinets."[45]

From then on all was easy; but, unlike Mme de Pompadour, who enjoyed chatting with Bernis, the King listened to him when he spoke of graver matters and was impressed by his intelligence, his good sense and his understanding. It must have been a relief for him to hear someone who, unlike the ministers, had neither faction nor past decisions to defend. Then, at the marquise's urging, Bernis was appointed Ambassador to Venice and, to the general surprise, he did a wonderful job. He settled the outstanding differences between France and the Most Serene Republic, charmed the Venetians and, more important, gathered priceless information about the various courts of Europe. He did so well, in fact, that it was decided to send him to Madrid, a key post; but first he stopped for a few months at Versailles.

He came back at a time when the Council was getting out of hand. In 1755, he wrote, there was "no unity in the Council, open warfare between M. d'Argenson and M. de Machault, gross disrespect in the discussions, no proper subordination. M. le prince de Conti, without being a minister, was consulted on almost everything,* Mme de Pompadour was openly at odds with the prince, and the King held the balance in the midst of these divisions. Add [to this] the display of the most scandalous luxury, the misery of the people, no true talent in the Council, not a courageous citizen at Court [and] no competent general on land or sea just before the onset of a war."[46] For reasons which will soon become clear, Bernis was deliberately painting the darkest picture possible, but he was only exaggerating, not inventing, except for one of his statements: the people were not miserable at all. Surprisingly, as he watched all this, the abbé felt he had the answers, but he dared not speak, unbidden, to the King; so he turned to his old friend. "Mme de Pompadour," he wrote, "was no longer that woman, surrounded only by amiable talents, who ruled France as the goddess of pleasure. The King, for some years, had lost his passion for her; she could now rely only on friendship, confidence and the ties of habit, which, among princes, are the strongest of all . . . I found Mme de Pompadour disgusted with the Court.

---

* As noted earlier, it was the prince de Conti who negotiated the return of the Parlement from Soissons.

She showed me the copies of the letters she had written the King asking his permission to withdraw from it and did not hide from me either those she wrote him about the business of state. The first letters convinced me only that she was in a bad temper and fed up . . . The others, on the contrary, I found admirable . . . I never would have thought that she was capable of telling the truth with so much energy and even such eloquence."[47]

We may perhaps surmise that when Bernis started to give her sound, well-reasoned and practical advice, Mme de Pompadour felt a not unsimilar surprise. Be that as it may, he now became her chief confidant. It was thanks to him that the marquise was able to reduce the role played by the self-serving, ambitious prince de Conti, who wanted to become King of Poland and behaved accordingly. Tell the King, Bernis suggested, that he should either call Conti into the Council or stop using him, since, in the current situation, his conflicts with d'Argenson simply paralyzed the government. It was a brilliant suggestion: no Prince of the Blood Royal had been allowed into the Council since Louis XIV first decided that their presence there gave them too much power; and Louis XV, who was well aware of Conti's ambition, had no intention of letting him in, so that, in fact, the prince's influence soon began to fade.

Mme de Pompadour knew almost as much as the King about the situation in France, and she told it all to Bernis. It is interesting, therefore, to find him repeating the maréchal de Noailles's earlier complaint about the sluggishness and inefficiency of government. Neither of them really provides the reasons for this, but we do not have to look very far to find one or, indeed, several. The ministers, who loathed one another, did their best to prevent any one of their number from doing so well that the King would give him more power, while at a lower level the machine ran smoothly. France was better administered than any other country in Europe, but it often had less actual direction from the top, and Louis XV, who continued to think that other people knew better, was still all too willing to take advice. Then, too, the government's work was impeded by the indiscretion of its members. Information was the lifeblood of intrigue, so it was passed on, stolen and leaked. It was, in fact, because Mme d'Estrades, the marquise's false friend, actually stole a State paper (presumably to show it to d'Argenson) that Mme de Pompadour was finally able to have her sent away from Court.

There was yet another reason why it was impossible for the King to arrive at a policy through normal discussion in the Council: with the exception of Louis XV himself and, up to a point, Machault, the ministers were blindly, ardently pro-Prussian. True, it had long been France's habit to be allied with Prussia against Austria, but already in the late thirties the cardinal de Fleury had had severe doubts as to whether the Prussian alliance still served the interests of France. The War of the Austrian Succession had ended these doubts perforce, but the King still thought a great deal about the question. Indeed, the main benefit of the Treaty of Aix-la-Chapelle had gone to Frederick II. Now, in 1755, the ministers' partiality notwithstanding, it began to look as if Prussia was about to switch alliances, exchanging France for England. This was a very serious matter since France and England were obviously about to go to war. Already the British Navy systematically attacked all

French ships, both commercial and military. In June, for instance, after announcing through his bullhorn that the two nations were at peace, a British commander fired upon and took two French warships, the *Alcide* and the *Lys*. Instead of retaliating in kind, Louis XV tried to negotiate, but in vain. The English were determined to fight, and no matter how much the King loved peace, it was clear that the situation was fast deteriorating.

Once again, that would mean a European war in which France would need allies. It was assumed that, as usual, Austria would side with England; Prussia was uncertain; so, as a first step, Louis XV turned to Spain. Because of its extensive American colonies, it had the second largest fleet in Europe, England's being the first. Late in 1754, the King, who felt little confidence in Rouillé, his new Foreign minister, wrote in his own hand to the new King of Spain, Ferdinand VI: "The tender friendship which unites us would not be such as it should and such as my heart wishes if we did not feel such reciprocal confidence as to communicate our feelings each to the other . . . The English have been, for all time, the constant and implacable enemies of our nations and our House; we have never had more dangerous adversaries . . . Without the sacrifices which Louis XIV, our common great-grandfather, made of his treasure and the blood of his subjects, without his constancy and courage, the English would have taken the crown of Spain and the Indies away from his posterity. It is the memory of these important events, deeply engraved in the mind of the late King Philip V, your father and my uncle, which has determined the constant friendship and tenderness which he always felt for France and myself; and this memory is the cause of my own intimate attachment to Spain. I am quite sure that Your Majesty feels the same way; it is this mutual accord of sentiment and interest which must tighten the bonds uniting our persons, our Houses, our states and our peoples."[48] Ferdinand VI, however, was wholly Spanish and felt no real connection with France; his wife was a strongly pro-British Portuguese princess and his most influential minister an Irishman. The answer he sent his cousin, while cordial, was vague in the extreme except for one piece of advice: France had best come to some sort of understanding with Great Britain, he wrote.

At the same time, the British concluded an alliance with Empress Elizabeth of Russia. In theory, it was purely defensive: the two states guaranteed the status quo in Germany. The English, of course, were thinking first of Hanover, George II's electorate. The Tsarina, worried by Prussian expansion, thought the treaty was directed against Frederick II, the only German ruler known to harbor territorial ambitions. Armed with this treaty, however, the British now turned to Frederick and pointed out that unless he joined the new alliance he might well be attacked on two fronts, by Austria on the west and Russia on the east. At this time, the Franco-Prussian alliance was due to be renewed, and Frederick was telling the French Ambassador that, of course, he intended to do so; but in January 1756 he signed the Treaty of Westminster, thus lining up with the British and against the French. This was done with the utmost secrecy. When a special French envoy, the duc de Nivernais, arrived in Berlin at the end of the month, the King behaved as if nothing had changed. He simply seemed curiously slow in getting down to the business at hand. It was months before Nivernais found out that he was being fooled.

Even before the Treaty of Westminster was signed, however, Louis XV, who was far more perceptive than his ministers, began to realize that Frederick II was likely, for the third time, to abandon France. Spain obviously couldn't be counted on, Russia and Great Britain were allied, and Austria was a potential enemy. It was just at this point that Count Stahremberg, the Austrian Ambassador to Versailles, came to see Mme de Pompadour; after saying a few words about the purpose of his visit, he handed her a letter and asked her to pass it on to the King. At first glance it might seem odd that one sovereign, and a very prudish one at that, should communicate with a formerly unfriendly fellow ruler through the good offices of just the kind of woman who, in Vienna, might well have ended up in a house for fallen women. In fact, Maria Theresa, on Stahremberg's advice, had made a remarkably clever move.

The Empress had two burning desires. She wanted to recover Silesia and, while she was at it, she wanted to humiliate the King of Prussia. That Austria could not do this unaided she knew full well. It was also becoming obvious to her that her closest ally, Great Britain, was going over to the enemy. The only possible ally left, therefore, was France.

France and Austria, however, were on the coolest of terms and the Empress knew that most of the Council at Versailles was rabidly anti-Austrian. Any overture to the Foreign minister would surely be repulsed, and repulsed publicly, which would be much worse. There was only one solution: someone must be found without an official position but with direct access to the King. As Stahremberg pointed out, that meant either the prince de Conti or Mme de Pompadour. After much hesitation, the Ambassador plumped for Mme de Pompadour: she was known to be absolutely discreet and wholly devoted to the King; she detested d'Argenson, the head of the pro-Prussian party; and, finally, Louis XV would be sure to keep the letter a secret since he would not want it thought that the gravest policies of state were decided in his (ex-)mistress's boudoir. On every count Stahremberg was right.

The letter itself was simple enough. It proposed a defensive alliance between France and Austria: if either country was attacked, the other would come to its aid. What Louis XV immediately understood, though, was that the defensive alliance was only a first step, and that Maria Theresa would eventually try to use it in such a way as to recover Silesia. In any case, like the Council, most of the French were anti-Austrian, and Frederick II might still renew the Franco-Prussian treaty. The situation was delicate in the extreme and required the nicest sort of judgment. Further, any exchange of drafts would entail a great deal of physical labor for which the King obviously had no time, since the matter was so explosive that it precluded the use of a copyist or secretary.

It was at this point that Louis XV thought of the abbé de Bernis, who was just about to set off for Madrid. Employing him as the intermediary would bypass the ministers; he had amply demonstrated his capacities as a diplomat during his embassy to Venice. The King, therefore, told Mme de Pompadour to show him the letter; she did, and the abbé was terrified. The immediate consequence of an Austrian alliance, he said, would be a general European war. Besides, he pointed out to the marquise, he had, after much effort, gained Rouillé's good opinion. If the Foreign minister found out that he was being preempted by Bernis, he would be sure to make

King Gustavus III of Sweden, who, with the help of the French Ambassador, carried through constitutional changes which saved Sweden from becoming a second Poland.

〜〜〜〜

King Frederick II of Prussia, France's untrustworthy ally in the War of the Austrian Succession and her foe in the Seven Years' War. He was the greatest general of the age.

J.B. Martin Inv. et Sculp.

Zéphyre.

Theatrical costumes: the warm South Wind on the left
the American Indian on the right

Indienne

These rococo fantasies, or others very like them,
were worn, among others, by Mme de Pompadour.

Mme du Barry after the portrait by Drouais. Louis XV's last official mistress here follows the fashion by wearing men's clothes, but there is no mistaking the power of her attractions.

him suffer for it, while the rest of the Court would consider him a traitor. "As I was thinking about all this," Bernis wrote, "the King, with whom I had never talked about affairs of state, came in and asked me suddenly what I thought of M. de Stahremberg's letter. I repeated to His Majesty what I had just said to Mme de Pompadour [i.e., about a European war]. The King listened to me with impatience, and when I was through he said, almost angrily: 'You are just like the others, the enemy of the Queen of Hungary.' "* Not at all, Bernis answered; on the contrary, he admired her greatly, but he still thought that an Austrian alliance would have fearful consequences. " 'Well, then,' the King replied with some emotion, 'we must simply be very polite to M. de Stahremberg and tell him we won't hear of this.'

" 'This is not what I think best, Sire,' I retorted. 'Your Majesty has everything to gain in finding out more about the intentions of the Austrian Court, but you must be very careful about the answer you give.' The King's face became more serene; he ordered me to listen to M. de Stahremberg in the presence of Mme de Pompadour, who was to be present only for the first conference . . . The King did not conceal from me that all his life he had wanted an alliance with Austria, that he thought it was the only way to establish a lasting and stable peace and to maintain the Catholic religion."[49] He then told Bernis that the Empress had asked that the talks be conducted in the deepest secrecy. In Vienna, only Maria Theresa, her husband, Francis I and Count Kaunitz, her chancellor, would know; in Paris, the three were to be Louis XV, Mme de Pompadour and Bernis.

Any truly ambitious man would have jumped at the chance to be the King's secret representative; Bernis, who could give good advice but lacked energy and courage, was simply terrified. As a first precaution, he asked to be given instructions written in the King's own hand so that he could later claim he had merely been obeying orders; that same day he received them. The talks were ready to begin, especially since Louis XV had made his feelings toward Frederick II very clear: he resented having had to put up with "numerous infidelities which might well be repeated . . . the unpleasant speeches the King of Prussia had made regarding the [French] government and matters which concerned him closely** . . . He was a little shocked by the levity which the Marquis of Brandenburg used towards the Crown of France† . . . From then on, the King treated me with a kindness and a familiarity which proved that he felt completely at ease with me, and that greatly abated the fear I had always felt in his presence."[50]

Since secrecy was essential, Bernis and Stahremberg took every possible precaution to avoid being discovered together. On the bank of the Seine, at the foot of Mme de Pompadour's de Château Bellevue, there was a pavilion hidden among the trees. Stahremberg came on one road and, dismissing his carriage and servants, walked the final mile; Bernis did the same (huffing and puffing) from another direction; and, miraculously, nothing leaked.

From the very first it was obvious that Stahremberg was acting in good faith; he immediately told Bernis about the negotiation between Prussia and Great Britain,

---

* Maria Theresa was now Empress, but the King obviously retained his old habits of speech.
** This was a reference to Frederick's attacks against Mme de Pompadour, whom he usually referred to as Petticoat III.
† Until Frederick's grandfather, Brandenburg, the central part of Prussia, had been a mere margravate.

which, until then, no one had suspected at Versailles, and he offered a general plan of alliance such as would assure a stable European peace. All this was to be cemented by a number of marriages between the Bourbons and the Habsburgs. As for the proposed treaty, it was straightforward enough. France would denounce its alliance with Prussia and do nothing to prevent Austria from reconquering Silesia; Maria Theresa would back the election of the prince de Conti to the Polish throne when August III expired, which he was expected to do in short order; the Duke of Parma, the husband of Madame Infante, would exchange Parma for a larger state in the Austrian Netherlands as soon as Austria had recovered Silesia; and, to prove her good faith, the Empress would allow French troops to garrison Ostend and Nieuport as soon as an English attack took place.

Prudently, at that first meeting, Bernis did no more than copy the Ambassador's proposal and answer that, in essence, he had no answer: he could only report to the King and then they would meet again. In fact, as he pointed out to Louis XV, Bernis immediately understood the plan's major flaw: while Maria Theresa was prepared to give up the Austrian Netherlands, which she barely controlled anyway, in order to regain Silesia, the recovery of that province would entail a war with Prussia into which France would surely be drawn. Besides, he said, it would be foolish to denounce the alliance with Prussia, and the King fully agreed; but an ambassador extraordinary should be sent to ascertain whether the alliance did, in fact, still exist. And since France had nothing to gain by becoming involved in another European war, the proposed agreement should be modified so that it could eventually be joined by the King of Prussia himself, thus guaranteeing the status quo throughout Germany. Since Maria Theresa was obsessed with the recovery of Silesia, it would obviously not be easy to convince her that her loss was definitive and that she could be friends with the "monster of Potsdam." Still, Bernis said, it was worth a try and he thought he might just be clever enough to do it.

Of course, the abbé was quite right: France had no reason to want a European war, but, on the other hand, if England declared war, as it was evidently about to do, the conflict was bound to spread. By November 1755, the hopes of keeping the peace were just about gone; and if she had to fight a Prusso-Hanoverian army because she was allied with France, Maria Theresa would certainly want Silesia as her reward. Since these issues were all so weighty, Bernis told the King that it was essential to let at least some of the ministers into the secret. After some resistance, Louis XV agreed, stipulating, however, that the comte d'Argenson was to be kept in the dark. Four ministers were chosen: Machault, who had recently become minister of the Navy; Séchelles, the contrôleur général; Rouillé, the Foreign minister; and the perennial Saint-Florentin, the minister of the Household.

The first result of this prudent and sensible move was a stream of complaints from Bernis, since, he claimed, it entailed endless work. He spent his days and nights copying out Stahremberg's proposals and his own, duplicating memoranda for the ministers, sending letters to the King; and while it is perhaps normal for a harassed negotiator to complain about his heavy task, Bernis went a good deal further: his health was ruined, he wrote, because he was unable to rest properly after having been bled (in fact, he lived on for another forty years); he lost his sleep; he suffered agonies from writer's cramp. All these moans were directed to the ever sympathetic Mme de Pompadour, and the poor sufferer was duly comforted; but the flaw in Bernis's character stood revealed: he had a congenital fear of responsibility, a lack of both stamina and courage, which hadn't mattered when he was Babet la bouquetière, or even Ambassador to Venice. Now that he was playing a key political role, though, these shortcomings became increasingly serious.

The negotiations continued throughout November, December and January, with the King watching over every development. Then, in February 1756, Frederick II, after prevaricating for six weeks, admitted to Nivernais that he had indeed signed a treaty of alliance with Great Britain and then, with breathtaking effrontery, he offered to sign one with France as well. It shouldn't have been surprising, really, since he was accustomed to breaking his word whenever it suited him. At that, the duc de Nivernais made a counteroffer: France was ready to renew the treaty, he said, but Frederick would have to break with Great Britain. Obviously, that was out of the question, and in April Nivernais returned to Versailles.

Prussia's declaration that it had become allied with England naturally put Bernis in the most difficult of situations. Before, France could—and did—use its alliance with Frederick as a negotiating ploy; now it found itself completely isolated, so that it needed Austria more than Austria needed France, since the former could always join England after all. That, at least, is what most people would have thought, but Bernis was smart enough to see that Maria Theresa was so obsessed by her hatred of Frederick that she would never join whatever side he was on. Thus, it was still possible, though certainly more difficult, to negotiate, and on May 1, 1756, a treaty was duly signed. It guaranteed the status quo in Europe and was purely defensive; any other prince (e.g., Frederick II) might join in; but if either France or Austria were to be attacked by Prussia, then the other would instantly come to its aid with a twenty-four-thousand-man army.

The reversal of alliances was greeted with general stupefaction. None of the foreign representatives at Versailles had realized that so momentous a change was even contemplated, let alone accomplished. Soon, however, other feelings replaced the initial surprise: rage, for instance, on the part of the Prussian Ambassador and his master, who had vainly tried to bribe Mme de Pompadour to keep France friendly towards Prussia; open joy for Stahremberg and the few members of the pro-Austrian party; and horror on the part of most everyone else at Versailles, d'Argenson first and foremost. As usual, this last took the form of personal attacks on Mme de Pompadour, who, supposedly, was drunk with pride because Maria Theresa, when corresponding with her, called her "my dear"* and had thus sold France down the river; and on the part of the King, who was so weak that he allowed his mistress to push him into betraying his duty; but it was all too late. The alliance was ratified. And if any other confirmation of its usefulness was needed, it came on May 18, when Great Britain declared war on France.

Even with its new ally, however, France was not ready to fight a war. The ministry was more divided than ever before, with d'Argenson, who was responsible for the Army, bitterly opposed to the new policy, and Rouillé, the Foreign minister, con-

---

* Maria Theresa, in actual fact, never wrote the marquise at all.

sumed with jealousy because Bernis was getting all the credit; indeed, it was the
abbé's opinion that Rouillé only stayed in office because his wife couldn't bear to
leave the Court. The fleet, although not negligible, wasn't strong enough to oppose
the British Navy without Spanish help. The high command of the Army was bickering as usual. The Parlement refused to register the new tax edicts without which the
war couldn't be financed. Only the King stood firm. "It is my own work and I think it
good,"[51] he wrote the comte de Broglie, the duc's brother. Now it was up to him to
prove that he was right, and the potential for disaster was enormous. France might
well find itself as beleaguered as it had been during those terrible years at the end of
Louis XIV's reign. He had hardly anyone he could count on, since even Bernis was a
weak reed; only a woman was left. In short order, Mme de Pompadour became an
unofficial but effective assistant prime minister. The King had chosen well after all.

Chapter Eight

A Few Acres of Snow

WHEN, in 1756, the Parlement de Paris refused to register the new tax edicts, it not only annoyed the King but also started a new French tradition. Firmly putting its own private quarrels before the needs of the nation, it acted so as to ensure, inasmuch as was in its power, the defeat of its own fatherland. That it did not succeed in the end was not its fault: had the King been less determined, had not a series of wholly unpredictable events occurred, the armies might well have starved for lack of supplies.

All through 1755 the government persisted with a halfhearted attempt at setting up the Grand Conseil, a limited court of appeals controlled by the Crown, as a rival to the Parlement. Once again, safe in the knowledge that the Parlement was there to stay, people simply shunned the alternate court. With the onset of the war and the consequent need for new taxes, the Parlement was ready for revenge. On July 7, an edict created a second vingtième (that 5 percent income tax) which was to end three months after the return of peace. The first vingtième, which had been collected for more than fifteen years, was to be extended for another ten. Immediately the Parlement protested: it might be willing to register the second vingtième, it said, but only if the first ended on December 31, 1761. Since the troops had to be paid, there was not a moment to be lost; the King held a lit de justice during which both taxes were actually registered. The next day, the Parlement protested again, which it had no right to do; and encouraged by this, the provinces, which still had—or had once had —their own representative bodies, the so-called *pays d'état*, pointed out that they were entitled to refuse paying until they had agreed to an *abonnement*, a set, unverifiable sum which was always inferior to what the actual tax would have produced. Since more than a third of the country consisted of pays d'état, it was easy to see that, even in the best of cases, the Treasury would be short of funds.

Having thus done what it could to hamper the war effort, the Parlement returned happily to its favorite amusement, the fight against the *Unigenitus* bull. Firmly ignoring the Church's recent compromises, the Parlement went right on hearing appeals against the bull from a variety of priests and lay persons. Once again the King was forced to intervene; once again he tried to impose a compromise. On December 13, 1756, he held yet another lit de justice at which he had the Keeper of the Seals, Machault, read a two-part speech. In the first part the bull was interpreted in such a way as to moderate its more extreme articles—a step towards the Parlement's position; but in the second the King simply promulgated a reform of the Parlement itself. Henceforth, Machault said, no conseiller of the Enquêtes or Requêtes (as opposed to the présidents) could vote on questions other than those of pure justice unless he had been in office for ten years; remonstrances were still authorized but edicts would become law the day after the King's response to them, irregardless of whether they had been accepted or refused; any further strike was forbidden. The last two provisions are clear enough; the first was due to the fact that the opposition to the King in the Parlement had largely been led by fiery young conseillers who had just bought their offices. Taking away their right to vote on the registration of edicts would singularly ease their passage.

Of course, this was merely a repeat of Fleury's attempt at containing the Parlement, and it was met with exactly the same weapon: a combination of resignations and strikes. What the conseillers most resented, of course, was the ten-year clause, which would, of itself, have brought peace back. At Versailles, the timorous Bernis bemoaned its existence, but the King stood firm. No doubt remembering Louis XIV, who had done so much to bolster royal authority, Louis XV told the Dauphin on December 22: "My authority is mine for my life only. I must keep it in full for you, my son. I am obligated to do so."[1] This was not only good politics, it was also good law. In France, the King, who was supreme while he lived, owned nothing: his possessions, his power, his crown were lent to him for the duration of his life. He could no more change the order of succession (as, for instance, Peter the Great had done) than he could abridge his successor's authority. Still, the fact remained that the country was at war with England and Prussia; and the Parlement, once again, was on strike.

This was all the more shameful in that the conflict was rapidly spreading to the whole of Europe. Frederick II, who understood the value of surprise, attacked Saxony in August without bothering to declare war. Since Saxony was a neutral country, it was a particularly shameful act.* The results were all too predictable. While Saxony had a perfectly respectable army, it could not compare with Prussia's, and Augustus III, its king, was no military genius. In short order Frederick managed to split the Saxon Army, defeat it and, to the horror of civilized people everywhere, compel its soldiers to serve in his own forces. The King fled to his kingdom of Poland; the Queen, who had remained in Dresden, was treated like an ordinary prisoner, guarded by men and searched: once again Frederick was breaking every rule of decent behavior—and taking a distinct pleasure in doing so.

All this was especially annoying to the French Government because it had disdainfully rejected, some four months earlier, Bernis's suggestion that France subsidize Dresden so that more troops could be enrolled. Had it done so, Saxony's resources might well have been denied to the King of Prussia, who plundered them mercilessly and who might, consequently, have been defeated. It was also particularly distressing for the Royal Family: the Dauphine, whom her husband loved passionately, was a

---

* It is perhaps not very difficult to see where a later German leader found at least some of his inspiration.

Saxon princess, and she was naturally appalled to hear that her native country was ravaged, her father in flight and her mother treated like a common criminal.

At least there was one compensation. The French Navy had always been the weaker of the two armed services. The money went to the Army, and the admirals had learnt that in time of war it was best to stay away from the British Navy. Now, in May 1756, a fleet of twelve ships of the line under amiral de La Galissonière sailed from Toulon to Minorca, then a British possession, landed an army corps under the maréchal de Richelieu, who besieged and, on June 27, took Port Mahon,* the island's fortress, while La Galissonière defeated an English fleet under Admiral Byng. The British were at first stunned, then outraged; upon his return, Byng was tried, convicted of treason and hanged (to encourage the others, Voltaire commented sardonically). The French—at least those who did not own a Parlement office—were elated.

Now that France was allied to Austria, it found that it had also gained two new friends: Russia, whose Empress loathed Prussia; and Sweden, which saw quite correctly that it stood to lose from Prussian expansion. Paradoxically, however, the one man who had carried through the negotiations was still no more than a private adviser to the King. The situation was so anomalous, in fact, that on January 2, 1757, the maréchal de Richelieu, more in favor than ever now that he had taken Port Mahon, patronizingly offered to help the abbé. Bernis was too experienced a courtier not to enjoy the irony of the situation: while Richelieu yearned to be called to the King's council but never was, he thought himself vastly superior to the abbé because he was a maréchal-duc and a First Gentleman of the Bedchamber. It was, however, Bernis who had the King's ear; with obvious delight he recounts the little scene that took place that day: "The maréchal de Richelieu . . . told me, a quarter of an hour before the King ordered him to call me into the Council: 'But why, when you have so much business to discuss with the King and his ministers, do you not ask for the entrées de la chambre? If you like, I will suggest it to the King.' I answered with a smile that I accepted his offer willingly. He was most astonished a moment later to hear the King tell me: 'Abbé de Bernis, take your place at the Council.' "[2]

Although this was a major step for the abbé—he was now a minister of State—Rouillé still remained Foreign minister, an obvious anomaly since, in effect, Bernis was in charge of his department. Still, Rouillé had accepted the alliance and the King hated to fire people. The situation was inherently unstable, however. Rouillé had become a mere shadow; d'Argenson was halfheartedly prosecuting a war he opposed while, as minister of Police, he allowed the same kinds of attacks on Louis XV and Mme de Pompadour that had cost Maurepas his position; as for Machault, he, too, had become a liability as the symbol of the conflict with the Parlement. To make it all worse, the war was unpopular—most people still thought of Austria as the enemy—and the King himself was beginning to lose his popularity.

How deeply the monarch was still loved, however, became blindingly clear on January 5, 1757. "This day," Barbier exclaimed in his diary, "has witnessed the most dreadful of events. The King has been assassinated, knifed . . . by a scoundrel. On Thursday morning, consternation was widespread in Paris; everyone was crying in the churches; but by the evening we had the happiness of learning with certainty that

---

* While the maréchal fought, his cook, desperate because there was neither cream nor butter, invented a new sauce made of oil, eggs and mustard. He called it sauce Mahonnaise, after Port Mahon, but we know it as mayonnaise.

the blow was neither deadly nor even dangerous."[3] Barbier was well informed: a slightly retarded man named Damiens had, in the late afternoon on Wednesday, walked up to the King and knifed him. The duc de Croÿ, who was in Louis XV's suite, saw what happened and promptly wrote it down.

"Around six in the evening, the sky being rather light but cloudy, there being a full moon and torches which dazzled the eyes, the King decided to return to Trianon, where everybody had remained. As he came down the last step of the small guard-room* to step into his carriage, leaning on his Grand and First Equerries, the duc d'Ayen and M. le Duc following him, the Captain of the Swiss Guard walking before him, a sufficient number of troops being lined up, a man sprang forth between two guards, whom he pushed, one to the right, the other to the left; he struck an officer with such strength that he made him fall, and came up, partly from behind, and struck the King on the right side with a knife that had a folding blade, using such force that the knife pushed the King forward, prompting him to say: 'Duc d'Ayen, someone has just punched me.'

"The man did all this with such speed that he ran back through the opening [between the guards] that he had made before those he had pushed could react and no one saw the blow, partly because of the torches, partly because we were all looking down at the last step.

"When he heard the King, the maréchal de Richelieu, who was behind, said: 'Who is that man wearing a hat?** The King turned to the side and, realizing it was the side where he had been hit, he felt the place with his hand and saw that it was covered with blood. He then said: 'I am wounded. Arrest him but do not kill him.'

"A footman, who was holding the carriage door open, saw the bleeding and shouted, 'The King is wounded.' Guards then seized the man and the King turned back. His attendants wanted to carry him but he said: 'No, I am still strong enough to go up myself,' and he walked back up the stairs easily, having until then shown much strength and great presence of mind. Back in his rooms, he saw the blood pouring out and thought that he was fatally wounded. 'Oh,' he said, 'I have been struck, I will not recover!' The loss of blood and the worry weakened him then, and he asked repeatedly for a priest and a surgeon. Since his entire household was at Trianon, for quite a long time he lacked everything. There were no sheets on his bed; he couldn't have a fresh shirt; only a robe could be found. Everybody was in a panic, running off in every direction. The best informed of those present said it was safer to let the blood run.† The King felt faint and thought he was dying. He asked urgently for a priest to hear his confession. The almoner on duty for the quarter came in. The King confessed in haste and asked strongly to be given a full absolution, promising to confess more fully if he had time. He was granted it.

"A surgeon then came in and washed the wound, but he didn't dare to probe it because the First Surgeon wasn't there. La Martinière, who had been at Trianon, finally arrived. He probed the wound and said that it wasn't deep and he didn't think that it could be dangerous, but everybody worried, as did the King, about the knife being poisoned. That made everyone worry twice as much as before. Mesdames

---

* Newly restored, the step can be seen today in the north corner of the cour de marbre.
** No one wore a hat in the King's presence. The fact that Damiens had not taken his hat off was enough to mark him as the assassin.
† Had the knife been poisoned, bleeding might have cleaned the wound.

came in because they had heard all the noise; finding the King wounded and bathed in his blood, they fainted, falling on the floor around the bed; some of them even stayed there for a long time before they came to. M. le Duc, his face awash with tears but retaining his presence of mind, saw to everything.

"The Queen came in, thinking that the King only had a colic, but seeing the blood, she also fainted. The King was still asking for a confessor. He was offered, in the absence of his own, a Court almoner who had an excellent reputation. The King confessed to him for a long time and asked for the last rites."[4]

In fact, La Martinière was right. The blade with which the King had been struck was some three and a half inches long and very sharp, quite long enough to reach a vital organ; but, luckily, January 5 was a very cold day and the King was wearing several layers of clothing, so the wound, though painful, was fairly shallow and poisonless. After a few days of weakness and fever, the First Surgeon announced, the King would recover fully; and with the arrival of the Household back at Versailles, it could be assumed that everything was back to normal.

That assumption, however, was mistaken. The very first evening, an attendant told Louis XV cheerfully that the wound was not deep, but the King answered: "It is deeper than you think, for it reaches the heart."[5] As always in the great crises of his life, he was remembering Fleury's teachings: a King was nothing without the love of his people; how much worse must he be, therefore, if one of his subjects tried to kill him. Instantly he sank into the deepest depression. Guilt, remorse, rejection all combined to make him feel still worse. The royal facade, upheld with such effort during his childhood, served as an insufficient shield for the sensitivity beneath. Now the shield had been pierced, and the unloved child was back in control.

As it happens, the King was all wrong. Robert-François Damiens, his would-be murderer, was a severely disturbed man, possibly slightly retarded, who had served as a footman in the houses of several officials of the Parlement, in particular that of the conseiller Béze de Lys, one of the fiercest opponents of the bull, the new taxes and the royal government. There, Damiens heard many fiery speeches denouncing the King, so he simply acted on them. He decided to knife the King as a warning, but probably did not even intend to kill him: under interrogation, he said he had just wanted to teach the King a lesson so that he would listen to the Parlement. Voltaire, who, like the rest of the French, was horrified, wrote Mme de Lutzelbourg: "The monster is a dog who will have heard a few dogs of the Enquêtes barking and will have caught rabies from them." He had a point.

The popular reaction was immediate: all cared about Louis XV, all abhorred Damiens. Immediately this was expressed in song: "C'est en vain qu'un monstre exécrable / Vomi par l'enfer en courroux / Frappe des rois le plus aimable . . . / Du haut des cieux, Dieu qui protége / Le roi chéri de ses sujets / Retient le bras d'un sacrilège. / Tendres sujets, séchez vos larmes / Louis ne perdra pas le jour / Dieu n'a permis vos alarmes / Que pour augmenter votre amour." ("In vain an execrable monster / spewed up by a raging hell / Strikes the most lovable of kings . . . / From high above, God who protects / the King beloved of his subjects / holds back the sacrilegious arm. / Tender subjects, dry your tears / Louis will not forsake the light /

God only permitted your alarms / to increase your love.")[6] There could be no doubt. In spite of the deluge of pamphlets attacking the King, he was still Louis the Beloved.

That, in itself, was a grave embarrassment to the Parlement. It would obviously do its popularity no good at all if it came out that some of its members had, unwittingly perhaps, inspired Damiens. Since the assault had taken place in a royal palace, it fell within the jurisdiction of a special official, the *prévôt de l'hôtel,* who had no reason to suppress Damiens's damning testimony; besides, the Parlement was still on strike. Nothing loath, however, it met in emergency session at five in the morning on January 6; then, fully aware that it was the only way to keep Damiens's revelations a secret, it begged the King to transfer the prisoner and the trial to them. Louis XV now held the perfect pretext for breaking the Parlement. All he had to do was refuse the request: in the wave of loathing which would have followed the full awareness of Damiens's inspiration, that institution could, no doubt, have been reduced to the subservient status it suffered under Louis XIV. At the same time, it must be remembered that Louis XV had just received the last rites and that he had just forgiven his enemies. Given the chance, he did exactly that and allowed the change of venue. That, in this case, christian charity was singularly misplaced can hardly be doubted. With a sigh of relief, the Parlement announced that it would indeed resume its functions, but only for the trial of Damiens; as for the rest, it would only stop striking if the King verbally suspended the Declaration of December 13. This Louis XV very properly refused to do, and by the end of the month he was exiling several leaders of the opposition.

The procedure against Damiens continued on its appointed course, however. He was questioned, tortured, tried and found guilty of lèse-majesté and parricide. Then he was tortured again*—to no avail, since he had already admitted everything— simply because the practice of justice as defined by the Parlement required it. On March 28, he was taken to the Place de Grève, in front of the Hôtel de Ville, there to have his right hand cut off, boiling lead poured onto his body and his tongue torn out, after which his arms and legs were tied to four horses. Because Damiens was unusually strong, pull as they might, the horses could not dismember him until the executioner finally incised his joints; and even then, it was quite a while before the wretched man died. Since the execution was public, it was watched by a huge crowd, some of whom, Casanova noted, were greatly enjoying themselves. Noticing that this was the case of a lady who stood before him at a window, he proceeded, he says in his memoirs, to lift her skirts and make that enjoyment mutual.

For the first few days after the attempt, while the King was constantly surrounded by his family, Mme de Pompadour was left utterly alone; indeed, she did not know how long she would be allowed to remain at Versailles. Like the other inhabitants of ce pays-ci, she immediately realized that the situation might turn into a repeat of that at Metz. Once before, when he thought he was dying, Louis XV had sent off his mistress in disgrace. Would Mme de Pompadour's fate follow the same course as Mme de Châteauroux's? It seemed all too possible. Still, there was a difference. The King was not actually her lover; they were no longer living in sin: it would therefore

---

* When, in 1787, Louis XVI prohibited the standard use of torture, the Parlement put up a tremendous howl.

be much harder for the Church to demand her dismissal. What seemed probable, however, was that the Dauphin and Mesdames, who were in constant attendance on their father, would convince him that he must send his friend away. As for how Mme de Pompadour felt, Bernis, who was there, tells us all about it.

"I went down to see her," he wrote. "She threw herself in my arms with cries and sobs which would have softened even her enemies, if courtiers were capable of feeling. I asked her firmly to gather all the strength of her soul and submit to Providence, adding that she should not listen to craven advice; that, as the King's friend, who had ceased being his mistress years ago, she must wait for his orders before leaving the Court, that being the keeper of many State secrets and the recipient of His Majesty's letters, she was not free to dispose of herself; that I would tell her, hour by hour, how the King was feeling . . . Very few people came to see her and no one was in a hurry to attend to her."[7] That unpleasant situation—to be expected, perhaps, for the first twenty-four hours—continued on and on. The marquise was not dismissed, but, then again, she heard nothing from the King, who was keeping to his bedroom. Naturally enough, as time passed and nothing changed, the anti-Pompadour forces at Court thought that their triumph was at hand, so they behaved accordingly. This was especially true of the comte d'Argenson, whose satisfaction was visible and much noticed; but even Machault, who could see which way the wind was blowing, now turned against his former friend. As for the marquise herself, Bernis noted: "After the first few moments of emotion and despair, [she] showed great courage and an apparent peace of mind throughout the eleven days during which the King left her without a consoling message."[8] And to his friend the comte de Stainville, far away in Rome, Bernis wrote: "The King has been assassinated* and the Court has seen in this dreadful event nothing more than the right moment to have our friend dismissed. All the intrigues were directed to the confessor. There is a tribe at Court that is always eager for the last rites."[9]

Depressed though he undoubtedly was, however, the King had not lost his wits, and, while he forbore to communicate with the marquise, he knew that as long as he didn't send her away she would be there, waiting to see him when he was ready. At last, on January 16, the day came. "It was nearly two," Dufort tells us, "and the cabinet was almost empty. The King was wearing his robe and a nightcap, and carried a stick on which he leaned a little. Sometimes he looked out the window, sometimes he stopped and daydreamed. The Dauphin, to whom the King had not said he could go, was talking to the marquis du Muy; the Dauphine dared not take her leave. Finally the King, sure that everyone must be having dinner, gave the Dauphine a sign that she could go; she came forth, curtsied to him as usual and left. She was accompanied by several ladies, among whom was the duchesse de Brancas. The King said to Mme de Brancas: 'Lend me your cape.' She took it off and gave it to him. He put it over his shoulders, walked once around the cabinet without saying anything, after having bowed to her and left, immediately turning towards his private apartments. The Dauphin, who was accustomed to following him, came forward; he had not reached the middle of the room before the King turned around and said: 'Don't follow me.' [When, some two hours later, Louis XV came back], he was not

---

* "Assassination" here refers only to the act itself; it does not presuppose the King's death.

the same man. Instead of a sad and severe look, his face was calm, his gaze pleasant. He was smiling and talking pleasantly. He spoke to all of us, joked about the cape he was wearing and left us, saying he was going to have his dinner and advising us to do the same; we had no trouble guessing that he had been to see Mme de Pompadour. A single conversation with a friend . . . had healed his spirit, which had been far more distressed than his body."[10] Dufort was right. Louis XV had indeed visited the marquise, who had convinced him that his people were very far from hating him.

The moment the courtiers realized that Mme de Pompadour was back in favor, they crowded in her antechambers as if the eleven days had never happened. This time, although she was kind to most, the marquise was determined to eliminate her worse enemies; since they were also opposed to the new alliance, her desire turned out to be good policy. Within twenty-four hours the comte d'Argenson received a holograph note from the King: "Monsieur d'Argenson, I no longer need your services and hereby order you to resign your offices as secretary of state for war, along with your other offices, and to withdraw to your estate of Les Ormes." That Mme de Pompadour had a share in this is quite sure; she may well have been responsible for the curt tone of the letter. But it is equally certain that d'Argenson could not have remained, even had he been the marquise's friend: he was too reluctant to prosecute a war of which he disapproved. Then, too, as minister of Police he had allowed the publication of violent attacks on Mme de Pompadour while encouraging street disorders as a way of convincing the King that the war was a mistake. He was replaced by Paulmy, his nephew and assistant.

Because Machault had just turned against the marquise, it was widely assumed that his simultaneous dismissal was her work; in fact, Louis XV was reluctantly dismissing a minister who had made too many enemies: Machault was attacked by the clergy, on whom he had tried to impose payment of the dixième; by the pays d'état for the same reason; and by the Parlement because of the December Declaration. His presence in the government simply made life too difficult, but, unlike d'Argenson, he was much missed by his master, who allowed him to keep his ministerial salary—twenty-thousand livres—and his precedence as Keeper of the Seals. He was replaced by a competent but uninspired administrator, Peyrenc de Moras.

These changes in the ministry were greeted with widespread enthusiasm. "We must admit that from the moment of the attempted assassination, the King has behaved like a hero," Barbier noted. "He has shown greatness of soul. He didn't know then what results such a wound might have, but he immediately and fearlessly gave his attention to spiritual matters as well as concerns of state. Ever since his recovery he has acted . . . like a true King."[11] No doubt Mme de Pompadour would have agreed; and yet they failed to see a radical vice in the way the King, now as before, chose his advisers. Because Louis XIV had promoted generation after generation of the same families to the ministry, this practice had come to seem normal and had been continued: Maurepas's father and grandfather had been in the government, as had Machault's. Unfortunately, Paulmy, a conscientious, hardworking man, simply did not have the capacities required of a minister in time of war, and Peyrenc de Moras, though he was a gifted administrator, had no idea about how the deficit should be handled. As a result, once again Louis XV found himself surrounded by less than competent ministers; and Peyrenc's successor, Silhouette, a former fermier général, proved so spectacularly inept that he spent only a few months in office and introduced a new word—usually defined as a shape seen in profile—into our vocabulary.

None of that prevented the King from working as hard as ever. Aside from all his normal cares, he had also begun to direct a separate, secret diplomatic service, known to only half a dozen men, the main object of which was to secure the election of a French candidate, the prince de Conti, to the throne of Poland. Much has been made of this *secret du roi;* in fact, it was no more than an attempt at overcoming the deficiencies of Rouillé and d'Argenson. In the event, the complexity of the rivalries which rent the great Polish nobles prevented any long-lasting success. Still, this service gave the King information his ministers tended to withhold, and while he paid for it in person, it only cost him the paltry sum of eighty thousand livres for the year 1756.

One of the unexpected boons of the secret du roi was the correspondence between the King and the comte de Broglie, the duc's ambitious brother. Here, as with the maréchal de Noailles some fifteen years earlier, Louis XV felt he had a way of bypassing his ministers' distortions; his assumption that most courtiers lied as a matter of course was all too accurate. The comte de Broglie, however, was not only truthful but also often blunt; and occasionally the King felt compelled to remind him who was the master. "I have seen quite clearly in all your letters, comte de Broglie, that you were having difficulty in adopting the new system I have chosen; you aren't the only one, but such is my will and you must work in support of it," Louis XV wrote firmly, referring to the new alliance; and he added two sentences which marked the end of the prince de Conti's hopes. "As for M. le prince de Conti, he is sulking because I told him I would not make him commander in chief of the army to be gathered on the Rhine. I thought the choice was mine; so much the worse for him, that is all I can tell you."[12] It was all clear enough; and in response to yet another complaint from Broglie, Louis XV replied on January 22, 1757, seventeen days after Damiens's attempt: "I am very pleased, comte de Broglie, that you make all the representations to myself and my ministers which you may think necessary, but always keep our intimate union with the Court of Vienna in sight; it is my work. I think it good and wish to uphold it."[13] There could hardly be a better answer to the calumnies, according to which the Austrian alliance had been due solely to Mme de Pompadour's influence.

However, while it was the King who determined policy, it was often Mme de Pompadour who helped to implement it. Louis XV, as the result of that first conversation in January, had found that he needed the marquise more than ever. He listened to her suggestions not only when it was a question of Court appointments but even when it was time to choose army commanders and ministers, and he asked her to deal with matters best handled by someone other than himself. Just how effectively she did this we are told by someone who didn't like her. The Président de Meinières was a Parlement man who belonged to the little group of extreme opponents. In 1756, he had tried to obtain an army commission for one of his sons. When he found that he was getting nowhere and complained, he was told to see Mme de Pompadour; having asked for an audience, he came to Versailles on January 26, 1757.

"Mme de Pompadour was standing near the fire," he wrote. "She looked me up and down with a disdain which will always stay engraved on my mind, her head inclined over her shoulder, without curtseying, and appraising me in the most intimidating manner possible.

"When I came close enough to her, she said in an angry voice to her footman: 'Bring a chair.' He put it opposite her and so close that my knees were not more than a foot away from hers . . . She sat as straight as a rod in her armchair." Coming straight to the point, she told Meinières that unless he took back his resignation—the Parlement's strike was taking the form of multiple resignations—nothing would be done for his son since that was the easiest way of punishing him. At that, the Président defended his devotion to the Parlement, mentioned what his colleagues would say if he were seen to give in and concluded that, therefore, he could not change his position.

"Mme de Pompadour started laughing and told me with the most admirable eloquence: 'I am always surprised to hear this talk about some pretended honor which is merely used as a pretext to oppose the King's wishes, his policy, his orders, all without seeing that true honor consists in carrying out the actual duties of one's position, and in putting a stop, as quickly as possible, to the disorder which has touched all the parts of the administration because of the lack of justice. That, Monsieur, is how you should define your honor, by admitting your wrongs . . . by trying, by changing your behavior so as to erase in the King's mind and those of his subjects the unfavorable impression that your actions have caused. No one, I think, is unaware that I hold the magistrates in great esteem, and I would give anything not to have to make such a reproach to this august tribunal, the first in this realm, to this court, which is always praising itself in the most pompous way in its writings and its remonstrances. What! It is this court, supposedly so wise, which is always trying to modify the government, which, in a quarter of an hour, goes all the way to this extremity! You follow nothing but your passions, your resentments, your blindness and your rage, and off go the resignations. It is with those madmen that you have resigned, M. de Meinières, and you place your honor in not wanting to be separated from them? You would rather see the ruin of the kingdom, the finances, the entire State? Ah, M. de Meinières, that is not the honor of a subject truly attached to his king, not even that of a good citizen . . . The King will be the master . . . Do not go charging the ministry with the King's particular and personal resentment, as you are always doing; this has nothing to do with them; this time, it is the King who is personally wounded and who, of himself . . . wants to be obeyed . . . I ask you, gentlemen of the Parlement, who you think you are to resist, as you have, your master's will? Do you think that Louis XV is not as great a King as Louis XIV?' " It was strong language. "I left," Meinières adds, "full of amazement and admiration."[14]

Unfortunately, admiration or no, Meinières, like his colleagues, continued to resist the King while in the provinces, the other eleven Parlements did their best to make the two vingtièmes as ineffective as possible. The clergy, too, now that Machault was gone, managed to squeeze an abonnement from Peyrenc de Moras. The attempt at

financial reform, that perennial struggle, had failed once again. This had two consequences, one short-term and highly visible, the other hidden but even more dangerous. The first was, obviously, a growing deficit, which hampered the war effort,
created constant difficulties for the government and made it look improvident; the
second was a general recognition that if, like the Nobility and Clergy, you were
strong enough to resist, you could quite easily avoid paying taxes. It was as a refusal
to pay an "illegal" tax that the English Revolution had started, and everyone knew
that it had ended with a king on the scaffold. That was hardly an encouraging
precedent. The people who were now fighting the vingtième—the Parlement and the
clergy—belonged to the upper classes and were, in effect, refusing to bear their part
of the common burden; yet, amazingly, they managed to convince the poor that they
were acting in their interest. A properly assessed vingtième would have lessened the
amount of tax paid by the poor and the lower middle class, but the fact was never
clearly perceived, so that it was in the very act of equalizing the tax load that the
government appeared to be oppressing the poor. This was obviously an impossible
situation.

All through the spring and summer of 1757, the deadlock continued. Neither the
King nor the magistrates were willing to give in; but while Louis XV was perfectly
happy to wait, his most important minister, who grew more timorous every day,
longed for a compromise. Convinced that the State was collapsing, the Treasury
failing, the armies disintegrating, Bernis naturally longed for internal peace. In fact,
his view of the situation was grotesquely pessimistic, but, with his accession to
power, the once-cheerful abbé had become a prophet of doom: clearly, the weight of
government was more than he could bear. At first, Louis XV resisted his pleas, but in
August, he finally gave in and accepted a halfway solution. The *Unigenitus* bull was to
have force of law and the December Declaration was to endure, but the King permitted the Parlement to present him remonstrances about both. The government having
thus duly caved in, the Parlement resumed its function on September 5; and Bernis,
who now corresponded with the comte de Stainville almost weekly, tried to justify
himself.

"Mme de Pompadour, my dear comte, is feeling very well," he wrote on September
24. "She was chagrined for a while by the arrangement with the Parlement; she
admits today that her pride for the King has suffered; but little by little she will feel
that the master's kindness strengthens his power and his authority."[15] And three
days later he added: "Our friend has almost cold-shouldered me for a few days
because of the arrangement with the Parlement; but I dare say that without it all was
lost. It is perhaps the greatest service I will ever render."[16] Bernis could hardly have
been more mistaken: in no time at all the Parlement was back to its old tricks.

In spite of Bernis's lamentations, at least the war in 1757 was going well. In the
spring, Frederick II invaded Bohemia and laid siege to Prague, but he was unable to
take the city and had to retreat; then, in June, he was beaten at Kolin by the Austrian
Field Marshal Daun. Within a month, the maréchal d'Estrées, who commanded the
French army in Germany, met the Anglo-Hanoverian army, led by the Duke of
Cumberland, defeated it and pushed it back from Westphalia: it is worth noting that,
as usual during the reign of Louis XV, the war was taking place outside French

borders, thus sparing the country from the ravages it had experienced during the
War of the Spanish Succession.

All through September, the good news continued: the maréchal de Richelieu, who,
fresh from his victory at Port Mahon, was replacing the maréchal d'Estrées, now
pursued Cumberland's army, caught up with it near the estuary of the Elbe River
and forced him to capitulate. It was a brilliant success, due in part to the quality of
the French army, no doubt, but also to Richelieu's dash and courage. With the
elimination of the French army, Frederick was left alone to face the French and the
Austrians: it should have been easy to end the war.

Then everything went wrong. Richelieu disobeyed orders and, typically sure that
he knew better, proceeded to do exactly the worst possible thing. The maréchal's
instructions were perfectly clear: he was empowered to accept the enemy's capitulation, but not to enter into any other kind of agreement. Unfortunately, Richelieu was
accustomed to disobeying orders. Instead of sending to Versailles for instructions, the
maréchal negotiated a separate truce with Cumberland: the Anglo-Hanoverians, instead of being made prisoner, simply took an oath to go home and not serve against
France anymore. Horrified as it was when it heard about this act of folly, the French
Government was powerless to remedy it. "M. de Richelieu, my dear comte, has
concluded a convention* a little too fast," Bernis wrote Stainville on September 20.
"Never has an act been less thoughtful or been carried through with fewer forms
. . . I greatly fear that it may create grave inconveniences which will outweigh the
advantages. Certainly the event is glorious in appearance and enables M. de Richelieu to march forward, but beware the consequences."[17] For once, Bernis was only
too right to complain. Within a matter of weeks, King George II refused to ratify the
Convention: the capitulation had been in vain. Worse still, instead of marching on to
Magdeburg—which he could easily have taken, since it was full of Saxon and Austrian prisoners who were ready to rise up at the time of a French attack—Richelieu
made his way to Halberstadt, where he spent seven weeks secretly negotiating with
Frederick II about the war contribution to be paid by Prussian subjects who lived in
the occupied territories.

Of course, Richelieu, who was far from foolish, had a good reason to act as he did:
during this time large sums were raised all over the area occupied by his army. This
was a normal procedure: Hanover, after all, was the property of the King of England;
what was unclear at the time was why this prevented him from continuing military
operations. The key to this riddle soon became apparent, however: of some sixteen
million livres that were raised that winter, the Treasury received a little over four
million. The rest vanished into the generals' pockets, with Richelieu taking the lion's
share; but others, like the duc d'Ayen and the maréchal de Maillebois, also received
significant sums. When, at the end of the war, the maréchal built himself an especially luxurious house at the end of his garden, the Parisians, who knew where the
money came from, dubbed it the Hanover Pavilion.

It is not very difficult to imagine what would have happened to the greedy
maréchal had he lived under Louis XIV; the only uncertainty is exactly what form his
punishment would have taken. Because Louis XV was too kind, because he hated to

* It is known as the Convention of Kloster-Zeven.

punish people, the maréchal endured nothing worse than a mild reprimand; but in this case the King would have done better to be harsh. Perhaps, to paraphrase the duc de Croÿ, Louis XV, in the 1750s, had all the qualities of a great king except for the necessary ability to punish.

All this would have been bad enough in an ordinary war; but here the French were facing a military genius who knew just how to take advantage of his enemy's mistakes. Frederick II made full use of the time given him by Richelieu; when, at last, he faced a French army, he was more than ready; and at this point Richelieu, who had been demoted and given the command of a smaller army, managed once again to do his country real harm. Another army had been entrusted to the prince de Soubise, that old friend of Mme de Pompadour's whom Richelieu disliked for that very reason. This force, together with a German army under the command of the Prince of Hildburghausen, now found itself face to face with the Prussians. Soubise, who seems to have had a perfectly accurate understanding of his own talents, begged Richelieu to come to the rescue. Richelieu, still smarting under his reprimand and all too willing to see a friend of Mme de Pompadour's humiliated, marched so slowly as to arrive too late. The result was one of the worst disasters ever suffered by a French army.

As it was, the prince de Soubise should have had quite enough men for a victory: he had twenty-four thousand French troops and thirty-six thousand Germans, these last a motley array of contingents sent by a number of German princes at Maria Theresa's request. Frederick II's army numbered some twenty-five thousand men, superbly armed and trained and led by the greatest general of his time. The allies, aside from their superior numbers, also had the best position: they occupied the hill of Rossbach, where they were protected by a series of strong retrenchments. Clearly, the Prussians had no hope of taking the hill, so Frederick relied on a stratagem: he feigned a retreat. Immediately Hildburghausen and Soubise started pursuing him. Worse, they started an enveloping movement to cut off the enemy's communications. Frederick had only been waiting for the allies to leave their retrenchments; as soon as they did, he turned his army around, so that just as Soubise thought he was about to attack the Prussian flank, he found the entire Prussian Army attacking his own. Immediately the German troops fled, taking some French regiments with them; the rest of Soubise's army resisted until the end of the day, but the odds were now too uneven: by nightfall the French force was virtually annihilated. And, to compound the disaster, a month later the Austrians, who had briefly occupied Berlin while Frederick was busy elsewhere, were beaten at Lenthe, in Silesia, and left more than thirty thousand prisoners behind. Once again, speed and intelligence had paid off. Frederick, who was quite incapable of beating a combined Franco-Austrian army, made sure the allies never had time to come together, and trounced them piecemeal, one at a time.

In Paris, the first reaction for many was satisfaction: Mme de Pompadour was unpopular, Soubise was her nominee, so Soubise's defeat meant a black eye for the marquise; and so people laughed and, as usual, sang: "Le prince dit, la lanterne à la main / J'ai beau chercher, où diable est mon armée? / Elle était là pourtant hier matin / Me l'a-t-on prise ou l'aurais-je égarée? / Prodige heureux, la voilà, la voilà! / O, Ciel, que mon âme est ravie! / Mais non, qu'est-ce donc que cela? / Ma foi, c'est l'armée ennemie." ("The prince [de Soubise], lantern in hand, says / I keep looking, where can my army be? / It was here, I'm sure, yesterday. / Has it been taken from me or have I mislaid it? / Happy miracle, it is here, it is here! / O Heavens, my soul is in rapture! / But, no, what can this be? / In faith, it is the enemy.")[18]

For Bernis, who had become Foreign minister in June, it was no laughing matter. On November 14 he wrote Stainville: "Our friend [Mme de Pompadour] is much to be pitied. The public would only have forgiven M. de Soubise's appointment if he had won a victory . . . M. de Soubise . . . should now accept with good grace the command of some important reserve. I think this both as a minister and as a friend"[19]; and, a few days later, he added: "All the courtiers saw in the defeat was *M. de Soubise* and not the State. Our friend has given him the strongest proofs of friendship and so has the King; she has also given proofs of reason and moderation."[20] Bernis was right in that she allowed Soubise to be superseded; and it is only fair to add that in 1758 he defeated a Hessian-Hanoverian army.

There can be no doubt that for once the marquise had made a very serious mistake: she was so accustomed to thinking in terms of Court favors and intrigues that she had considered an army command as just another plum to be awarded to a friend. Rossbach, at any rate, taught her that armies are not like courts: Soubise was the last of her frivolous appointments. Still, the situation was worrisome. France had a number of experienced generals but it lacked a strong minister of War and a talented commander in chief. As a result, confusion piled upon confusion as every officer, his eye firmly on promotion, tried to ruin his rivals, while the Court factions fought in favor of their protégés. Bernis soon complained of this to Stainville, who had become his chief confidant and adviser: "I agree with you, my dear comte, that if our military plans continue to be as chaotic as they are now, our enemy, by his talent, will ruin our system. But who have we here to lead the military? The maréchal de Belle-Isle keeps writing memoranda which no one reads at the war office, Duverney [a very rich financier related to Mme de Pompadour] is also producing memoranda which M. de Richelieu, his friend, ignores. The discipline among officers and men depends absolutely on the secretary of state for war, who is afraid of making powerful enemies and who fears energetic solutions because he can see that the King doesn't like them." And, of course, Bernis added his usual lament: "What, then, is left me, who am in charge of the political side? To forecast, to report disasters."[21] Bernis was right: Paulmy was far too aware of his uncle's disgrace to take chances, so that he ended up by being completely ineffective; but even his replacement, in 1758, by the maréchal de Belle-Isle did little to improve matters.

The abbé did have one solution in mind, though, which he naturally confided to Stainville: "The idea of appointing a Prime Minister scares everybody, so there is no ministry to speak of . . . We need someone to keep the parts and the whole together."[22] As usual, Bernis was perceptive; unfortunately, the prime minister he had in mind was none other than himself. Seldom can a man have so misunderstood his own capacities: unable as he was to face the responsibilities of a Foreign minister, he would no doubt have promptly collapsed if the King had been foolish enough to take his hints.

Once again, therefore, Louis XV found himself faced with a minister whom he had trusted earlier but who had now become a burden instead of a support: just as Bernis had pushed for a surrender to the Parlement, so now he began to plead for peace at any price. Already in January 1758, he was writing Stainville, now Ambassador to Vienna: "My advice is to make peace and to start with a truce on land and sea. As soon as I know what the King thinks of this idea . . . which good sense, necessity and logic have presented to me, I will give you the details. In the meantime, try to explain to M. de Kaunitz [Maria Theresa's chancellor] two equally true notions: the King will never abandon the Empress, but he mustn't sink with her; our respective mistakes have transformed a great plan . . . into an assured ruin . . . The more I contributed to this great alliance, the more I must be believed when I speak for peace."[23] Given the fact that Frederick II was now under attack by France, Austria and Russia, whose combined forces were vastly superior to his, this was sheer cowardice, and Louis XV saw it as such. Luckily, he could still rely on Mme de Pompadour. Discarding her earlier faith in the abbé, she now backed the King to the hilt. He felt that the war must go on, that suing for peace in 1758 would be disastrous, and so did she; it was no more than common sense. Of course, she was reviled by the still vigorous pro-Prussian party: her head had been turned by Maria Theresa's amiability to her, they said, and she was bleeding France dry for the most frivolous of reasons.

These accusations, nonsensical as they were, nevertheless received a wide hearing; mistresses, like ministers, had always been unpopular. Now this unpopularity began to affect the King, who was represented as weak, infatuated and oblivious to the welfare of his people. To the courtiers who financed songs and pamphlets, these accusations were merely a useful tool, a convenient lie which they didn't believe themselves; nor did it occur to them they might be endangering the regime which gave them so much. To them, this was simply a Court intrigue like any other, a way of displacing the favorites of the day and replacing them with their own candidates; but, in fact, the foundations of the French Revolution were laid during the Seven Years' War.

Unwittingly, because he was so weak, Bernis strengthened the Court opposition. The paradox here, though, is that at the same time he was pestering the King for more power: his ambition pushed him on, while his pessimism made him admit he was incapable of using properly what power he already had. "I had hoped that the same trust in me which caused me to be chosen [as Foreign minister] would allow me to make my advice prevail . . . I am more listened to, perhaps, than the others, but my influence is no greater when the time comes to make decisions."[24] Bernis complained to Stainville. There could be no finer tribute to the King: like his great-grandfather, Louis XV now felt strong enough to take advice but make his own decisions. And although he did not know it yet, the abbé was writing the wrong person: Stainville was wholly in favor of the war, the alliance and fighting on; he told not just Bernis but Mme de Pompadour, who, of course, passed his letters on to the King, so that even as Bernis was fading, the marquise realized that there was at least one strong, capable man who was ready to take over.

By the spring of 1758, Bernis had reached a state of total frenzy. He wanted peace immediately but continued to beg Stainville for advice, even though he knew it would go against his own preferences, and he strained his relationship with Louis XV and Mme de Pompadour dangerously by constantly begging for favors. In February, the always indulgent monarch gave him a new, rich abbey, thus greatly increasing his income, and made him a Knight of the Saint Esprit, but that still wasn't enough: not only did Bernis want to be Prime Minister, he also demanded a cardinal's hat. For so subtle a courtier, it was an amazing misreading of the King's feelings. A prime minister who was also a cardinal would have been a second Fleury, the very situation the King was most determined to avoid; and, compounding his error, instead of just begging the King to nominate him to the purple, he actually told his master that the Pope wanted to make him a cardinal and was only waiting for the King's request out of sheer courtesy. Even Bernis, however, realized that he had failed to convince: "The King told me that he felt quite sure that I would never be obsessed by [the cardinal's hat] and that if the Pope felt like awarding it to me, apparently he would warn him."[25]

While Bernis was thus angling for his promotion, he nearly found himself altogether undone. He owed his contact with the King, and therefore his office, wholly to Mme de Pompadour's recommendation; now it looked as if Louis XV had fallen in love with a pretty young woman, the marquise de Coislin, who belonged to an old aristocratic family and longed to replace the apparently eternal Pompadour. By the middle of March, it was obvious that Mme de Coislin had become the King's mistress and the Court held its breath; but, once again, affection and trust triumphed over lust: when Louis XV found out that Mme de Coislin was using her new position to humiliate Mme de Pompadour, he simply dismissed her, much to the rage of the pro-Prussian party.

Still, new measures—and new men—were becoming a clear necessity. In Germany, the comte de Clermont, whose appointment owed much to his valor in Flanders under the maréchal de Saxe, had been given a mentor in the person of the incompetent comte de Mortagne, and the result of that mistake came swiftly: in March, the French were defeated by Frederick at Crefeld. Clermont remarked bitterly: "I could have managed this quite well by myself," and once again the generals fell to quarreling. By April Bernis, more overwhelmed than ever, was asking for help. The Council was down to four members—Bernis; the maréchal de Belle-Isle, who had just replaced Paulmy at the war ministry; the maréchal d'Estrées; and the perennial Saint-Florentin—so the abbé asked that the King add a new member. "That proposal," he wrote "displeased [Mme de Pompadour]. She answered me angrily: 'Why must you have new ministers? Aren't you the master now?'

" 'It is, Madame, because I neither am nor want to be the master, and even less to look as if I am, that I ask for help and advice.' "[26] Eventually he was heard: on July 2, Puysieulx, the former Foreign minister, and Berryer, who had been in charge of Paris and was a friend of the marquise's, were admitted to the Council, but they did not make much difference.

More than ever, therefore, the King found himself alone, and although he was increasingly displeased with Bernis, he didn't know where to find his replacement. Nor could he take comfort in the military operations: even when, after Crefeld, the disasters ceased, it became clear that a new, hardly preferable pattern was being set. The three allied armies converged on Berlin, but because they lacked a unified command, and because Apraxin, the Russian general, was, to say the least, unenthusiastic,* the King of Prussia managed to fight each of the three armies separately to a standoff. There is much to be said against Frederick's unprincipled behavior, but it cannot be denied that all through the war he displayed the most dazzling tactical and strategic genius. He was sometimes beaten, but he won far more battles than he should have, given the strength of his army, and after a defeat he always managed to recoup his losses. It is just barely conceivable that if the allies had appointed a supreme commander they might have overcome Frederick, but that was never even a remote possibility. Even the French failed to achieve the unity of command within their own forces. Belle-Isle, a seasoned soldier but a born intriguer, ran the war ministry to the best of what he saw as his own private interest, while the other generals—Soubise, Richelieu, Broglie, Contades—all loathed one another and wanted nothing so much as to see the others fail.

Louis XV was fully aware of this, but he, too, had been raised at Court. From his earliest years he had seen precisely this kind of rivalry, and while he deplored it, he didn't think it could be suppressed or ended. Still, he was beginning to look at Bernis with an ever more critical eye, and no wonder: the Foreign minister had transferred a good part of his attention from the war to his own promotion. On April 21, 1758, he wrote Stainville: "Our friend told me I must beware that the King take umbrage at my elevation . . . but he has never been more at ease with me than since our first explanation about the hat and the consent he then gave to my promotion. As for Mme de Pompadour, she is enchanted by it all."[27] He could not have been more blind. The marquise resented her protégé's greed and his pessimism; the King was resolved not to have a cardinal in the Council. As it was, time kept passing without any news from Rome. "Please conclude my Roman business," Bernis wrote Stainville on May 6, "for if it becomes known, I will be exposed to every kind of calumny"[28]; and, a week later: "The Pope is dead, there is a castle in the air at an end . . . I would be easily consoled for myself, but it would be a misfortune for the government. That position would have given me more influence, dignity and safety."[29] Away in Vienna, Stainville, a man to whom ambition was hardly unknown, must have been smiling: it was now only a question of time before Bernis went too far, and since so few men of talent were committed to the new alliance, it stood to reason that a change in the ministry would benefit him.

This became even more probable as Bernis, greatly to the King's disgust, continued to whine for peace. He spoke to the Council as he wrote to Stainville, so he himself tells us. It is not difficult to imagine Louis XV and Mme de Pompadour's feelings when they heard something like his missive of June 6; it is nothing but a long moan. "We have reached the last stage of decadence," he wrote Stainville. "Neither Montmartel nor Boullongne can find another écu.** Our army's shame is almost at its peak . . . We have no government. My representations are useless . . . The public abhors the system because it abhors the war. I receive anonymous letters

* He was probably receiving bribes from the English.
** A three-livre silver coin.

threatening me with being torn limb from limb by the people . . . Our friend runs at least as great a risk . . . I have witnessed a secret plot being formed in all parts of the State against the new alliance and its authors. We have been universally betrayed . . . Peace has never been more necessary or more difficult to arrange"[30]; and later that month, underlining his words for greater emphasis, he added: *"Give us peace at any cost."*[31]

By mid-summer, with the King still determined to fight on, Bernis had a new idea. At last he had been granted his cardinal's hat, although the actual pontifical brief did not arrive in Paris until November. Breathing a sigh of relief at still being on good terms with Mme de Pompadour—he had discovered that some courtiers were saying that he, Bernis, was plotting her dismissal so as to be all-powerful—the abbé now decided he needed help. "I think you could do better than I as Foreign minister," he wrote Stainville, *"considering this from the point of view of the alliance* . . . And then, united as we are, we would become the strongest, and my red hat, once I was away from the ministry, would no longer frighten people . . . You have energy and you will communicate it better than I."[32] What Bernis had in mind was a situation where he would be, in effect, Prime Minister, a member of the Council, with Stainville as his assistant; where he would continue to make all appointments himself, decide on policy and then leave it to the new minister to do the actual work. As it happened, the King, too, thought that a change was overdue, but he never thought of making Bernis Prime Minister, nor did Stainville himself want to become Bernis's flunky.

On August 25, it became clear that something was in the wind: the King created Stainville a duc, and the happy man chose to be known as duc de Choiseul. Whatever reluctance Louis XV may still have had to change ministers in the middle of a war was soon overcome by Bernis himself. In between complaints that his pontifical brief was taking forever to come, he sent Mme de Pompadour letters on September 19, 26, 29, October 4 and October 6 which all read like this one, the first of the series: "I warn you, Madame, and ask you to warn the King, that I can no longer be answerable to him for my work. My head is always shaken or confused . . . If the King wants to keep me, he must give me relief."[33] Seldom if ever has a man become Prime Minister by whining that he was overworked, and Bernis proved no exception. Still, on October 9, in a long holograph letter, Louis XV gave him one last chance; it was also a masterly exposition of the policy he had adopted.

"I am sorry," the King wrote, "that the business for which I have made you responsible should so affect your health as to render you incapable of bearing the weight of your work.

"Certainly no one wants peace more than I, but I want a solid and honorable peace; I am willing to sacrifice my interests for it, but not those of my allies. Work in consequence of what I am telling you, but let us not rush anything. The campaign is now nearing its end.* Let us wait for that event; it may give us a better occasion not to go and lose everything by so foully abandoning our allies. It is only when peace comes that we will be able to retrench on all kinds of expenses, principally the depredations in the Army and Navy, which is impossible in the middle of a war like this one. Let us be content with curbing the abuses and preventing impossibly large

---

* Campaigning, in the eighteenth century, started in March and ended in November.

expenditures without turning everything topsy-turvy, as we must do when we have peace. I permit regretfully that you turn the foreign ministry over to the duc de Choiseuil [sic], whom I think the only man capable of taking it on right now, since I absolutely will not change the system I have adopted and do not even want to hear a possible change suggested."[34]

That the King was appointing Choiseul only reluctantly cannot be doubted: he had not forgotten the new duc's role in the Choiseul-Romanet affair and had disliked him ever since. It was obviously one thing to have this brilliant, energetic man as his ambassador in Vienna: there Choiseul could do the most good without the King ever seeing him, but it was quite another to have him at Versailles attending the Council and working daily with the King. Still, there was no choice: Choiseul was far and away the best candidate.

He was also a man of many, often contradictory, qualities. A member of an old Lorraine family, he was excessively proud of his lineage, but he had married the granddaughter and heiress of a very rich, very plebeian financier; a brilliant conversationalist, he was also capable of nurturing long-term, deeply laid designs; immensely vain, he depended entirely on the good graces of a woman—Mme de Pompadour— to reach the place he coveted. As he was, he surprised people and often conquered them, except when he had so infuriated them by his frivolity that they would have nothing more to do with him; and he always made news. "The duc de Choiseul" a contemporary noted, "had an ugly, even a revolting face; but his wit, light and pleasant, easily made up for the unpleasant impression given by his appearance. An impetuous character who wanted to bend everything to his slightest wish; a deep understanding, which let him see all the possibilities and showed him how to make them happen; a great prodigality, even when he was not yet successful, which grew with the position he reached; an inconceivable charm in his conversation, and a manner all his own of repairing on the instant the mistakes his first impulse had caused him to make, a talent which, more than once in the course of his great fortune, gave him as supporters people who had only come to him to complain or tell him about their discontent; enormous resources of mind; a little too much indifference about the means he used to reach his goal; no sense of economy, either for himself or for the State when he controlled it; more enthusiasm than ability to hate— such was the duc de Choiseul. He had many mediocre protégés and few declared enemies . . . Women complained about his audacity . . . a failing easily explained by his numerous conquests."[35] After Bernis's eternal complaints, it is easy to see why this brilliant, energetic, resourceful man appealed to Mme de Pompadour. Within a matter of days, the King realized that he had at last found a minister after his own heart.

Indeed, the duc had every agreeable quality. "All that family was most cheerful, so that the marquise, who was easily bored, now found the most amusing of company among those whom she trusted; she had become very close to them, so much so that she never left them and dined three times a week at the duc de Choiseul's . . . The Choiseuls were in fashion and the duc was galloping towards the first place."[36] Full of plans and ideas though he was, Choiseul understood the necessity of also making himself popular. Naturally, Mme de Pompadour came first; it took very little time before she realized that she could relax. Choiseul saw her daily and told her all the news; he discussed every major decision with her, every appointment. She and he shared the same goal: they wanted France to be powerful and prosperous; as a result, the marquise left much business to him and devoted herself instead to making the King's life pleasanter.

Choiseul was far too intelligent to rely solely on the marquise's favor. He realized that at first Louis XV didn't like him and set about making himself a friend as well as a minister. In this he succeeded; but the King might one day get tired of him, so, anticipating twentieth-century politics, the duc tried to build himself the widest constituency possible, both at Court and in Paris. "He was as munificent in his ministry as he had been in his embassies; never has minister led a grander life," Dufort noted. "At that time we had our dinner at precisely two o'clock and all the foreigners with an introduction and all the courtiers were allowed in. The larger table sat thirty-five and another was ready but not seen. A valet de chambre counted the people coming in and as soon as their number reached thirty-five, the other table was set. His extraordinarily abundant plate was magnificently worked and the silver made it dazzling . . .

"All at Court took on a new face. The *petits appartements* became more brilliant, the Princes of the Blood paid court more assiduously. New balls to which the entire Court was invited were invented to break the routine; a new ballroom was built and we had quadrilles danced in costumes of every period and every country . . . The King was there one night, in the central box with Mme de Pompadour, Mme de Brancas and Mme d'Esparbès, the duc de Choiseul, the duc de Gontaut, his brother-in-law, and the prince de Beauvau, who was Captain of the Guard. Mme de Pompadour sat in an armchair on the right; the two other ladies, one behind the other, on the opposite side; the King in the middle; the others behind. The King hadn't been there a half hour when he stood up, ordered the duc de Choiseul to sit down in his place and remained standing behind, playing familiarly with his hair and treating him with the greatest affability. All the onlookers concluded that [the duc] had reached the highest peak of favor, for the King never forgot himself in public."[37] Still, while the reality of power was at Versailles, Choiseul understood full well that events are often what they seem rather than what they are, and that the contemporaries, like posterity, would judge him more often on what people said than on what he actually did; so he set about courting, with enormous success, the salons and intellectuals. Soon Mme du Deffand, who had invented the very notion of salon and had helped mold public opinion in France and abroad, was raving about the new minister. Voltaire, who knew an enlightened man when he saw one, joined the chorus, as did d'Alembert. Soon everyone knew that the duc de Choiseul was the incarnation of the Enlightenment, a tolerant, sceptical man who looked askance on the Church, had no use for old-fashioned sentiment, and made as brilliant a life for himself as he could. The corollary to that, of course, was the immediate appearance of an anti-Choiseul party led by the Dauphin and Mesdames, who were horrified by the duc's anticlericalism; but no one much listened to them.

At first, the new minister worked together with Bernis, but then the pontifical brief arrived. On December 8, 1758, Bernis, kneeling before the King, received his red hat; on the thirteenth, he was dismissed from all his offices and exiled to his abbey of Vic-sur-Aisne; from then on, he was never again concerned with the business of state.*

It was now all up to Choiseul—and not a moment too soon. As usual, the war was not going well. For a while it seemed as if Choiseul's talents might actually change the course of events. At the beginning of the campaign of 1759, on April 13, the duc de Broglie won a great victory over the Anglo-Hanoverians at Bergen, thus preventing a planned invasion of Alsace, but soon afterwards Contades was beaten at Minden by Frederick II: it was back to the usual seesaw. As a result, Broglie's victory loomed even larger. He was made a Marshal of France by Louis XV, a Prince of the Holy Roman Empire by Maria Theresa, and was promised the command in chief of the French armies for 1760. At the same time, he found that a number of the promotions he had recommended had been denied him: the prince de Soubise's friends, horrified that someone else was doing well, were busy telling the King that the victory had been grossly exaggerated. For the rest of the campaign the French armies remained on the defensive, but at least they were successful: an attempt against Cassel was defeated by the comte de Broglie, another against Göttingen also failed. It was back to the stalemate after all.

That it should be so was not surprising. Even Choiseul could not tighten the alliance, find new generals and raise more money in just a few months. And because the war was taking place so far away—in Saxony, Westphalia and Hesse—it never became quite real for the French. Many people found it irritating and humiliating that a league of France, Russia and Austria couldn't crush the Anglo-Prussians; they blamed the government, Mme de Pompadour and the King; but there was no question of real sacrifices. Unlike the wars of Louis XIV, during which parties of enemy soldiers had ranged almost all the way to Paris, the current conflict never touched most people's lives at all. Paradoxically, however, while Louis XV was freely blamed because France was not victorious, no one seemed to reflect that he deserved praise for not allowing the country to be invaded. His, in fact, was the first reign in many centuries during which not a single Frenchman had to suffer enemy occupation—no mean achievement; but because that state of affairs had begun to seem perfectly normal, and because the King considered it beneath him to justify himself, he was given no credit for a condition which the French soon had good cause to remember with longing.

Briefly, in 1759, it looked as if Choiseul might triumph after all. On August 13, the combined Russian and Austrian armies crushed Frederick II at Kunersdorf, near Frankfort on the Oder. It looked as if Prussia was finished. Berlin was occupied. Frederick, in his despair, considered suicide. "I have no more resources," he wrote one of his ministers, "and, without lying, I think all is lost."[38] The French Ambassador in Vienna, Choiseul's cousin, begged the Austrians to pursue the beaten King, pointing out that the object of war is not so much the occupation of territory as the crushing of the adversary. A smart follow-up would have resulted in the King's capture and the end of the war: the Prussian Army was down to three thousand men;

* He was eventually made Ambassador to the Holy See, a post he filled until his death with conspicuous splendor.

instead, the Austrian generals, who well understood that Maria Theresa wanted Silesia first and foremost, settled down to besiege its fortresses, thus giving Frederick time to raise new forces. As for the Russians, whether or not Grand Duke Peter, who worshiped Frederick, was communicating their war plans to the Prussians, as he later boasted, one thing was certain: the Tsarina Elizabeth was in poor health and the Grand Duke, her heir, would reverse her policies as soon as he came to the throne. Russian generals, therefore, thought it wise to fight hard enough to satisfy the Tsarina but not so hard as to alienate their future emperor. In 1760 Saltykov, the Russian commander, again occupied Berlin, but it was a last thrust and mattered little except to the Berliners, who had to pay a special tax.

The French, now under the maréchal de Broglie, were still fighting the Anglo-Hanoverians without discernible results. In January 1761, the maréchal de Belle-Isle died. Louis XV trusted Choiseul and was reluctant to take on another intriguing soldier—the choices were either Broglie, who was impossibly arrogant, or d'Estrées, who was impossibly spineless; so the King called Choiseul's cousin, Praslin, back from Vienna, made him a duc and gave him the foreign ministry, while Choiseul himself took on both the war and the navy ministries. While Praslin was serious, competent and hardworking, he was never more than his cousin's assistant; the letters to foreign courts might be signed Praslin, but they expressed Choiseul's policy.

Unfortunately, the first act of the new minister proved to be a serious mistake: Soubise having won a small battle the year before, he was once again championed by Mme de Pompadour, who prided herself on her loyalty to her friends; so Choiseul decided to split the Army in two, with half going to Soubise and the other half remaining under Broglie. Naturally enough, Broglie was infuriated, but he received a direct order from the King and had to obey. The all too predictable consequence of this act of folly promptly followed: instead of trying to beat the enemy, the two commanders each tried to show that the other was an incompetent fool; and on July 17 they allowed a Hanoverian army a wholly undeserved escape from what would have been a crushing defeat. Broglie, never a good-tempered man at best, blamed Soubise and refused to communicate further, thus infuriating Choiseul and making a bad situation worse. When, in January 1762, Broglie returned to Versailles and attacked both the minister and Soubise in a long, widely distributed memorandum, he was swiftly dismissed and exiled to his estates, thus leaving the incompetent Soubise in command. Once again, it all ended in a song: "Si je suis pauvre général / Je suis un brave maréchal / Je sais exposer ma patrie / Et braver des miens le mépris . . . / Poisson soutient Soubise / La France paiera nos sottises." (If I'm a wretched general / I am a brave marshal / I know how to put my country at risk / and brave my friends' contempt . . . / Poisson upholds Soubise / France will pay for our mistakes.")[39]

At least on the diplomatic front Choiseul made progress; but here, too, no immediate effect could be expected. Convinced that France alone could never defeat the sea power of England, he negotiated an alliance with the two other Bourbon kings who ruled over Spain and Naples. The Family Pact was signed in August 1761, but, unfortunately, the Spanish fleet left much to be desired. It fought at the side of the French Navy but failed to overcome the British; indeed, it was not until twenty years later that the advantages of the alliance finally ripened; and then the result was the freedom of the United States. In any event, whatever good the Family Pact might be doing was overborne by a greater loss: on January 5, 1762, the Tsarina of Russia died and was succeeded by her nephew, Peter III, who predictably annulled the alliance with Austria and instead became Frederick II's virtual slave. With the Franco-Austrian camp thus diminished, it was obviously time for compromise, since what couldn't be achieved with the Russians was unlikely to succeed without their help. Frederick, too, was heartily sick of the war, and so were the English. With George III's accession to the throne, Pitt, who had been the driving force behind the war, was replaced by the peace-loving Lord Bute; and in Vienna, Maria Theresa, convinced that she was unlucky, gave up Silesia for good.

Choiseul had another, perhaps more important, reason to end the conflict: while on land France was neither victorious nor vanquished, at sea it had endured nothing but defeats. Once again, events proved that France could not fight on both land and water.

The French fleet, as it happened, was a perfectly respectable force, probably the second best in Europe; unfortunately, it was the British Navy which occupied first place. It was no surprise, really: Great Britain being an island, all its trade must go by sea, thus providing it with a large number of experienced sailors; besides, it was accustomed to protecting its own bottoms, and had built up its fleet accordingly. Because Pitt understood perfectly where the national strength lay, the main war effort had gone to the Navy, while Hanover, George II's electorate, provided most of its Continental Army. France, on the other hand, lacked both expertise and funds. The Navy department, managed first by Maurepas and then by Machault, had been run efficiently but only as a minor component of France's military panoply. When Machault was dismissed, it seemed like a good idea to appoint an admiral, Massiac, to the ministry. Unfortunately, the new minister proceeded to demonstrate that, as a later French statesman was to remark, war is too serious a business to be entrusted to the military. Massiac's main occupation, while in office, was to quarrel with the civilians who ran the procurement agencies, and his replacement by Berryer did not help much: a competent and honest administrator, Berryer managed to bring order back into the ministry but was quite unable to strengthen the Navy.

These shortcomings, severe enough in themselves, were aggravated by the lack of competent admirals. La Galissonière, who had defeated Admiral Byng, died in 1765; his successor, the marquis de Conflans, had neither La Galissonière's genius nor any confidence in his own fleet, so that French ships spent most of their time avoiding the enemy, only to be beaten when, by accident, they met it. Since France was primarily a Continental power, this naval inferiority might not have mattered very much but for one crucially important fact: all through the seventeenth and eighteenth centuries it had acquired a very sizable Colonial empire. Canada, Louisiana (then three times the size of today's state), many islands in the West Indies and large tracts of territory in India were French, and a very profitable trade had developed between them and the mother country. Now, in spite of valiant local efforts and the spending of some two hundred million livres, England's naval superiority enabled it to take over the French colonies: that, quite as much as the stalemate in Central Europe, was an intolerable situation.

Both Louis XV and Choiseul, even if they felt no great friendship for Frederick II, realized that, more than ever, England was France's chief enemy, but one which could not be defeated in the current war. They agreed, therefore, that while peace must be sought, it should be followed by a rehabilitation of the Navy, which would allow France to take its revenge one day. Here, too, the minister proved to be the King's man. Having arrived at the same conclusions as his master, he carried out visibly and energetically the policies closest to the King's heart: it was no wonder if, in 1762, he was more in favor than ever. And since he was also busy making sure he was popular where it mattered, pamphlets which normally derided the ministers now turned laudatory, no matter how the war went; thus, in mid-May people were singing to a minuet tune: "Quand Choiseul / D'un coup d'oeil / Considère / Le plan entier de l'Etat / Et seul, comme un Sénat, / Agit et délibère; / Quand je vois / Qu'à la fois / il arrange / Le dedans et le dehors, / Je soupçonne en son corps / un ange." ("When Choiseul / with one glance / considers / the entire body of the State / and alone, like a senate, / acts and deliberates; / when I see / that at once / he arranges / the inside and the out, / I suspect he harbors / an angel.")[40] In one way, this popularity was an asset for the entire government; but what it entailed—and even if the King realized this, he didn't care—was an exaltation of the minister's reputation as the only competent man at Versailles. The more Choiseul was praised, the more it looked as if Louis XV only ratified the decisions of his brilliant nominee, and very few people realized that this wasn't the case at all.

It was, in any event, reassuring to have Choiseul in charge of the peace negotiations, which opened late in 1762. The Treaty of Paris, which was signed on February 10, 1763, and closed the Seven Years' War, was, at the time, widely considered to be a triumph of diplomatic cleverness. France, it is true, lost Canada altogether, Cape Breton Island, most of its Indian possessions, most of Senegal; it ceded Louisiana to Spain as a compensation for the latter's loss of Florida, which went to England; but it retained the key West Indian islands, whose sugar (and slave) trade enriched ports like Bordeaux; it kept five key cities in India, so that there, too, commerce—in silk, ivory, spices—could continue as before; and it was granted fishing rights in North American waters. As for Continental borders, they stood almost exactly where they had been before the conflict; France, in particular, remained unchanged.

Later French historians, many of whom belonged to the right or extreme right, have bemoaned the loss of France's colonies in 1763 and blamed Louis XV accordingly. Now that the age of Colonial empires has ended, it is difficult to share their point of view: in losing these distant territories but retaining its Colonial trade, France had, at any rate, avoided future wars of independence like the one Great Britain was to experience just twelve years later. Already in 1774, it had become clear that colonies were not always so compliant as to represent a net benefit to the mother country. Voltaire himself, the most intelligent man of his time, said he was quite indifferent to the loss of a few acres of snow; he was referring, of course, to Canada. As for Choiseul, he bragged about having outsmarted the English, a claim which, at that very moment, was causing considerable unease in London.

Still, the peace was unpopular among the people for the simple and sufficient reason that no one could claim that it was victorious. Frederick II, after all, had demonstrated that all the might of France could not crush him, and Maria Theresa, France's ally, had gained nothing either. What everyone forgot, however, was that France, while sometimes gaining, had also often lost pieces of its actual territory in the various treaties concluded before the eighteenth century. This time, just as it was untouched by the war, France was spared by the peace; but since it is always easier to blame a scapegoat than to settle for a reasonable compromise, the entire onus of the war was put on Mme de Pompadour. Choiseul, who had negotiated the Treaty of Paris, received nothing but applause; the marquise, who was considered responsible for the war, was reviled; and, of necessity, some of her unpopularity carried over onto the King.

Whatever his people might think, Louis XV was well aware that at sea France had been defeated, and he started planning for his revenge the very moment the peace was signed. Within two weeks of that event, he was writing: "The peace we have just concluded is neither good nor glorious: no one realizes it better than I. But, given the unfortunate circumstances, it could be no better, and I can assure you that if we had continued fighting, we would have had to accept a worse peace next year. As long as I live I will never give up my alliance with the Empress and will never be tied to the reigning King of Prussia.

"Let us make do with what we have and so prepare ourselves as not to be overcome by our real enemies."[41] Early in April, he set a new process in motion in a letter to the comte de Broglie, who was still managing the secret du Roi. "My intention," he wrote, "is to gather information on the coast and the interior of England that will ease the execution of plans which the circumstances might render necessary someday, far in the future I hope. I approve the idea you have communicated to the Sieur Tercier [through whom this correspondence was carried] to find a capable and intelligent officer who will undertake the necessary reconnaissance and report to you . . . I recommend that you keep this an absolute secret."[42] This was followed by at least five complementary letters on the same subject within the next four months.

Although Louis XV and Choiseul were in complete agreement about the need to prepare for a future war against England, the duc would have been more than surprised if he had seen those letters: at the moment, both Broglie brothers were exiled to their estates in Normandy, and it was hardly customary for the King to be corresponding with a disgraced subject. In fact, the punishment was more apparent than real: the Broglies had produced an extremely insolent and abundantly leaked memorandum to the King in January 1762, and they had been chastised accordingly; but, in fact, ever since the early fifties the comte had been head of the secret du Roi, the King's secret diplomacy. The secret had a straightforward, but, as it turned out, impossible goal—the election of a French prince to the Polish throne—and since first Puysieulx and then Rouillé had been less than enthusiastic about the attempt, Louis XV simply set up his own secret agency. While the various envoys to Poland, who often appeared to be mere underlings, went through a variety of complex maneuvers with fluctuating success, the plain fact was that geography came first. France was very far away and Russia, Prussia and Austria shared a common border with Poland; thus, under pressure the Poles had elected Augustus III of Saxony as their king against the French candidate. In 1763, it was obvious that Augustus did not have long to live, so another election was in the offing.

For a while, early that year, Louis XV, in his letters to Tercier, had favored the election of one of the Dauphine's brothers, Prince Xavier of Saxony. "What I desire for the next election in Poland," he wrote in March 1763, "is that the Poles make a free choice; [I would prefer] one of the brothers of Mme la Dauphine, Xavier rather than the others, in no event the eldest, but all this without our being visibly involved. If they want the prince de Conti, I won't be opposed to him."[43] In May, these lukewarm instructions were made even cooler. "As for more money [to buy the electors], in no case can you expect it, nor that a single soldier will be moved for this election. All I want is that the Polish nation's wishes be realized and that it be free, but Russia is terribly close."[44] By November the situation was clear; in yet another holograph letter Louis XV wrote Tercier: "The Elector of Saxony has been told [by Catherine II] that she advised him to desist because he could never be elected unanimously, but she lets him understand that if there is any division, she will send troops to ensure the right kind of unanimity . . . You know I will not go back to war for the sake of Poland."[45]

In the event, the King was perfectly right. Augustus died in December, Russian troops were sent "to keep the peace" in March, and they ensured the election of the Russian candidate, Stanislas Poniatowski, on September 7. Since Peter III had been killed in a coup d'état and was replaced by his wife, now the Tsarina Catherine II, and since Poniatowski had been her lover, the Poles mistakenly consoled themselves with the belief that now, at last, they were safe from Russian intervention. They could not have been more mistaken: Catherine's favors extended to her current lover and no further.

What, then, had been the point of the secret du Roi? Clearly, with or without his successive foreign ministers, Louis XV had been unable to change the course of Polish affairs. There was, however, another reason, which historians have so far ignored, for continuing the network of secret agents: Louis XV had learned, from his earliest childhood, to distrust his ministers. They often misrepresented the facts to him, sometimes lied outright, or simply pretended to obey him while really pursuing their own, different policies. Even with Choiseul at the peak of his favor, the problem remained. It takes a wise and subtle man to realize that even the best of ministers must have serious faults; Louis XV knew that Choiseul was indiscreet and prone to take an overly optimistic view of many situations. By maintaining the secret du Roi, he could check up on his minister, make sure that he knew the truth and that secret plans—the sending of a spy to England, for instance—remained secret.

In July 1763, for instance, the baron de Breteuil, who was just back from Saint Petersburg, where he had been a notably unsuccessful ambassador, received a letter from the King. "I have asked the comte de Broglie, along with the Sieur Tercier, to gather from you all details relative to your mission, and my intention is that you give them a detailed memorandum on the situation of this empire . . . When you have finished that, you may start working on Sweden . . . [and I order you] to observe the most absolute secrecy."[46] This last was essential: the whole point of the secret du Roi was that the ministers knew nothing of its existence. When it looked as if one of its agents, the comte de Guerchy, might reveal it to the duc de Praslin, the King wrote Tercier: "If Guerchy were to break the secret, it would be against me that he was acting and he would be lost."[47]

The wisdom of maintaining the secret du Roi is obvious enough; that same principle could also apply to an altogether different category of business. When, in 1757, it seemed possible that the Protestants would take advantage of the war to rise up against the government, the King used Mme de Pompadour as his letterbox, but he alone, and without his mistress' knowledge, settled what might have been a major catastrophe.* The Protestants were still suffering from the civil disabilities imposed on them by Louis XIV and aggravated by M. le Duc. Anyone caught attending a Protestant service, for instance, was normally sent off as a convict to row on the King's galleys, a fate rather worse than the death it preceded. Although both the holograph letters from the King and the reports from Berryer, whom he chose as his representative, are deliberately vague and cryptic, it seems almost certain that the prince de Conti,** furious at being refused the post of commander in chief, was cautiously offering to lead the rebellion if it actually occurred. Obviously, this was a grave situation: if it was mishandled, civil war might result. In August 1757, the King gave Berryer a written order to put the Grand Judge of the Swiss† in charge of contacting the Protestants; this was the perfect choice since the Grand Judge was a Protestant himself. When, in November, Berryer gave up his office of lieutenant [chief] of Police for Paris to enter the ministry, the King ordered him to keep working on the Protestants' problem—but still in secret. In December, Louis XV was again writing him: "I order you to see the Sieur Herrenschwand, the Grand Judge of the Swiss, as often as necessary so as to know everything that concerns the Protestants of my kingdom, and to report to myself alone."[48] In the event, a number of leading Protestants who had been condemned to the galleys were pardoned and released, while the loyal members of the sect were encouraged visibly to support the government and the war, but no one except the King, Berryer and Herrenschwand realized that there had ever been any danger: it is as good an example as any of the care and efficacity with which Louis XV ruled the realm.

In the same way, the King went on controlling personally the finances of the State. In 1761, for instance, Bertin, the contrôleur-général, received a holograph note: "Please gather as soon as possible reliable and detailed information on the abuses in the administration of the provinces relative to the taxes on the corvées.‡

"Similarly, instructive memoranda on that administration in the pays d'état.

"Also on the administrative setup of the Dauphiné and the Franche-Comté.* Transmit these orders to the first meeting of the committee of ministers so that we may take the most appropriate measures to reach our several goals and be informed of the progress accomplished. Let the manner of proceeding be examined, discussed

---

* This account is based on the King's correspondence preserved in the Bibliothèque Nationale, Paris; it has not been given in any other work on the life or reign of Louis XV.
** Although never actually named—he is always referred to as the prince—there was no one else of that stature, with sufficient daring and intelligence, to lead a rebellion.
† A judge who was competent in all cases affecting members of the Swiss Guard or even Swiss traders residing in France.
‡ Rather than actually building roads, which the corvée implied, the peasants often paid a small tax.
* Two provinces which had retained an unusual amount of self-government.

and settled before you see me about it."[49] This was obviously a key matter since taxes, as usual, were coming in little and late, but Louis XV also looked after smaller questions. On January 4, 1762, in response to a request from the duc de Chaulnes, he allocated thirty thousand livres for the school of the Chevau-légers of the Guard, adding to the warrant: "Good for this one time only."[50] Just how closely the King kept track of his ministers' work, in fact, showed clearly three days later. "M. de Saint-Florentin is not here, so I have opened your letters after having been told of your carriage accident," Louis XV wrote Bertin. "Since you cannot come here, and there is nothing urgent, I permit you to wait until next Sunday, on which day I will see the deputies of the Chambre des Comptes at the usual hour . . . M. de Saint-Florentin is in Paris; it is necessary that you see him promptly, or that you write him, for the letter to the Chambre must be sent tomorrow at noon."[51] Clearly, the King did not rely on his ministers to keep the State functioning.

There was, however, a standard way of fooling even hardworking kings, one which even Louis XIV had sometimes been unable to resist: flattery. Only, with Louis XV, probably because of his own diffidence, it just didn't work. "His Majesty having gone to see the new offices of the war ministry [now run by Choiseul], a few days ago, he went in everywhere and, in M. Dubois's room, having found a pair of glasses, he picked them up. 'Let us see,' the King said, 'if they are as good as the ones I use.' A paper, no doubt written on purpose, was also at hand. It was a letter in which one could read a pompous encomium of the monarch and his minister (the duc de Choiseul). His Majesty, quickly putting down the glasses, said: 'They are no better than mine; they enlarge everything too much.' "[52] And in much the same tone, the King wrote Tercier in February 1764, in response to a begging letter: "I give bishoprics neither because of the name [i.e., family] nor because someone is in favor, but to those who will, I think, work best for the Church and the peace of the realm"; and then he added a typically deprecatory touch: "I am very far from being infallible."[53]

It was, in fact, this feeling that he was prone to error which made the King appreciate Choiseul's self-confidence. The minister, according to the duc de Croÿ, "has a hold on the King through his pleasing manner, his boldness and his decided tone—just what the King needed—as well as by the facility with which he works."[54] Indeed, working with Choiseul was actually pleasant. Unlike his predecessors, who saw nothing but problems, the duc seemed to thrive on difficulties; and besides coping with everyday questions, he was also capable of developing the kind of grand strategy that France needed so badly.

This was to rest on two complementary treaties: the alliance with Austria would help keep the peace in Central Europe and balance the influence of Prussia, while the Pacte de Famille would enable France eventually to take its revenge on England. The first order of business, therefore, was to link Habsburgs and Bourbons by family ties. Joseph II, Maria Theresa's son and co-Emperor, married the Infanta Isabella, while the heir to the Spanish throne, the Principe de Asturias, wed her sister Maria Luisa, both daughters of Madame Infante and Don Philip of Parma; the Archduke Leopold, Grand Duke of Tuscany, married a Spanish princess; the Archduchess Maria Carolina went to Naples as the wife of King Ferdinand IV,* while it was

---

* Ferdinand IV was the second son of Charles III of Spain and the brother of the Principe de Asturias.

understood that when the Dauphin's eldest son reached the appropriate age, he, too, would be given one of Maria Theresa's daughters. All in all, Choiseul's idea was impressive: no one was likely to attack a block which included France, Spain with all its colonies, Austria, Tuscany and Naples. At the same time, the minister made it very plain to Charles III that he expected Spain to improve its navy and do better the next time: it had hardly been a help during the Seven Years' War.

No number of allies, however, could make up for France's own deficiencies, so Choiseul, with almost passionate energy, set about reforming the armed forces. In a satirical song written at Christmas 1763, he is described as mad for change: "Rempli de son mérite, / Entrant le nez au vent, / Choiseul parut ensuite / Et d'un ton turbulent / Dit, sans aucun égard, changeons cette cabane; / Je veux culbuter tout ceci / Je réforme le boeuf aussi / Et je conserve l'âne." ("Full of his own merit, / walking with his nose in the air, / Choiseul came in next / and in a lively voice / said, without concern, let us change this hut; / I want to tear all this down / I'm firing the ox as well / and keeping the donkey.")[55] The "hut" in question is, of course, the stable in which Jesus was born.

In fact, Choiseul managed to create so effective a military organization that it lasted until the 1820s; indeed, Napoleon's victories, while they were obviously due in part to his genius, would not have been possible without it. Surrounding themselves with competent officers and engineers, Choiseul and Praslin, who kept exchanging ministries, improved the naval academy at Brest and the map-keeping office of the Navy, while finding funds for the construction of new ships of the line. In 1763, at the end of the war, only forty damaged ships remained; by 1771, France had sixty-five frigates, while the ports of Cherbourg, Rochefort and Toulon were bulging with supplies. The organization of the Navy, drastically changed, was codified in a lengthy ordinance of March 25, 1765. The ports received new fortifications with new artillery to make them effective, while in 1769 the duc de Praslin created a corps of marines which proved its worth just a few years later during the siege of Yorktown.

Following earlier efforts—the creation of the Ecole Militaire, the edict ennobling officers—Choiseul set about improving the Army. Until the reforming ordinance of December 5, 1762, no two regiments had had the same number of men; recruiting was left to the captains, who tended to be corrupt and inefficient; officers served only for half the years. During the winter months the troops, left to themselves, were housed with the local population and never exercised. Now the King recruited the men directly: it was more efficient and ensured the men's loyalty to the Sovereign. Barracks were built to house the Army, and officers were made to serve all year round so that training could go on continuously. The size of the regiments, their structure, their number of officers were made uniform. Military hospitals were created and the men's pay improved. A camp was built near Compiègne for exercises of all kinds, so that in time of war competent generals would lead reliable troops. The artillery itself, almost nonexistent by the end of the war, was recreated from scratch. Four different sorts of guns were now made: light cannons capable of being moved very quickly, heavy siege pieces, fortress cannons and coastal pieces. All this, while initiated and controlled by Choiseul, was done with the King's detailed approval;

Louis XV made a point, as well, of never missing the military exercises at Compiègne, so that, year by year, he witnessed the improvement of his armed forces.

Unfortunately, standing armies are expensive and the war had been run on a deficit. While the Treasury had borrowed to meet its needs, it had done so at what was then considered ruinous rates ranging from 10 to 14 percent. Once again, the key to financial stability was the Parlement. At the same time, Choiseul was determined to prove himself capable of subduing that usually fractious body. Since it was a question of pleasing the Parlement without, however, reviving the disputes caused by the *Unigenitus* bull, Choiseul looked around and, a freethinker himself, he found the perfect offering.

The Jesuits, in the eighteenth century, were still very much the order founded by Ignatius Loyola: fully obedient to the Pope, they represented the cutting edge of Catholic orthodoxy. As such they were the sworn enemies of the Jansenists, and partly responsible for the issuing of the bull. Besides this, enough in itself to make the Parlement loathe them, they traditionally provided kings all over Europe with their confessors. The distance from this fact to supposing that the order was a sort of international power behind the throne was a very short step, and this presumption did not add to their popularity. They were, however, admirable teachers, so that their schools, widely considered the best in Europe, were attended by the children of the upper classes. At the same time, because they had houses all over the world, and because they literally owned Paraguay, the Jesuits had become international bankers as well as property holders. It was in this particular capacity that they suddenly appeared before the Parlement de Paris.

In 1741 the Jesuit Father La Valette had gone off to the order's house in Martinique, which was a French possession. On arrival, he found the establishment burdened with debt, so in order to make extra money he started to trade in sugar and slaves—a dubious enough enterprise for a man of the cloth. As it turned out, his business prospered—until, that is, a combination of a hurricane, an epidemic and the seizure of his ships by the British threw him into bankruptcy. Among his creditors was a Marseille trading house, Lionci et Gouffre, to whom he owed the enormous sum of a million and a half livres. Lionci et Gouffre sued not only Father La Valette but also the whole French Jesuit order on the grounds that it was responsible for all its members' enterprises. After due deliberation, the Marseille Commercial Tribunal agreed.

Aghast, the Jesuits appealed to the Parlement de Paris in its capacity as the court of last appeal; this seemed safe enough since most of its conseillers and présidents had been raised in Jesuit schools. As it turned out, however, the Jesuits would have done better to pay the million and a half livres. Once the Parlement had a good reason to look at an order that had oppressed the Jansenists, it was a reasonable presumption that it would not limit itself to a mere commercial matter. Sure enough, when the suit was called at the Grande Chambre on April 6, 1761, one of the judges, the abbé Chauvelin, rose and pointed out that the very constitutions of the order now came under the court's cognizance since the responsibility of the order for its members must be ascertained. He didn't have to remind his colleagues that, as a corollary, they also had the power, in their capacity of keepers of the laws, to scrutinize these constitutions so as to ensure their conformity to French legislation; but he did point out that he felt obligated, as a Christian, as a Frenchman, as a subject of the King and as a magistrate, to call the court's attention to a number of dangerous articles he had noticed in the order's rules. No sooner was the request made but it was granted.

A first inkling of the Parlement's intentions came astonishingly soon: just a month after the suit was called, the Jesuits were condemned to pay the million and a half livres plus damages of a hundred and fifty thousand livres. It took a little longer before the report on the constitutions was ready, but when, on July 3, the Attorney General, Joly de Fleury, came before the Grande Chambre, it was to say that because the Jesuits owed absolute obedience to their General,* they constituted a danger to the safety of the State and the freedom of private persons. At this point Chauvelin intervened again with a summary and quotes from various political theories which the Jesuits had endorsed at one time or another. That the books he quoted were some hundred and fifty years old seemed to make no difference: they advocated such principles as the legitimate assassination of insufficiently pious kings, and that was enough. Reminding his audience of the killings of Henri III (1589) and Henri IV (1610), and a recent attempt against the King of Portugal, Chauvelin went on to say that Damiens—who knew no language but French—had no doubt been incited to murder by reading a book long out of print published by a German Jesuit. The consequences now came swiftly: on August 6, the Parlement condemned the order and ordered its schools closed by October 1.

Of course, the accusations were a farrago of nonsense, and so most everyone realized. Whatever the Jesuits' faults or merits, they were being condemned unjustly; but mere denials of justice had never worried the Parlement. Still, the closing of the schools applied only within that court's jurisdiction. It was now up to the provincial Parlements: they could do the same thing if they chose and, with some delay, most of them did: Rennes, Rouen, Aix, Bordeaux, Perpignan, Metz, Pau, Toulouse, Dijon and Grenoble followed Paris. Nancy, Colmar, Besançon and Douai simply abstained. The Parlement de Provence, which sat at Aix, even went Paris one better: before hearing the suit, it confiscated the Jesuits' possessions, an extraordinary instance of assessing a penalty on a yet unconvicted body; and when one of the présidents protested against this insult to every rule of legal procedure, he was condemned to perpetual banishment for having insulted his fellow magistrates.

Because the parlements made sure that their decisions were fully publicized, along with the apparently damning quotes from Jesuit books, their decision was immensely popular; as for the order, when it tried to defend itself, it found that its publications were seized or banned. Even so, the King, who liked the Jesuits, was fully aware that the order was being railroaded; and since he also considered the whole fuss to be yet another self-interested move on the part of the Parlement, he decided to call the issue to his council, thus taking over jurisdiction. At this point Choiseul intervened. The war, he pointed out, was not over yet, so it was not a good idea to antagonize the Parlement when money was needed so very badly, a view with which Lamoignon, the Keeper of the Seals, wholeheartedly agreed. Still, the King, while willing to let the

* The General was the head of the order; he resided in Rome.

order go, tried to save the Jesuits as individuals so that they could go on teaching and confessing. He delayed the October 1 closing date of the schools by six months and asked the Pope to modify any part of the Jesuit constitution that might be construed as breaking French law. The Pope, not unnaturally, refused and in 1762 the Jesuit houses were closed one by one. Then, on August 6, a new decision of the Parlement forbade the individual Jesuits to wear the habit of their order and to correspond in any way with their superiors; it also made them legally unable to teach, hold a benefice or any other public trust without an oath of fidelity to the King, which included a promise to defend the liberties of the Gallican Church against the Pope. Finally, in March 1764 all the Jesuits were banished from the kingdom. This was too much for Louis XV. In an edict dated November of that year, he formally allowed individual Jesuits to live in France as private persons. As d'Alembert wrote Voltaire: "These are fanatics who are slitting other fanatics' throats, but we must let them do it: all these imbeciles who think they are serving religion are actually serving the cause of reason."[56] Together, the Parlement and Choiseul had started a major European movement: by 1767, the Jesuits had been expelled from all the states ruled by a Bourbon; seven years later, the Pope himself abolished the order.

While Choiseul actually cooperated with the Parlement in its war against the Jesuits, there was a whole section of the Royal Family and the Court that felt outraged and insulted: the Dauphin, Mesdames, the anti-Pompadour faction, the Queen —all saw this as the most dastardly of sacrileges. They had always detested Choiseul because he was the marquise's man; now they loathed him even more, and he relied increasingly on the support of the Paris salons; besides, he felt confident—rightly— of the King's favor.

While all these grave matters naturally took much of the King's time and attention, the ceaseless ceremony of the Court continued unchanged; indeed, the sacrosanct etiquette had become the one institution that no one wanted to reform. Week after week, year after year, Louis XV continued to dine in public—he was famous for the elegance with which he opened his soft-boiled eggs—dress and undress before the courtiers granted the entrées and go through the ritual of the presentations. In compensation, he hunted as much as ever and paid even more attention to his new buildings. As for Mme de Pompadour, she was so powerful, so firmly established, that no one seriously tried to get her dismissed anymore. The Court, in fact, seemed frozen in its perennial routines, while Choiseul was too successful to leave his rivals any hope of replacing him.

This stability was soon to be broken, however: death, in the eighteenth century, was never very far away. Madame Infante, Louis XV's favorite daughter, had come for yet another prolonged stay at Versailles in 1757. As ambitious as ever, she thought she could use Bernis, with whom she was on the best of terms, to encompass the exchange of Parma for a larger state. As it turned out, Bernis was soon gone and the war brought her no nearer to her goal, but, to her father's delight, she stayed on. Then, in late November 1759, she caught smallpox. The disease soon proved to be of the most virulent kind, and on December 5 she died. She was only thirty-two years old. The King, of course, was deeply grieved, and after mourning her for months he redirected the affection he had felt for her to his grandson in Parma, Don Ferdinand.

"You may be sure that I am delighted when I hear people speak well of you because I love you and kiss you very tenderly although we are far away from each other,"[57] Louis XV wrote his grandson in September 1762. Don Ferdinand was only eleven years old and it was the start of an abundant correspondence. Sealed in red wax and dried with gold sand, the letters became even more frequent after the death of Madame Infante's widower, Don Philip, in July 1765. As soon as the King was told that his fourteen-year-old grandson had become an orphan, he wrote: "I am pleased that you feel as deeply as you should the irreparable loss which you have just sustained. Always remember him, and everything he told you, and trust those he has placed near you. I promise I will help you with advice; as for the continuation of my [financial] assistance, my protection and my love, never doubt them as long as you continue to deserve them. You are now in a great position, though at the head of a very small state; always ask our Sovereign Judge for his help in governing it wisely. I wrote to Spain as soon as I heard about your father's death and hope that the King, your uncle, will not forget in his nephew the love he had for his brother. I kiss you most tenderly, my very dear grandson."[58] No doubt Louis XV remembered his own orphaned childhood.

The loss of Madame Infante had been a severe blow. As the summer of 1763 passed into winter, it became all too clear that he had another, still worse, loss to fear: although Mme de Pompadour was only forty-two, she had been very unwell for some time. It is difficult for us to tell, given the hopeless inadequacy of medicine in the eighteenth century, exactly what was wrong with the marquise, but it sounds very like heart failure: she was constantly out of breath, felt weak, had swollen legs, lost her appetite and, all in all, began to look like a very much older woman. In her last portrait, painted by Drouais, we can see the transformation: in less than twenty years, the slender, ravishing young woman has become more than matronly.

No matter how unwell she might feel, Mme de Pompadour insisted on living exactly as she had always done. She did have a sort of elevator—a flying armchair, it was called—installed so that she no longer had to walk up the stairs of Versailles, but otherwise kept up her many activities. The truth was, however, that she was worn out. It wasn't only the life of the Court, though that was exhausting enough; for a few years now, ever since Choiseul's accession to the ministry, she had sloughed off many of her political tasks. More important, because she had become the King's mistress by sheer willpower, because keeping that position had meant an endless wariness, Mme de Pompadour found herself unable to let life provide. Nothing, she was sure, would go right unless she saw to it personally: added to everything else, it was simply too much. No doubt she had been sustained by her love for Louis XV, but even so her life was too exhausting. Early in 1764, she became seriously ill.

"At Court, Mme de Pompadour's illness stopped everything," the duc de Croÿ noted. "It had begun, on February 29, by a bad cold on the chest. The seventh day of the illness, she was thought to be safe when she developed a strong miliarial fever, and on the eleventh a strong putrid fever was noticed. She was very ill, the worry grew, the King was almost always with her. On March 10, she was near death; they say that on the ninth day of her illness she confessed to the priest from the Madeleine . . . Everybody agreed that she was kind and seemed to take an interest in her . . .

"On April 13, her situation looked absolutely desperate . . . During the night of the fourteenth to the fifteenth she was given the last rites even though she was at Versailles* . . . She showed much courage and ready acceptance of death.

"His Majesty had seen her the day before, but he no longer saw her after she had received the last rites. For a long time she had been merely his friend, and he was the one who told her she needed the last rites. She could no longer remain in bed because her chest illness choked her: she always sat in an armchair, unable to breathe.

"A little before her death, the marquise said good-bye and sent away MM. de Soubise, de Gontaut and de Choiseul, saying: 'It is coming close; leave me with my confessor and my maids.' She called back M. de Soubise and gave him her keys. She arranged everything, called back her business manager and told her to call her carriage so that she could be taken to her Versailles house.

"She died on April 15 . . . at seven at night . . . She was widely regretted, for she was kind and had helped those who had come to her."[59]

Not only had the King, out of religious feeling, been forced to let her die without him: now, no sooner had she breathed her last but she must be removed. Dufort described the event. "The duchesse de Praslin told me: 'I saw two men pass by carrying a stretcher. When they came closer (they passed right under my window) I saw that it was the body of a woman covered only with so thin a sheet that the shapes of the head, the breasts, the belly and the legs were clearly visible. I sent to ask: it was the body of that poor woman who, according to the strict rule that no dead person can remain in the Palace, was being carried to her house.' "[60] Mme de Praslin was not the only one watching. The desolate King also waited for a last look at his friend. "It was six o'clock at night, in winter, and a dreadful storm was raging. The King took Champlost by the arm; when he arrived at the mirrored door of the *cabinet intime* which gives out onto the balcony facing the avenue, he told him to close the entrance door and went with him out onto the balcony. He kept absolutely silent, saw the carriage drive into the avenue and, in spite of the bad weather and the rain, which he appeared not to feel, he kept looking at it until it went out of sight. He then came back into the room. Two large tears were still running down his cheeks, and he said to Champlost only these few words: 'These are the only respects I can pay her.' "[61]

At Court, the dead woman was swiftly forgotten. "There is no more talk here of her who is gone than as if she had never existed,"[62] the Queen wrote a friend on April 20. She was right, of course, or mostly so: Choiseul missed his protectress for a while, Soubise and Gontaut their friend, Marigny his sister. For all the other courtiers, a place was now vacant, and Choiseul's sister, the duchesse de Gramont, promptly and unsuccessfully tried to fill it. Still, no one thought that the marquise's death would entail any great political change; Choiseul was too deeply entrenched for that. Within a few months, the dead woman's possessions, including the gold-

---

* No one except the King and members of his family was allowed to die in a royal palace. Allowing Mme de Pompadour to stay on broke one of the firmest prescriptions of the etiquette.

and-lacquer desk that Maria Theresa sent her, were sold at auction on Marigny's orders. Bellevue, which had been hers for her life only, reverted to the Crown.* One man alone missed her: Louis XV. Although etiquette forbade his mourning in public, there could be no doubt about the depth or duration of his bereavement. For nearly twenty years Mme de Pompadour had been everything to him; now he was alone.

* Ironically, it was given to Mesdames, who had so despised the marquise, by Louis XVI in 1775.

Chapter Nine

The State Reborn

AFTER Mme de Pompadour's death, Louis XV found himself in an unpleasantly familiar situation: the duchesse de Ventadour, the Regent, the maréchal de Villeroy, Mme de Châteauroux—all, in their time, had served as a prop for his diffidence; and all had been withdrawn. Then, with the advent of the marquise, the King had found the ideal helper. She, too, was gone. Would he now look for someone new to lean on? The Court, of course, assumed that he would, and that, as he grew older—he was, after all, reaching his mid-fifties—the new mistress would become more and more powerful. The choice, therefore, was crucial, and the candidates did their best to catch the King's fancy. Still, the first attempts failed miserably: Choiseul's sister, the duchesse de Gramont, who had offered herself before Mme de Pompadour had been a week in her grave, was firmly repulsed, but, nothing loath, she tried again and again. To the minister the lady's attempts may have seemed not only praiseworthy but likely to be crowned with success: he was almost alone at Versailles in thinking her attractive; indeed, rumor had it—probably falsely—that he was her lover. Anyone with a less prejudiced eye, however, could see that Mme de Gramont was plain, awkward, very tall (a major defect in a century which prized grace rather than strength) and, most important, she was also rude, domineering and quick to anger. These failings were so well known, in fact, that she had been quite unable to find a husband, finally settling for a debauched and ruined duc who promised to depart as soon as the wedding ceremony was over.

Aside from Choiseul's fondness for his sister, it was obviously very much in his interest to have a reliable, trustworthy replacement for Mme de Pompadour. He could hardly forget that he owed his place to the marquise, and since he was himself given to exert his influence unfairly, he assumed that the new mistress, whoever she turned out to be, would do the same. The Court being what it was, the lady must be either his friend or his foe; there was no position in between. The latter possibility must, obviously, be avoided; but even if the new mistress proved to be his friend, this time she must be dependent on Choiseul rather than the other way around: now that the minister's protectress was dead, he intended to have no other. It was thus a grave annoyance to him when the King proved impervious to Mme de Gramont's offers, or, indeed, to a succession of pretty young women whom the duc sent forth at regular intervals. Since Choiseul loathed being thwarted, he promptly took his revenge by maligning the King, something he would not have even dared to contemplate in Mme de Pompadour's lifetime.

Of course, there could be no question of his doing so to Louis XV's face, but stories—anonymous stories—began to emerge. They all had a common theme—the King's stupidity—while invariably Choiseul's genius served as the counterpoint. Their aim was perfectly clear: besides giving the duc an outlet for his anger, they were to create a situation such that a change in ministry would become unthinkable: the King being incapable, only Choiseul could keep France strong, prosperous and happy. In fact, the minister had rather more shortcomings than his sovereign. That, in spite of his other, often admirable qualities, Choiseul had a tendency to be frivolous and smug no one doubted; and his vanity, although carefully concealed by a veil of exquisite manners, was just as important a part of his character. As long as Mme de Pompadour lived, she had kept the minister within bounds; once she was gone, he let his success go to his head. Luckily for him, Louis XV was absolutely indifferent to the gossip of the Paris salons, and he had known so many vain people, starting with the maréchal de Villeroy, that Choiseul's own conceit seemed to him perfectly natural. Still, despite what people said at Mme du Deffand's evenings or the maréchale de Luxembourg's afternoons, he kept the minister on a tight rein. Increasingly, Choiseul found himself carrying out policies he had opposed at first. Not unnaturally, he resented it.

In itself, this habitual self-assertiveness of the King's was something new. In earlier years he had given his ministers all the headway they wanted, until the day he finally dismissed them. That transformation, and the fact that, as the months passed, he failed to take a new mistress, should have warned Choiseul that he was dealing with a new man, but the minister was far too busy with the tasks of government, with intrigue and with display to see what was happening. Of course, Louis XV still needed sex, but for that he had the Parc aux Cerfs as well as countless one-night affairs, usually with pretty young women recruited for him by Lebel, his valet de chambre. He still liked being in company, so he held his suppers just as often as before; but he no longer felt unable to carry on without help. It was, surely, Mme de Pompadour's greatest gift to the man she loved that she had enabled him finally to develop the self-confidence he had always so sorely lacked. If he now dispensed with a maîtresse déclarée, it was partly, no doubt, to avoid the Court intrigues which always accompanied the selection of a favorite, but it was also because, at last, he could stand alone.

As always when a royal mistress died, the Court assumed that the King would spend more time with his family—the Queen, the Dauphin and Mesdames. Only, Louis XV had grown accustomed to the kind of society Mme de Pompadour knew how to provide, and compared to that his family seemed horribly dull. The Queen had become even more limited with the years; no one outside her little circle could bear her company. The Dauphin, although not devoid of either culture or intelligence, was as terrified of his father as ever, and that hardly made him good company. As for Mesdames, they tried their best; unfortunately, Madame Louise, whom Louis XV loved the best, spent much of her time in religious exercises; Mesdames Victoire and Sophie were slow-witted and dull, so that left only Madame Adélaide, who was unfortunately yearning for political influence. She was bright, vivacious and energetic, but also blunt—she called Mme de Pompadour *Maman-putain,* ("Mama whore"), for instance—and bad-tempered; she also lacked persistence, and espoused the most reactionary, ultra-Catholic viewpoints, so she was forever embarking on campaigns that were doomed to failure from the very start: by 1765, it was obvious that the Jesuits wouldn't be recalled and that Choiseul wouldn't be dismissed.

Still, the King had his old friends—Ayen, Richelieu, Meuse, Soubise, among others; he saw a lot of Choiseul; he hunted as much as ever; and he embarked on a regular correspondence with his orphaned grandson, Don Ferdinand, Duke of Parma. Sometimes the letters only run a few lines, as if the King wanted Don Ferdinand to realize that he was often in his thoughts. On August 25, 1765, for instance, off went a weather report: "I don't know whether it is hot in Parma," Louis XV wrote, "but here we have been dying of the heat for eight days; the night before there had been a frost on the ground."[1] Sometimes the letters convey affection. "I answer three of your letters today, my dear grandson," the King wrote on October 6. "They do not bore me; on the contrary, they have given me much pleasure because of the trust and tenderness you show me."[2] By November, however, the tone changes. Although the King's relationship with his son cannot be called close, it was certainly loving, besides which Louis XV was convinced that the Dauphin would, when the time came, make an excellent sovereign. Once previously the Dauphin had greatly alarmed his father when he had contracted smallpox, but now he was suffering from consumption,* an even more deadly disease, so that there was very little chance of his recovering. All through the end of October and the beginning of November, the Dauphin got steadily worse, while displaying the most admirable strength of mind, which was, no doubt, sustained by his strong religious feelings. On November 17, the King wrote Don Ferdinand: "I am your grandfather by a daughter whom I loved dearly and lost. I am about to lose my son as well; last Wednesday he received the last rites; imagine how I must feel."[3]

The Dauphin still lingered for a while, but then, on December 20, he died, and on the twenty-first the King wrote: "The date, my dear grandson, will tell you the full extent of my sorrow; forgive me, I can say no more."[4] On December 30, he added: "You must have your prayers changed,** but there is every probability (after everything we have seen) that he will not need them, and that instead it is he who is praying for us, which we desperately need, for his loss has been a dreadful blow to me and my whole kingdom . . . I am going to Choisy to avoid the [New Year's] compliments which, this year, I could hardly bear."[5] As for the kingdom, Louis XV was right, of course: the fifty-six-year-old monarch's successor was now a child of twelve; but what is striking is the directness, the intensity of his sorrow which the King continued to express in letter after letter.

"It is . . . probably around [the New Year] that you will have heard the sad, unbearable news which will surely have preceded my short but terrible letter which, even so, cost me much just to write," Louis XV noted on January 6, 1766. "Since our loss . . . we are now deep in winter, and without an end in sight,"[6] The winter, we

---

* The eighteenth-century name for tuberculosis.
** I.e., to include a prayer for the Dauphin's soul.

may surmise, was as emotional as it was real: the beginning of January, after all, is not normally expected to end the cold season. Two weeks later, the King goes right on: "I try distracting myself as best I can since here there is no remedy [for my sorrow], but I cannot grow used to not having a son, and when they bring me my grandson,* what a difference for me . . . Our winter is terrible and refuses to end."[7] And a week later: "You cannot tell me you love me too often, and I intend to deserve your love by the way I treat you."[8] Then, on February 8, the wound is bleeding anew: "We went this morning to the service for the Knights of the Saint Esprit who died within the last year. There were only two.** My tears and yours dispense me from naming them to you."[9]

For the next two years, death continued to strike the Royal Family. In March 1768, some fifteen months after her husband, the Dauphine also died of consumption, leaving her five children in the King's care. A little later, it was the Queen's turn: on June 24, 1768, Marie Leczinska joined her son and daughter-in-law. That Louis XV was deeply affected is unquestionable. He greatly missed the Dauphine, of whom he was very fond. As for the Queen, he had developed the sort of relationship to her that one might be likely to have with an old, dull but kindly aunt who lives in one's own house: one is used to her presence and feels real affection for her. Then, too, Marie Leczinska was a link to the King's youth: apart from the maréchal de Richelieu and the immovable Saint-Florentin, there was hardly anyone left who remembered the Regency.

The sorrow the King felt at his son's death did not, however, prevent him from doing his duty. He was as conscientious as ever in supervising expenditures, for instance. More important, now that peace made it possible, he was determined to assert his control over the Parlement. That the task would be difficult hardly needs saying: the whole history of the reign was there to prove it; but now, to make the situation worse, Louis XV faced the opposition, veiled but determined, of his principal minister. Choiseul had staked out his position as a liberal freethinker from the first. However questionable the methods adopted in the expulsion of the Jesuits, there can be little doubt that weakening the powerful grip of the Church was all to the good; and, in a number of other ways, Choiseul's attitude resulted in real progress, not the least of which was a relaxation of the censorship. "Finally the Encyclopédie is published as a whole," Bachaumont noted in March 1766. "It is probable . . . that the government is looking the other way and that everything is being done with its tacit approval."[10] He was quite right, of course: the minister corresponded regularly with Voltaire and was on friendly terms with the philosophers. His concurrent alliance with the obscurantist Parlement de Paris thus seemed extremely odd.

There were several good reasons for it, however. The duchesse de Choiseul was related to a number of the great Parlement families, so by indulging that institution the duc was being friendly to his cousins by marriage, and it was one of the most firmly established habits of the ancien régime that whoever was most powerful would protect the rest of the extended family. Then, as they cooperated in the dissolution

---

* The future Louis XVI.
** The Dauphin and the Duke of Parma, father of Don Ferdinand.

of the Society of Jesus, the judges and the minister had found that they had much in common: the desire to restrict the King's independence and the enmity of the reactionary party at Court. Of course, Choiseul was a liberal, while the Parlement remained firmly opposed to change, but in expelling the Jesuits the courts had made themselves look far more advanced than they really were. Finally, and most important, was the fact that Choiseul was secretly encouraging the Parlement in its attempts to appropriate the King's authority.

At first glance, it may seem a little surprising to see a principal minister working behind the scenes to undermine the authority of his own government. In fact, the duc knew that he need fear no attack against him personally, and it suited him very well to see the King's powers questioned: the more intractable the problem became, after all, the more he, Choiseul, would be needed, whereas if everything went smoothly the King might well decide to dispense with his services; so he encouraged the parlements of Paris and of Rennes to keep the religious controversy simmering while obstinately refusing to register any tax edict.

There is hardly any need to recapitulate the tiresome litany of the Parlement de Paris's resistance to royal authority, but recently that of Rennes had gone it one better. Brittany had become part of France in the fifteenth century when its Duchess married the King of France, but three hundred years later the province still considered itself an independent country which happened to share a sovereign with France. As a result, it always resisted taxation in the name of its ancient traditions. Now, however, it had moved on to a state of virtual rebellion against the Royal Governor, the duc d'Aiguillon, because he tried to enforce the law and ensure the payment of the vingtième. By 1766, the situation there was such that any royal backsliding would have resulted in outright anarchy.

Already in 1765, Louis XV had decided that the pretensions of the two parlements, Paris and Rennes, had become intolerable, but when the problem came up in the Council, Choiseul recommended inaction; then, when he saw that the King was determined to assert his authority, he did his best to delay any actual move, claiming, for instance, that a lit de justice could not be held unless the Chancellor were present—a legally untenable position. Since Lamoignon, who held that office,* had been exiled in October 1763 precisely because he supported the Parlement, it was obvious that he could not be recalled to preside over the humbling of his cherished institution. Better legal advice prevailed, however, and the King was ready to act, when the Dauphin's death stopped everything.

It was easy to predict that the King would not be deflected from his course: not only did he feel, rightly, that the Parlement was attempting to usurp his powers, but he could also reread a memo which the Dauphin had given him some years earlier. The parlements, his son had written, were trying to "convince the kingdom that, oblivious to the people's misery, you waste their blood and their treasure; that, considering only your own pleasure, you are establishing a crushing despotism; that without [the parlements] all the laws would be annulled and the State in an uproar . . . An unbreakable firmness is the only way to preserve . . . your authority: it is

---

* Chancellors held their office for life; if they displeased the King, their functions were taken over by a Keeper of the Seals, who could be dismissed at will.

sad to have to make others fear you, but sadder still to be in fear yourself."[11] With astonishing accuracy, the Dauphin was foreseeing the calamities which were to bring his son to the scaffold; but Louis XV was not Louis XVI, and he acted in time.

It was not until February 28 that the King could, once again, face the problem, but then three successive councils, on February 28, March 1 and 2, settled the dispositions to be taken and the course to be followed during the lit de justice. There can be no doubt that what happened next reflected the King's own policy, and while his speech to the Parlement was written by Joly de Fleury, the Attorney General, it was modified and rewritten by the King himself. As delivered to the lit de justice of March 3, 1766, it was nothing less than a clear, majestic definition of absolute monarchy. As such, and because it was Louis XV's last attempt to settle the long drawn out conflict, it is worth quoting at some length.

Before doing so, however, some terms require elucidation. Recently, the separate chambers within the Parlement de Paris had proclaimed their "union," i.e., their capacity (and right) to act as one body; more recently, they had extended this union to include the rebellious Parlement de Rennes. This was an unprecedented move and could present the government with a far more formidable opposition than ever before. It was also perfectly illegal. This is what Louis XV meant when he referred to the "system of unity" or the "reunion."

"What has happened in my parlements of Paris and Rennes in no way concerns my other parlements," the King began in a clear, firm tone. "I have treated these two courts as befitted my authority and I need account for this to no one.

"I would have no other answer to so many remonstrances which have been brought to me if their reunion, the indecency of their style, the temerity with which the most erroneous principles are upheld and the affected use of new expressions to characterize these did not reveal the pernicious consequences of this system of unity which I have already proscribed and which some wish to establish in principle even as they put it into practice." So far, Louis XV was merely reprimanding a group of factious magistrates. Now he went on to explain and define, as clearly as ever it was done, the principles on which the government was founded.

"I will not suffer anyone," he said, "to introduce into the monarchy an imaginary body which could only disrupt its harmony. The magistrates do not constitute a body or order separate from the three orders of the realm.* The Magistrates are my officers . . .

"It is in my person only that the sovereign power resides; its particular characteristic is the spirit of wisdom, justice and reason; it is from myself alone that my courts hold their existence and their authority; the plenitude of this authority, which they exercise in my name, remains always within me; it is to myself alone that the legislative power belongs, exclusively and without limits; it is through my authority alone that the officers of my courts proceed, not to make but to register and publish my laws, and that they may remonstrate whatever is part of the duty of good and faithful advisers; the public order in its entirety emanates from me; I am its supreme guardian; my people are at one with me only, and the rights and interests of the nation, which some have dared represent as a body separate from the monarch, are neces-

* The Clergy, the Nobility and the Third Estate.

sarily united with mine and rest in my hands alone." It was a masterful, and legally correct, exposition, spoken with so awesome a majesty as to be literally crushing: all through the great hall of the Parlement, the magistrates, heads bent, sat in obvious fear, and even the usually mocking Choiseul, watching from a box, found himself silenced.

Still Louis XV went on. "If, after I have scrutinized your remonstrances, and in full knowledge of the question, have persisted in my intentions, my courts should persevere in their refusal to obey instead of registering by the King's express command, the formula used to express duty and obedience; if they try to annihilate by their own efforts laws which have been solemnly registered; if, finally, when my authority has been forced to show itself to its fullest extent,* they still dare to fight on by using defensive decisions, suspensive oppositions or through the irregular method of cessation of services or resignations, then confusion and anarchy will replace the legitimate order and the scandalous spectacle of a contrary rival to my own power will reduce me to the sad necessity of using all the power I have received from God to preserve my people from the fearful consequences of such attempts.

"Let the officers of my courts, therefore, weigh attentively what I am still good enough to tell them."[12] And the very next day, to a deputation of the Parlement de Normandie, the King continued: "I have read all your remonstrances; never send me another like these again; my people are obedient and quiet; the agitation you describe exists only among you."[13]

Amazingly, Louis XV was right. The surface discontent which had accompanied the last years of the war had now subsided. France was at peace and more prosperous than ever, while the weight of taxation remained light. As for the magistrates' popularity, its shallowness was clearly revealed by the widespread joy with which the King's speech was greeted. Immediately dubbed *le discours de la flagellation* ("the flagellation speech") because the parlements, like a disobedient child, had just received a whipping, it united such disparate elements of the population as the artisans, the middle class and the intellectuals in a great burst of approval which expressed their resentment at the magistrates' pride and corruption. Voltaire, ever the spokesman for enlightened opinion, praised the speech to all his friends: he had experienced at first hand the shortcomings of the parlements when he defended the unjustly accused Calas. What Voltaire, and now many others, realized was that the parlements had in fact become a new feudal aristocracy, immensely powerful, immensely rich and responsible to no one but themselves. Just as, in an earlier century, the kings had earned their popularity by fighting the demands of the great nobles, so now Louis XV, by attacking the new *privilégiés,* was at one with his people. As a sure sign of this new attitude, songs began to circulate mocking the parlements.[14]

The flagellation speech was also a blow for Choiseul. Once again, in fact, Louis XV was using his favorite method: his adoption of a necessary policy was also a warning for the minister who had opposed it; but, as usual, the duc failed to see that his position was growing precarious. Of course, he had one good reason to feel secure: overtly he was more powerful than ever since the deaths of the Dauphin, and then the Dauphine, removed the last counterbalance to his influence.

---

* I.e., in a lit de justice.

Unfortunately, in spite of his intelligence and his energy, Choiseul, as the years passed, became increasingly reckless. In domestic politics this was translated into support of the parlements and the well-meaning but incapable contrôleur général, Laverdy—although it is only fair to add that the minister was just as improvident when it came to his own finances. Similarly, his foreign policy—he had taken back the foreign ministry in 1765—was based on a rather unfortunate mixture of bravado and carelessness; and once again Poland provided the trap.

Louis XV understood quite well that France, in spite of its traditional links with that anarchy-ridden country, could do nothing to protect it against the self-destructive tendencies encouraged by its eager and hungry neighbors. By 1766, it was becoming obvious that Catherine II and Frederick II were in cahoots, and that their friendship was likely to result in serious territorial losses for Poland. This Choiseul determined to stop without, however, considering how it was to be done; and when, in February 1767, a number of Polish nobles rose against the Russians, who, through King Stanislas Poniatowski, were in effect ruling the country, he publicly endorsed their cause. However, since Austria was not about to oppose Russia, and Prussia was delighted with the trend of events, Choiseul found himself reduced to Turkey in his search for a helpful power; but Turkey, which then had common borders with both Russia and Poland, was in no shape to defeat Catherine's armies.

Of course, the King still had his secret du Roi. In 1767, its main agents were Vergennes, who was ambassador to the Porte; Havrincourt, ambassador to Holland; Breteuil, ambassador to Sweden; Rossignol, consul in Russia; and Hennin, the envoy to Geneva, and he understood the situation perfectly. In mid-November 1768, he wrote to Monet, who was his link with the comte de Broglie: "The Turks will decide the fate of Poland; but I fear it will be ruined no matter what,"[15] and a few days later he declined a well-intentioned but ill-advised suggestion of Monet's to try and elect Don Ferdinand of Parma to the Polish throne. He was right, of course: the Poles and the Turks were crushed by the Russian Army and Choiseul was left looking like an impotent fool. This was all the more unfortunate in that it began to drive a wedge between France and Austria.

Maria Theresa, as everyone knew, thought of Frederick II as the devil incarnate, not least, perhaps, because he was a freethinker; but by 1769 she no longer ruled alone: after the death of Francis of Lorraine, it had been necessary to elect a new emperor; naturally, that turned out to be Maria Theresa's eldest son, Joseph. The hereditary lands still remained the Empress's own, but since Joseph II was her heir, she began, very gradually, to share the government with him, and he quite admired Frederick II, both as a general and as a reformer. Besides, with Poland obviously ripe for the taking, it was very much in Austria's interest to remain on good terms with its two neighbors, Russia and Prussia, so that it, too, could achieve some territorial gains. In 1769, therefore, Joseph II met Frederick at Neustadt and was seen to be on the best of terms with him. This boded ill for Choiseul since Louis XV was as attached as ever to the Austrian alliance, which was now weakened by the minister's support for Poland.

All this was bad enough; but then, in the summer of 1768, Choiseul was driven into a real frenzy by the King's new affair. This was unreasonable, to say the least, since the new favorite, who was still a long way from becoming a maîtresse déclarée, cared nothing for politics and rather admired the minister. Choiseul was careful to say that he objected to her only on the grounds that she was not worthy of the King, but that was the most transparent of justifications, although the past of the new mistress certainly was unconventional. The illegitimate daughter of a monk and a seamstress, Jeanne Bécu was born in Lorraine in 1743; now she was twenty-five years old. She was bright, well educated and had excellent manners. "Although," Talleyrand wrote some years later, "Mme de Pompadour was brought up and lived in the financial society of Paris, which was then rather distinguished, she had common manners, vulgar ways of speaking . . . Madame du Barry [as Jeanne Bécu soon became] . . . although less well brought up, always managed to speak correctly . . . She liked to talk and had mastered the art of telling stories rather amusingly."[16]

It was, however, not her conversation which had excited Louis XV's interest. Whatever her other merits—and she had a number—she was dazzlingly beautiful and sexy. Colleval, one of her visitors, wrote: "She was nonchalantly sitting, or rather lying, in a big armchair and wore a white dress with pink garlands which I can never forget. Madame du Barry, one of the prettiest women in a court where beauties were legion, was the most seductive of all because of the perfection of her entire person. Her hair, which she often dressed without powder, was of the most beautiful blond, and so abundant that she hardly knew what to do with it. Her wide open blue eyes had a frank and caressing look . . . Her nose was adorable, her mouth very small and her skin of a dazzling whiteness."[17] What Colleval doesn't say is that her bust was famous, and frequently displayed by deeply décolleté dresses.

Besides her looks and her figure, Jeanne Bécu, who had been calling herself Mme du Barry for some time, had another great asset: if we are to believe the many men who had slept with her, she was reported to have great talents for making love. That, in fact, was also her greatest problem: before reaching the King's bed, she had for some three or four years been a high-class prostitute whose pimp, the vicomte du Barry, sold her to a variety of clients. In return for her efforts, he provided her with a luxurious, relatively idle life and a chance to meet some of the lesser intellectuals, men like Crébillon, Moncrif (Marie Leczinska's friend) and Collé, who came for supper and taught her to hold her own in a salon. And there, both as a guest and, very probably, a client, she met the maréchal de Richelieu, who, in turn, introduced her to Lebel, the King's valet de chambre.

Lebel, of course, realized that she would provide his master with a few very pleasant nights, so he made sure that Louis XV saw the pretty Jeanne, and soon the affair was under way. It could hardly go very far, everyone agreed. After all, Mme de Pompadour, a mere bourgeoise to be sure, had been a rich and respectable married woman. Mme du Barry was little better than a streetwalker and thus irredeemably, utterly unpresentable. Of course, although she had taken on her protector's name, she was still unmarried, which, if anything, made it worse. Then, on September 1, 1768, an event took place discreetly which stunned all those who heard about it. The vicomte du Barry had an elder brother, the comte Guillaume du Barry, whose title was perfectly genuine: the du Barrys were a good, if impoverished, family—so poor, in fact, that the comte had been unable to find a suitable wife. Now he was brought

from his province, married to Jeanne—whose father, the monk, performed the ceremony—and departed, much the richer, as soon as the sacramental words had been
pronounced. The former prostitute was now, for good and all, Madame la comtesse
du Barry and could, therefore, be presented at Court. As for the maréchal de Richelieu, who had, in a manner of speaking, discovered her, he was in seventh heaven:
she would, he thought, be a second edition of Mme de Châteauroux.

He could not have been more mistaken. Mme du Barry, who was, indeed, properly
grateful, did no more than smile at him. She felt unfitted for a political role, serious
business bored her and, besides, she understood perfectly well that the last thing that
Louis XV wanted from her was advice, so the maréchal failed, yet again, to enter the
Council. Choiseul, who was, of course, informed of all this, now chose to remain
obstinately blind. Perhaps because he was egged on by his sister, perhaps because
Richelieu had belonged to the anti-Pompadour faction, but more probably because he
thought the young woman was bound to acquire influence (she never did), he decided to fight her. This little war was, as usual, fought on two fronts: gossip and
insolence at Court, pamphlets and songs in Paris. In no time at all, the King was
painted in the vilest colors as an old, impotent debauchee, a used-up lecher whose
faltering lust was revived by the wiles of a whore. Unpleasant as the anti-Pompadour
songs had been, the new crop went a good deal further; among the least obscene is
this: "Vous verrez le doyen des rois / Aux genoux d'une comtesse / Dont jadis un écu
tournois / Aurait fait votre maîtresse / Faire auprès d'elle cent efforts / Dans la route
lubrique / Pour faire mouvoir les efforts / De sa machine antique. / Mais c'est en vain
qu'il a recours / A la grande prêtresse / Au beau milieu de son discours / il retombe en
faiblesse." ("You will see the dean of kings / at the knees of a countess /
who once would have become / your mistress for a small coin / making a hundred
efforts / on the road of sex / to move the springs / of his ancient machine / but in vain
he has recourse / to the grand priestess / right in the midst of his discourse / he
lapses back feebly.")[18]

It is perfectly typical of Choiseul that in his rage he chose to attack the sovereign
to whom he owed everything; perhaps he should have remembered how similar
methods had affected the careers of men like d'Argenson and Maurepas; but it seems
probable that he thought he would actually induce the King to give up his mistress.
He began to realize how wrong he was when, in December 1768, Mme du Barry was
given rooms at Versailles near the King's own, although it is fair to note that no one
really believed that the former prostitute would actually be presented at Court; and,
of course, if she wasn't presented, she couldn't become a maîtresse déclarée. Besides,
the King himself was fully aware of his new love's antecedents. According to a
perhaps apocryphal but representative anecdote, at about this time Louis XV said to
the duc de Noailles: "I'm told that I'm Sainte-Foix's successor."

"Yes, sire," the duc replied. "Just as Your Majesty is Pharamond's successor,"
Pharamond, according to legend, being the founder of the French monarchy some
thousand years earlier. Still, he didn't care: the comtesse, aside from pleasing him in
bed, was also fulfilling one of his most essential needs, that of a cozy, intimate circle,
a home. In a court that had grown sadder year by year since 1764, this was a major

contribution: once again Louis XV could look forward to walks, entertainments and suppers with a charming young woman who amused him and made him feel at ease.

Although Mme du Barry was obviously quite different from Mme de Pompadour, the two women shared one essential quality: kindness. "As for the duc de Choiseul, [Mme du Barry] showed regret that she couldn't have been his friend and told us about all the efforts she had made to win him over; she told us that without his sister, the duchesse de Gramont, she would have managed it. She complained about no one and never said anything nasty . . . 'I only wanted to oblige everyone,' she said."[19] Given the constant attacks she had to bear, the comtesse's attempts are not without merit, especially since Choiseul was the bitterest of enemies. The news that Mme du Barry was to be officially presented on April 22, 1769, nearly drove him mad. He did his best to ensure that not a single lady at Court would agree to perform the neces- sary role of a sponsor, but he was no match for the King, who simply called in the maréchale de Mirepoix and offered to pay her gambling debts if she served as the sponsor. Delighted, the maréchale agreed, and Mme du Barry, more beautiful than ever, was presented to His Majesty, to Mesdames and to the Dauphin.*

Naturally, that only made Choiseul angrier. Now that the comtesse was officially part of the Court, Mme de Gramont and her close friend, the princesse de Beauvau, embarked on a campaign of deliberate rudeness, slighting Mme du Barry at every turn. There was a whole new spurt of obscene songs and pamphlets, and Choiseul deliberately ignored a letter in which Louis XV, after telling him that he trusted him and wanted to keep him in office, went on to say that Mme du Barry pleased him and that he only wanted peace. It wasn't much to ask for, but Choiseul, seized by his overweening pride, continued on his anti–du Barry campaign. Since, at the same time, he was encouraging the Parlement in its continued opposition, while his foreign policy was proving ineffective and possibly dangerous, his behavior looks like sheer self-destruction. In fact, he was relying on his perception of human nature and the proximity of a great event.

Having conquered Mme de Pompadour's esteem, then the King's, when they had originally disliked him, Choiseul was convinced that he could control just about anybody—and that, of course, included Louis XV. He would never be dismissed, he often told his confidants, because the King was too lazy, too afraid of business, and because he, Choiseul, was too popular. As for the great event, it was nothing less than the crowning of the new system of alliances: in May 1770, just a year after Mme du Barry's presentation, the Dauphin, who would be sixteen years old, was to marry the Archduchess Marie Antoinette. It was perfectly obvious, Choiseul thought, that the minister who had brought such an event about could not be sent away without injuring the alliance itself. Thus, having nothing to fear, he divided his energies between the war against the favorite and his plans for a wedding of dazzling splen- dor.

This, at least, pleased the King. As he overcame his shyness, Louis XV began to enjoy the great ceremonies of the Court. For a while, now, there had been no first lady at Versailles: the advent of a new one must be properly celebrated. Besides, the Dauphin's marriage always made for the grandest of celebrations, so the King gave

---

* The eldest son of the late Dauphin, the future Louis XVI.

his minister a free rein. Since, in any event, Choiseul never worried about overspending, the preparations were lavish in the extreme.

In January 1770, people already began to enjoy the first fruits of all this when they came to view the two carriages which were about to go off to Vienna for the use, on her travels, of the Archduchess. "There are two berlines . . . One is covered with a flat velvet, crimson on the outside, on which the four seasons are embroidered in gold on the main panels, with all the attributes relating to the festivities. The other is covered in blue velvet and adorned with the four elements, also embroidered in gold. There are no paintings at all,* but the work is of a fineness, a subtlety which makes it practically a fine art. The roofs are very rich; one of the two even seems too heavy. The imperial is topped by bouquets of flowers in gold of every shade; they are worked with just as much care. The carriages are so well suspended that they sway with every move . . . M. le duc de Choiseul, as Foreign minister, has ordered these magnificent coaches."[20]

Curiously, Choiseul's bitterest enemies were delighted by the Archduchess's arrival: Mesdames, although they had opposed the alliance and now made nasty wisecracks about the little Austrian,** realized that she could be used as a tool to fight Mme du Barry; this was Madame Adélaïde's own idea, and she couldn't wait to put it into practice. Of course, like many of the princess's positions, it suffered from a certain lack of consistency: because she was an ultra-Catholic, Madame Adélaïde hated Choiseul, who, besides having expelled the Jesuits, had also been Mme de Pompadour's friend; therefore, to the surprise of many, she forced herself to be civil, at least some of the time, to Mme du Barry because she thought the comtesse would be the lever with which to dislodge Choiseul. At the same time, she had nothing but contempt for the former prostitute and resented her father's having a mistress. The Dauphine, she thought, could be used to make Mme du Barry's life miserable, and perhaps even dislodge her. Since, however, it was clear that the Dauphine would support Choiseul, who had brought about her marriage, the whole plan was clearly self-defeating; but, soured by her lack of beauty, influence or a husband, Madame Adélaïde never saw much beyond the nastiness of the moment. It was, in fact, typical of her that when she was told about her sister Madame Louise's departure from Versailles, she asked venomously: "Left? And with whom?"[21] although she knew quite well that after much soul-searching, the princess had entered a Carmelite convent. Still, that, too, might help: since the King was particularly fond of Madame Louise, it was hoped he might turn to the new Dauphine instead, and that the young woman, in turn, would do Mesdames' bidding.

When, in May, the young Marie Antoinette arrived, she was an immediate success: slender, graceful, immensely attractive, she had blue eyes, auburn hair, a dazzling complexion, wonderful manners and immense charm. She was still a little flat-chested, as Louis XV noted, but she had barely reached the age of fourteen and was likely to fill out. All in all, everyone agreed, the Dauphin was lucky, and even that rather dour young man, although he didn't say much, managed to look quite pleased.

---

* Carriages were often adorned with scenes painted by the likes of Boucher and Van Loo.
** L'Autrichienne, that term of hatred used so frequently after 1789, actually originated in Mesdames's apartment.

At first everything went well. At supper with the King and the Royal Family, Marie Antoinette asked about the function of that ravishingly pretty lady down at the end of the table. Her dame d'honneur, the comtesse de Noailles, answered tactfully that she was there to amuse the King, to which the Dauphine answered that, in that case, she would be her rival. It was an endearing error, and Marie Antoinette's eagerness to please the King—she was, of course, following her mother's instructions—boded well for the future. The King was so pleased with his granddaughter-in-law that he began to think of marrying an archduchess himself. On June 6, he wrote Broglie: "Let [Durand] take a good look at her figure, from head to foot and without leaving out anything he can see of the Archduchess Elisabeth; let him also find out about her character, all in deepest secrecy and without arousing suspicions in Vienna."[22] It was only a fantasy: the sixty-year-old King did not really want to marry a girl who was over forty years his junior; but it does show how taken he was with the Dauphine.

He was also delighted with the wedding festivities. There was a banquet, as usual, plus balls, fireworks, operas and plays, all quite splendid, although Marie Antoinette complained that the entertainments chosen by the maréchal de Richelieu, whose year it was to be First Gentleman of the Bedchamber, were dreadfully old-fashioned. Best of all, there was the new theater designed by Jacques Ange Gabriel. A masterpiece of trompe-l'oeil and glowing color, the columned, semicircular auditorium was technically the most advanced in Europe as well as the most beautiful. Made entirely of wood, shaped and painted like marble, bronze and lapis lazuli, it was a composition in pale gray, light and dark blue and pink. Upon its inauguration, it was immediately acclaimed as the supreme achievement of eighteenth-century design, a place it has retained to this day. Within four months of that triumph, the King's new house in the park of Versailles, the Petit Trianon, which was also designed by Gabriel, was ready. In its chastely classic ornaments, its simplicity of form, and in the harmony of its proportions it proved that when a great architect worked for a king who was also a connoisseur, perfection was indeed within reach. It is also worth noting that both the theater and the house were perfect examples of the new neoclassical style: although he had been brought up in a rococo world, Louis XV at sixty was still sufficiently flexible to patronize a radically new style.

Of course, all these festivities turned out to be expensive. Turning one day to his new contrôleur général, the abbé Terray, the King asked how he found his festivities at Versailles. "Ah, Sire, impayables!"[23] the abbé answered, punning on a word which means both "extraordinary" and "impossible to pay." The great cost of the fetes, however, upset no one else, least of all Choiseul, who was beginning to have other worries: it was a serious blow to his preeminence that the King should have fired the incapable but docile Laverdy and replaced him with Terray, a rude, uncouth and highly capable minister who was horrified by the mounting deficit, felt no particular loyalty to Choiseul, and was yearning to reform the tax system. Already in 1768, the former chancelier, Lamoignon, had traded his resignation against the payment of his debts by the King; his successor, René de Maupeou, was a hardworking jurist who belonged to a Parlement family and had indeed been Premier Président of the Parlement de Paris for five years; but he was a true monarchist, acute enough to see that unless things changed, the system was bound to collapse. As a result, he was firmly opposed to the Parlement's encroachments; with Choiseul as principal minister, he remained relatively powerless, but he was clearly not in the duc's corner.

Still, the festivities went on. On May 30, the City of Paris gave a great fireworks display at the edge of the Place Louis XV.* "The main decor," we are told, "represents the Temple of Hymen [the goddess of marriage], preceded by a magnificent colonnade. This temple stands before the statue of Louis XV. It is surrounded by a kind of parapet whose four angles are flanked by dolphins [emblems of the Dauphin] who seem ready to emit a storm of fire. Rivers on the four facades will also give out floods and cascades of the same nature. The temple is topped by a pyramid supporting a globe. Many pieces of fireworks are set around the decor. Past the statue, towards the river, is a structure from which the final bouquet will erupt."[24] As it turned out, the rockets in that structure caught fire prematurely and started whizzing toward the tightly packed crowd, which then tried to flee, but because the rue Royale, one of the main exits, was under construction, it was scarred by holes and trenches. Panic erupted; by the time it was all over, 132 people had been crushed or trampled to death: it was not a good omen for the future, people said, that so terrible a catastrophe should have marred the Dauphin's wedding.

Be that as it may, the King continued to be pleased with the Dauphine. On June 15, Mercy-Argenteau, the Austrian Ambassador, wrote Maria Theresa to tell her this, adding: "The King finds her sprightly and a little immature," adding, "but that is right for her age."[25] Indeed, even when it came to Mme du Barry, whose real function she finally discovered, Marie Antoinette behaved with tact and wisdom. "Mme du Barry thought it necessary to go and pay court one morning to Her Royal Highness; that princess received her without affectation; it all happened in a dignified way and so as to displease no one."[26] A month later, the Ambassador wrote, the King was still perfectly satisfied, but although Marie Antoinette had only been at Versailles for two months, a storm was already brewing. Not unnaturally, the young Dauphine, upon finding herself in the most sophisticated court in Europe, looked for someone other than the Austrian Ambassador to give her advice. Her husband, as she promptly discovered, was quite unable to provide it, so she looked for older relatives and, unfortunately, found them. To their delight, Mesdames were now in a position to make trouble, and they did their best to poison the Dauphine's mind. Already on July 9, Marie Antoinette wrote her mother: "The King is infinitely kind to me and I love him tenderly, but what a pity that he should have such a weakness for Mme du Barry, who is the most stupid and impertinent creature imaginable. She played cards with us every night at Marly; twice she found herself next to me, but she didn't speak to me and I didn't try to start a conversation with her; but when it became necessary, still, I spoke to her."[27]

By September, Mercy could see what was happening. "Mesdames," he wrote to the Empress, "because of the way they were raised, are shy and lacking in all the pleasing qualities, and they would like to be imitated by Madame la Dauphine . . . A few days ago, the Paris city administration and the Estates of the Languedoc came to compliment the Royal Family. Mesdames, upon being consulted by Madame la Dauphine, tried to convince her that on such occasions no answer was to be made,

* Today, the Place de la Concorde.

and that they always remained silent."²⁸ Luckily, Marie Antoinette didn't listen to them, but their scheme is clear: they would use the Dauphine to dislodge Mme du Barry while inducing her to behave in such a way as to make herself unpopular. This, to be fair, was mostly Madame Adélaide's doing; at the same time, she was trying to turn the Dauphine against Madame Victoire—for amusement, one can only presume —as well as against the comtesse de Provence, the wife of the Dauphin's brother.

All these little conflicts, unimportant in themselves, naturally filtered back to the King and saddened him: he was all too accustomed to Choiseul's war on Mme du Barry; when, suddenly, the Dauphine started to snub the favorite, he was really upset. Then, too, there was the problem of the Dauphin's lack of sexual enthusiasm: although Marie Antoinette was attractive and willing, the marriage, after some four months, remained unconsummated. Although people in the eighteenth century normally felt no qualms about revealing the details of their sex lives, this time the King seemed a little embarrassed. Rather than talking to the Dauphin himself, he sent his doctor, upon which it became clear that the young man was suffering, at the very least, from timidity, which was attributed, in part, to youth. Since the Dauphin's unwillingness to perform affected the succession to the throne, the King was right to worry, but the doctors advised him to be patient: the Dauphin, they said, was simply a little late in his development; give him time and all would be well.

Upsetting as all this may have been, however, Louis XV had graver worries: Choiseul's foreign policy was meeting with failure after failure. After having utterly —and predictably—failed to help Poland, the duc was now intent on revenge. France, he announced, must make her weight felt, so he began to encourage Spain to take a much stiffer tone in its negotiations with England over the possession of the Falkland Islands. That he was risking a European war for the sake of some impossibly remote and barren islands doesn't seem to have worried him at all, but Louis XV, who could see trouble coming, began to show his unhappiness, and the Austrian Ambassador, although attributing it wrongly to Maupeou's supposed intrigues, promptly noticed it. In mid-September, he wrote the Empress to warn her of this; and although he expected Choiseul to stay in office, he added: "One cannot ignore the fact that [the duc] has many shortcomings, especially a lack of seriousness and a little inconsequence."²⁹

All this was bad enough, but there was much more to come. As usual, Choiseul was secretly urging the Parlement to resist the King. The specifics, this time, resulted from the earlier disturbances in Brittany: the Parlement de Rennes, not content with preaching rebellion, had also indicted the Governor, the duc d'Aiguillon. Since the latter was a Peer of the Realm, he could only be tried by the Parlement de Paris in which the other Peers would then be sitting; so the procedure was transferred to Paris. At that point the King intervened. Not only was d'Aiguillon perfectly innocent, but it was also obvious that if a governor could be tried and convicted for obeying the King's orders, then soon the monarch would find no one to serve him. In a rare assumption of his judicial capacity, therefore, the King presided in person at the Council of State's* session during which the indictment was called up and quashed. That should have been the end of the business, since no one denied that the King

---

* The equivalent of the United States Supreme Court.

had the legal right—akin to that of pardon—to do what he had just done, but, naturally, the Parlement ignored the procedure and continued its pretrial hearings with Choiseul's full, if discreet, approval.

Once again, the Parlement was ignoring both the law and the King's stated will. In November, therefore, an edict, written by Maupeou, came down from Versailles. In essence, it repeated exactly what the King had said in the flagellation speech. Instantly the Parlement refused to register the edict and sent the Premier Président d'Aligre to the King with remonstrances. The King read them, threw them in the fire and ordered that registration take place the next day. To no one's surprise, it didn't. Instead, as so often happened before, there were more remonstrances, followed by a lit de justice, protests, lettres de jussion, and a strike: 1766 had been all for nothing. And if, once again, the Parlement resisted boldly, it was, as everyone knew, because it had Choiseul's support and thus felt perfectly safe: the Minister would force the King to back down and all would be well.

It was at this point, in mid-December 1770, that the efforts of Mme de Pompadour bore fruit. The King, looking about him, saw danger from without and rebellion from within, both due to the policies of his minister. The choice was clear: he could assume that Choiseul knew best, keep him in office, knuckle under to the Parlement and embark on a rerun of the Seven Years' War; or he could assert his own better sense by taking over the government directly, changing France's foreign policy, and taming the Parlement once and for all. The first choice, while incomparably easier since it required no action, would be shaming; the second meant a series of upheavals and the kind of drastic reform which Louis XV had, until now, always tried to avoid. Consulting only his duty—to himself, to the monarchy and to France—and strengthened by the self-confidence Mme de Pompadour had given him, the King made the only possible decision. On December 24, to everyone's amazement, he dismissed Choiseul and Praslin.

As usual, the former ministers were exiled to their country houses, in Choiseul's case the sumptuous château of Chanteloup, near Tours. But now an unprecedented event followed. Instead of shunning all the members of the Choiseul clan, many courtiers made a beeline for Paris, where the duc had stopped for a few days. The King, upon being asked whether he permitted visits, answered: "I neither permit nor forbid them." It was enough, and the line of carriages outside the hôtel de Choiseul grew spectacularly long: clearly the duc had done his propaganda well and thoroughly; but, far away in Ferney, Voltaire, clear-eyed as ever, wrote approving letters to all his friends: he, too, could see that Choiseul was heading straight for an unnecessary war and, by supporting the Parlement, lining himself up with the most reactionary elements in France. For once, though, no one listened to him; and since Choiseul was convinced he owed his fall to Maupeou's intrigues, a great many pamphlets began appearing against him. These marked a new low in invective; worse, they predicted his murder in tones clearly meant to encourage any potential killer.

Naturally, Choiseul did not confine himself to financing and inspiring anti-Maupeou pamphlets; he also made sure that the King himself was reviled in sheet after sheet. The theme was easily found: the dismissal of the enlightened Choiseul was due wholly to the sexual wiles of Mme du Barry: France was losing its guiding genius because he had failed to court the whore who was bringing shame to an elderly monarch; as a result, Louis XV, who, as usual, disdained all self-justification, has been blamed for dismissing Choiseul in a fit of senile infatuation. Virtually the reverse is true: an aging, tired monarch who cared only for Mme du Barry and was inclined to let the rest slide would have kept Choiseul in office. It took an independent-minded and vigorous ruler, in fact, to take so bold a step as the dismissal of a hugely popular minister.

The very day Choiseul received the letter which sent him off to Chanteloup another document was sent from the King's study. It went to Charles III of Spain. "The treaty which unites us, my dear brother, has been sealed in blood and friendship, and I am too happy with the indivisible glory and interests which it has established between your crown and mine not to fulfill with the greatest good will all its obligations," Louis XV wrote. "It is in a spirit of sincerity that I have examined with the most scrupulous care the measures best fitted to the current state of your disagreements with England . . .

"Our true glory, my dear brother, for I do not distinguish mine from yours, consists far less in the promise you are today demanding of England than in the certainty of the means we can use together to force it one day to give up its unjust desires. I consider that delay holds nothing but advantages for us: it is especially essential to me so that I may complete the operations through which I have already successfully begun to amend my finances, and to give me the means of supporting Your Majesty's views and the good of the alliance with an activity and a vigilance proper to the dignity of my crown. All the measures which I have taken so far in my ports, my coastlines and my colonies are purely defensive. I must even warn you that these defensive measures are the only ones I could take if, against my hope, Your Majesty persisted in a policy which I only oppose the better to later ensure its success, which I wish for as earnestly as you do, and which haste alone can keep us from attaining . . .

"Let us rather choose the moment [to make war]; it is on the proper choice of this moment that the success of the war will depend. I urge Your Majesty to pay special attention to this crucial thought.

"The advice I give you is that of a relative, a friend and an ally who sees no separation between your interests and his."[30]

This firm but tactful letter had an immediate effect: there was no war over the Falklands and, therefore, no European war. As it turned out, the moment mentioned by Louis XV did come in 1778, and then, together with the Americans, France and Spain took their revenge on Great Britain. At the same time, the King made it very plain that, with or without Choiseul, he was as intent as ever on maintaining the Austrian alliance, so that after a few days of alarm Maria Theresa was reassured; but even she believed that the minister's fall was due largely to Mme du Barry. It is enlightening to see how even the best-informed and shrewdest of ambassadors can misunderstand a situation: at one with most everyone, Mercy wrote the Empress on January 23, 1771: "The haughtiness and indiscreet language of the duchesse de Gramont and of the princesse de Beauvau, her intimate friend; the weakness with which the duc de Choiseul followed their every desire; the open war he had allowed himself to wage against the favorite; the bold comments he made to his master about that woman; and still more the biting and public jokes he told about her—all that had, for some time, caused the King to feel disgusted with his minister. The latter's enemies kept up and encouraged that feeling; finally they used it to convince the King that the duc de Choiseul was encouraging the parlements to disobey him."[31]

That last sentence, of course, went straight to the heart of the matter. Having ensured that peace would remain unbroken, the King, with Maupeou's help, now turned his attention to the Parlement. During the night of January 19 to 20, musketeers were sent to every conseiller and président; to each they handed the King's order to state, without delay or obfuscation, whether they were ready to return to work: they were to answer simply either yes or no. More than half of the magistrates answered negatively or refused to answer at all: so far, there was nothing new. The next morning all the opponents met in an extraordinary session, presided over by Ferré, an old conseiller who had sat in the Parlement since 1708. Cheerfully, he told his colleagues that he had already, in the course of his long career, received fourteen lettres de cachet without being harmed by them, so that he was now awaiting the fifteenth with perfect equanimity. Thus comforted, the strikers told their more reasonable colleagues that anyone who didn't join them would be ostracized until, finally, 132 judges—there were 170 altogether—refused to obey the King's orders. Late on the twentieth a decision of the Council confiscated their offices, while letters from the King enjoined them to leave Paris forthwith. On the twenty-first the 38 remaining magistrates, in a gesture of solidarity with their colleagues, joined the strike; but immediately they, too, were exiled.

The usual deadlock had been reached and people expected the usual solution to follow: eventually there would be a compromise settlement and all would continue as before. This time, however, it was noted that the rebels were actually sent to rather uncomfortable residences: instead of Pontoise or, as in 1753, Soissons, many of them found themselves in tiny villages whose inns lacked the luxuries to which they were accustomed, so they naturally painted their "martyrdom" in the darkest colors. Indeed, to read their letters, one would think that they had been sent to an eighteenth-century equivalent of a concentration camp. Still, the conflict seemed to be moving down the same old road. Once again, the King set up a new court, this time the Council of State,* which he addressed on January 29. "Messieurs," he told them, "I need you so that the course of justice in my Parlement be interrupted no longer. I know your zeal and your attachment to my person and count on them. You may count on my protection as you carry out your new functions, and on the marks of my affection."[32] Once again, everything was set up to replace the Parlement; once again the new tribunal found itself idle because everyone assumed that, sooner or later, the Parlement would return.

The only novelty, in fact, was that this time the government faced an even more formidable opposition than in 1756. The Princes of the Blood Royal—the duc d'Orléans, the prince de Conti, the comte de Clermont, the comte d'Eu—who knew that

---

* The Council of State was a quasijudicial body which functioned as a court of last appeal; the business of government took place mostly in the Council of Despatches and partly in the Council of Finances, both regularly attended by the King.

they could always count on the Parlement to defend their privileges, announced publicly that they refused to be judged by the Council of State and even went so far as to send remonstrances to the King, who declined to read them. Then, too, the provincial parlements flew to the rescue of their exiled colleagues. From Rouen came remonstrances in which the King was told that resistance to his policies was both a right and a duty for the magistrates, that the exiled members of the Parlement de Paris alone could sit as judges, that their replacements were, in effect, traitors. Aside from the extreme violence of the tone, this was all so much nonsense: a King, some four hundred years earlier, had created the Parlement, not the other way around; and the purchase of their offices hardly gave the magistrates the right to speak in the name of the nation.

As it was, the generalized revolt of the parlements, along with a variety of antiquated, redundant tribunals like the cour des Aides, gave Louis XV and Maupeou their chance: compromise, that oft-tried solution, had clearly become impossible; now, at long last, it might be possible to set up impartial, prompt and cost-free courts. By 1771, everyone knew that the parlements automatically favored their relatives and friends; that suits dragged on for at least two, but often as many as ten or fifteen, years, partly because the judges were lazy, partly because complicated procedures were far more profitable than simple ones; and that, finally, justice could be bought since bribes were perfectly legal. Now the old system had finally broken down, and the King could significantly improve his subjects' life while removing a selfish and obstinate impediment to reform.

Already on February 25, Maupeou, in a speech to the Council of State, made it very plain that this time the Parlement would not return. "His Majesty," he said, "could have limited himself to repairing the losses of the magistrature . . . but from the saddest events his wisdom will bring forth a happier order and one for which our fathers had long yearned. Venality,* introduced by the force of circumstance, seems to dishonor the most august of functions by forcing a man to buy the right to fulfill it."[33] Henceforth, he announced, judges, instead of owning their offices, would be appointed by the King, from whom they would receive a salary; their independence from the government would be guaranteed by giving them their office for life; justice would be free, the judges being forbidden to accept any gift from people who resorted to their courts. As for the salaries, they were large for the Premier Président, who was to receive 20,000 livres a year, the same amount as a minister of state, adequate for a président, who would get 6,000 livres, but, at 2500 livres, meager for the conseillers.

Of course, the new Parlement was to be quite different from the old. First, while it would still register the King's edicts and keep the right to present remonstrances, it lost the right to defer registration after the King had either accepted or refused the remonstrances; and these last were to remain unpublished. Further, the huge jurisdiction of the Parlement de Paris was broken up: it had reached as far as the Auvergne and, in an era of slow communications, caused endless delay; now, while a Parlement would still sit in Paris, it would be augmented by five councils located in Blois, Châlons, Clermont-Ferrand, Lyon and Poitiers. Two other Parlements, those

---

* The process through which judges bought their office.

of Rouen and Douai, were abolished and replaced by councils, while a number of other courts, useless institutions which had lived on since the Middle Ages, were purely and simply dissolved. Even the new Parlement de Paris was smaller and more effective than the old: to no one's surprise, 75 judges did more work than the previous 170. In April, the new institution was solemnly inaugurated with a speech in which Maupeou drew the line between independence and sedition.

To the former Parlement's chagrin, these drastic reforms were greeted either with relief or simply with indifference. The magistrates had expected the people to rise in their defense, the realm to be the scene of commotion and revolt; none of these longed-for reactions happened. In fact, enough of the former judges agreed with the King's policy so that he had no difficulty staffing the new courts; rather, the number of applicants far exceeded that of the offices; and as the new Premier Président, the King chose Bertier de Sauvigny, a great legal mind and first-rate administrator. There could be very little doubt that the new Parlement was off to a good start. As for the rebels' last hope, namely, that once again the new courts would find themselves deserted, this time it was thoroughly quashed. The King made it very plain that he would never call back the old parlements and people believed him. When, for instance, there were rumors in mid-March that Choiseul would return to office and bring the Parlement back with him, Louis XV wrote the comte de Broglie: "What a stupid tale is that of [Choiseul]'s return to the foreign ministry! And how wicked that of the Parlement's return."[34]

Far from contemplating Choiseul's recall, in fact, the King was, slowly but surely, putting together a new ministry. By June it was complete. Maupeou, of course, remained chancelier; the abbé Terray, now finally able to reform the system, kept his place as contrôleur général. A technical minister, Bertin, who had been running the departments of Agriculture, Mining and the Merchant Marine with noted efficacity, was also retained, and Saint-Florentin, now created duc de La Vrillière, stayed on as Minister of the King's Household, a post he had occupied since the very beginning of the reign. Elsewhere there were changes. The duc d'Aiguillon became Foreign minister, partly as compensation for his troubles with the parlements, partly because he was quick, intelligent, committed to the Austrian alliance and willing to take orders from the King. It should perhaps also be mentioned that he had become a close friend of Mme du Barry's, so naturally gossip had it that he owed his promotion to being her lover, a patent untruth since the comtesse, aside from being faithful, never once ventured to suggest a political appointment. As minister of War, the King chose a highly competent officer, the marquis de Monteynard, who continued Choiseul's improvements. Finally, the Navy went to a superb administrator, Bourgeois de Boynes, whose efficacity was to be proved some years later when the French at long last defeated the British Navy. All in all, these were competent, hardworking men who, with the possible exception of d'Aiguillon (a cousin of the maréchal de Riche-lieu), were quite independent of any Court coterie. The two leaders were unquestionably Maupeou and Terray, but all stayed in place until the end of the reign.

Naturally, the ousted magistrates, the Princes of the Blood Royal and a few other malcontents resorted to the usual weapons. Since, to their fury, no one seemed to mind the new order of things, they decided to attack the King's person. It was easy enough, after all, to describe him as the besotted and impotent lover of a money-hungry whore. The new tide of pamphlets, usually printed abroad, ranged all the way from obscene songs to imaginary but inflammatory news: "The rumor is that the young vicomte du Barry is imprisoned at Pierre-Encise because he gave the comtesse of the same name a reason to worry about her health,* which she has passed on to the King in the same manner" was a typical example; or again: "The King's attachment for Mme du Barry comes from the prodigious efforts of which she has rendered him capable thanks to an amber concoction with which she daily perfumes her inside."[35] More classic, perhaps, was a song like this one: "France, quel est donc ton destin / D'être soumise à la femelle / Ton salut vint de la Pucelle / Tu périras par la catin." (France, what then is your fate / You are ruled by the females / You were saved by a virgin** / You will be destroyed by a whore.")[36] Curiously, these productions, while undoubtedly weakening the heretofore almost religious awe in which the monarchy was held, actually have had a greater effect on posterity than on Louis's contemporaries. Seen from the twentieth century, any institution which resists an absolute king seems praiseworthy. Historians have, in consequence, portrayed the scene following the dismissal of the old Parlement as one of despair mixed with barely contained rebellion. Nothing, in fact, could be further from the truth: the people were delighted; the lawyers, after a token resistance, discovered that their jobs had become easier; and the intellectuals welcomed the reform. Of course, the new judges were described by their predecessors in the most insulting terms, but that really didn't make much difference. "Although people had little esteem, then, for the new Parlement," the duc de Croÿ wrote about 1772, "it was functioning beautifully: never had there been so many famous trials, so that this Parlement, where no one had wanted to go, was, because of this, made so fashionable that it was always crowded. It is an unimaginable spectacle to see how it became established in just one year."[37]

Now that resistance to progress had ceased, it became at long last possible to reform the iniquitous and inefficient tax system. From the very first, Louis XV had made it clear that the new institution was there to stay. By 1773, the former judges had been reimbursed for the value of their offices; but already in 1771 the abbé Terray started on his great work, safe in the knowledge that his new edicts would be registered without fuss. A former conseiller in the Parlement—he had been the only member not to resign in 1756—Terray had been discovered by Laverdy, the former contrôleur général, who appreciated his thorough understanding of government finance and his unflagging energy. Arriving at his office by 6 A.M., he had finished his paperwork by ten, and could then spend the day seeing all comers. Early in 1771, without wasting a minute, he set about balancing the budget.

Of course, that meant braving a torrent of unpopularity. Ever since the death of Orry, two concurrent trends had brought the State to the edge of bankruptcy. On the one hand, taxes were not only insufficient to meet current needs, they were also never paid in full because all the parlements had encouraged resistance and evasion. On the other, thousands of salaries were paid to the holders of antiquated sinecures,

---

* I.e., a venereal disease.
** Joan of Arc.

while the expenses of the Court mounted. Clearly, any thoroughgoing reform must attack both problems.

For many years, the Treasury had suffered from the fact that the poor paid taxes and the rich didn't: aside from the obvious unfairness of the system, it was also self-defeating. In November 1771, therefore, Terray reestablished the vingtièmes—they had expired some years before—on a new basis: the first vingtième, or 5 percent income tax, was to be permanent; the second vingtième was to last ten years only. For that period, therefore, everyone in France would pay a 10 percent income tax, but it would go back down to 5 percent in 1781. To our modern sensibility, it hardly seems like an unbearable burden, and the poor, in 1771, were not heard to complain, but the rich, who were accustomed to paying no taxes at all, filled the air with their lament. They complained even more when they found out that for the first time in living memory, Terray actually meant the new law to be obeyed. There were to be no exceptions and no abonnements through which it had been possible to contract for a fraction of the tax actually due. People would pay what they owed, and the nobility like the rest. To that end, Terray ordered that all France be surveyed—most income still came from agriculture—while carefully checking all tax returns and prosecuting fraud, but in a fair and humane way. While instructing his collectors to allow no excuse or evasion, he also made sure that, where there was uncertainty, the taxpayer was given the benefit of the doubt. Within months, the money began to come in.

That, in itself, had several positive consequences. First, if the Treasury stopped borrowing, it could reduce the amount of interest it was paying out. Then, the accumulated debt could now be funded and slowly diminished: the bulk of it, which consisted of short-term notes, was to be paid off by 1781. Further, by providing for regular and sufficient collections, Terray made sure that French policy would never again be hampered by financial shortages; and, finally, this new solvency paved the way for the reduction, and then the abolition, of the more obnoxious minor taxes on which the Treasury had heretofore depended. Fiscal fairness is a key element of good government: this, with the King's knowledge and encouragement, is what Terray was beginning to establish. That the privilégiés should be made to bear their share of the tax burden was nothing short of a revolution, so naturally the abbé was loathed by the courtiers, who suddenly found themselves paying 10 percent on their pensions as well as their regular income. It was the only, the best, way of consolidating the government while allaying popular discontent.

At the same time, waste had to be reduced, so now that he could afford to buy them back, Terray abolished hundreds of unnecessary offices which had been created for the sole purpose of selling them and thus getting the Treasury fresh money. Now these useless salaries were eliminated, while Court expenses were held down. By 1774, with the debt shrinking, the budget was largely in balance. To be fair, however, that happy result was not only due to Terray's efforts: the policies inaugurated by Fleury in the 1720s had borne fruit. The prosperity which he had fostered had continued and expanded: never had France been so rich; never had so many of its peasants lived so well. Of course, the cities felt the consequence of this, while all the manufacturing and artisanal trades prospered beyond anything ever known before. This was especially marked in cities like Paris, Lyon, Bordeaux and Marseille, where whole new areas were built up in splendid style. As a result of this, the new taxes yielded even larger returns than Terray had expected. It was a sign of the times that, over the length of the reign, in an inflation-free period, the sum paid yearly by the Ferme générale more than doubled, growing from a little over 60 million livres in 1715 to 132 million by 1775.

It is not, perhaps, very surprising that the reforms, both judicial and financial, should have been greeted by howls of abuse: too many people in a position to make themselves heard had an interest in the old system. Then, too, some of the Paris salons which should have supported Maupeou and Terray attacked them because they had "stolen" Choiseul's place, but this froth of insults cannot conceal the key fact: starting at the end of December 1770, Louis XV, true to the idea of a King's responsibility he had learned from Fleury half a century earlier, and able, at last, to trust his own instincts, had set about changing the very shape of the monarchy. He had not merely tamed the Parlement but actually ended it; he had renovated the State's finances and set the government on a course of progress and renewal—all at an age when people usually cling to the status quo. It was no mean achievement.

All this naturally absorbed a good deal of the King's attention, but without distracting him from foreign affairs. There, his unchanging rule was that the Austrian alliance must be maintained. In October 1773, for instance, he wrote: "I have made that alliance and it will continue as long as the Empress lives and the Emperor [Joseph II] as well. I have reason to be pleased with him. I want no war, I have made this plain enough."[38] As a result, the Foreign minister had his task all set; nor, until 1772, was there any sort of serious crisis. Still, it was becoming evident that some sort of partition of Poland was in the offing. As in the fifties and sixties, Louis XV realized that France was simply too far away to help, and already in May 1771 Mercy made it very plain to the comte de Broglie that while Austria intended to leave Stanislas Poniatowski on the throne, it was likely to appropriate some of the Polish borderlands.

As soon as d'Aiguillon became Foreign minister, he decided, like most of his predecessors, to help the Poles, but this time unofficially. Recalling Dumouriez, who had been sent to Warsaw by Choiseul, he appointed a military man, the marquis de Vioménil, as ambassador and told him to so organize the Poles that they would resist any attempt at partition. This Vioménil did with relative success. He brought a patriotic party together and, with the help of a few hundred French volunteers, kidnaped King Stanislas and took over the fortress of Cracow; but, as usual, the Poles were too divided to put up any serious resistance to invasion. In due course, Vioménil found himself forced to free Stanislas and evacuate Cracow. Some of the volunteers, who had been taken prisoner, were freed at Maria Theresa's request and the expected happened. On August 5, 1772, together with Russia and Prussia, Austria attacked Poland. Torn between the realization that seizing foreign provinces was immoral and the feeling, strongly reinforced by Joseph II, that her duty to the State came first, the Empress, as Frederick II said ironically, cried and cried as she took and took.

This first partition of Poland was greeted in France with indignation, and the government was reviled for doing nothing to stop it. Here, said the pro-Prussian party, was the bitter fruit of the Austrian alliance: France was now so powerless that it could not even stop this act of international piracy. In fact, had France been allied with Frederick II instead, the situation would have been exactly the same, since Prussia helped itself to quite as large a share of Poland as Austria; indeed, with its three neighbors agreeing to partition it, Poland was clearly doomed. As it was, d'Aiguillon, who had made secret overtures to Frederick earlier in the year—without result—could do nothing but complain. Mercy saw it all quite clearly. In September, he wrote Maria Theresa: "The . . . arrangements relative to Poland are mortifying for the French minister; but I believe I can assert that the Most Christian King sees the arrangements from a more reasonable viewpoint, and more justly, and they will not modify his feelings on the current system."[39]

At least farther north France was able to save an old ally. After a moment of glory at the beginning of the century under the reign of Charles XII, Sweden, exhausted by its efforts and hampered by an unworkable constitution, had sunk into near anarchy. The King was powerless, the nobles divided: it all began to look very like Poland, and there, too, greedy neighbors thought of helping themselves—in this case, Prussia and Russia. This France was determined to avoid, partly because it had been Sweden's ally for some 150 years, partly because Catherine and Frederick were quite powerful enough as it was.

Luckily, the French Ambassador, the comte de Vergennes,* was a man of exceptional quality. An agent of the secret du Roi, he was in close touch with the King, who was, in this case, at one with d'Aiguillon, so Vergennes did his effective best by encouraging and financing a royalist party whose solution was to scrap the constitution and reinstate a strong monarchy. Early in 1772, with the help of King Gustavus III, who resented being an impotent figurehead as much as he feared annexation by his neighbors, a coup was carried out, the old Senate dissolved and a strong, centralized government introduced. The Swedes, who had realized that they were in danger of losing their independence, applauded the new system. It was a success for France and helped make up for the partition of Poland.

At the same time, the efforts begun by Choiseul continued in both Army and Navy. Year by year, the fleet grew stronger, better organized and better armed, while the idea of a descent into England remained one of the King's most secret but most cherished projects. For the moment, Louis XV still wanted peace, but he was only waiting for the time when France and Spain could take their revenge on the British. That, in the meantime, his government gained financial and political strength could only comfort him, and he also found pleasure in the fact that the Court was more brilliant than ever. Then, too, Mme du Barry saw to it that his life was as pleasant as possible: as he entered his sixties, Louis XV had reason to feel like a much younger man.

* Appointed Foreign minister by Louis XVI, he was in office all through the War of Independence, and a staunch pro-American.

Chapter Ten

Not Time Enough

ALTHOUGH the Court of Versailles had long been a byword for glamour, luxury and elegance, it fascinated Europe more than ever in the seventies. Led by an apparently ageless and indefatigable King, it moved from fete to fete in a variety of breathtaking settings. The new generation of the Royal Family, as it came into its own, added greatly to the gaiety and liveliness of the atmosphere: the Dauphin remained a heavyset, dull young man who cared for little besides hunting, but the Dauphine was full of sparkle, and the Dauphin's two brothers, the scholarly comte de Provence and the frivolous comte d'Artois, had all the charm of youth. Then, of course, there was Mme du Barry, prettier than ever and covered with diamonds.

Although, like a true eighteenth-century woman, the comtesse promptly had her apartments in the various palaces redecorated, she cared little for the arts or literature. Here was no second Mme de Pompadour, but rather someone who loved luxury and intended to have the best of everything; indeed, as one looks at Mme du Barry's collections, one begins to realize that, rather like certain birds, she liked everything that shone: gold, precious stones and porcelain; and while, in another century, this predilection might have produced rather grim results, it was the comtesse's luck that in her lifetime it was virtually impossible to buy an ugly object. Thus, when she ordered herself a porcelain service, it naturally came from Sèvres and was a miracle of cheerful elegance; when she bought new furniture, it was designed by Carlin and liberally adorned with Sèvres porcelain plaques. Her new house at Louveciennes was a neoclassical building designed by Ledoux and situated on a hill outside Paris, with the obligatory panoramic view. It managed to combine the cool stateliness of the neoclassical style with the soft colors, abundant draperies and jewellike detail which were just then coming into fashion. It was typical of the comtesse's taste, however, that the main house simply wasn't enough: there was also a garden pavilion "which was so famous for its taste and the richness of its ornamentation" that in the middle eighties it dazzled Mme Vigée-Lebrun, who had come to paint the comtesse's portrait. "The first time," the artist wrote, "Mme du Barry showed it to me, she said: 'It is in this room that Louis XV did me the honor of being my guest at dinner' . . . the salon was ravishing, one saw the most beautiful views from it and the mantelpieces, the doors were all adorned in the most dazzling way; the locks were as admirable as the greatest masterpieces of jewelery and the furniture was of a richness and elegance beyond all description."[1] As in the case of Bellevue, Louveciennes was built on Crown land: at Mme du Barry's death, therefore, it would revert to the royal domain; but, for all that, it had cost well over a million livres.

Indeed, the comtesse made no bones about it: she liked money, in great quantities, for what it could buy, and Louis XV indulged her rather the way one does a favorite child. First, there was a huge annual pension, 1,200,000 livres ($5,625,000), to which the King added an irrevocable annual income of 150,000 livres ($675,000); then, the favorite was allowed to draw on the Treasury for all her household expenses—items like the wages for her hundred servants; or the costumes for Zamor, her black page, in silver, pink, blue or white silk, taffeta and velvet; and then, because she loved gems, there were frequent gifts of diamonds, rubies and emeralds. With all that, however, Mme du Barry managed to spend her income, and rather more, every year: there were carriages, carved, gilded and painted, to be bought; and a full (twelve dozen of everything) silver service for her table; and, of course, her Sèvres service; and, most important of all, her dresses. In one year alone, she ran up bills amounting to 170,000 livres ($765,000) at Mlle Bertin's, a coming young designer, while spending more than 100,000 livres on lace and silk alone; but first and foremost came her great passion for jewelery.

Most spectacular, perhaps, was the bodice completely covered with diamonds, shaped into flowers, bows and ribbons, which had cost 450,000 livres ($2,025,000), especially when it was combined with a diamond necklace of dazzling proportions. Besides these, she owned over 140 large diamonds, 700 smaller ones, 300 very large pearls, 3 enormous sapphires and 7 huge and renowned emeralds, as well as a plethora of lesser stones and gold adornments. It can hardly be doubted that, covered with her jewels, she must have been an extraordinary vision, but while the King enjoyed the part of the magician who, with a touch of his magic wand, makes every wish come true, he also loved Mme du Barry for her other qualities: she was cheerful, easily amused, kind; she loved to play at being hostess; she was always ready to make herself pleasant; and, of course, she had lost none of her physical attractions. Few things can be more invigorating to a man over sixty than to be admired by a ravishing young woman; and admire him she did: her behavior during and after his reign proved it abundantly, as did one of her rare recorded comments about the Revolution: if Louis XV had still been alive, she sighed, none of this would be happening.

It was thus particularly upsetting to the King when another young woman of whom he was fond, the Dauphine, started waging war against the favorite. At first, although cool, Marie Antoinette had been polite, speaking to the comtesse whenever necessary and confining her scathing appraisals of the "creature" to the ladies of Mesdames' circle. Soon, however, she decided that as the first lady at Versailles (even if she was only sixteen) it was her duty to set standards; so, in the most obvious ways she began to snub the comtesse, ultimately ignoring her altogether, and, of course, the Court noticed it. Soon it was the main topic of gossip: how long, people wondered, would the Dauphine keep it up? Mesdames, of course, were delighted, and in the course of her daily visits they urged her on. Mme du Barry at first tried not to notice; then, for a while, she suffered in silence; but, finally, the situation became too obvious. Something had to be done, but neither the comtesse nor the King knew what: Louis XV was reluctant to speak to the Dauphine himself, so at first he tried a few hints, but they did no good at all. Next, he called in Mercy, the Austrian Ambassador, and rather embarrassedly pointed out to him that the Dauphine was making everyone's life very unpleasant. Mercy, who cared nothing for a young girl's whims but a great deal for the alliance, went to see the Dauphine and bluntly told her to be polite to Mme du Barry. Outraged, Marie Antoinette replied that there could be no question of her speaking to the creature: had the Ambassador forgotten he was addressing an archduchess who was also the future Queen of France? Besides, she pointed out, the King himself hadn't said anything, and that meant that he really approved of her behavior. Aghast, Mercy bowed himself out and promptly appealed to the Empress.

Like Mercy, Maria Theresa thought the alliance was more important than her daughter's little games, so on September 30, 1771, she sent off a letter so strongly worded that she told Mercy he could suppress it if he thought it too harsh. Mercy, who by then had gauged the pride and obstinacy of the Dauphine, handed the letter on.

"The Ambassador," the Empress wrote, "has confirmed that you are entirely led by your aunts [Mesdames] . . . I respect them, I like them, but they have never known how to earn the respect or affection of their family or the public and you want to go the same way. That fear, that shyness about speaking to the King,* that best of fathers, or to the people [Mme du Barry] with whom you have been advised to speak! Own up to your shyness, to that fear of saying merely good morning; a word on a dress, on a bagatelle costs you so many grimaces, pure grimaces, or else it's even worse. You have allowed yourself to become such a slave that reason, and even duty, no longer convince you. I cannot keep quiet anymore . . . After Mercy told you what the King wished and your duty demanded, you have dared to disobey him: what good reason can you offer? None. You must know and see the Barry only as a lady received at Court and in the King's circle. You are his first subject, you owe him obedience and submission. You must show the Court and courtiers that your master's will is done. If humiliation or familiarities were demanded of you, neither I nor anyone else would advise you to risk them, but an indifferent word, a few looks, not even for the lady but for your grandfather, your master! And you disobey him so visibly on the first occasion you have of obliging him! . . . Let us see now for whom you have done this; it is through a shameful compliance to people who have subjugated you, treating you as a child, arranging horse and donkey rides with children and dogs: these are the great causes which make you prefer them to your master and which, in the long run, will make you ridiculous, so that you will be neither liked nor respected . . . Your only goal must be to please and obey the King."[2]

Frivolous and obstinate though she was, Marie Antoinette feared her mother, but even then it was a while before the letter had the desired effect, especially since Madame Adélaide kept repeating that, no matter what anyone might think, the King simply didn't care how other people treated the favorite. On October 13, in fact, the Dauphine answered the Empress: "I have good reason to think that the King himself does not want me to speak to the Barry; besides, he has never talked to me about it.

---

* Mercy had advised her to approach the King directly and ask for his orders.

He has shown me more affection since he knows I have refused, and if you were able to see everything that happens here as I can, you would realize that this woman and her clique would not be satisfied with a word, and that I would have to speak to her again and again . . . I do not say that I will never speak to her, but cannot agree to speak on a precise day at a precise time because she would mention it in advance and look triumphant."[3] It was perfectly clear: in what she saw as a contest between herself and the favorite, Marie Antoinette was too proud to give in.

Maria Theresa, however, who heard weekly from Mercy, knew that Louis XV was becoming increasingly annoyed, and that if he had indeed been very affectionate to the Dauphine, it was because he thought it might help her to swallow her pride. It still took another letter from the Empress, and more objurgations from Mercy, but at last an agreement was reached. On January 1, 1772, Mme du Barry, like the rest of the Court, filed past the Dauphine, who, with a visible effort, looked at her and said: "There are many people at Versailles today, Madame." The comtesse, kind as always, was careful not to gloat, the King was relieved and peace returned to the Royal Family.

For the next two years, life at Court remained quiet, even though Marie Antoinette neatly managed to avoid speaking to Mme du Barry. There were the usual intrigues, of course, but it was obvious that the King intended to keep both favorite and ministers in place. The comte d'Artois married a Piedmontese princess with all the usual celebrations. The Dauphine, because she represented youth and the future, began to be genuinely popular, and the Dauphin seemed to become a little more amiable as the result of his wife's influence, even if he was still unable to consummate his marriage. As for the King, the passing years seemed, if anything, to make him grow younger. He hunted as energetically and as often as ever; he continued to preside over cheerful, lively suppers; the movements from château to château occurred just as often as before. More importantly, his political reforms were obviously taking root. By the spring of 1774, the new Parlement was functioning as smoothly as if it had always existed, the Treasury was at ease and the Debt shrinking. After the partition of Poland, no new crisis endangered the peace: Louis XV could enjoy life in the full consciousness that, by his efforts, he had prevented the virtual dissolution of the State, which had seemed a distinct possibility only three years earlier. Still, appearances to the contrary notwithstanding, he was no longer a young man*; his doctors warned him to take less violent exercise and begged him not to make love quite so often. Sensibly, given the state of medical knowledge, the King paid no attention to them; and then, at the end of April 1774, suddenly, he was seen to change.

At first, it was simply assumed that he was suffering from one of those periodic bouts of fever which assaulted him throughout his life, and Mme du Barry naturally did everything she could to comfort him in that opinion, out of kindness and not, as most courtiers supposed, to avoid dismissal. Still, all the precedents were in everyone's mind: Metz, when Mme de Châteauroux had tried keeping the King from the Court, only to be ignominiously sent away; Damiens's attempt when Mme de Pompa-

---

* A man of sixty-four, in the eighteenth century, seemed far older than he would today because life expectancy was much shorter.

dour had waited through days of silence. If now Louis XV were to be seriously unwell again, what would he do? And if he sent Mme du Barry away and recovered, would he call her back? It was not easy for the great noncommitted mass of courtiers to decide how they were to behave, so all watched anxiously while the anti–du Barry party muttered darkly about the state of the patient's soul. Still, there were a few old friends who simply cared for Louis XV as a person, and one of these, the duc de Croÿ, carefully recorded what he saw day by day.

"For eight days," he wrote, "the King often looked and felt very unwell. On Tuesday, April 26, he was having supper at Trianon with the lady [Mme du Barry] and the usual courtiers, but he found the food unappetizing, so he didn't eat. On Wednesday the twenty-seventh, he hunted, but because he felt cold and the weather was damp, he broke with his custom and followed the hunt in a carriage, without ever being able to warm up, and he also had a slight fever. On Thursday, the twenty-eighth, the fever was higher and accompanied by nausea. La Martinière, the First Surgeon, was called . . . [and] told him that since he was ill he must return to Versailles, making him get into a carriage at the end of the day; the King was wearing his robe with a coat over it.

"As he entered the carriage, the King said: 'At the gallop' and, in fact, he went from the courtyard of Trianon to that of Versailles in just three minutes . . . All night his fever was high and accompanied by a severe headache . . . To ease the pain he was given opium.

"Lemonnier [one of the King's doctors] decided on his own to have him bled on the morning of the twenty-ninth . . . Bordeu and Lorry came and had him bled again at three . . .

"The King was in a small camp bed in the middle of the room: he had just been changing his clothes and his bed was being remade because he had been sweating a little . . . I heard him speak several times. His voice was hoarse, which I took as a sign that his fever was still high . . . People were told to leave because his room was becoming too warm; the doctors and the normal attendants alone added up to a large crowd. All the Royal Family came in and out often during the day . . .

"Around ten-thirty at night, the doctors, as they gave him a drink, thought that he looked flushed. They said: 'Bring the light, the King can't see his glass.' Nudging one another, they pretended nothing was wrong and gathered for a conference at the end of the room. A quarter of an hour later, they came back and, under different pretexts, such as the need to see his tongue, they examined him and realized that there was an open eruption of smallpox . . . Once the pustules were out, the King was exhausted but much quieter . . . He didn't yet know what ailed him."[4]

So far, Louis XV had only been really ill for three or four days, and the signs all looked good: while there were several varieties of smallpox, most were really dangerous before the eruption of the pustules, and most people who died did so then; once the eruption was over, the patient had a very good chance of recovery as long as he wasn't suffering from a particularly virulent form of the disease, the *petite vérole confluente*. It seemed, therefore, quite probable that after an unpleasant siege the King would get well. The doctors, however, taking his age into account, felt that he might lack the stamina to beat the illness and, as a result, were far less confident than they appeared to be. That discrepancy was of the gravest importance: if the King was in real danger, then Mme du Barry would have to leave; if not, she could stay, and many people had much to lose if the wrong decision were made. As for the doctors themselves, they trod a very fine line: if the comtesse was sent away but the King recovered and she returned, then, obviously, they would find themselves in very hot water; but if they let the King become so ill that he was no longer able to confess and be shriven, it would be still more serious. Naturally, the anti–du Barry party began to look hopeful, while her supporters, headed by the maréchal de Richelieu, who had played a similar role at Metz, and the duc d'Aiguillon went around saying that the King was already on the road to recovery and hinting that the usually forgiving comtesse was ready, this time, to remember the names of those who had wished her gone. At least that night the Court watched one selfless act: Mesdames, who had never had smallpox and were therefore sure to catch it if they came near their father, moved into their father's room and took turns keeping him company. Even more bravely, Mme du Barry, who had not had the disease either, and whose beauty was everything to her, also stayed by the King's side for most of the day and night.

"On April 30th," Croÿ continues, "the abundant eruption went well. There were no worrying symptoms. Thus, no one dared worry the King [by telling him the truth] since he was already very apprehensive. They told him that he was only suffering from a miliary fever . . . He kept showing his pustules and looking surprised, but everyone reassured him by looking confident . . . and since no one mentioned confession so as not to upset him, he didn't dare talk about it himself, and all remained as it had been."[5] What the duc means, of course, is that Mme du Barry still kept him company. The next day, May 1, nothing changed. That afternoon, the Archbishop of Paris came for a visit, but, fully aware of the stakes, he said nothing about confession or the last rites and simply chatted for a while with the King. Needless to say, he was praised by the maréchal de Richelieu and severely criticized by the anti–du Barry party.

"On May 2 . . . at one, we came in as if for the normal lever . . . The King then seemed very quiet, but his head was red and very swollen . . . The rest of the day went for the best . . . so that the King talked of this and that . . . and even seemed quite cheerful . . .

"Mme du Barry was encouraged to stay by her supporters, but she kept saying: 'I am upsetting the whole family, why can't I be allowed to leave?' But because the King was so used to her presence, it made her feel that she was helping him, and so she seemed to sacrifice herself by staying on . . . The King said several times: 'If I hadn't had smallpox when I was eighteen, I would think that I had it now.' "[6] Louis XV was, of course, referring to his serious illness of October 1728, when he was widely thought to have had smallpox; like the measles, that illness immunizes its sufferer. If indeed the King had had smallpox in 1728, he couldn't be suffering from it in 1774: it was no wonder he believed his doctors' lies.

Still, Louis XV was both sensible and brave. "On May 3, at one-fifteen . . . the King looked at the pustules on his hand with great attention and said: 'It is smallpox' . . . Nobody answered him, and he turned around, saying: 'Well, as to that, it is surprising.' He meant that he had it again and that people were trying to conceal it from him.'"[7] At that Bordeu, who was a du Barryite, told the King firmly that he was wrong: it was not smallpox. That was a brazen lie, of course, and, coming from a Catholic, a particularly grave one since the King was now risking his soul.

"On May 4 . . . people said the smallpox was going back in,* which is always fatal . . . We were allowed in [to the King's room]. He seemed less swollen and red to me. He spoke quite as usual but in a worried tone, and the way he does when he is annoyed.

"I first thought of looking at the courtiers' faces, and I have seldom seen so striking a spectacle. All those—and they were numerous and well known—who belonged to the lady's party showed rage and despair. All those who cared about the King alone exhibited anguish and pain."[8] It was no wonder. The preceding evening, at long last, in answer to Louis XV's reiterated affirmation that he must be suffering from smallpox, the maréchal de Broglie and the Archbishop of Paris had remained silent. It was enough; and since he was well versed in the practice of medicine, the King immediately understood that he was doomed. At eleven forty-five, therefore, "he told Mme du Barry: 'Now that I know what my condition is, I will not repeat the scandal of Metz. Had I known what I know now, you would not have come in. I owe myself to God and my people. You had, therefore, better leave tomorrow.' She fainted [and, when she revived] went out."[9] In fact, instead of waiting until the next day, swiftly and discreetly Mme du Barry went straight to her carriage.

"Towards midnight [the King] said: 'Go and get Mme du Barry.' Laborde told him: 'She has left.'

" 'Where has she gone?' he asked.

" 'To Rueil, sire.'

" 'Ah, already!' " And, according to Laborde, two large tears then ran down the King's cheeks. "That night, he asked to get up, but the pain from the pustules on the soles of his feet made him faint . . .

"On Thursday, May 5, all went well . . . On Friday, May 6, during the night there was some agitation, with moments of delirium . . . At nine in the evening, the face seemed darker, which might have been due to the scabs on the pustules.

"Saturday . . . was decisive. It was a triumphant night from the religious point of view, without a single weakness. The order, the decisiveness and the firmness with which [the King] behaved were amazing and showed the greatest courage."[10] It was then that, with great discretion, the King confessed, received absolution and was given the last rites, upon which "the cardinal [de la Roche-Aymon] said: 'Gentlemen, the King has asked me to tell you that he begs God's forgiveness for having offended Him, and for the scandal he caused his people [a reference to Mme du Barry]; if God gives him health, he will look to penitence, to sustaining our religion and to relieving his people.' The King then said: 'I wish I had had the strength to say it myself.' He also said a little while later to Madame Adélaide: 'I have never felt better, or more at peace.' "[11]

Later that day, the King's illness took a turn for the worse. He was racked by a high fever, his face changed. That evening, he lapsed into delirium again and was acknowledged to be near death. On the ninth, at three in the morning, "he got much

* If some of the pustules, instead of suppurating freely, closed up too soon, then there was no hope.

worse; the scabs and dried pustules became black . . . and it was noticed that an inflammation of the throat prevented him from swallowing."[12] Within hours, scabs formed on his eyelids and blinded him. "Far from fearing death, as people thought he would, he displayed a courage all the more heroic in that it was simple, quiet and modest, and the most perfect Christian acceptance joined to the greatest tranquility . . .

"He was lying on his camp bed in the middle of the room, all curtains wide open, brilliantly lit by a quantity of candles held by the priests, who were wearing their surplices and kneeling around the bed . . . His face, swollen by the scabs, was the color of bronze . . . His chest was immobile, his mouth open, but his face was not misshapen and showed no agitation; in a word, it looked like a Moor's, a negro's head, dark and swollen.

"The Bishop of Senlis, standing, recited the last prayers . . . All the other people present also stood and looked horrified, but . . . there was, overall, more etiquette than feeling.

"On May 10 . . . he remained conscious until noon and showed, as before, the greatest patience, firmness, quiet and acceptance. At three-fifteen he expired."[13] Immediately the courtiers ran out of the bedroom where the body had already begun to decompose.

Across a courtyard, in a room where they stood alone, the Dauphin and Dauphine had been watching a candle set in the King's window. Suddenly they saw it go out and heard a noise like thunder: it was the Court racing to pay them homage; but when the doors were flung open, the panting mob stood frozen: there, kneeling on the floor before them, the new King and Queen, tears running down their cheeks, were crying: "Protect us, O God, we are too young to reign!"

Within days, however, Louis XVI and Marie Antoinette had changed their minds. The swiftness of the transition was epitomized by the indecent haste with which the body of the late King had been bundled away. Already decomposing and emitting a dreadful stench, it had been quickly thrust into a coffin and driven to Saint Denis, the burial place of French royalty, as the Court hurriedly left the Palace, both to escape contagion and because the sacrosanct etiquette required it; but without wasting a moment, the new rulers had Mme du Barry arrested and sent to a remote convent. Then, as soon as was practicable, the ministry was dismissed. Louis XVI had meant to call back Machault, whom his father had greatly esteemed, but he listened to Madame Adélaide's advice and sent for Maurepas instead: the new minister, now aged but as frivolous as ever, was just about the worst possible choice. All the reforms of the previous three years were annulled. The old Parlement was recalled, the tax edicts modified. Within three years, the deficit once again became unmanageable. The Revolution was on its way.

Afterword

"HE had a unique memory and presence of mind; his understanding was extraordinary. He never said anything false . . . He was kind, an excellent father and relative, and the most honest man in the world. He was knowledgeable in the sciences and especially competent in astronomy, physics, chemistry, botany, but all with the greatest modesty. Overall, modesty was a virtue which in him almost became a vice: always seeing more clearly than the others, he always thought he was wrong. I have often heard him say: 'I would have thought this (and he was right) but I'm told it isn't so and must be wrong' . . .

"He never willfully said anything nasty or harsh . . . All he lacked was the ability to decide by himself . . . Louis XIV was too proud; he wasn't proud enough . . . He thought only his mistresses loved him enough to tell him the truth. In his despair at the death of Mme de Châteauroux, he exclaimed: 'Who will tell me the truth now, and criticize me?' "[1] So wrote the duc de Croÿ after Louis XV's death; and he no doubt missed the late King all the more as he saw the petty nastiness and the weak obstinacy of his successor.

It is easy enough, in retrospect, to discover Louis XIV's mistakes, easier still to make the long list of Louis XVI's misjudgments, but when it comes to Louis XV, the task is incomparably harder. It is no wonder that his detractors have chosen to focus on his personal life: it is to this we owe the hackneyed and wholly inaccurate cliché of the weak womanizer giving in to his mistresses' whims. It is more difficult to understand how anyone could have invented the grotesque "after me the deluge" when, in fact, Louis XV spent the last years of his reign in a valiant effort to reform the regime. Although historical speculation must, by definition, remain idle, it is not difficult to suppose that if Louis XV had lived on for a few more years the Revolution would never have occurred. By 1774, he had removed its two immediate causes, the anti-reform Parlement and the unfair, inefficient tax system. Perhaps, in the end, Louis XV's gravest shortcoming was that he died too soon.

Even so, his fifty-nine-year reign was the second longest in French history, and while he cannot be held responsible for the policies implemented when he was still a child, his personal rule, starting a little before Fleury's death, stretched over some thirty-five years. How, then, should he be judged?

No matter which point of view one chooses, it is difficult not to give him very high marks indeed. First, and perhaps most important, he avoided the catastrophic wars which marred the reigns of practically all his predecessors. Under Louis XV, France, for the first time in centuries, remained secure and protected behind its borders: to judge the magnitude of this particular achievement, it should be remembered that France (to start with the sixteenth century) was invaded, and ravaged under Francois I, Henri II, Henri III, Henri IV, Louis XIII, Louis XIV, the First Republic, Napoléon, Napoléon III and the Third Republic. And such wars as there were under Louis XV were fought without unbearable costs in either men or money. Throughout the period from 1740 to 1774, the taxes remained at a reasonable level, no matter what the Parlement claimed. The dreadful famines which struck as recently as 1710 ceased, largely because the government preserved and distributed supplies more efficiently. Never in its history had France been so peaceful or so prosperous: surely Louis XV deserves some praise for this very considerable achievement.

Then, too, it was during his reign that French culture set the standards for the rest of the world. Catherine the Great, Maria Theresa, Frederick II, and most anyone with any pretension to culture read, wrote and spoke French whenever possible. When it came to literature, philosophy, painting, sculpture, architecture and fashion, everyone looked to Paris. The most enchanting women, the most illustrious intellectuals, the most inspired cabinetmakers were all French and owed everything to the atmosphere of tolerant and civilized interest which Louis XV encouraged.

Still, no one is perfect, and Louis XV, like the rest of us, had faults. In his own lifetime people would have said that the chief of these was too great a liking for women. That Louis XV, after his first period as a faithful husband, had a great many mistresses cannot be denied: the number runs to the hundreds, perhaps even higher, and from a Catholic point of view it implies constant and reiterated sinning. If, however, we look at the King's sex life from a more tolerant—and more reasonable—point of view, that particular failing hardly seems very important. Just because Louis XV loved women neither diminished his care for the welfare of France nor his affection for his family. It is, further, hard to see why he should not have enjoyed himself as he pleased. Like our own, the eighteenth century was an era of sexual freedom, and Louis XV was simply behaving like most of his courtiers, male or female.

With all that, however, Louis XV was almost disabled, for most of his life, by one crucial flaw: his lack of self-confidence. Had he been better able to assert himself, he could probably have spared France the War of the Austrian Succession, the parlements would have been crushed—and consequently the reforms introduced—much earlier, and a number of inefficient ministers relieved of their posts sooner. Still, it adds greatly to the interest of the King's story that after a long struggle he succeeded in overcoming his diffidence. Starting in December 1770, Louis XV abundantly proved that he had gained the ability to make difficult decisions and stick to them.

When all is said and done, therefore, the facts speak for themselves. France, in 1774, was larger, more prosperous and very much happier than it had been in 1715: there can be no better epitaph for a King who was also a kind father, a good friend, a faithful lover and the most civilized of men.

Notes

Chapter 1

1. Dangeau, XVI, 136.
2. Ibid,, XVI, 126.
3. Ibid., XVI, 129.
4. Ibid., xvi, 136.
5. Marais, I, 160.
6. Ibid., I, 167.
7. Ibid., I, 201.
8. Saint-Simon, XI, 165ff.
9. Ibid., XI, 178.
10. Ibid., XI, 183.
11. Dangeau, XVI, 169.
12. Ibid., XVI, 200.
13. Ibid., XVI, 235.
14. Ibid., XVI, 273.
15. Egret, 9.
16. Madame, duchesse d'Orléans, letter of September 27, 1715.

Chapter 2

1. Madame, duchesse d'Orléans, letter of January 3, 1716.
2. Saint-Simon, XI, 218.
3. Ibid., XIV, 102.
4. Madame, duchesse d'Orléans, letter of November 1, 1717.
5. Ibid., letter of October 2, 1718.
6. Quoted in Sars.
7. Saint-Simon, XIV, 23ff.
8. Madame, duchesse d'Orléans, letter of October 2, 1718.
9. Villars, II, 37.
10. Saint-Simon, XVI, 56.
11. Ibid., XI, 175.
12. Ibid., XI, 298.
13. Ibid., XVI, 415.
14. Marais, I, 318.
15. Saint-Simon, XVI, 416.
16. Bibliothèque Nationale, Paris, Fonds Français, 1756.
17. Saint-Simon, XVI, 437ff.
18. Marais, I, 105.
19. Ibid., II, 47.
20. Madame, duchesse d'Orléans, letter of July 31, 1721.
21. Marais, II, 83.
22. Ibid., II, 182.
23. Barbier, I, 146.
24. Marais, II, 184.
25. Ibid., II, 186.
26. Barbier, I, 147.
27. Marais, II, 253.
28. Ibid., I, 437.
29. Ibid., II, 299.
30. Ibid., II, 310.
31. Madame, duchesse d'Orléans, letter of June 11, 1722.
32. Ibid., letter of March 26, 1722.
33. Marais, II, 319.
34. Ibid., II, 321.
35. Ibid., II, 324.
36. Ibid., II, 328.
37. Saint-Simon, XIX, 6.
38. Bibl. Nat., Fonds Français, 2325.
39. Ibid.
40. Villars, II, 53.
41. Marais, II, 370.

CHAPTER 3

1. Saint-Simon, XIX, 208.
2. Walpole, letter of December 6, 1723.
3. Cited by Thirion.
4. Ibid.
5. Walpole, letter of January 13, 1724.
6. Villars, III, 130.
7. Clérembault-Maurepas, année 1724.
8. Villars, III, 136.
9. Barbier, I, 365.
10. Walpole, letter of November 28, 1724.
11. Saint-Simon, XV, 317.
12. Daudet, 259.
13. Walpole, letter of December 24, 1725.
14. Ibid.
15. Quoted in Piépape.
16. Walpole, letter of December 24, 1725.
17. Villars, III, 217.
18. Ibid.
19. Quoted in Piépape.
20. Ibid.
21. Villars, III, 214.
22. Ibid., III, 222.
23. Quoted in Thirion.
24. Ibid.
25. Villars, III, 242.
26. Walpole, letter of June 12, 1726.
27. Walpole, letter of June 18, 1726.
28. Bibl. Nat., Fonds Français, 487, NA.
29. Quoted in Sars.
30. Walpole, letter of September 28, 1726.
31. Barbier, I, 426.
32. Ibid., I, 431.
33. Walpole, letter of November 19, 1727.

CHAPTER 4

1. Bibl. Nat., Fonds Français, 6803.
2. Barbier, II, 37.
3. Ibid., II, 41.
4. Ibid., II, 153.
5. Ibid., II, 53.
6. Pollnitz, III, 1ff.
7. Barbier, III, 338.
8. Pollnitz, III, 35ff.
9. D'Argenson, I, 113.
10. Pollnitz, II, 134.
11. Barbier, II, 247.
12. Ibid., II, 238.
13. Quoted in Egret.
14. D'Argenson, I, 136n.
15. Clérembault-Maurepas, année 1732.
16. Ibid., année 1733.
17. Barbier, III, 125.

18. D'Argenson, II, 1.
19. Ibid., II, 121.
20. Ibid., I, 321.
21. Ibid., I, 284.
22. Ibid., I, 291.
23. Ibid., III, 193.
24. Hénault, 217.
25. Toussaint, unpublished ms., unn. pp.
26. D'Argenson, I, 220.
27. Ibid., I, 265.
28. Barbier, III, 154.
29. Luynes, I, 263.
30. Ibid., III, 84.
31. Ibid., I, 163.
32. Ibid., I, 168.
33. Ibid., I, 196.
34. Ibid., I, 169.
35. Ibid., I, 287.
36. Ibid., I, 317.
37. Ibid., I, 273.
38. Bouffonidor, I, 129.
39. Ibid., I, 127.
40. D'Argenson, III, 45.
41. Luynes, I, 402.
42. Ibid., I, 297.
43. Ibid., I, 280.
44. Ibid., I, 225.
45. Ibid., II, 269.
46. Ibid., I, 308.
47. Ibid., IV, 244.
48. D'Argenson, II, 4.
49. Ibid., II, 181.
50. Ibid.
51. Ibid., II, 211.
52. Toussaint.
53. Ibid.
54. Luynes, III, 77.
55. Ibid., III, 104.
56. Luynes III, 78.

CHAPTER 5

1. D'Argenson, III, 1.
2. Ibid., III, 2.
3. Ibid., III, 27.
4. Ibid., III, 142.
5. Croÿ, *Nouvelle Revue*, III, 10ff.
6. Barbier, III, 247.
7. D'Argenson, II, 219.
8. Bibl. Nat., Fonds Français, 487, NA.
9. Brancas.
10. Luynes, IV, 265.
11. Ibid., IV, 267.
12. Ibid., IV, 268.
13. Brancas, late November 1742.

14. Ibid., December 28, 1742.
15. Quoted in Sars.
16. D'Argenson, IV, 49.
17. Quoted in Sars.
18. Ibid.
19. D'Argenson, IV, 49.
20. Ibid., IV, 50.
21. Ibid., IV, 62.
22. Correspondence Noailles, letter of November 20, 1742.
23. Ibid., letter of November 26, 1742.
24. Ibid., letter of early January 1743.
25. Bibl. Nat., Fonds Français, 487, NA.
26. Luynes, IV, 407.
27. Bibl. Nat., Fonds Français, 487, NA.
28. Croÿ, 45.
29. Barbier, III, 421 and 438.
30. Luynes, IV, 447.
31. Ibid., IV, 467.
32. Brancas, introduction.
33. Lordat, May 6, 1743.
34. Bibl. Nat., Fonds Français, 12767.
35. Ibid.
36. Ibid.
37. Correspondence Noailles, May 8, 1743.
38. Ibid., May 20, 1743.
39. Ibid., June 4, 1743.
40. Ibid., June 29, 1743.
41. Ibid., July 5, 1743.
42. Ibid., July 8, 1743.
43. D'Argenson, IV, 83.
44. Correspondence Noailles, July 13, 1743.
45. Ibid., July 24, 1743.
46. Brancas, letter of July 17, 1743.
47. Bibl. Nat., Fonds Français, 12767.
48. Ibid.
49. Ibid.
50. Barbier, III, 475.
51. Bibl. Nat., Fonds Français, 487, NA.
52. D'Argenson, IV, 98.
53. Lordat, May 4, 1744.
54. Bibl. Nat., Fonds Français, 12767.
55. Ibid.
56. Barbier, III, 513.
57. Brancas, letter of June 3, 1744.
58. Barbier, III, 518.
59. D'Argenson, IV, 103.
60. Lordat, July 6, 1744.

CHAPTER 6

1. Luynes, VI, 13.
2. Ibid., VI, 39.
3. Ibid., VI, 39ff.
4. Ibid.

5. Ibid.
6. Barbier, III, 536ff.
7. Ibid.
8. Luynes, VI, 48.
9. Barbier, III, 533.
10. Bibl. Nat., clipping.
11. Barbier, III, 547.
12. Lordat, November 15, 1744.
13. Luynes, VI, 95.
14. Correspondence Noailles, August 30, 1744.
15. Bibl. Nat., Fonds Français, 487, NA.
16. Luynes, VI, 145.
17. Ibid., VI, 162.
18. Ibid., VI, 181.
19. Ibid., VI, 182.
20. Barbier, IV, 13.
21. Luynes, VI, 354.
22. Ibid., VI, 355.
23. Bibl. Nat., Fonds Français, 9184, NA.
24. Correspondence Pompadour, XXVff.
25. Barbier, IV, 32.
26. Valfons, 133.
27. Bulletin des Comités Historiques, 1849, tome 1.
28. Barbier, IV, 37.
29. Luynes, VI, 440.
30. Tessan, 38 (unpublished ms.).
31. Luynes, VI, 442.
32. Barbier, IV, 41.
33. Ibid., VI, 493.
34. Croÿ, *Nouvelle Revue,* III, 26.
35. Barbier, IV, 97.
36. Croÿ, I, 56ff.
37. Croÿ, *Nouvelle Revue,* III, 35.
38. Ibid., III, 36.
39. Valfons, 189.
40. Lordat, April 3, 1746.
41. Croÿ, I, 93.
42. Ibid., I, 86.
43. Croÿ, *Nouvelle Revue,* III, 43.
44. Ibid., III, 122.

CHAPTER 7

1. Dufort, I, 123.
2. Ibid., I, 125.
3. Croÿ, *Nouvelle Revue,* III, 213.
4. Ibid., III, 209.
5. Ibid., III, 207.
6. Ibid., III, 278.
7. Correspondence Pompadour, January 3, 1751.
8. Barbier, IV, appendix.
9. Croÿ, *Nouvelle Revue,* III, 144.

10. Quoted in Egret.
11. Barbier, V, 125.
12. Ibid., V, 324.
13. Correspondence Pompadour, October 19, 1750.
14. Croÿ, *Nouvelle Revue,* III, 340.
15. Tressan, 329.
16. Dufort, I, 103.
17. Correspondence Pompadour, September 29, 1751.
18. Dufort, I, 101.
19. Ibid., I, 104ff.
20. Ibid.
21. Correspondence Pompadour, September 29, 1751.
22. Croÿ, *Nouvelle Revue,* III, 388.
23. Correspondence Pompadour, December 5, 1751.
24. Ibid., October 1752.
25. Ibid., March 1749.
26. Barbier, IV, 487.
27. Correspondence Pompadour, January 3, 1751.
28. Barbier, IV, 289.
29. Mitford, 162.
30. Correspondence Pompadour, April 1, 1751.
31. Ibid., December 7, 1752.
32. Ibid., December 28, 1749.
33. Ibid., March 1, 1750.
34. Ibid., January 12, 1753.
35. Dufort, I, 138.
36. Mitford, 207.
37. Croÿ, *Nouvelle Revue,* III, 392.
38. Dufort, I, 116.
39. Croÿ, I, 335.
40. Croÿ, *Nouvelle Revue,* III, 378.
41. Ibid., III, 393.
42. Dufort, I, 71ff.
43. Ibid., I, 227.
44. Ibid., I, 99.
45. Bernis, 118.
46. Ibid., 204.
47. Ibid., 207.
48. Gaxotte, 244.
49. Bernis, 226.
50. Ibid., 227ff.
51. Gaxotte, 250.

Chapter 8

1. Luynes, XV, 345.
2. Bernis, 312.
3. Barbier, VI, 425.
4. Croÿ, I, 364ff.
5. Gaxotte, 173.
6. Clérembault-Maurepas, année 1757.
7. Bernis, 354.
8. Ibid., 356.
9. Bernis, II, 111.
10. Gaxotte, 174.
11. Barbier, XV, 468.
12. Broglie, *Secret,* I, 226.
13. Ibid., I, 231.
14. Correspondence Pompadour, 181ff.
15. Bernis, II, September 24, 1757.
16. Ibid., September 27, 1757.
17. Ibid., September 20, 1757.
18. Clérembault-Maurepas.
19. Bernis, II, November 14, 1757.
20. Ibid., II, November 22, 1757.
21. Ibid., II, December 22, 1757.
22. Ibid.
23. Ibid., II, January 6, 1758.
24. Ibid., II, January 25, 1758.
25. Ibid., II, March 17, 1758.
26. Ibid., II, 77.
27. Ibid., II, April 21, 1758.
28. Ibid., II, May 6, 1758.
29. Ibid., II, May 13, 1758.
30. Ibid., II, June 6, 1758.
31. Ibid., II, June 24, 1758.
32. Ibid., II, August 1, 1758.
33. Ibid., II, September 19, 1758.
34. Ibid., II, October 9, 1758.
35. Montbarey, I, 200.
36. Croÿ, *Nouvelle Revue,* III, 411.
37. Dufort, I, 243ff.
38. Gaxotte, 256.
39. Bachaumont, I, 63.
40. Ibid., I, 88.
41. Broglie, February 26, 1763.
42. Ibid., April 7, 1763.
43. Ibid., March 17, 1763.
44. Ibid., May 19, 1763.
45. Ibid., November 18, 1763.
46. Ibid., July 13, 1763.
47. Ibid., November 11, 1763.
48. Bibl. Nat., Fonds Français, 1799, NA.
49. Bibl. Nat., Fonds Français, 6498, NA.
50. Ibid.
51. Ibid.
52. Bachaumont, I, 116.
53. Broglie, February 3, 1764.
54. Croÿ, II, 17.
55. Bachaumont, I, 373.
56. Gaxotte, 302.
57. Louis XV, *Lettres à . . . Ferdinand,* September 20, 1762.
58. Ibid., July 30, 1765.

59. Croÿ, *Nouvelle Revue,* III, 430.
60. Dufort, *Mémoires.*
61. Ibid.
62. Hénault, *Mémoires,* 421.

CHAPTER 9

1. Louis XV, *Lettres à . . . Ferdinand,* August 26, 1765.
2. Ibid., October 6, 1765.
3. Ibid., November 17, 1765.
4. Ibid., December 21, 1765.
5. Ibid., December 30, 1765.
6. Ibid., January 6, 1766.
7. Ibid., January 20, 1766.
8. Ibid., January 27, 1766.
9. Ibid., February 3, 1766.
10. Bachaumont, III, 15.
11. Gaxotte, 339.
12. Flammermont, 25ff.
13. Ibid.
14. Bibl. Nat., Fonds Français, 15021.
15. Broglie, II, 299.
16. Talleyrand, 63.
17. Quoted by Gaxotte.
18. Bouffonidor, I.
19. Dufort, II, 23.
20. Bachaumont, V, 71.
21. Campan, 48.
22. Broglie, June 6, 1770.
23. Bachaumont, V, 141.
24. Ibid., V, 142.
25. Arneth and Geffroy, June 15, 1770.
26. Ibid.

27. Ibid., July 9, 1770.
28. Ibid., September 19, 1770.
29. Ibid.
30. Quoted in Boutaric.
31. Arneth and Geffroy, January 23, 1771.
32. Gaxotte, 451.
33. Ibid., 453.
34. Broglie, March 18, 1771.
35. Théveneau de Morande.
36. Bachaumont, V, 301.
37. Croÿ, II, 20.
38. Quoted in Boutaric.
39. Arneth and Geffroy, I, 353.

CHAPTER 10

1. Bernier, 92.
2. Marie Thérèse, *Correspondence . . . Marie Antoinette,* 55ff.
3. Ibid., 60ff.
4. Croÿ, III, 83ff.
5. Ibid.
6. Ibid.
7. Ibid.
8. Ibid.
9. Ibid.
10. Ibid.
11. Ibid.
12. Ibid.
13. Ibid.

AFTERWORD

1. Croÿ, III, 108ff.

Bibliography

The classification numbers of all unpublished sources quoted in this book are given in the notes. Aside from these, the author has used the resources of the département des manuscrits of the Bibliothèque Nationale, Paris, and those of the Archives Nationales, Paris.

Antoine, Michel. *Le Discours de la flagellation.* Paris, 1955.

Argenson, marquis de. *Journal et mémoires,* Paris, 1856.

Arneth et Geffroy, eds. *Correspondance secrète entre Marie Thérèse et le comte de Mercy-Argenteau.* Paris, 1874.

Bachaumont, Louis Petit de. *Mémoires secrets.* London, 1777.

Barbier, Edmond. *Chronique de la régence et du règne de Louis XV.* Paris, 1857.

Bernier, Olivier. *The Eighteenth-Century Woman.* New York, 1981.

Bernis, cardinal de. *Mémoires et lettres.* Paris, 1878.

Bouffonidor. *Les Fastes de Louis XV.* Villefranche, 1783.

Boutaric, L. *Louis XV: Correspondance secrète.* Paris, 1866.

Brancas, duchesse de. *Mémoires.* Paris, 1890.

Broglie, duc de. *Le Secret du Roi,* Paris, 1878.

Bulletin des comités historiques. Paris, 1849.

Campan, Jeanne. *Mémoires.* Paris, 1826.

Clérembault-Maurepas. *Recueuil,* ed. Raunié. Paris, 1879–86.

Croÿ, duc de. *Journal inédit.* Paris, 1906.

Croÿ, duc de. *Mémoires,* in *Nouvelle Revue Rétrospective.* Paris, 1895.

Dangeau, Philippe, marquis de. *Journal.* Paris, 1856–60.

Daudet, Chevalier. *Journal historique . . . du marriage du roy. . . .* Chalons, 1725.

Dufort de Cheverny, J. N. *Mémoires sur les règnes de Louis XV et Louis XVI.* Paris, 1886.

Egret, Jean. *Louis XV et l'opposition parlementaire.* Paris, 1970.

Flammermont, Jules. *Le Chancelier Maupeou et les parlements.* Paris, 1883.

Gaxotte, Pierre. *Le Siècle de Louis XV.* Paris, 1935.

Hénault, Président. *Mémoires.* Paris, 1855.

Levron, Jacques. *Louis XV.* Paris, 1973.

Ligne, prince de. *Mémoires.* Bruxelles, 1860.

Lordat, Marie-Joseph, comte de. *Lettres à son oncle.* Paris, 1908.

Louis XV. *Correspondance de Louis XV et du maréchal de Noailles.* Paris, 1865.

———. *Lettres à l'Infant Ferdinand de Parme.* Paris, 1938.

Luynes, duc de. *Mémoires sur la cour de Louis XV.* Paris, 1860.

Marais, Mathieu. *Journal et mémoires.* Paris, 1863.

Marie Leczinska. *Lettres de la reine Marie Leczinska et de la duchesse de Luynes au Président Hénault.* Paris, 1886.

Marie Thérèse. *Correspondance entre Marie Thérèse et Marie Antoinette.* ed., Georges Girard. Paris, 1933.

Mitford, Nancy. *Madame de Pompadour.* New York, 1968.

Montbarey, prince de. *Mémoires autographes.* Paris, 1826.

Nouvelles à la main. Bibliothèque Nationale, Département des manuscrits, Fonds Français 3712.

Orléans, Madame, duchesse de. *Lettres.* Paris, 1890.

Piépape, Général de. *Histoire des princes de Condé au XVIIIième siècle.* Paris, 1911.

Pollnitz, baron de. *Lettres et mémoires.* Amsterdam, 1737.

Pompadour, Mme de. *Correspondance.* Paris, 1876.

Saint-Simon, duc de. *Mémoires.* Paris, 1874.

Sars, comte Maxime de. *Le Cardinal de Fleury.* Paris, 1942.

Talleyrand, prince de. *Mémoires.* Paris, 1891.

Théveneau de Morande. *Le Gazetier cuirassé.* London, 1771.

Thirion, H. *Madame de Prie.* Paris, 1905.

Toussaint, M. *Anecdotes curieuses de la cour de France sous le règne de Louis XV.* n. p., n. d. (obviously the late 1780s).

Tressan, Louis-Elizabeth de la Vergne, comte de. *Souvenirs.* Paris, 1897.

Valfons, marquis de. *Souvenirs.* Paris, 1860.

Villars, maréchal duc de. *Vie écrite par lui-même.* Paris, 1784.

Walpole, Horatio, Lord. *Memoirs,* ed., William Coxe. London, 1820.

Index